70-442: PRO: Designing and O...
...ss by Using Microsoft SQL Serve...

O9-BSU-474

Objective	Chapter and Lesson
Designing Efficient Access to a SQL Server Service (1.0)	
Design appropriate data access technologies.	Chapter 1, Lessons 1 and 2
Design an appropriate data access object model.	Chapter 1, Lesson 3
Design a cursor strategy for a data access component.	
■ Decide when to use cursors.	Chapter 3, Lesson 2
■ Decide how to maximize cursor performance.	Chapter 3, Lesson 2
■ Detect which applications are using cursors and evaluate whether to remove them.	Chapter 3, Lesson 2
Design caching strategies.	
■ Select ADO.NET caching.	Chapter 3, Lesson 1
■ Design custom caching functionality.	Chapter 3, Lesson 1
■ Design a refresh strategy for cached data.	Chapter 3, Lesson 1
Design client libraries to write applications that administer a SQL Server service.	
■ Design server management objects (SMO) applications.	Chapter 4, Lesson 1
■ Design replication management objects (RMO) applications.	Chapter 4, Lesson 1
■ Design automation management objects (AMO) applications.	Chapter 4, Lesson 1
■ Design SQL Server Networking Interface (SNI) for asynchronous queries.	Chapter 4, Lesson 1
Design queries that use multiple active result sets (MARS).	
■ Decide when MARS queries are appropriate.	Chapter 4, Lesson 2
■ Choose an appropriate transaction isolation level when you use MARS.	Chapter 4, Lesson 2
■ Choose when to use Asynchronous queries.	Chapter 4, Lesson 3
Designing a Database Query Strategy (2.0)	
Write and modify queries.	
■ Write queries.	Chapter 2, Lesson 1
■ Modify queries to improve query performance.	Chapter 2, Lesson 2
Design queries for retrieving data from XML sources.	
■ Select the correct attributes.	Chapter 2, Lesson 3
■ Select the correct nodes.	Chapter 2, Lesson 3
■ Filter by values of attributes and values of elements.	Chapter 2, Lesson 3
■ Include relational data, such as columns and variables, in the result of an XQuery expression.	Chapter 2, Lesson 3
■ Include XML attribute or node values in a tabular result set.	Chapter 2, Lesson 3
■ Update, insert, or delete relational data based on XML parameters to stored procedures.	Chapter 2, Lesson 3
■ Debug and troubleshoot queries against XML data sources.	Chapter 2, Lesson 3
Design a cursor strategy.	
■ Design cursor logic.	Chapter 3, Lesson 3
■ Design cursors that work together with dynamic SQL execution.	Chapter 3, Lesson 3
■ Select an appropriate cursor type.	Chapter 3, Lesson 3
■ Design cursors that efficiently use server memory.	Chapter 3, Lesson 3
■ Design cursors that minimize blocking.	Chapter 3, Lesson 3
■ Design a strategy that minimizes or eliminates the use of cursors.	Chapter 3, Lesson 3
Designing Error-Handling Routines (3.0)	
Design code that validates input data and permissions.	Chapter 5, Lesson 1
Design code that detects and reacts to errors.	Chapter 5, Lesson 2
Design user-defined messages to communicate application events.	Chapter 5, Lesson 1

Objective	Chapter and Less
Designing a Transaction Strategy (4.0)	
Manage concurrency by selecting the appropriate transaction isolation levels.	Chapter 6, Lesson 1
Design the locking granularity level.	Chapter 6, Lesson 2
Design transaction scopes.	Chapter 6, Lesson 2
Design code that uses transactions.	Chapter 6, Lesson 2
Performance Tuning a Database and a Database Application (5.0)	
Optimize and tune queries for performance.	
■ Evaluate query performance.	Chapter 7, Lesson 1
■ Analyze query plans.	
■ Modify queries to improve performance.	
■ Test queries for improved performance.	
■ Detect locking problems.	Chapter 7, Lesson 1
■ Modify queries to optimize client and server performance.	Chapter 7, Lesson 1
■ Rewrite subqueries to joins.	Chapter 7, Lesson 1
■ Design queries that have search arguments (SARGs).	Chapter 7, Lesson 1
■ Convert single-row statements into set-based queries.	Chapter 7, Lesson 1
Optimize indexing strategies.	
■ Design an index strategy.	Chapter 7, Lesson 2
■ Analyze index use across an application.	Chapter 7, Lesson 2
■ Add, remove, or redesign indexes.	Chapter 7, Lesson 2
■ Optimize index-to-table-size ratio.	Chapter 7, Lesson 2
Scale database applications.	
■ Specify a data-partitioning model.	Chapter 8, Lesson 1
■ Design queries that target multiple servers.	Chapter 8, Lesson 1
■ Implement scale-out techniques like federated database, service broker, distributed partitioned views.	Chapter 8, Lesson 1
■ Design applications to distribute data and workload transparently.	Chapter 8, Lesson 1
■ Identify code or processes that can be moved to a different tier to improve performance.	Chapter 8, Lesson 1
■ Rewrite algorithms to improve efficiency.	Chapter 8, Lesson 1
Resolve performance problems.	
■ Analyze application performance across multiple users.	Chapter 8, Lesson 2
■ Capture workload information.	Chapter 8, Lesson 2
■ Find out the causes of performance problems.	Chapter 8, Lesson 2
■ Specify resolutions such as: changing algorithms, scaling up, and scaling out, terminating a session.	Chapter 8, Lesson 2
Optimize data storage.	
■ Choose column data types to reduce storage requirements across the enterprise.	Chapter 7, Lesson 3
■ Design appropriate use of varchar across the enterprise.	Chapter 7, Lesson 3
■ Denormalize entities to minimize page reads per query.	Chapter 7, Lesson 3
■ Optimize table width.	Chapter 7, Lesson 3

MCITP Self-Paced Training Kit (Exam 70-442): Designing and Optimizing Data Access by Using Microsoft® SQL Server™ 2005

Sara Morgan and Tobias Thernström
of GrandMasters

PUBLISHED BY
Microsoft Press
A Division of Microsoft Corporation
One Microsoft Way
Redmond, Washington 98052-6399

Library of Congress Control Number: 2007922585

Printed and bound in the United States of America.

1 2 3 4 5 6 7 8 9   QWT   2 1 0 9 8 7

Distributed in Canada by H.B. Fenn and Company Ltd.

A CIP catalogue record for this book is available from the British Library.

Microsoft Press books are available through booksellers and distributors worldwide. For further in
mation about international editions, contact your local Microsoft Corporation office or contact Micro
Press International directly at fax (425) 936-7329. Visit our Web site at www.microsoft.com/mspi
Send comments to tkinput@microsoft.com.

Acquisitions Editor: Ken Jones
Developmental Editor: Karen Szall
Project Editor: Maria Gargiulo
Editorial Production: nSight, Inc.

Body Part No. X13-62481

Dedication

*To my Mom and Dad, who have always been a tremendous inspiration for me.
I am nothing without you both. I love you.*

–Sara Morgan

To my fiancée, Frida, my mother, Viveca, and the memory of my father, Bertil.

–Tobias Thernström

*To my wife, Mary, who patiently endured the late nights and long weekends that were spent
on this effort, and to Nikki the Rottweiler, who tried her best to help but just
couldn't get the syntax down.*

–Ted Malone

About the Authors

Morgan

Sara Morgan, an independent author and consultant based in Baton Rouge, Louisiana, is an MCSD and MCDBA and is certified in SQL Server 2000 and Visual Basic .NET. She specializes in developing leading-edge Web-based applications using Microsoft technologies. Since graduating from Louisiana State University with a degree in quantitative business analysis, she has been developing software for a variety of industries, including a not-for-profit hospital, a financial company offering mortgages, a major retailer, a software company that writes legislative software, and an application service provider.

Sara has written articles for *MSDN Magazine, Enterprise Development, .NET Development, Visual Studio Magazine*, and DevX.com. She has also co-written *MCTS Self-Paced Training Kit (Exam 70-529): Microsoft .NET Framework 2.0 Distributed Application Development* (Microsoft Press, 2006) and *MCPD Self-Paced Training Kit (Exam 70-547): Designing and Developing Web-Based Applications Using the Microsoft .NET Framework*. Sara's articles about enhanced computing and her latest research efforts can be found at *http://www.custsolutions.net.*

as Thernström

Tobias Thernström has enjoyed the company of SQL Server for over 10 years. He is a senior database architect and trainer at Rbam AB (*www.rbam.se*), a professional software services company located in Sweden. Tobias has been involved in the development of several SQL Server certifications provided by Microsoft. He is an MCT and co-founder of the Swedish SQL Server User Group (*www.sqlug.se*).

Ted Malone

Ted Malone has been working with SQL Server since the days of OS/2 and has developed database systems ranging from small to extremely large. Ted is currently product strategy architect for Configuresoft, Inc. (*http://www.configuresoft.com*), a Colorado Springs, Colorado–based software development firm and Microsoft Gold ISV Partner that specializes in delivering enterprise management tools for Fortune 1000 corporations. Ted is the vice president of the Rocky Mountain SQL Server Users Group and a frequent contributor to the Professional Association for SQL Server. Ted was also a contributing author to *SQL Server Security* (McGraw-Hill Osborne Media, 2003) as well as a contributor to several SQL Server 2005 study guides.

In his free time, Ted enjoys the Colorado wilderness with his family and dogs. Ted is a avid pilot with more than 4,000 hours of flight time and enjoys riding his motorcycle ever possible.

ntents at a Glance

ble of Contents

hat do you think of this book? We want to hear from you!

Microsoft is interested in hearing your feedback so we can continually improve our books and learning resources for you. To participate in a brief online survey, please visit:

www.microsoft.com/learning/booksurvey/

What do you think of this book? We want to hear from you!

Microsoft is interested in hearing your feedback so we can continually improve our books and learning resources for you. To participate in a brief online survey, please visit:

www.microsoft.com/learning/booksurvey/

Introduction

This training kit is designed for software developers who plan to take the Microsoft Certified IT Professional (MCITP) Exam 70-442: Designing and Optimizing Data Access by Using Microsoft SQL Server 2005. The primary objective of this exam is to certify that developers and database administrators know how to design efficient access to SQL Server 2005 databases. We assume that before you begin using this kit, you have spent at least three years doing database development work. We also assume that you have worked on multiple phases of a software development project, including design, development, deployment, and post-production/maintenance. The Preparation Guide for Exam 70-442 is available at the URL *http://www.microsoft.com/learning/exams/70-442.mspx*.

The labs in this training kit will use SQL Server 2005 Enterprise Edition. A 180-day evaluation edition is included on the companion DVD. If you do not have access to this software, you can download a 180-day trial of SQL Server 2005 through *http://www.microsoft.com/sql/downloads/trial-software.mspx*. You can also consider purchasing SQL Server 2005 Development Edition, which contains all required features.

By using this training kit, you will learn how to do the following:

- Design efficient access to a SQL Server service.
- Design a database query strategy.
- Design error-handling routines.
- Design a transaction strategy.
- Performance tune a database and a database application.

Hardware Requirements

We recommend that you use a test workstation, test server, or staging server to complete the exercises in each lab. However, it would be beneficial for you to have access to production-ready data in your organization. If you need to set up a workstation to complete the practice exercises, the minimum system requirements follow:

- Personal computer with a 600 MHz Pentium III compatible or faster processor
- 512 MB of RAM or more (1 GB or more recommended)

- 350 MB free hard disk space for the SQL Server installation
- 450 MB additional free hard disk space if you plan to install SQL Server Books (and sample databases
- CD-ROM drive or DVD-ROM drive
- Super VGA (1,024 x 768) or higher resolution video adapter and monitor
- Keyboard and Microsoft mouse or compatible pointing device

Software Requirements

Note that you will need SQL Server 2005, and in some cases, Microsoft Visual Studio 2(complete the labs included with each chapter. Although these products can be installe(production server, it is not recommended that you do so. Instead, install these product execute the labs in each chapter on a single development machine. The following softw required to complete the lab exercises:

- One of the following operating systems:
    - ❏ Microsoft Windows 2000 Server SP4
    - ❏ Windows 2000 Advanced Server SP4
    - ❏ Microsoft Windows Server 2003, Standard Edition SP1
    - ❏ Windows Server 2003, Enterprise Edition SP1
    - ❏ Windows Server 2003, Datacenter Edition SP1
- SQL Server 2005. For instructions on downloading and installing SQL Server Enterprise Edition, see the "Installing SQL Server" section of this Introduction.
- Visual Studio 2005 or Visual Studio 2005 SP1. A free 90-day evaluation of Visual S Professional Edition is available for download from the MSDN Web site at *h* *msdn2.microsoft.com/en-us/vstudio/bb188238.aspx*. Visual Studio 2005 SP1 work: Visual Studio 2005 Standard Edition, Professional Edition, and Team Edition available from the Microsoft Download site.
- The *AdventureWorks* database; available as a separate download with the SQL Server samples from *http://www.microsoft.com/downloads/details.aspx?FamilyID=e719ecf* *-4312-af89-6ad8702e4e6e&DisplayLang=en*.
- Microsoft Data Access Components (MDAC) 2.8; available for free download from *www.microsoft.com/downloads/details.aspx?FamilyID=6c050fe3-c795-4b7d* *-185d0506396c&DisplayLang=en*.
- Microsoft Web Application Stress Tool; available for free download from the Mic Download Center at *http://www.microsoft.com/downloads/details.aspx?familyid=E2C* *-062A-439E-A67D-75A89AA36495&displaylang=en*.

- Microsoft Internet Explorer 6.0 SP1 or later.
- Internet Information Services (IIS) 5.0 or later.

alling SQL Server 2005

A 180-day evaluation of SQL Server 2005 Enterprise Edition is available on the companion DVD or is available for download by performing the following instructions.

1. Browse to *http://www.microsoft.com/sql/downloads/trial-software.mspx* and click the "Download SQL Server 2005" link. You will need to complete a registration form that requires you to have a .NET Passport account.

2. Read and follow the instructions on the download page to download the SQL Server 2005 Enterprise Evaluation Edition. Locate the correct download file for your environment.

3. Once the install executable has been downloaded to your local machine, execute the downloaded file (SQLEVAL.EXE) and click Run to extract the setup files to your local development machine.

4. Browse to the location where you extracted the setup files. Execute Setup.exe from the Servers folder to begin the installation process.

5. Select I accept the licensing terms and conditions and click Next.

6. Click Install from the Installing Prerequisites dialog box. Once complete, click Next to continue.

7. The installation will then perform a system configuration check. In the Welcome dialog box, click Next to begin the installation.

8. Once the System Configuration Check is complete, click Next.

9. Enter and name and company information in the Registration Information dialog box and click Next to continue.

10. Click Next to accept the defaults in the Feature Selection dialog box.

11. Click Next and accept the defaults in the Instance Name dialog box.

12. Click Next and accept the defaults in the Logon Information dialog box.

13. Click Next and accept the defaults in the Error and Usage Report Settings dialog box.

14. Click Install in the Ready to Install dialog box and wait for the installation to complete.

15. You will also have to download and install the *AdventureWorks* database, which is referenced in some of the chapter labs.

Installing Visual Studio 2005

Visual Studio 2005 Professional Edition is required to run some of the lab files provided book. To download and install a free 90-day evaluation edition of Visual Studio 2005 I sional Edition, refer to the following instructions:

1. Browse to *http://msdn2.microsoft.com/en-us/vstudio/bb188238.aspx* and click the I load link for the Visual Studio 2005 Professional 90-day trial. You will need to cor a registration form that requires you to have a .NET Passport account.

2. Read and follow the instructions on the download page to download the Visual 2005 Evaluation Edition. Locate the correct download file for your environment.

3. Once the ISO image file has been downloaded to your local machine, copy it to a DVD-R, which will result in an exact copy of the installation media. Even thoug copy is fully functional, the license is only valid for 90 days.

4. Once copied to a DVD-R, you can browse to the DVD drive and begin the installat executing the Setup.exe file.

5. Click Install Visual Studio 2005. The installation will begin by copying required files to a temp directory. When it is complete, click Next to continue the installati

6. Select the I accept the licensing terms and conditions check box and click Next t tinue the installation.

7. Click Install in the Select features to install dialog box and accept the default instal Once complete, click Next to continue. The installation will take several minutes to plete; the time will vary depending on the speed of your development machine.

Installing the AdventureWorks Database

You will need to download and install a sample database for Adventure Works, a fic retailer that is referenced in some of the labs in this book. To install the sample database to the following instructions:

1. Browse to *http://msdn.microsoft.com/vstudio/express/sql/default.aspx* and click the I load icon.

2. Select the SQL Server 2005 Samples download and follow the instructions on the load page to save the **case-insensitive collation DB** installation package (Adve WorksDBCI.msi) to your local development machine.

3. Once the installation package has finished downloading, double-click the executal and click Run to execute the Installer.

4. Click Next in the Welcome dialog box.

5. Select I accept the terms in the license agreement and click Next in the License dialog box.
6. Click Next and accept the defaults on the Destination Folder dialog box.
7. Click Install in the Ready to Install dialog box.
8. Click Finish in the Wizard Completed.

ılling Microsoft Web Application Stress Tool

The Microsoft Web Application Stress Tool is used to simulate multiple user requests to a Web site. To install this tool, refer to the following instructions:

1. Browse to *http://www.microsoft.com/downloads/details.aspx?familyid=E2C0585A-062A-439E-A67D-75A89AA36495&displaylang=en*, and click Download.
2. Select Run, and wait until the download completes and the installation begins. The setup file may take several minutes to download.
3. You should receive a security warning. Select Run to continue the installation.
4. Select Yes in the license agreement dialog box.
5. Select Next to install to the default destination directory.
6. Upon completion, the installation will display the readme documentation. Select OK and then select Finish to complete the installation.

e Scenarios

In the case scenarios at the end of each chapter, you will apply what you've learned in that chapter. If you have difficulty completing this work, review the material in the chapter before beginning the next one. You can find answers to these questions in the Answers section at the end of this book.

Scenarios and the 70-442 Exam

Of the approximately 200 practice test questions included on the companion CD, 180 are based on case scenarios. Case scenario-based practice test questions provide a way to assess whether the certification candidate understands the information that he or she has learned. Each case scenario describes a fictional company that is facing some dilemma. The case scenario will be exhaustive and will feature both technical and non-technical details. You need to be able to analyze and interpret not only the technical issues, but the business needs as well.

You will need to read each case scenario more than once. It is a good idea to read through the case scenario quickly the first time. Try to identify the major obstacle(s) facing the fictional company. Then read the questions associated with this case scenario. There are approxir 10 questions for each scenario.

On the next pass, pick out details that will help you answer the questions. Note portions case scenario that relate to specific questions. It will be necessary to read the scenarios oughly and to absorb as much information as possible rather than reading only the se that you think are relevant.

Case Scenario Structure

Each case scenario contains several sections that cover different aspects of the fictiona pany. The first part of the scenario will provide background information, such as an ove of the company and any changes the company plans to make. It might also reveal any problems the company is currently facing.

In many cases, the existing environment, including details regarding both software and ware, is described. Because this exam involves optimizing SQL Server, you should exp see information regarding the databases and database servers. You might also see inform about the network and server infrastructure.

There will also be sections describing the company's business requirements, including g or technical requirements. The technical requirements section specifies technical c involving security, maintainability, availability, and recoverability.

Using the CD and DVD

A companion CD and an evaluation software DVD are included with this training kit. The panion CD contains the following

- **Practice tests** You can practice for the 70-442 certification exam by using tests c from a pool of approximately 200 realistic exam questions. These questions giv many different practice exams to ensure that you're prepared to take the real thin
- **Labs** Many chapters in this book include sample files associated with the lab exe at the end of every lesson. Most exercises have a project or solution that you can complete the exercise and a version of the completed exercise for your review. To the sample files on your hard disk, run Setup.exe in the Labs folder on the comp CD. The default installation folder is \My Documents\Microsoft Press\MCIT Paced Training Kit Exam 70-442.
- **An eBook** An electronic version (eBook) of this book is included for times whe don't want to carry the printed book with you. The eBook is in Portable Documer

mat (PDF), and you can view it by using Adobe Acrobat or Adobe Acrobat Reader, available from http://www.adobe.com.

The evaluation software DVD contains a 180-day evaluation edition of SQL Server 2005 Enterprise Edition, needed to run the lab files in this book

to Install the Practice Tests

To install the practice test software from the companion CD on your hard disk, perform the following steps

1. Insert the companion CD into your CD drive and accept the license agreement. A CD menu appears.

NOTE If the CD menu doesn't appear

If the CD menu or the license agreement doesn't appear, AutoRun might be disabled on your computer. Refer to the Readme.txt file on the CD-ROM for alternate installation instructions.

---

2. Click the Practice Tests item and follow the instructions on the screen.

to Use the Practice Tests

To start the practice test software, follow these steps:

1. Click Start, All Programs, Microsoft Press Training Kit Exam Prep. A window appears that shows all the Microsoft Press training kit exam prep suites installed on your computer.
2. Double-click the practice test that you want to use.

Practice Test Options

When you start a practice test, you choose whether to take the test in Certification Mode, Study Mode, or Custom Mode.

- **Certification Mode** Closely resembles the experience of taking a certification exam. The test has a set number of questions, it's timed, and you can't pause and restart the timer.
- **Study Mode** Creates an untimed test in which you can review the correct answers and the explanations after you answer each question.
- **Custom Mode** Gives you full control over the test options so that you can customize them as you like. You can click OK to accept the defaults, or you can customize the number of questions you want, how the practice test software works, which exam objectives

you want the questions to relate to, and whether you want your lesson review
timed. If you're retaking a test, you can select whether you want to see all the que
again or only those questions you missed or didn't answer.

In all modes, the user interface you see when taking the test is essentially the same bu
different options enabled or disabled, depending on the mode.

After you click OK, your practice test starts.

- To take the test, answer the questions and use the Next, Previous, and Go To butt
  move from question to question.

- After you answer an individual question, if you want to see which answers are co
  along with an explanation of each correct answer—click Explanation.

- If you'd rather wait until the end of the test to see how you did, answer all the que
  and then click Score Test. You'll see a summary of the exam objectives you chose a
  percentage of questions you answered correctly overall and per objective. You cai
  a copy of your test, review your answers, or retake the test.

When you review your answer to an individual practice test question, a "References" s
lists where in the training kit you can find the information that relates to that questic
provides links to other sources of information. After you click Test Results to score your
practice test, you can click the Learning Plan tab to see a list of references for every obj

How to Uninstall the Practice Tests

To uninstall the practice test software for a training kit, use the Add Or Remove Pro
option in Windows Control Panel.

Microsoft Certified Professional Program

The Microsoft certifications provide the best method to prove your command of c'
Microsoft products and technologies. The exams and corresponding certifications are
oped to validate your mastery of critical competencies as you design and develop, or
ment and support, solutions with Microsoft products and technologies. Computer profes:
who become Microsoft-certified are recognized as experts and are sought after industry
Certification brings a variety of benefits to the individual and to employers and organiz

---

MORE INFO   All the Microsoft certifications

For a full list of Microsoft certifications, go to *http://www.microsoft.com/learning/mcp/default.r*

---

hnical Support

Every effort has been made to ensure the accuracy of this book and the contents of the companion CD. If you have comments, questions, or ideas regarding this book or the companion CD, please send them to Microsoft Press by using either of the following methods:

E-mail: tkinput@microsoft.com

Postal Mail:

Microsoft Press
Attn: MCITP Self-Paced Training Kit (Exam 70-442): Designing and Optimizing Data Access by Using Microsoft SQL Server 2005, *Editor*
One Microsoft Way
Redmond, WA 98052–6399

For additional support information regarding this book and the CD-ROM (including answers to commonly asked questions about installation and use), visit the Microsoft Press Technical Support Web site at http:/www.microsoft.*com/learning/support/books.* To connect directly to the Microsoft Knowledge Base and enter a query, visit *http://support.microsoft.com/search.* For support information regarding Microsoft software, please visit *http://support.microsoft.com.*

luation Edition Software Support

The 180-day evaluation edition provided with this training kit is not the full retail product and is provided only for the purposes of training and evaluation. Microsoft and Microsoft Technical Support do not support this evaluation edition.

Information about any issues relating to the use of this evaluation edition with this training kit is posted to the Support section of the Microsoft Press Web site at *http://www.microsoft.com /learning/support/books*. For information about ordering the full version of any Microsoft software, please call Microsoft Sales at (800) 426-9400 or visit the Microsoft Web site at *http:// www.microsoft.com.*

esigning a Data Access Strategy

The first step in working with data is to design a data access strategy. The same strategy should apply to all applications that access data, so it is important that you consider all potential data sources. If you spend the time carefully considering your options before you begin coding your applications, it will be much easier to manage those applications in a consistent way.

Designing an effective data access strategy involves decisions such as determining what network protocol to use and what connection method to utilize. The decisions that you will need to make depend on whether you need to connect to Microsoft SQL Server 2005 through Hypertext Transfer Protocol (HTTP) endpoints or whether a connection needs to be made to HTTP Web services using custom Simple Object Access Protocol (SOAP) methods. You also must consider whether you need to design connections between multiple instances of SQL Server 2005. This chapter will cover all these issues, along with determining which type of data access method to utilize.

Exam objectives in this chapter:
- Design appropriate data access technologies.
- Design an appropriate data access object model.

ore You Begin

To complete the lessons in this chapter, you must have:

- A computer that meets or exceeds the minimum hardware and software requirements listed in the Introduction at the beginning of this book.
- Microsoft SQL Server 2005 installed, as well as the SQL Server 2005 AdventureWorks sample database.
- Microsoft Visual Studio 2005, Microsoft Visual C# 2005 Express Edition, or Microsoft Visual Basic Express Edition installed.
- Experience designing and working with databases in SQL Server 2005. You should know which tools are provided with SQL Server 2005, such as SQL Server Management Studio and SQL Server Configuration Manager.
- Experience installing an instance of SQL Server 2005 and a basic understanding of how to configure network libraries.
- A basic understanding of creating and consuming Web services.
- Experience creating Windows-based applications using Visual Studio 2005.

Lesson 1: Designing Data Access Technologies

Estimated lesson time: 60 minutes

Today's database systems need to be connected to a variety of applications running on
more platforms. To access these disparate systems, database developers need to unde
the different data access technologies available to them. This lesson will review these te
ogies and suggest ways that they can be applied.

Selecting a Network Protocol

Connecting to a SQL Server database requires you to configure both a network protoc
a network library. When you install an instance of SQL Server 2005, several network lil
are installed as dynamic-link library (DLL) files. Each *network library* enables you to pas
across the network through packets. These libraries must be installed to support a par
protocol; some network libraries support multiple protocols.

The *network protocol* selected is critical to determining how SQL Server 2005 interacts w
network and can have an impact on the way that you integrate SQL Server 200£
Microsoft Internet Information Services (IIS). You will need to configure network prc
after the setup has completed. You do so using the SQL Server Configuration Manager

SQL Server 2005 enables you to configure one of four different network protocols. You c
what protocols are available for your instance of SQL Server by expanding the *SQL Serve*
Network Configuration node in SQL Server Configuration Manager, as shown in Figure

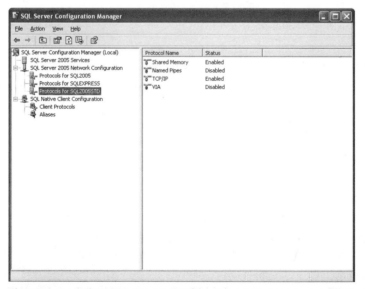

Figure 1-1   Using SQL Server Configuration Manager to configure network protocols for the

From here, you can configure each network protocol for a particular SQL Server 2005 instance. The network protocols available are as follows.

- **Shared Memory** This is the most straightforward protocol and is simply enabled or disabled. This protocol is typically used only when the connection between client and server is occurring on the same machine.
- **Named Pipes** This protocol allows you to specify a pipe that SQL Server will listen on. It ensures that the Windows authentication process will occur each time a connection is established. The named pipes protocol was designed for a local area network (LAN), and in this environment, it can perform well. This is the fastest protocol to utilize when the application and server reside on the same machine.
- **TCP/IP** This popular protocol was designed to support communication over the Internet and is the fastest protocol when it comes to transmitting data across wide areas. TCP/IP is a good choice when dealing with a slow network or across a wide area network (WAN).
- **VIA** This special protocol only applies to Virtual Interface Adapter (VIA) hardware.

Prior to SQL Server 2005, there were more protocols available, but the number of protocols has been reduced. Typically, you will only need to consider named pipes or TCP/IP. The protocol depends on the type of network on which your application will be running.

Network protocols need to be configured on both the client and server end. Figure 1-1 shows a screenshot of where you would configure the network protocols that the server uses to listen on. You can use the same tool to configure the client side. You do so by expanding Client Protocols within the *SQL Native Client Configuration* node, as shown in Figure 1-2.

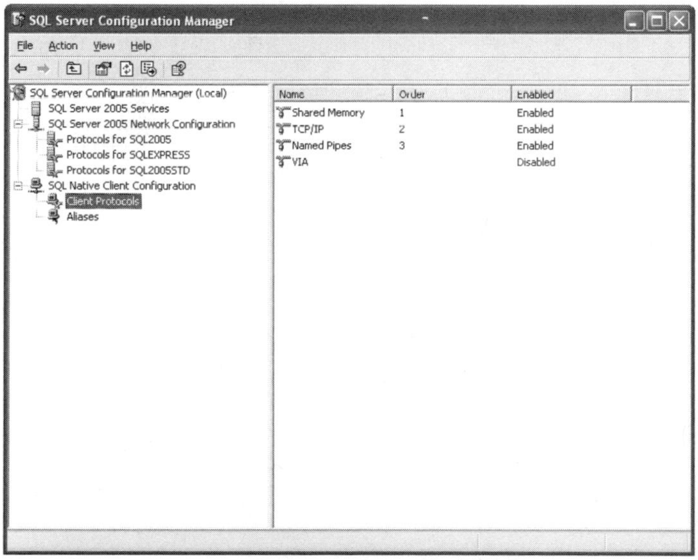

Figure 1-2   Using SQL Server Configuration Manager to configure network protocols for the client

From here, you can set the sequence in which enabled protocols are used when making nection. A connection with the protocol ordered as 1 will be attempted first. If this conn fails, it will move to the protocol ordered as 2. In Figure 1-2, shared memory is listed as th protocol. Using the shared memory protocol is fine if the server and client reside on the machine. But if you know that the client always needs to attach by using another pro such as TCP/IP, you need to change the order on the client machine by using SQL Serve figuration Manager.

It is possible to use the connection string to specify a particular protocol. Only the spe protocol will be considered, and it will not fail over to the next protocol if a connection c be made. To specify the TCP protocol, you prepend your SQL Server connection strin; the tcp prefix. This is followed by the server name, instance name, and optionally, the number. The format is as follows:

```
tcp:<servername>\<instancename>,<portnumber>
```

or

```
tcp:<ipaddress>\<instancename>,<portnumber>
```

Following is an example of what the connection string would look like if you wanted t nect to a local instance of SQL Server using a TCP connection through port 1431:

```
//C#
string connString = @"server=tcp:.\sqlexpress,1431;Integrated
Security=SSPI;initial catalog=AdventureWorks";
```

```
'VB
Dim connString As String = "server=tcp:.\sqlexpress,1431;
Integrated Security=SSPI;initial catalog=AdventureWorks"
```

Selecting a Data Provider

Developers working with the Microsoft .NET Framework are most likely familiar ADO.NET. This *application programming interface* (API) is tightly integrated with the Framework and enables you to provide data access for managed code applications. ADC uses providers to access specific data sources, such as SQL Server or Oracle. The API, represents a set of functions developers can use to access application functionality, pr features that are useful when designing applications for the .NET Framework, such as memory cache.

Database developers might also be familiar with Microsoft Data Access Components (M This connectivity library has passed through several versions in the years since it was intro with the Windows 98 operating system. MDAC provides developers with multiple APIs that can be used to connect to a wide variety of data sources.

MDAC 2.8 is available as a free download from MSDN at *http://msdn2.microsoft.com/en-us /data/aa937730.aspx*. This version is already available with the Windows XP Service Pack 2 (SP2) operating system, but if you are unsure of which version you have, you can download a utility named Component Checker from the same location as MDAC.

You might not be familiar with SQL Native Client (SNAC), which was introduced with SQL Server 2005. SNAC also provides access to a variety of data sources, but additionally, it enables you to take advantage of certain functionality made available with SQL Server 2005. The new features include database mirroring and the ability to query Multiple Active Result Sets (MARS), provide query notifications, and utilize *EXtensible Markup Language* (XML) data types. XML is a simple and extensible format used to represent data.

SNAC provides stricter error handling than MDAC, and errors that would be reported generally with MDAC might reveal more information with SNAC. For this reason, applications that are upgraded from MDAC to SNAC might behave unexpectedly if error handling is not specifically addressed.

SNAC does not allow you to access some of the beneficial features of MDAC, such as connection pooling, memory management, and client cursor support. SNAC also does not implement ActiveX Data Objects (ADO), although it does enable you to access the functionality of ADO. If you need to support a SQL Server database prior to version 7.0, you will have to use MDAC.

SNAC does wrap the *Object Linking and Embedding* (OLE) *DB* provider and *Open DataBase Connectivity* (ODBC) driver into one DLL, which enables the DLL to perform more quickly and to be secured more easily. ODBC and OLE DB are used to access a variety of data sources other than SQL Server. To take advantage of the new features available with SQL Server 2005, you need to use the SNAC for new application development. It is not necessary to upgrade existing applications to SNAC unless you plan on taking advantage of the new SQL 2005 features, such as MARS queries.

Exam Tip   Make sure you understand the differences between each data provider and which is more appropriate in certain scenarios. Specifically, note the differences between SNAC and MDAC.

Developers have more than one option when selecting a data provider for their applications. The one you select depends on the platform you are targeting and the language you are using. Table 1-1 lists the Microsoft recommendations for selecting a data provider.

Table 1-1   Recommended Uses for Data Providers

Data Access Technology	Recommended Use
MDAC	Use if you are writing native code targeting Windows or if you need to wr classic ASP application, Visual Basic 6.0x COM application, or C++ applic
SNAC	Use if you need to access the latest features in SQL Server 2005 using OD OLE DB.
ADO.NET	Use if you are writing a managed code application for the .NET Framewo

How to Connect by Using ADO.NET

ADO.NET is tightly integrated with the .NET Framework and can be used to build data applications using any of the supported languages. It is comprised of two main areas:

- **Providers** Represent each data source available to your application. There is a pr for SQL Server and another one for Oracle. Third-party companies can create pro for other databases as well.
- **Services** Represent what is done with the data returned by a provider. For exa there is one service that provides an in-memory cache so that data can be main inside a dataset.

ADO.NET is included with the .NET Framework, so you do not have to do anything spe access it. Everything you need is provided in the *System.Data* namespace. You will have a reference to the specific namespace required. The namespace you use is dependent data source you are trying to access. For example, if you are trying to access a SQL Ser database, you will set a reference to the *System.Data.SqlClient* namespace. Refer to Table determine the correct namespace to reference. The following code would need to be pla the top of any code file that makes a connection to the database:

```
//C#
using System.Data.SqlClient;

'VB
Imports System.Data.SqlClient
```

Table 1-2   Namespaces and Objects Used to Connect to Data Sources

Data Source	Namespace	Object Name
SQL Server database, version 7.x	*System.Data.SqlClient*	*SQLConnection*
OLE DB database or SQL Server database, version 6.5 or earlier	*System.Data.OleDb*	*OleDbConnection*
ODBC database	*System.Data.Odbc*	*OdbcConnection*
Oracle client	*System.Data.OracleClient*	*OracleConnection*

Each provider has a connection object that is used to establish a connection with the data source, as shown in Table 1-2. You will need to create an instance of the connection object and then set the connection properties before opening the connection. You set the connection properties through a connection string. The connection string will vary depending on the data source, but for most data sources, you will need to specify the server name, database name, and any authentication credentials.

Following is an example of the code needed to open a connection to the SQL Server 2005 database for the fictional company named Adventure Works.

```
//C#
//Open the Connection to SQL Server Express
string connString = @"server=.\sqlexpress;Integrated Security=SSPI;initial
            catalog=AdventureWorks";
sqlConn = new SqlConnection(connString);
sqlConn.Open();
```

```
'VB
'Open the connection to SQL Server Express
Dim connString As String = "server=.\sqlexpress;Integrated
                      Security=SSPI;initial catalog=AdventureWorks"
sqlConn.ConnectionString = connString
sqlConn.Open()
```

to Connect by Using MDAC

MDAC consists of multiple APIs that ship with the Windows operating system. You have a choice of three interfaces:

- ODBC
- OLE DB
- ADO

Open Database Connectivity

ODBC provides a way for developers to connect to any kind of data source and is the widely accepted method of data access. Using software drivers, it enables you to access ety of data sources, such as a Microsoft Office Access database, a Microsoft Office Excel s sheet, and a Microsoft Visual FoxPro database. Any third-party database vendor can v software driver that adheres to the ODBC standards in order to provide an interface to data.

ODBC requires you to set up a *Data Source Name* (DSN), which identifies the correct dri utilize. The name of the DSN will be used in the connection string employed to connect database. To create a DSN, click Start, Control Panel, Administrative Tools, Data Sc (ODBC). The Drivers tab will list all the ODBC drivers available for your computer, as s in Figure 1-3.

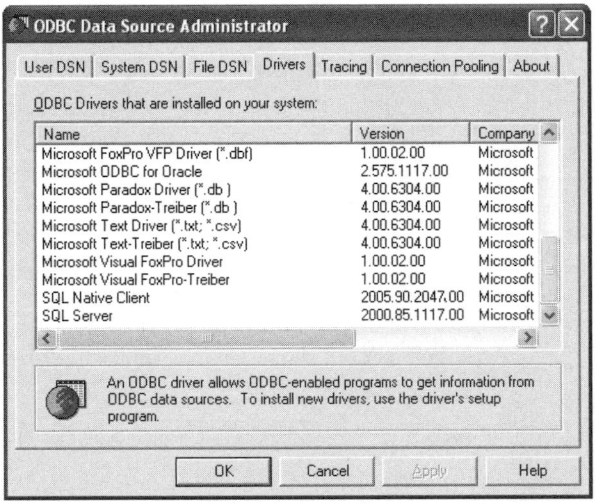

Figure 1-3   Drivers tab in the ODBC Data Source Administrator utility

You can create one of the following DSN types:

- **User DSN**   Can only be used by the current user on the current machine.
- **System DSN**   Can be used by all users on the current machine.
- **File DSN**   Connection details are stored in a file that can be shared with multiple

The first step in creating a DSN is to select a driver and therefore identify the type c source. The connection information required for the DSN will vary depending on what was selected. Once the DSN is created, you can reference the DSN in the connection such as the one that follows, which references a DSN called "myDSN":

```
"DSN=myDSN;Uid=myUID;Pwd=myPwd"
```

If the DSN was a file DSN, the string would appear as follows.

```
"FILEDSN=c:\dataConn.dsn;Uid=myUid;Pwd=myPwd"
```

In both of these connection strings, the authentication credentials were added to the string. *Authentication* is the process of verifying that the user has access to the requested resource. Depending on the database you are accessing, you might not have to specify a user ID and password.

ODBC cannot be used by scripting languages such as Microsoft Visual Basic Scripting Edition (VBScript) and JScript, so the following code example is provided in C++. Connecting to an ODBC data source with C++ code involves allocating an environment and connection handle. You can then use the *SQLConnect* function to establish a connection to the database. The following is an example of the code you would need to make a connection using ODBC and a user DSN named "myDSN" :

```cpp
//C++
// Allocate environment handle, allocate connection handle,
// connect to data source, and allocate statement handle.
void direxec::sqlconn(void)
{
    unsigned char chr_ds_name[SQL_MAX_DSN_LENGTH];    // Data source name
    RETCODE rc;             // ODBC return code
    unsigned char szData[MAX_DATA];    // Returned data storage
    SDWORD cbData;         // Output length of data
    HENV henv;             // Environment
    HDBC hdbc;             // Connection handle
    HSTMT hstmt;           // Statement handle

    //Initialize the chr_ds_name with the name of the DSN
    _mbscpy(chr_ds_name,(const unsigned char *)"myDSN");

    SQLAllocEnv(&henv);
    SQLAllocConnect(henv,&hdbc);
    rc=SQLConnect(hdbc,chr_ds_name,SQL_NTS,NULL,0,NULL,0);

    // Deallocate handles, display error message, and exit.
    if (!MYSQLSUCCESS(rc))
    {
        SQLFreeEnv(henv);
        SQLFreeConnect(hdbc);
        error_out();
        exit(-1);
    }

    rc=SQLAllocStmt(hdbc,&hstmt);

}
```

IMPORTANT   Using ODBC with Visual Basic .NET and Visual C# .NET

Typically, you will only use ODBC or OLE DB when your development language is C++. Howe
you have a compelling reason to use ODBC with Visual Basic .NET or Visual C# .NET, an add
component is provided. For more information about using ODBC with Visual Basic .NET or V
C# .NET, refer to the MSDN articles at *http://support.microsoft.com/kb/310985/* and *http://sup*
.microsoft.com/kb/310988.

Object Linking and Embedding Database

Like ODBC, OLE DB can also be used to access a variety of data sources. However, it do
require the user to create a DSN. Typically, OLE DB is considered the fastest and most c
tent option when accessing data using the C++ language.

OLE DB 2.0 utilizes a concept where data providers act as an intermediary and serve c
an application. To connect to a data provider, you must first create an instance of th
source object. The provider is uniquely identified with a *class identifier (CLSID)* that is
in the registry. Similar to a globally unique identifier (GUID), the CLSID consists of a I
integer that is represented as a string of hexadecimal digits. The following C++ code d
strates how you would create an instance of a provider using their CLSID and then in
that provider using the *Initialize* method:

```
//C++
// Create an instance of the OLE DB Initialization Component.
CoCreateInstance(CLSID_MSDAINITIALIZE, NULL, CLSCTX_INPROC_SERVER,
    IID_IDataInitialize,(void**)&pIDataInitialize);

// Create an instance of CLSID_MSDASQL with supported Services.
pIDataInitialize->CreateDBInstance(CLSID_MSDASQL, NULL,
    CLSCTX_INPROC_SERVER, NULL, IID_IDBInitialize,
    (IUnknown**)&pIDBInitialize);

// Initialize the DataSource object by setting any required
// initialization properties and calling IDBInitialize::Initialize
    CHECK_HR(hr = myDoInitialization(pIDBInitialize));
```

There are many considerations when connecting to a data source using OLE DB. For
information about how to query data using OLE DB, refer to the "OLE DB Programmer
erence" at *http://msdn2.microsoft.com/en-us/library/ms974412.aspx*.

ActiveX Data Objects

Based on OLE DB, ADO enables you to easily access data using programming language
as Visual Basic, Active Server Pages (ASP), and JScript. ADO uses a hierarchical object

and enables developers to query a database and return data into a *recordset* object. If your application needs to access data using Visual Basic (not Visual Basic .NET) or the scripting languages VBScript and JScript, you need to use ADO.

Before you can create a connection using ADO, you need to reference the ADO libraries in your project. If you are using a Visual Basic project, you will need to select References from the Project menu. From Available References, browse to the location of the MDAC library, as shown in Figure 1-4.

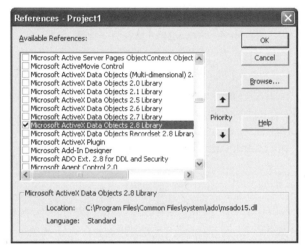

Figure 1-4   References dialog box used to set a reference to the latest MDAC library

Once the library reference has been set, you can refer to the ADO objects in your Visual Basic code. ADO provides a connection object, which represents a session with a specific data source. The connection object uses a connection string to specify the connection parameters. You can utilize a DSN connection or a DSN-less connection. For a DSN-less connection, all the connection information is specified within the connection string itself.

The following Visual Basic code can be used to open a connection to a SQL Server database using a DSN-less connection string:

```VB
'VB
Dim conn as ADODB.Connection
Set conn = New ADODB.Connection
conn.ConnectionString = "Provider='sqloledb';Data Source='MySqlServer';" & _
        "Initial Catalog='Northwind';Integrated Security='SSPI';"
conn.Open
```

How to Connect by Using SQL Native Client

SQL Native Client was introduced with SQL Server 2005. It contains the SQL ODBC and SQL OLE DB provider and also enables you to connect using ADO. SNAC was intro so developers can take advantage of the new features in SQL Server 2005.

How you handle the connection depends on which type of application you have. You wil to change the provider name specified in the connection string. The following conne string can be used by ODBC, OLE DB, or ADO to access a SQL Server database namec using a trusted connection and *without* using the SNAC provider:

```
"Provider=SQLOLEDB;Server=(local);Database=Pubs;Integrated Security=SSPI;"
```

This is the connection string you are probably used to seeing, and it is the one you shoul tinue to use, unless you need to take advantage of the new features available with SQL 2005. If you want to use the SQL Native Client with ADO, you will need to use a differer vider. You will also need to use the *DataTypeCompatibility* keyword so that the new data available with SQL Server 2005 are accessible in ADO. For example, the following conne string can be used for an ADO application using the SQL Native Client:

```
"Provider=SQLNCLI;DataTypeCompatibility=80;Server=(local);
Database=Pubs;Integrated Security=SSPI;"
```

If you are using ODBC or OLE DB, you do not have to include the *DataTypeCompatibili* word, but you will need to keep the *SQLNCLI* value as the provider.

Managing Password Policies

Prior to SQL Server 2005, there was no way to force a user to change their SQL Server password. This was considered a security issue. Now, administrators have the option c ging a user logon so that the password must change or it will eventually expire. This er an administrator to set up a user logon so that the user must change the password a logon; this helps to ensure that only the user knows the password.

BEST PRACTICES   Configure Password Expiration whenever possible

Although it is not necessary for all logons to be configured with password expiration or for the to change the password, it is recommended that you set up logons this way whenever possi

---

Figure 1-5 shows password expiration being set using SQL Server Management Studio time the user logon is created. Password expiration can also be done programmaticall the logon has been created. You would accomplish this by executing the T-SQL com ALTER LOGIN.

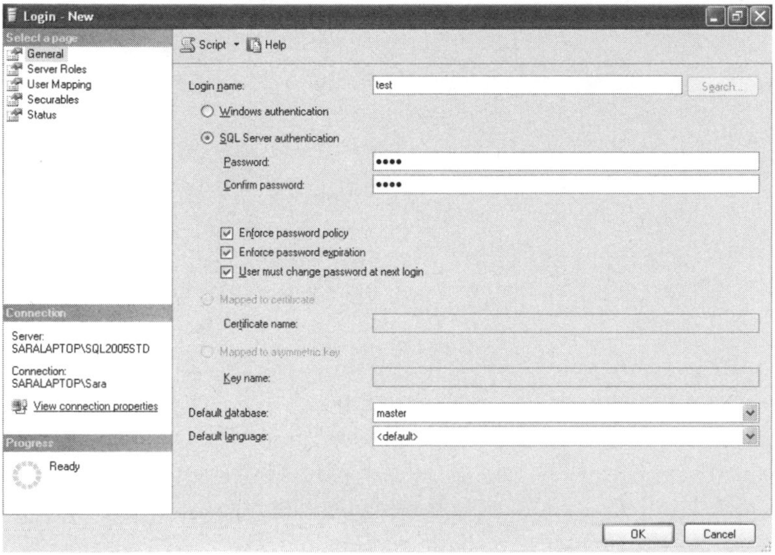

Figure 1-5   Login – New dialog box used to create a user login in SQL Server Management Studio

Because SQL Server 2005 enables you to force a password change, you can create an application for help desk employees to reset passwords while maintaining the integrity of the password. The application would use the ALTER LOGIN command to issue the password reset. The syntax for this command would be similar to the following.

```
ALTER LOGIN Test WITH PASSWORD='NewPassword', MUST_CHANGE
```

The MUST_CHANGE parameter ensures that the user must change her password the next time that she attempts to log on.

Connecting to a SQL Server Service

In this lab, you will connect to a SQL Server service using one of two different methods. In the first exercise, you will use ADO.NET to connect to an instance of SQL Server 2005. In the second exercise, you will connect to the same SQL Server instance, but this time, you will use the new SQL Native Client provider.

The completed code examples, in both Visual Basic and C#, are available in the \Labs\Chapter 01 folder on the companion CD.

IMPORTANT   Lab requirements

You will need to have SQL Server and Visual Studio 2005 installed before you can complete the exercises in this chapter. Refer to the Introduction for setup instructions.

▶ **Exercise 1: Connect Using ADO.NET**

In this exercise, you will connect to a local instance of SQL Server 2005 using ADO.NET. this, you will first create a simple Windows forms application using Visual Studio 2005

1. Open Microsoft Visual Studio 2005.
2. On the File menu, select New, Project.
3. In the New Project dialog box, expand the *Other Project Types* node, and select Visu dio Solutions.
4. Type **TK442Chapter1** for the name of your blank solution, place it in a directory o choosing, and then click OK.

   A new solution file will be created, and you can now add multiple projects to this tion. You will add one project for each lab included in this chapter.
5. On the File menu, select Add, New Project. Select Windows Application as the ten and type **Lab1** as the project name. Set the language by selecting Visual Basic, Visu or Visual J# from the language drop-down list box. By default, Visual Studio will the language specified when it was first configured.
6. From the Toolbox, drag a button control onto the Form1 design surface. Use the f ing properties for this control:

   Name = btnOpen

   Text = "Connect using ADO.NET"
7. Right-click Form1 from Solution Explorer, and select View Code. At the top of the file, add the following statement.

   ```
   //C#
   using System.Data.SqlClient;
   ```

   ```
   'VB
   Imports System.Data.SqlClient
   ```
8. Paste the following code below the Form1_load method. Modify connection stri match your environment.

   ```
   //C#
   private void btnOpen_Click(object sender, EventArgs e)
   {
       try
       {

               //Open the Connection to SQL Server Express using ADO.NET
               string connString = @"server=(local);" +
                           "Integrated Security=SSPI;" +
                           "Database=AdventureWorks";
               sqlConn = new SqlConnection(connString);
               sqlConn.Open();
   ```

```
            MessageBox.Show("Connection was successful");
    }
    catch (Exception ex)
    {
        MessageBox.Show(ex.Message);
    }
}
```

'VB

```
Private Sub btnOpen_Click(ByVal sender As System.Object, ByVal e As
System.EventArgs) Handles btnOpen.Click
        Try

            'Open the Connection to SQL Server using ADO.NET
            Dim connString As String = "server=(local);" & _
                                    "Integrated Security=SSPI;" & _
                                    "Database=AdventureWorks"
            Dim sqlConn As New SqlConnection
            sqlConn.ConnectionString = connString
            sqlConn.Open()
            MessageBox.Show("Connection was successful")

        Catch ex As Exception
            MessageBox.Show(ex.Message)
        End Try

End Sub
```

9. Save the project, and press Ctrl+F5 to build the project without debugging.

   Ensure that the project builds with no errors. Form1 should appear with the button you created.

10. Click the button to open a connection to the *AdventureWorks* database in your local instance of SQL Server. You should receive a message box that states, "Connection was successful." If you do not receive this message, you must resolve any errors before continuing.

11. Open Microsoft SQL Server Management Studio, and connect to the local instance of SQL Server.

12. Click New Query, and type the following SQL statement to query for open connections:

```
SELECT
    connect_time,
    connection_id,    session_id,
    client_net_address,
    auth_scheme
FROM
    sys.dm_exec_connections
order by connect_time desc
```

You should see a record for the connection that was just created.

▶ **Exercise 2: Connect Using SQL Native Client**

In this exercise, you will connect to the same instance of SQL Server, but this time, you w
the SQL Native Client provider. You will do this using ADO, which will require you to add
erence to the MDAC library.

IMPORTANT   Exercise Requirements

You will need to have SQL Server and the latest version of the MDAC library installed b
you can complete this exercise. Refer to the Introduction for setup instructions.

---

1. Return to the project that was created in Exercise 1. If you did not complete Exer
    you now need to complete steps 1 through 4 of Exercise 1 before continuing wit
    exercise.

2. Select Project, and Add Reference.

3. Select the COM tab, and scroll to the Microsoft ActiveX Data Objects 2.8 library c
    nent. Select that component, and click OK. This will allow you to use the ADO libr
    your code.

4. Return to the Form1 designer and drag a button control from the Toolbox on
    Form1 design surface. Use the following properties for this control:

    Name = btnOpenSNAC

    Text = "Connect using SQL Native Client"

5. Paste the following code below the Form1_load method. Modify connection stri
    match your environment.

```csharp
//C#
private void btnOpenSNC_Click(object sender, EventArgs e)
        {
            try
            {
            conn = new ADODB.Connection();
            string connString = @"Provider=SQLNCLI;" +
                            @"Data Source=(local);" +
                            "Initial Catalog=Adventureworks;" +
                            "Integrated Security=SSPI;" +
                            "DataTypeCompatibility=80;";
            conn.Open(connString,"" ,"", 0);
            MessageBox.Show("Connection was successful");

            }
            catch (Exception ex)
            {
                MessageBox.Show(ex.Message);
            }
        }
```

```vb
'VB
Private Sub btnOpenSNC_Click(ByVal sender As System.Object, ByVal e As
System.EventArgs) Handles btnOpenSNC.Click
        Try

                Dim conn As New ADODB.Connection
                conn.ConnectionString = "Provider=SQLNCLI;" _
                & "Data Source=(local);" _
                & "Initial Catalog=AdventureWorks;" _
                & "Integrated Security=SSPI;" _
                & "DataTypeCompatibility=80;"
                conn.Open()
                MessageBox.Show("Connection was successful")

        Catch ex As Exception
                MessageBox.Show(ex.Message)
        End Try
    End Sub
```

6. Open or return to Microsoft SQL Server Management Studio, and connect to the local instance of SQL Server.

7. Click New Query, and type the following SQL statement to query for open connections, or execute the same query from Exercise 1:

```sql
SELECT
    connect_time,
    connection_id,     session_id,
    client_net_address,
    auth_scheme
FROM
    sys.dm_exec_connections
order by connect_time desc
```

You should see a record for the connection that was just created.

Quick Check

1. Which popular network protocol is often used when transmitting data across a slow network?

2. Which data provider enables you to perform Multiple Active Result Set (MARS) queries?

3. Which three interfaces are available with the MDAC library?

4. When would it be a good idea to utilize ADO.NET as your data provider?

Quick Check Answers

1. TCP/IP was designed to support transmissions across the Internet and is a go performer across a wide area network or a slow network.

2. SQL Native Client is a data provider that was introduced with SQL Server 2005 was created to support some of the new features available with SQL Server 20 such as MARS queries, database mirroring, query notifications, and the XML d type.

3. MDAC supports ODBC, OLE DB, and ADO. ODBC and OLE DB are useful wh you need to query data sources outside of SQL Server, especially if you are p gramming in C++. ADO is your only option if you need to program using a scri ing language like VBScript or JScript.

4. It is a good idea to use ADO.NET as your data provider when you are developi managed code for the .NET Framework.

son 2: **Designing a Data Access Connection**

Estimated lesson time: 60 minutes

Expanding on the data access technologies reviewed in the last lesson, this lesson will cover designing connections between SQL Server and heterogeneous clients. It will also cover what needs to be done to connect to XML Web services and another instance of a SQL Server service.

igning Connections for Heterogeneous Client Computers

Not all computers that connect to your SQL Server service will be using a Windows operating system. It is not uncommon to have some users in your enterprise using other platforms, such as UNIX or Linux. However, non-Windows users can still connect to your SQL Server service through HTTP endpoints.

IMPORTANT **SQL Server Enterprise Edition Required for HTTP Endpoints**

You cannot create an HTTP endpoint using SQL Server Express Edition. You must have the standard edition or higher to create endpoints and complete the lab in this lesson.

HTTP endpoints allow you to expose data directly from your SQL Server without having to create an intermediary interface. This also enables non-Windows consumers to access the same data that Windows consumers can. You can create a stored procedure or user-defined function that exposes data both to internal company applications as well as external partners or customers that might be running on other platforms, such as UNIX.

HTTP endpoints can be created as TCP or HTTP. This indicates the protocol that will be used to send the data across the network. TCP is applicable when there is a need to create endpoints for database mirroring or service brokering. HTTP is the protocol to use when providing native XML Web services through SQL Server.

You must be a member of the sysadmin role to create endpoints. Endpoints are created using the CREATE ENDPOINT statement in a SQL query window. The following is an example of an HTTP endpoint named GetProducts, which is used to retrieve product information from the *AdventureWorks* database using a stored procedure named GetProductListing:

```
CREATE  ENDPOINT GetProducts
    STATE = STARTED
AS HTTP (
      SITE = 'localhost',
      PATH = '/sql/products',
      AUTHENTICATION = (INTEGRATED),
      PORTS=(CLEAR)
```

```
    )
FOR SOAP (
    WEBMETHOD 'GetProductListing'
    (
                name='AdventureWorks.dbo.GetProductListing',
                schema=STANDARD
    ) ,
      WSDL = DEFAULT,
      DATABASE = 'AdventureWorks',
      BATCHES=ENABLED
    )
```

The first thing to notice about this statement is that the STATE is set to a value of STAF
This indicates that the endpoint listener will be active shortly after it is created. If we di
specify this, the statement would execute, but the endpoint would not be availab
requests. Alternative values for this option are STOPPED and DISABLED.

In the CREATE ENDPOINT statement, specify that this will be an HTTP endpoint and i
will use INTEGRATED authentication. By selecting integrated authentication, either NTI
Kerberos can be used as part of the authentication challenge. Endpoints can be set with c
more of the following as authentication options:

- **Basic** Uses a base64-encoding strategy, and is not considered secure unless you
  use a *Secure Socket Layer (SSL)* port, which represents a secure connection to encry
  data. An SSL certificate will contain the IP address and port information.
- **Digest** Uses a username and password that is then encoded with a one-way ha
  algorithm. This will map to a valid Windows domain account.
- **Integrated** Indicates that authentication will occur using either NTLM or Ker
  authentication methods.
- **NTLM** Uses a challenge-response protocol; this is the authentication mechanism
  by Windows 95, Windows 98, and Windows NT 4.0.
- **Kerberos** Uses a standard Internet authentication method and is supported by
  dows 2000, Windows XP, or Windows 2003.

Selecting CLEAR as the port means you will be going through the default port 80, which
a secure channel. To use a secure channel, you would change the ports option to SSL, bu
would also need to register a secure certificate on the server hosting SQL Server 2005.

The GetProducts endpoint will retrieve data using the GetProductListing stored proce
The stored procedure represents the Web method for the native XML Web service. The
ProductListing stored procedure executes a query against the *AdventureWorks* databas
appears as follows:

```
CREATE PROCEDURE dbo.GetProductListing
AS

  SELECT name,
       productnumber,
       listprice
  FROM production.product
GO
```

Data will be returned from the endpoint in the Simple Object Access Protocol (SOAP) format. *SOAP* is a transport protocol that provides a standard way to send messages between applications. Allowing the endpoint to use SOAP as the transport protocol is specified in the FOR portion of the CREATE statement and is the best choice when returning data across the Internet. The FOR clause is used to specify the payload for the endpoint. Alternatively, the FOR clause could have been set as Transact-SQL (TSQL), service broker (SERVICE_BROKER), or database mirroring (DATABASE_MIRRORING).

By specifying the WSDL = DEFAULT switch, you are able to expose the Web Services Description Language (WSDL) to potential consumers. At this point, the PATH option is used to indicate where to locate the WSDL for the endpoint. You can get information about what the endpoint returned by querying the WSDL file at *http://localhost/sql/products?WSDL*.

By enabling batches for the GetProducts endpoint, you are allowing ad hoc SQL to be executed against the endpoint. The SOAP request will need to contain the *<sql:sqlbatch>* element. Within this element is another element named *<BatchCommands>* that contains one or more SQL statements. There can also be a *<Parameters>* element to specify any optional parameters needed for the queries. The following is an example of a SOAP request that contains an ad hoc query:

```
<?xml version="1.0" encoding="utf-8" ?>
<soap:Envelope xmlns:soap="http://schemas.xmlsoap.org/soap/envelope/"
xmlns:xsi="http://www.w3.org/2001/XMLSchema-instance"
xmlns:xsd="http://www.w3.org/2001/XMLSchema">
<soap:Body>
<sqlbatch xmlns="http://schemas.microsoft.com/sqlserver/2004/SOAP">
<BatchCommands> SELECT EmployeeID, FirstName, LastName FROM Employee WHERE
EmployeeID=@x FOR XML AUTO;
</BatchCommands>
<Parameters>
  <SqlParameter Name="x" SqlDbType="Int" MaxLength="20"
 xmlns="http://schemas.microsoft.com/SQLServer/2001/12/SOAP/types/SqlParameter">
    <Value xsi:type="xsd:string">1</Value>
    </SqlParameter>
  </Parameters>
</sqlbatch>
```

```
</soap:Body>
</soap:Envelope>
```

The SOAP request includes a query that returns employee data as an XML stream for a [ular employee. Because the employee ID needs to be passed in as a parameter for the (the <Parameters> element is included.

Enabling batches for an endpoint enables users to execute any query against the dat: This enables them to get data beyond what is returned from the Web method assigned endpoint. Essentially, they are able to execute any query allowed by the SQL Server pe sions. If you decide to enable batches for HTTP endpoints, ensure that the user acc accessing those endpoints have proper permissions assigned.

Designing Connections for HTTP Web Services

In the previous section, you saw how HTTP endpoints are created to return data directly an instance of SQL Server. This is all part of a new capability offered with SQL Server known as native XML Web services. Essentially, you are able to use HTTP and SOAP to d Web services from SQL Server 2005 directly. This enables you to bypass IIS and the ne create Web services using Visual Studio 2005.

IMPORTANT   IIS Not Required for Endpoints on Windows Server 2003

If you are creating endpoints on a Windows 2003 Server server, you do not need to have IIS installed. SQL Server 2005 will utilize the http.sys module in the Windows Server 2003 kernel

---

Using Web services to host your SQL Server data is great when you have a large amount o that needs to be retrieved quickly and efficiently. Examples of this include online produ(alogs, staff listings, stock results, and music listings.

The use of Web services can also be helpful in the generation of reports. You can easily (a stored procedure to generate the data needed and then expose it using Web services ir Server 2005. The data can then be consumed by another application or just embedded ir Excel document. By using Excel as the display mechanism, you do not have to worry : creating a special application that acts as an interface to your data.

Only authenticated users are allowed to access your native XML Web services. There is no port for anonymous users, so all incoming SOAP requests must be authenticated. Yo choose to handle security using the Windows user logon or the SQL Server logon. In the ple code created earlier, the endpoint was directed to use Windows authentication.

If Windows authentication is used, no additional SOAP authentication headers are req You only need to worry about additional SOAP authentication if you use SQL Server to a rize your users. If you do use SQL authorization, you will need to utilize Web services security using Web Services Enhancements (WSE). You will also need to modify the Transact-SQL statement used to create your endpoint. If you decide to use SQL authentication, you will need to set an option in the FOR clause that specifies that the logon type will be mixed. The following is an example of a CREATE ENDPOINT statement that uses SQL authorization.

```
CREATE  ENDPOINT GetProducts
   STATE = STARTED
AS HTTP (
     SITE = 'localhost',
     PATH = '/sql/products',
     AUTHENTICATION = (BASIC),
     PORTS=(SSL)
   )
FOR SOAP (
     WEBMETHOD 'GetProductListing'
   (
               name='AdventureWorks.dbo.GetProductListing',
               schema=STANDARD
   ) ,
     LOGIN_TYPE = MIXED,
     WSDL = DEFAULT,
     DATABASE = 'AdventureWorks',
     BATCHES=ENABLED
   )
```

When you create an endpoint using the CREATE ENDPOINT statement, you automatically have access to it, but for other SQL Server users to see and access it, you must specifically grant them access. To do this, you will use the GRANT statement. In the following example, a user named TestUser in the MyDomain domain has been granted access to the endpoint named GetProductListing:

```
GRANT CONNECT ON ENDPOINT::GetProductListing TO [MyDomain\TestUser]
```

If the endpoint was created using the default WSDL option, clients can use the WSDL document to generate proxy code. The *proxy code* contains the instructions for how the Web service should be called and what interface it is using. This will be used by the client application to access the Web service method. The WSDL document contains information about the Web service, such as the method name, what parameters are used, and what return values are provided.

Using Microsoft Visual Studio 2005, you can add a Web reference to the endpoint using a URL. If the client application is an ASP.NET project, the reference is added by selecting Add Web Reference from the Website menu. You will then see a dialog box similar to the one shown in Figure 1-6. If the client application is a Windows application project, the reference is added by selecting Add Web Reference from the Project menu. You would then select the link

for Web services on the local machine. In the URL text box, you would type the path
WSDL file for your SQL Web service. (For the previous example, this was *http://localhos*
products?WSDL.) This will generate the necessary proxy code for your client application

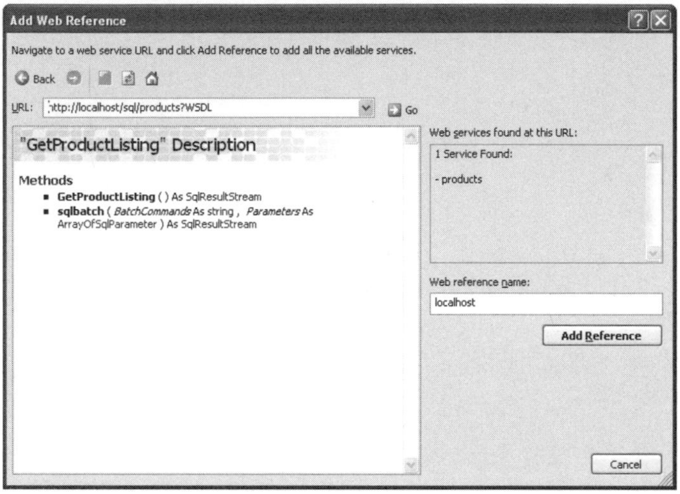

Figure 1-6   Add Web Reference dialog box for an ASP.NET project created with Visual Studio

Once the Web reference has been added, you can access the Web method exposed by the
service. You will need to pass in the necessary authentication credentials because this is a
Server requirement. The following code could be used to access the GetProducts endpoi
ated earlier:

```
//C#
SQL.GetProducts ws = new SQL.GetProducts();

ws.Credentials = new System.Net.NetworkCredential("Administrator",
"Pass@word", "MyDomain");

object[] objList = ws.GetProductListing();
DataSet ds = new DataSet();
//Loop through the array of objects returned until
//you get to the dataset
foreach (object o in objList)
{
   if (o is DataSet)
   {
     ds = (DataSet)o;
   }
}

'VB
```

```
Dim ws As New SQL.GetProducts

ws.Credentials = System.Net.CredentialCache.DefaultCredentials

Dim ds As New DataSet
Dim objList As Object() = ws.GetProductListing
'Loop through the array of objects returned until
'you get to the dataset
Dim o As Object
For Each o In objList
   If o.GetType.ToString = "System.Data.DataSet" Then
      ds = o
   End If
Next
DataGridView1.DataSource = ds.Tables(0)
ws = Nothing
```

igning Connections for Another SQL Server Instance

SQL Server 2005 enables you to install multiple instances of the SQL Server service. The additional instances are known as *named instances*, and each will be assigned a unique name, which is used to identify it. You will need this name when creating the connection string used to connect to the additional instance. If the instance was installed on a port number other than the default, you will also need to specify the port number with the instance name.

For example, the following connection strings can be used to connect to a named instance of the SQL Server service that has been assigned to port number 1431:

```
//C#
string connString = @" server=.\SERVER02,1431;" & _
                       "Integrated Security=SSPI;" & _
                       "Database=AdventureWorks"
```

```
'VB
Dim connString As String = "server=.\SERVER02,1431;" & _
                           "Integrated Security=SSPI;" & _
                           "Database=AdventureWorks"
```

With SQL Server 2005, you can create linked servers, which allow you to execute commands against an OLE DB source. The data source could be a heterogeneous data source, such as Oracle, or just another instance of the SQL Server service.

You can create a linked server using SQL Server Management Studio or a SQL script. To create a linked server using SQL Server Management Studio, expand the *Server Objects* node from the Object Explorer pane. From here, you should see a node called *Linked Servers*. You create a new linked server by right-clicking the *Linked Servers* node and selecting New Linked Server.

The New Linked Server dialog box shown in Figure 1-7 enables you to specify the server as SQL Server or Other data source. If the server type is SQL Server, you need to type instance name in the Linked Server text box.

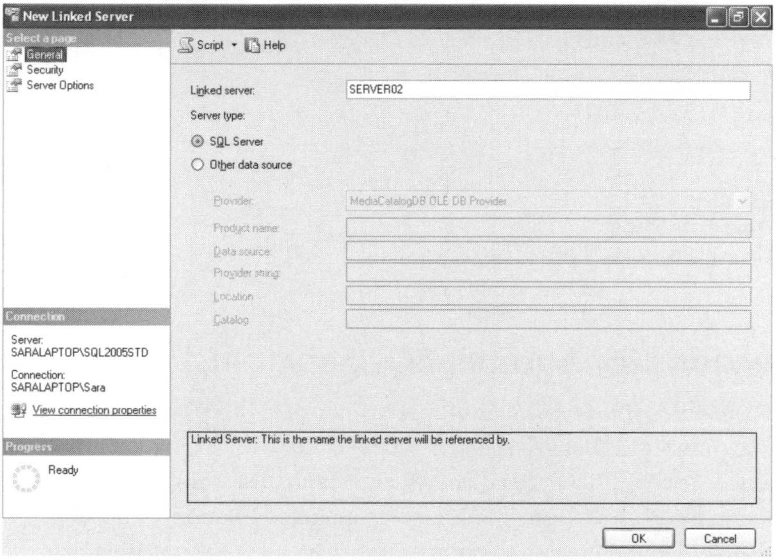

Figure 1-7   Add New Linked Server dialog box in SQL Server Management Studio

After the linked server has been created, you can execute queries and commands against the linked server using a four-part name. The name appears as *linked_server_name.c .schema.object_name*.

Its four parts are:

- **linked_server_name**   Name of the linked server as it was specified in the New Li Server dialog box. For a SQL Server linked server, this is the instance name.
- **Catalog**   For a SQL Server linked server, this is the name of the database.
- **Schema**   For a SQL Server 2005 instance, this refers to the user-schema, which is lection of database entities that forms a single namespace. For earlier versions of Server, this portion of the four-part name is the database owner, such as dbo.
- **Object_name**   This is the object being accessed, which is typically a table name. It also be another object, such as a view or a user-defined function.

Lab: Creating and Consuming HTTP Endpoints

In this lab, you will create an HTTP endpoint that is used to get information about engine employees from the *AdventureWorks* database. In the first exercise, you will create the I endpoint on SQL Server 2005. In the second exercise, you will create a Windows forms project that references the endpoint and displays the data returned in a *dataGridView* control.

The completed code examples, in both Visual Basic and C#, are available in the \Labs\Chapter 01 folder on the companion CD.

▶ Exercise 1: Create an HTTP Endpoint

In this exercise, you will create a stored procedure to retrieve engineering employee information. The stored procedure will be referenced by a newly-created HTTP endpoint.

1. Open Microsoft SQL Server Management Studio, and connect to the local instance of SQL Server.

2. Click New Query, and type the following SQL statement to create a stored procedure named GetEngineeringEmployees. Ensure that you receive a message stating the commands completed successfully.

```
CREATE PROCEDURE dbo.GetEngineeringEmployees
AS

SELECT e.employeeid,
       e.title,
       c.firstname,
       c.middlename,
       c.lastname
FROM humanresources.employee e
LEFT JOIN person.contact c
    ON e.contactid = c.contactid
LEFT JOIN humanresources.employeedepartmenthistory ed
    ON e.employeeid = ed.employeeid
WHERE ed.departmentid = 1
    AND (startdate < getdate() AND enddate is null)
GO
```

Select the *AdventureWorks* database from the Available Databases drop-down list, and then click Execute.

3. In the same query window, type the following SQL statement to create an HTTP endpoint named GetEngineeringList. Ensure that you receive a message stating the commands completed successfully.

IMPORTANT Stop IIS to Complete Exercise

If the machine you are using for this exercise has IIS installed on it, you will have to stop the IIS Admin Service to be able to create your endpoint. Otherwise, you will receive an error stating that the port is already bound to another process. Go to Services in Control Panel to stop the IIS Admin Service. When you restart the IIS Admin Service, be sure to also restart the World Wide Web Publishing Service.

```
CREATE  ENDPOINT GetEngineeringList
STATE = STARTED
AS HTTP (
    SITE = 'localhost',
    PATH = '/sql/employees',
    AUTHENTICATION = (INTEGRATED),
    PORTS=(CLEAR)
)
FOR SOAP (
    WEBMETHOD 'GetEngineeringEmployees'
    (
            name='AdventureWorks.dbo.GetEngineeringEmployees',
            schema=STANDARD
    ) ,
    WSDL = DEFAULT,
    DATABASE = 'AdventureWorks',
    BATCHES=ENABLED
)
```

Select the *AdventureWorks* database from the Available Databases drop-down list, then click Execute.

4. Open Internet Explorer, and type the URL *http://localhost/sql/employees?WSDL*

IMPORTANT   Possible delay

There could be a delay in the creation of the WSDL document for your endpoint. If you an error, wait a few seconds and try typing the URL again.

---

5. Inspect the WSDL document displayed in the browser window. Select Find, and search for GetEngineeringEmployees. Note that the XML associated with the stored cedure only occupies a small portion of the document.

▶ **Exercise 2: Consume the HTTP Endpoint**

In this exercise, you will create a Windows forms application using Visual Studio 2005, add a reference to the HTTP endpoint created in Exercise 1.

1. Open Microsoft Visual Studio 2005.

   If you completed the lab from Lesson 1, you can skip to step 4.

2. On the File menu, select New, Project.

3. In the New Project dialog box, expand the *Other Project Types* node, and select Visual dio Solutions. Type **TK442Chapter1** for the name of your blank solution, and place a directory of your choosing. A new solution file will be created, and you can now multiple projects to this solution. You will add one project for each lab included i chapter.

4. On the File menu, select Add, New Project. Select Windows Application as the template, and type **Lab2** as the project name. Set the language by selecting Visual Basic, Visual C#, or Visual J# from the language drop-down list box. By default, Visual Studio will select the language specified when it was first configured.

5. From the Project menu, select Add Web Reference.

6. From the Web Reference dialog box, type the URL *http://localhost/sql/employees?WSDL* and then click Go.

7. You should see the *GetEngineeringList* method displayed in the methods pane. Note that you also have access to a method named *sqlbatch*. This method is available because the endpoint was created using the BATCHES=ENABLED option.

8. Type SQL as the Web reference name, and click the Add Reference button to add the reference.

9. From the Toolbox, drag a button control onto the Form1 design surface. Use the following properties for this control:

    Name = btnWebService

    Text = "Connect to Web service"

10. From the Toolbox, drag a *dataViewGrid* control onto the Form1 design surface. Leave the properties with the default values.

11. Right-click the Form1 file from Solution Explorer, and select View Code. Paste the following code into the code window:

```
//C#
private void btnWebService_Click(object sender, EventArgs e)
        {
            try
            {
                SQL.GetProducts ws = new SQL.GetEngineeringList();

//Use the credentials of the user that is logged in
                ws.Credentials = System.Net.CredentialCache.DefaultCredentials;

                object[] objList = ws.GetEngineeringEmployees();
                DataSet ds = new DataSet();
                //Loop through the array of objects returned until
                //you get to the dataset
                foreach (object o in objList)
                {
                    if (o is DataSet)
                    {
                        ds = (DataSet)o;
                    }
                }
                dataGridView1.DataSource = ds.Tables[0];
```

```
        }
        catch (Exception ex)
        {
            MessageBox.Show(ex.Message);
        }

    }
```

```vb
'VB
Private Sub btnWebService_Click(ByVal sender As System.Object, ByVal e As
System.EventArgs) Handles btnWebService.Click
        Try
            Dim ws As New SQL.GetEngineeringList

            'Use the credentials of the user that is logged in
            ws.Credentials = System.Net.CredentialCache.DefaultCredentials

            Dim ds As New DataSet
            Dim objList As Object() = ws.GetEngineeringEmployees
            'Loop through the array of objects returned until
            'you get to the dataset
            Dim o As Object
            For Each o In objList
                If o.GetType.ToString = "System.Data.DataSet" Then
                    ds = o
                End If
            Next
            DataGridView1.DataSource = ds.Tables(0)
            ws = Nothing

        Catch ex As Exception
            MessageBox.Show(ex.Message)
        End Try


    End Sub
```

12. Save the Lab2 project by going to the File menu and selecting Save All.

13. Right-click the Lab2 project from Solution Explorer, and select Set As Startup Proj

14. Press Ctrl+F5 to build the project without debugging. Ensure that the project build
cessfully. Form1 should appear after the project compiles and executes. You shou
an Open Web Service button; click this button. The data results are displayed in the
ViewGrid control, as shown in Figure 1-8.

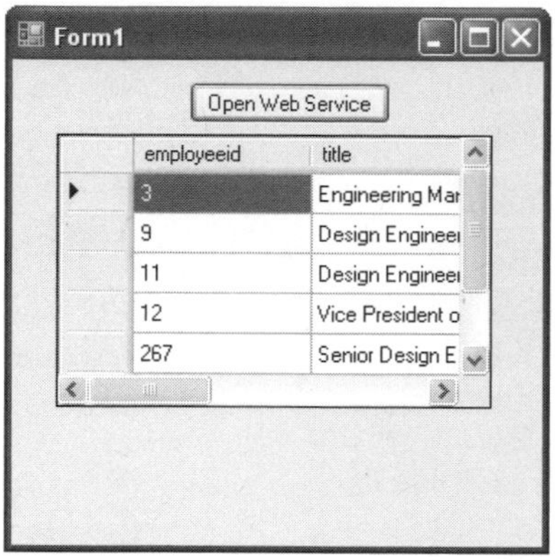

Figure 1-8 Form1 as it displays a list of all engineering employees from the *AdventureWorks* database

---

Quick Check

1. Which protocol enables you to expose SQL Server data to heterogeneous clients?
2. When creating an HTTP endpoint, which option must be set to allow consumers to execute ad hoc queries against the endpoint?
3. When creating an HTTP endpoint, which option must be set to allow consumers to view a WSDL document associated with the endpoint?
4. When executing a query against a linked server, how is the data source identified in the query statement?

Quick Check Answers

1. HTTP is the protocol, and you can create HTTP endpoints using the CREATE ENDPOINT statement. This enables you to expose SQL Server data as a Web service to clients that might not be running on the Windows platform.
2. You must set the BATCHES=ENABLED option in the CREATE ENDPOINT statement to allow consumers to execute ad hoc queries. Which queries can be executed will still be controlled by the level of access granted to the consumer making the request.
3. You must set the WSDL = DEFAULT option in the CREATE ENDPOINT statement for the WSDL document to be generated. This document can be used by consumers to generate a proxy that is used to connect a client application to the endpoint.
4. The linked server name is identified through a four-part name whose parts appear as follows:

   linked_server_name.catalog.schema.object_name

Lesson 3: Designing a Data Access Object Model

Estimated lesson time: 45 minutes

Database developers must often decide between several data access object models. To an appropriate data access object model, he or she must know what type of data needs retrieved. This lesson will cover the different models available and what considerations sl be made when selecting one.

What is the ADO Object Model?

The ActiveX Data Objects (ADO) object model is a data access technology that define objects used to access the data. It provides a high-level interface, so you can get to your d; quickly and easily as possible. And, it lets you access data from a wide variety of data so

The model has evolved over the years; some developers might remember using previou; models known as Data Access Objects (DAO) or Remote Data Objects (RDO). These m relied on a complex and deep hierarchical data structure. The ADO object model is a 1 model that simplifies many of the steps involved with connecting and accessing data f data source.

You may recall from Lesson 1 that there are two versions of ADO available. There is the that is part of the MDAC and then there is ADO.NET, which is part of the .NET Frame Both use similar concepts regarding connections and some of the other basic objects, bu use different structures and models.

For both data access methods, you must make a choice between using a connected or di nected model. This will determine the type of data object into which you return your dat; difference between a connected and disconnected model has to do with whether a conne to the data source is maintained after the data object has been populated. Each metho distinct advantages and disadvantages; which method to use depends on the applic requirements.

Using a Disconnected Model with ADO.NET

The idea of a disconnected model was driven primarily by the need for efficiency and sc; ity while still allowing for maximum functionality. Let's say you have an application th; plays and manipulates data from a data source. If you choose a connected model, yo; maintain a connection to the data source even after the data has been passed to the ap tion. This connection will consume memory and resources on the application server. 1 application is being accessed by multiple simultaneous users—say, thousands of them could significantly alter the ability of your application server to perform well. You will likely notice slowdowns as the number of user connections increases.

The disconnected model, which disconnects the client from the data source as soon as the data is returned, is ideal for applications that need to cache data locally for a large number of simultaneous users. In this model, the client will connect with the data source and return a snapshot of the data required. It will then disconnect from the client and only reconnect when changes need to be made or data refreshed from the data source.

The key object in ADO.NET that supports the disconnected model is the *DataSet*. The *DataSet* object is an in-memory representation of the data as it existed on the data source at the time the query was executed. It can contain data from several different tables that are linked together through relationships. This enables you to maintain data from both the parent and child tables within the same *DataSet* object.

The *DataSet* maintains a structure that is similar to the database structure. It is hierarchical and contains collections for tables, rows, columns, constraints, and relationships. The type of *DataSet* offered with ADO.NET is very different than the one that comes with ADO. With ADO, you cannot have multiple tables inside a single *DataSet*. You can return data from multiple tables, but there won't be any relationships that define how the data results relate to each other.

DataSets can be beneficial in the following situations:

- To easily populate data-bound controls in Windows and Web-based applications
- To process data from multiple tables and potentially different data sources while maintaining the relationships between these tables
- To cache data locally for operations such as sorting or filtering
- To pass data through application tiers or through an XML Web service

DataSets can be created using the Data Source Configuration Wizard or with the Dataset Designer. This can be useful when creating a *typed dataset*, which is a *DataSet* that maintains the schema information and is easier to maintain and less prone to errors.

Of course, *DataSets* can also be created programmatically because the *DataSet* object is just derived from a class in the .NET Framework. To create a *DataSet*, you start by creating a new instance, such as in the following code:

```
//C#
DataSet dsEmployees = new DataSet("Products");
```

```
'VB
Dim dsEmployees As New DataSet("Products")
```

To get data into your *DataSet*, you need a data source. This is defined by using the *DataA*
object. ADO.NET offers two data adapters: one specifically for SQL Server, and another
other databases. If you are querying a SQL Server database, you want to use the *SQL*
Adapter. In addition to the *SQLDataAdapter* object, you need a *SQLConnection* to represe
connection to the database and a *SQLCommand* object to represent the action taken a
the database. Before you can access these objects, you need to set a reference at the top o
code file to the *System.Data.SqlClient* class, such as in the following code statement:

```
//C#
using System.Data.SqlClient;
```

```
'VB
Imports System.Data.SqlClient
```

You can then create instances of the *SQLDataAdapter*, *SQLConnection*, and *SQLCom*
objects, as in the following code:

```
//C#
SqlDataAdapter adapter = new SqlDataAdapter();
SqlConnection conn = new SqlConnection(connString);
```

```
'VB
Dim adapter As New SqlDataAdapter()
Dim conn As New SqlConnection(connString)
Dim cmd As New SqlCommand(queryString, conn)
```

In this sample code, a *SQLCommand* object was created using a query string. This query
could have contained an actual Transact-SQL statement such as SELECT * FROM Produ
it could contain the name of a stored procedure. This will represent the action that is
against the data source which, in this case, is a query.

BEST PRACTICES Wrap Database Code in a *Try...Catch* Block

It is a good idea to wrap the portion of your code that accesses the database inside a *try...c*
block. You can then place any cleanup code in the Finally portion of this block. For *DataAdc*
and *Connection* objects, you can specifically call the *Dispose* method to ensure that all systen
resources are released.

If changes need to be made to the data in a *DataSet*, they will be made to the in-memor
of the data. The changes will not be propagated back to the data source until the *U*
method for the *DataAdapter* object is called. The following code is an example of s
changes made to the dsProducts *DataSet* back to the data source defined with the *DataA*
named adapter:

```
//C#
adapter.Update(dsProducts.Tables[0]);
```

```
'VB
adapter.Update(dsProducts.Tables(0))
```

g a Connected Model with ADO.NET

ADO.NET also provides objects that maintain a connection to the data source until they are specifically closed and released. The *DataReader* object is part of ADO.NET's connected model, and it returns a read-only, forward-only stream of data from a data source. Because it is read-only and forward-only, it can be quite efficient for applications that only need to display data and not manipulate it or cache it locally.

Deciding whether to use a *DataSet* or a *DataReader* depends on the requirements of the application. If the application needs to cache data locally so that it can be updated, the *DataSet* is a good choice. If the data returned will only be read and not manipulated, a *DataReader* is generally the most efficient choice. This is especially true if the amount of data returned is too large to be cached in-memory.

Using a *DataReader* object does require that the developer specifically close the resource when it is no longer needed, but if this is done as soon as possible, the *DataReader* can be an efficient form of data access. As long as you do not require the functionality available with the *DataSet*, it is more efficient to return data to a *DataReader* object.

To use the *DataReader* object, you still need a connection to the database using either the *SQLConnection* or *OleDbConnection* objects. You can also still use the *SQLCommand* or *OleDbCommand* objects to handle the action performed against the data source. The *DataReader* object you select is also determined by the data source. The following *DataReader* objects are available:

- *SQLDataReader*
- *OleDbDataReader*
- *OdbcDataReader*
- *OracleDataReader*

You will use the *ExecuteReader* method of the command object to return data into the chosen *DataReader* object. The following code is an example of a *SQLDataReader* populated with data from a *SQLCommand* object named *cmd*:

```
//C#
SqlDataReader reader = cmd.ExecuteReader();
```

```
'VB
Dim reader as SqlDataReader = cmd.ExecuteReader()
```

In some cases, you might want to return data as an XML stream. In this case, you will u
XmlReader object to obtain a read-only, forward-only stream of data in an XML format. Yc
still use the same connection and command objects used to populate a *DataReader*, but :
case, the query will use the FOR XML AUTO clause to return the data as XML. You wi
need to add an additional reference at the top of your code to the *System.Xml* namespac
example, the following code could be used to populate an *XmlReader* object with XMI
from the products table in the *AdventureWorks* database:

```
//C#
string queryString = "select name, productnumber, listprice " +
                                "from production.product " +
                                "FOR XML AUTO";
SqlCommand cmd = new SqlCommand(queryString, conn);
XmlReader xreader = cmd.ExecuteXmlReader();
```

```
'VB
Dim queryString As String = "select name, productnumber, listprice " + _
                                "from production.product " + _
                                "FOR XML AUTO"
Dim cmd As SqlCommand = New SqlCommand(queryString, conn)
Dim xreader As XmlReader = cmd.ExecuteXmlReader()
```

Lab: Selecting a Data Access Object Model

In this lab, you will connect to a database using both the disconnected and connected n
from ADO.NET. In the first exercise, you will create a Windows forms project that ret
data from the database using a *DataSet*. In the second exercise, you will use the same Wir
forms project from Exercise 1, and you will retrieve data in a *SQLDataReader* and displ
results in a message box.

The completed code examples, in both Visual Basic and C#, are available in the \Labs\
ter 01 folder on the companion CD.

▶ Exercise 1: Retrieve Data Using a Dataset

In this exercise, you will create a new Windows forms project named Lab 3 and add it
existing solution created in previous lessons. You will connect to the *AdventureWorks* dat
retrieve product data for all products, populate a *DataSet*, and then use that data to po
a *dataGridView* control.

   1. Open Microsoft SQL Server Management Studio, and connect to the local insta
       SQL Server.

2. Click New Query, and type the following SQL statement to create a new stored procedure named GetProductListing:

```
USE [AdventureWorks]
GO
/****** Object:  StoredProcedure [dbo].[GetProductListing]    ******/
SET ANSI_NULLS ON
GO
SET QUOTED_IDENTIFIER ON
GO
CREATE PROCEDURE [dbo].[GetProductListing]
AS

select name, productnumber, listprice
from production.product
GO
```

3. Open Microsoft Visual Studio 2005. If you completed the Lesson 1 lab or the Lesson 2 lab, you can skip to step 6.

4. On the File menu, select New, Project.

5. In the New Project dialog box, expand the *Other Project Types* node, and select Visual Studio Solutions. Type **TK442Chapter1** for the name of your blank solution, and place it in a directory of your choosing. A new solution file is created, and you can now add multiple projects to this solution. You will add one project for each lab included in this chapter.

6. On the File menu, select Add, New Project. Select Windows Application as the template, and type **Lab3** as the project name. Set the language by selecting Visual Basic, Visual C#, or Visual J# from the language drop-down list box. By default, Visual Studio will select the language specified when it was first configured.

7. From the Toolbox, drag a button control onto the Form1 design surface. Use the following properties for this control:

Name = btnDataset

Text = "Open Dataset"

8. From the Toolbox, drag a *dataViewGrid* control onto the Form1 design surface. Leave the properties with the default values.

9. Right-click the Form1 file from Solution Explorer, and select View Code. Paste the following code into the code window, modifying connection strings to match your environment:

```
//C#
private void btnDataset_Click(object sender, EventArgs e)
{
    DataSet dsProducts = new DataSet("Products");
    SqlDataAdapter adapter = new SqlDataAdapter();

    //Initiate the connection to SQL Server
```

```
String connString = @"server=.\SQL2005STD;" +
                        "Integrated Security=SSPI;" +
                        "Database=AdventureWorks";
SqlConnection conn = new SqlConnection(connString);

//Define the query that will be executed
SqlCommand cmd = new SqlCommand("GetProductListing", conn);

try
{
    //Populate the adapter with results of the query
    adapter.SelectCommand = cmd;
    adapter.Fill(dsProducts);
    //Set the datasource for the dataViewGrid control on the form
    dataGridView1.DataSource = dsProducts.Tables[0];

}
catch (Exception ex)
{
    MessageBox.Show(ex.Message);
}
finally
{
    if (adapter != null)
    {
        adapter.Dispose();
        adapter = null;
    }
    if (cmd != null)
    {
        cmd.Dispose();
        cmd = null;
    }

    if (conn != null)
    {
        if (conn.State == ConnectionState.Open)
        {
            conn.Close();
        }
        conn = null;
    }
}

}
```

'VB
```
Private Sub btnDataset_Click(ByVal sender As System.Object, ByVal e As
System.EventArgs) Handles btnDataset.Click

    Dim dsProducts As New DataSet("Products")
```

```
Dim adapter As New SqlDataAdapter()

    'Initiate the connection to SQL Server
    Dim connString As String = "server=.\SQL2005STD;" & _
                                "Integrated Security=SSPI;" & _
                                "Database=AdventureWorks"
    Dim conn As New SqlConnection(connString)

    'Define the query that will be executed
    Dim cmd As New SqlCommand("GetProductListing", conn)

    Try
        'Populate the adapter with results of the query
        adapter.SelectCommand = cmd
        adapter.Fill(dsProducts)

        'Set the datasource for the dataViewGrid control on the form
        DataGridView1.DataSource = dsProducts.Tables(0)

    Catch ex As Exception
        MessageBox.Show(ex.Message)
    Finally
        If Not (adapter Is Nothing) Then
            adapter.Dispose()
            adapter = Nothing
        End If

        If Not (cmd Is Nothing) Then
            cmd.Dispose()
            cmd = Nothing
        End If

        If Not (conn Is Nothing) Then
            If (conn.State = ConnectionState.Open) Then
                conn.Close()
            End If
            conn = Nothing
        End If

    End Try

End Sub
```

10. On the File menu, select Save All to save the Lab3 project.
11. Right-click the Lab3 project from Solution Explorer, and select Set As Startup Project.
12. Press Ctrl+F5 to build the project without debugging. Ensure that the project builds successfully. Form1 should appear after the project compiles and executes. You should see an Open Dataset button; click this button. The data results are displayed in the *dataView-Grid* control.

► **Exercise 2: Retrieve Data Using a *DataReader***

In this exercise, you will add a button to the Windows forms project named Lab 3 that w:
ated in Exercise 1. You will connect to the *AdventureWorks* database, retrieve product d:
products with a shipment level less than 50, populate a *SQLDataReader*, and then
through the results and display them in a message box.

1. Open Microsoft Visual Studio 2005.

2. Open the project, created in Exercise 1, named Lab 3.

3. From the Toolbox, drag a button control onto the Form1 design surface. Use the f
    ing properties for this control:

    Name = btnDataReader

    Text = "Open DataReader"

4. Right-click the Form1 file from Solution Explorer, and select View Code. Paste t
    lowing code into the code window, modifying connection strings to match your en
    ment:

```csharp
//C#
private void btnDataReader_Click(object sender, EventArgs e)
    {
        //Initiate the connection to SQL Server
        String connString = @"server=.\SQL2005STD;" +
                            "Integrated Security=SSPI;" +
                            "Database=AdventureWorks";
        SqlConnection conn = new SqlConnection(connString);
        conn.Open();

        //Define the query that will be executed
        string queryString = "select name, productnumber, listprice " +
                            "from production.product " +
                            "where safetystocklevel < 50";
        SqlCommand cmd = new SqlCommand(queryString, conn);

        SqlDataReader reader = null;
        try
        {
            //Execute the command and return a datareader
            reader = cmd.ExecuteReader();

            //See if the object has data and if it does
            //format a string with the results and display
            //it as a message box
            String ret = "";
            if (reader.HasRows)
            {
                do
                {
```

```csharp
                while (reader.Read())
                    ret += reader.GetString(0) + " - " +
                            reader.GetString(1) + " (" +
                            reader.GetDecimal(2) + ")" +
                            "\n";
            }
            while (reader.NextResult());

        }
        else
        {
            MessageBox.Show("No rows returned.");
        }

        MessageBox.Show(ret);
    }
    catch (Exception ex)
    {
        MessageBox.Show(ex.Message);
    }
    finally
    {
        if (reader != null)
        {
            reader.Close();
            reader = null;
        }

        if (conn != null)
        {
            if (conn.State == ConnectionState.Open)
            {
                conn.Close();
            }
            conn = null;
        }
    }
}
```

'VB
```vb
Private Sub btnDataReader_Click(ByVal sender As System.Object, ByVal e As
System.EventArgs) Handles btnDataReader.Click

        'Initiate the connection to SQL Server
        Dim connString As String = "server=.\SQL2005STD;" & _
                                    "Integrated Security=SSPI;" & _
                                    "Database=AdventureWorks"
        Dim conn As New SqlConnection(connString)
        conn.Open()
```

```vb
'Define the query that will be executed
Dim queryString As String = "select name, productnumber, listprice " + _
                            "from production.product " + _
                            "where safetystocklevel < 50"
Dim cmd As New SqlCommand(queryString, conn)

Dim reader As SqlDataReader
Try
    'Execute the command and return a datareader
    reader = cmd.ExecuteReader()

    'See if the object has data and if it does
    'format a string with the results and display
    'it as a message box
    Dim ret As String = ""
    If reader.HasRows Then
        Do While reader.Read()
            ret += reader.GetString(0) + " - " + _
                reader.GetString(1) + " (" + _
                Convert.ToString(reader.GetDecimal(2)) + ")" + _
                Chr(10) + Chr(13)
        Loop
    Else
        MessageBox.Show("No rows returned.")
    End If
    MessageBox.Show(ret)

Catch ex As Exception
    MessageBox.Show(ex.Message)
Finally
    If Not (reader Is Nothing) Then
        reader.Close()
    End If

    If Not (conn Is Nothing) Then
        If (conn.State = ConnectionState.Open) Then
            conn.Close()
        End If
        conn = Nothing
    End If
End Try
End Sub
```

5. On the File menu, select Save All to save the Lab3 project.

6. Right-click the Lab3 project from Solution Explorer, and select Set As Startup Proj

7. Press Ctrl+F5 to build the project without debugging. Ensure that the project build
    cessfully. Form1 should appear after the project compiles and executes. You shou
    an Open DataReader button; click this button. The data results are displayed in a
    sage box.

Quick Check

1. What data object is used in the ADO.NET disconnected model?
2. In what situation is it best to use a *DataSet* object?
3. In what situation is it best to use a *DataReader* object?
4. What object with the connected model is used to return XML data?

Quick Check Answers

1. The *DataSet* object is used in ADO.NET to return data to an in-memory local cache representation of the data from the data source. The client is then disconnected and will only reconnect when updates need to be passed back to the data source.
2. A *DataSet* object is appropriate in situations where data is coming from multiple tables and/or multiple data sources. It is useful for populating data-bound controls and when there is a need to cache data for sorting or filtering. It can also be used to pass structured data through Web services.
3. A *DataReader* object is appropriate in situations where data does not need to be cached locally. If data just needs to be provided quickly, one time, and in a read-only and forward-only fashion, then a *DataReader* can be very efficient.
4. Like the *DataReader*, the *XmlReader* provides a read-only, forward-only view of the data. But in the case of the *XmlReader*, the data is in an XML format.

---

e Scenario: Selecting a Data Access Strategy

You are a database developer for a large bank that is currently upgrading several classic ASP applications to the .NET Framework. The new applications will access a SQL Server that was recently upgraded from SQL Server 2000 to SQL Server 2005. This is the only data source that the application needs to access. The original applications used Visual Basic script to access business logic stored in DLLs built with Visual Basic 6.0.

The development manager has asked you to review the first application to be upgraded and make recommendations for what technologies the new application will utilize. The application is a Web application used by customers to access account information. He tells you that the first upgrade will be a test run for the remaining upgrades, and he would like to see it done as quickly as possible. What recommendations do you make to the manager regarding data access?

Suggested Practices

Objective 1.1: Design appropriate data access technologies

- **Practice 1**   Locate non-SQL data sources in your organization, such as Access data or Excel spreadsheets. Create a test .NET Windows application that makes a conn to these data sources using the MDAC data providers discussed in Lesson 1. U ODBC and ADO APIs to create the connection. Pay attention to differences in the nection strings for each provider.

- **Practice 2**   Create an HTTP endpoint that references the stored procedure crea Lab 1 for Lesson 2. This time, alter the values for the CREATE ENDPOINT statem that it returns data as T-SQL instead. Also, make a change so that batches ar enabled. Note the differences in the output that is generated.

Objective 1.2: Design an appropriate data access object model

- **Practice 1**   Create a test Windows .NET application that reads data from a non-SQ source using the *ODBCDataReader* object. The application should iterate throug data and display the results in a *DataGridView* control.

- **Practice 2**   Create a test Windows .NET application that will access the *Adventure* database and execute the following query:

```
SELECT name, productnumber, listprice
FROM production.product
             FOR XML AUTO
```

The application should use an *XMLDataReader* object to return the data as an stream. Display the data on the Windows form using either a *listbox* control, *textbo* trol, or message box.

References

- Learning ADO.NET
  http://msdn2.microsoft.com/en-us/data/aa937699.aspx
- Learning Microsoft Data Access Components (MDAC)
  http://msdn2.microsoft.com/en-us/data/aa937703.aspx
- Learning SQL Native Client
  http://msdn2.microsoft.com/en-us/data/aa937705.aspx
- Usage Scenarios for SQL Server 2005 Native Web Services
  http://msdn2.microsoft.com/en-us/library/ms345140.aspx

- How to Use the ODBC.NET Managed Provider in Visual Basic .NET and Connection Strings
  http://support.microsoft.com/kb/310985/
- How to Use the ODBC.NET Managed Provider in Visual C# .NET and Connection Strings
  http://support.microsoft.com/kb/310988
- SQL Server OLE DB Programmers Reference
  http://msdn2.microsoft.com/en=gb/library/aa198360(SQL.80).aspx
- ADO.NET: More than a Matter of ABCs "Connected and Disconnected Modes"
  http://www.samspublishing.com/articles/article.asp?p=102202&seqNum=2&rl=1
- Comparison of ADO.NET and ADO
  http://msdn.microsoft.com/library/default.asp?url=/library/en-us/vbcon/html /vbconADOPreviousVersionsOfADO.asp

apter Summary

- SQL Server 2005 supports the following four network protocols: Shared Memory, Named Pipes, TCP/IP, and VIA. You can specify a particular network protocol in the connection string.
- The Microsoft Data Access Components (MDAC) library is the appropriate data provider when you are writing native code that targets Windows or you need to provide data access for an ASP application, Visual Basic 6.0x COM, or C++ application.
- The SQL Native Client (SNAC) was introduced with SQL Server 2005 and can be used to access new SQL Server features, such as MARS queries, database mirroring, and the XML data type.
- ADO.NET is the appropriate data access provider when providing data access to a managed code application for the .NET Framework.
- Non-Windows users can connect to SQL Server 2005 through HTTP endpoints. This is a way of exposing data from SQL Server through Web services. Endpoints can be set with one or more of the following authentication methods: Basic, Digest, Integrated, NTLM, or Kerberos.
- In a disconnected model, the client is disconnected from the data source after the *DataSet* has been populated. A data adapter is used to fill the *DataSet* with data retrieved from a command object.
- In a connected model, the client remains connected to the data source until the connection is specifically closed. The *DataReader* object is used to return a read-only, forward-only stream of data.

esigning Database Queries

Microsoft SQL Server 2005 is designed to handle small to large enterprise-level databases. However, it does little good to have data in a database unless you know how to extract portions of that data. It is critical for every database developer and administrator to know how to query a SQL Server 2005 database.

Lesson 1 will begin with writing database queries, which covers everything from query basics to writing functions and remote queries. Lesson 2 will move on to writing specialized queries, which involves using query hints and writing full-text queries. Lesson 3 will feature retrieving data from Extensible Markup Language (XML) sources and will cover how to write an XQuery (an XML querying language) expression.

Exam objectives in this chapter:

- Write and modify queries.
  - ❑ Write queries.
  - ❑ Modify queries to improve query performance.
- Design queries for retrieving data from XML sources.
  - ❑ Select the correct attributes.
  - ❑ Select the correct nodes.
  - ❑ Filter by values of attributes and values of elements.
  - ❑ Include relational data, such as columns and variables, in the result of an XQuery expression.
  - ❑ Include XML attribute or node values in a tabular result set.
  - ❑ Update, insert, or delete relational data based on XML parameters to stored procedures.
  - ❑ Debug and troubleshoot queries against XML data sources.

Before You Begin

To complete the lessons in this chapter, you must have:

- A computer that meets or exceeds the minimum hardware requirements listed i Introduction at the beginning of this book.
- SQL Server 2005 installed, as well as the SQL Server 2005 *AdventureWorks* sa database.
- Experience designing and executing queries in SQL Server Management Studio.
- Experience creating and working with XML data.

son 1: Writing Database Queries

Estimated lesson time: 90 minutes

SQL Server 2005 provides several methods for extracting data from a database. You can use special operators to aggregate and combine data. In addition to the data available within the database, you can query remote or heterogeneous data using linked servers. This lesson will cover the different ways you can write database queries.

te SELECT Queries

The SELECT statement is the primary means of querying a relational database. This is a Transact-SQL statement that can be simple or quite complex depending on which clauses are applied to the SELECT statement. The basic structure of this statement is as follows, in which those statements surrounded by square brackets are optional:

```
SELECT <comma-delimited list of expressions or column names>
[INTO <table name>]
FROM <tables, views, or linked servers>
[WHERE <search condition(s)>]
[GROUP BY <comma-delimited list of columns>]
[HAVING <search condition(s)>]
[ORDER BY <comma-delimited list of columns> <ASC or DESC>]
```

Notice that the only portions of the statement that are required are the SELECT and FROM clauses. The simplest SELECT statement would look something like the following:

```
SELECT * FROM Person.Contact
```

The previous query requested that all rows, due to the wildcard symbol (*), should be retrieved from the Person.Contact table. Most queries that you write will not be this simple, and there are many considerations that need to be made when designing complex queries.

Performing Joins

One of the most frequently used operations in a SELECT statement is a join. Because most databases are normalized, it is often necessary to retrieve data from multiple tables. *Normalization* is the process in which data is separated into multiple related tables. Joins enable you to create a result set that is derived from one or more tables. A join relates tables based on a key column, such as a primary key or a foreign key. You want the column specified in your join clause to contain values common to both tables. For the *AdventureWorks* database, you can join the Person.Contact table to the HumanResources.Employee table to retrieve an employee's title. For example, the following query returns the first name and last name from the Person.C〈 table and then the title from the HumanResources.Employee table:

```
SELECT con.FirstName, con.LastName, emp.Title
FROM Person.Contact con
JOIN HumanResources.Employee emp
   ON con.ContactID = emp.ContactID
```

There are several types of joins, and which one is used depends on what data needs returned. Which join type is used can affect the number of rows that are returned. The 〈 ent join types are as follows:

- **INNER**   This is the default join type and is used if you do not specify a join type. I〈 cates that all matching rows from both tables should be returned. When this join t〈 used for the previous query 290 rows are returned.
- **FULL**   In this case, you could have rows returned from either the right or left tabl〈 do not meet the join condition. When this happens, the table that does not meet th〈 dition will return a null value for output columns. When this join type is used for th〈 vious query 19,972 rows are returned, which is the number of rows i〈 Person.Contact table.
- **LEFT**   In this case, you could have rows returned from the left table that do not me〈 join condition. The rows from the left table will return null values. When this joir〈 is used for the previous query, 19,972 rows are returned, which is the number of ro〈 the Person.Contact table.
- **RIGHT**   In this case, you could have rows returned from the right table that do not〈 the join condition. The rows from the right table will return null values. When thi〈 type is used for the previous query, 290 rows are returned.

Using Subqueries

Sometimes, it might be necessary to use a subquery within your SELECT statement. Su〈 ries are nested queries that can be used within SELECT, UPDATE, INSERT, and DELETE〈 ments. Typically, they are used in place of a column in the select list, but they can also be 〈 in the WHERE or HAVING clauses. Subqueries can be nested several levels deep, up to 3〈 els, but doing so would consume a lot of memory and would be hard to read and mai〈 The subquery is always surrounded by parentheses.

In many cases, a subquery could be used in place of a join. For example, the following query could replace the one used previously to return the first name, last name, and title of all employees:

```
SELECT con.FirstName, con.LastName,
  (SELECT emp.Title
     FROM HumanResources.Employee emp
     WHERE con.ContactID = emp.ContactID) As Title
FROM Person.Contact con
```

In this case, the query would return 19,972 rows and would function much the same as a LEFT or FULL join. When you join one or more tables, regardless of the method, you need to be careful to verify that you return the data that you expect. Just because the query executed successfully and returned results does not mean that it returned the data your application requires.

Using Linked Servers

In some cases, it might be necessary to retrieve data from heterogeneous data sources. *Distributed queries* enable you to access multiple data sources using the OLE DB data provider. This type of capability is important in large companies that might have data located in several different data sources. The data sources could reside on the same computer and in different instances of SQL Server, or they could reside on separate computers. The data source could be something other than a relational database, such as a Microsoft Office Excel spreadsheet. The data could also be from another type of database, such as Oracle or Sybase.

To access a remote or heterogeneous data source, you will first need to create a linked server. Once the linked server is defined, you can perform queries and updates against the data source. Linked servers can be created and accessed through Microsoft SQL Server Management Studio. Once you have connected to your SQL Server instance, you can expand the *Server Objects* and *Linked Servers* nodes. Any previously defined linked servers will be listed here. Within the *Providers* node is a list of several supported data providers. (See Figure 2-1.) Table 2-1 lists each of these data providers along with the data source with which it is associated.

Figure 2-1   Supported data providers listed below the *Providers* node in Object Explorer

Table 2-1   Data Providers Available for Linked Servers

Data Access Provider	Data Source
ADsDSOObject	Used to query an LDAP database using Active Directory
DTSPackageDSO	Used to query a Data Transformation Package (DTS) pac in SQL Server 2000
EMPOLEDBVS71	Used to query the VSEE Versioning Enlistment Manager P data source
MediaCatalogDB, MediaCatalog-MergedDB, MediaCatalog-WebDB	OLE DB provider used to access the media catalog used by DTS runtime
Microsoft.Jet.OLEDB.4.0	Used to access data sources, such as Excel spreadsheets a Microsoft Office Access databases
MSDAIPP.DSO	Used to get documents in Microsoft Internet Information vices (IIS) virtual directories
MSDAOSP	Used to query hierarchical rowsets from XML data
MSDASQL	OLE DB data provider for ODBC
MSDMine	OLE DB data provider for data mining services
MSIDXS	OLE DB data provider for Microsoft Indexing Server
MSOLAP	OLE DB data provider for accessing an Online Analytical i cessing (OLAP) database

Table 2-1   Data Providers Available for Linked Servers

Data Access Provider	Data Source
MSUSP	OLE DB data provider used for searching a Microsoft Office Outlook database
SQLNCLI	Used to query remote instances of SQL Server using the new data provider for SQL Server 2005
SQLOLEDB	OLE DB provider for SQL Server
SqlReplication.OLEDB	OLE DB provider for SQL Server Replication
SQLXMLOLEDB	OLE DB provider that exposes XML functionality to ActiveX Data Objects (ADO)
SQLXMLOLEDB.4.0	OLE DB provider that exposes XML, version 4.0 functionality to ADO

To create a linked server, right-click the *Linked Servers* node and select New Linked Server. From the New Linked Server dialog box, you will configure the linked server. Figure 2-2 shows how to use the Microsoft.Jet.OLEDB.4.0 DB Provider to configure a linked server named Employees. In this case, the data is an Access database named Employees.mdb.

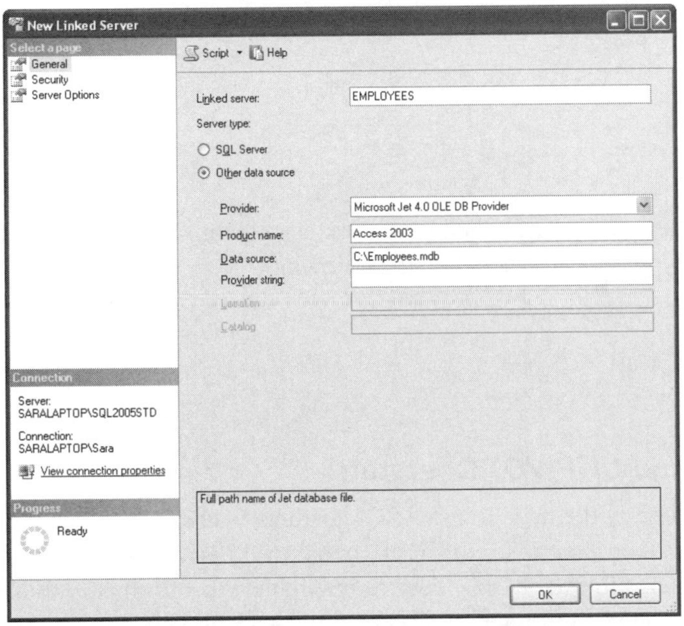

Figure 2-2   New Linked Server dialog box used to configure a linked server that points to an Access 2003 database

Once the linked server has been created, you will see the name appear below the *Linked S* node. At this point, you can execute queries against this data source using the New C window in SQL Server Management Studio. For example, you could issue the follc Transact-SQL command from a query window:

```
SELECT * FROM EMPLOYEES...Employee
```

This previous statement would return all records from the Employee table. The SELECT ment uses a four-part name, where the first part is the named of the linked server, and th part is the table name. Because an Access database does not have catalog and schema n you just use periods to represent those portions of the name.

How you structure the query will vary depending on the data source. For example, if yc querying an Oracle database as a linked server, you would still use a four-part name because Oracle has only one catalog per database instance, the structure of the query v look like the following:

```
LinkedServerName..OwnerUserName.TableName
```

Alternatively, you can create a linked server using Transact-SQL and the sp_addlinkeds built-in stored procedure. The syntax used for this stored procedure is as follows:

```
sp_addlinkedserver [@server='Server Name'],
    [@srvproduct='Product Name'],
    [@provider='Provider Name'],
    [@datasrc='Data Source'],
    [@location='Location'],
    [@provstr='Provider String'],
    [@catalog='Catalog']
```

For example, if you had used sp_addlinkedserver to create the linked server named Em ees, the Transact-SQL would have looked like the following:

```
sp_addlinkedserver 'EMPLOYEES',
    'Access 2003',
    'Microsoft.Jet.OLEDB.4.0',
    'c:\Employees.mdb'
```

Using the *PIVOT* and *UNPIVOT* Operators

The *PIVOT* operator is one of the new Transact-SQL features available in SQL Server 20 enables you to generate an output table, which can then be used as input for a cross-tab re The *PIVOT* operator is used in the FROM clause to manipulate one of the input-table ex sions. The result is that one column might be aggregated and then returned as multipl umns in the output table.

The *PIVOT* operator provides an alternative method for aggregating data into multiple columns. Previously, you would have needed to use CASE statements to accomplish the same results. The following is an example of a Transact-SQL statement that uses the PIVOT statement to return a count of purchase orders by vendor for each year:

```
SELECT VendorID, [2001] As '2001', [2002] As '2002',
  [2003] As '2003', [2004] As '2004'
FROM (SELECT VendorID, PurchaseOrderID, YEAR(orderdate) as ChangeYear
  FROM Purchasing.PurchaseOrderHeader) r
PIVOT
(
Count(r.PurchaseOrderID)
  FOR ChangeYear
    IN ([2001], [2002], [2003], [2004])
)
As Results
Order By VendorId
```

The query should return 86 rows that are ordered by the VendorID. Table 2-2 shows the first five results.

Table 2-2 Query Results When Using the *PIVOT* Operator

Vendor	2001	2002	2003	2004
1	0	3	14	34
2	0	4	13	34
3	0	3	13	34
4	0	4	13	34
5	0	3	13	34

Another operator, named *UNPIVOT*, does the opposite of the PIVOT statement. It will return results as rows instead of aggregated columns. This type of operator would be useful if you had results from a *PIVOT* operator stored in a table, and you needed to view the results differently. *UNPIVOT* does not return the data as it originally appeared, because the original data was aggregated, but it does return the data in an alternative format.

Using the *APPLY* Operator

The *APPLY* operator is also a new Transact-SQL feature in SQL Server 2005. Like the *PIVOT* operator, *APPLY* is also used in the FROM clause. However, it is used to apply a *table-valued*

function to each row in the outer table. A table-valued function is just like an ordinary
defined function, except that it returns a table as a result. The *APPLY* operator can be
the following:

- **OUTER APPLY**   Returns all rows that return a result set and will include NULL val
  the columns that are returned from the table-valued function.
- **CROSS APPLY**   Returns only rows from the outer table that produces a result set.

To understand how the *APPLY* operator works; assume you wanted to return the total d
purchase orders for all employees in a certain year. To use the *CROSS APPLY* opera
accomplish this, you would first create a table-valued function, such as the following:

```
CREATE FUNCTION fnGetPurchaseOrderTotal(@EmpID int, @Year varchar(4))
RETURNS @RetTable TABLE (TotalDue money)
AS

BEGIN

WITH OrderTree(total)
AS
(
   SELECT sum(totaldue) as OrderTotal
   FROM Purchasing.PurchaseOrderHeader
   WHERE EmployeeID = @EmpID
   AND YEAR(OrderDate) = @Year
)

INSERT INTO @RetTable
   SELECT * FROM OrderTree

RETURN
END
```

You would then create a query that used the *CROSS APPLY* operator to join the results
table-valued function. This would be done on a row-by-row basis. The following exa
shows how a query that needs to return employees hired in the year 2002 would look:

```
SELECT c.LastName + ', ' + c.FirstName as Employee,
   CONVERT(varchar, tot.TotalDue,1) as 'Total Due'
FROM Person.Contact c
JOIN HumanResources.Employee e
   ON c.ContactId = e.ContactID
CROSS APPLY fnGetPurchaseOrderTotal(e.employeeid,2002) as tot
WHERE tot.TotalDue IS NOT NULL
ORDER BY tot.TotalDue desc
```

This query would return 12 results, which are ordered according to the Total Due, from largest to smallest, in Table 2-3.

Table 2-3   Query Results When Using the *APPLY* Operator

Employee	Total Due
Sandberg, Mikael	620,215.34
Meisner, Linda	552,326.62
Miller, Ben	463,360.53
Hill, Annette	456,909.57
Pellow, Frank	430,733.40
Ogisu, Fukiko	424,454.80
Hee, Gordon	423,910.48
Hillmann, Reinout	423,825.96
Kurjan, Eric	303,465.26
Hagens, Erin	251,473.99
Rao, Arvind	236,225.88
Word, Sheela	82,975.17

IMPORTANT   Set database compatibility

To take advantage of both the *APPLY* and *PIVOT* operators, the database compatibility level needs to be set to 90 (the SQL Server 2005 default setting).

Using the *EXCEPT* and *INTERSECT* Operators

Prior to SQL Server 2005, the options for combining result sets included joins and the *UNION* operator. We reviewed the join statement earlier; the *UNION* operator can be used to combine the results of two or more SELECT statements if they have the same structure.

SQL Server 2005 offers two additional operators, *EXCEPT* and *INTERSECT*, that can be used to combine and limit result sets. These operators are used to compare the results of two or more SELECT statements and return values that are common to the two. The *EXCEPT* operator returns any distinct values from the left-side query, and the *INTERSECT* operator returns distinct values from both the left-side queries and right-side queries.

The queries that are compared must contain the same columns and structure in order comparable. But, this can be a useful way of joining two result sets based on distinct v For example, the following query can be used to identify which products have at least on ument assigned to them:

```
Select ProductID
FROM Production.Product
INTERSECT
SELECT ProductID
FROM Production.ProductDocument
```

This query will return 31 records even though there are 32 records in the Production.Pr Document table. This is because one of the products is associated with two document this query will only return distinct values.

Exam Tip Make sure you focus on the new operators presented in this chapter, such as *P* *UNPIVOT, CROSS APPLY, OUTER APPLY, EXCEPT,* and *INTERCEPT.*

Using Ranking Functions

SQL Server 2005 offers four ranking functions that can be used to indicate where eac falls in the result sets ranking. This can be useful if you need to build an array or rank s results. The four functions are as follows:

- **ROW_NUMBER** Used to return the row number sequentially as it appears in the set. The function can use both an order and partition clause. The ranking will star the number 1.

- **RANK** Used to return the rank of each row within the partition of the result se function also uses an order and partition clause. The ranking will add one to the ra the number of ranks that preceded it. With this function, you can have two or more that receive the same rank.

- **DENSE_RANK** Used to return the rank of each row within the partition of the resu The function also uses an order and partition clause. The ranking will add one rank plus the distinct rows that preceded it, so the ranking will be sequential.

- **NTILE** Used to return data based on groups that are then numbered starting a This function accepts an integer that specifies the number of groups that each par will be divided into.

The following is an example of the *ROW_NUMBER* function, which is used to return th number for rows ordered by the contact's last name:

```
SELECT e.EmployeeID,
  ROW_NUMBER() OVER(ORDER BY c.LastName) as RowNumber,
  c.FirstName, c.LastName, e.Title
FROM HumanResources.Employee e
JOIN Person.Contact c ON e.ContactID = c.ContactID
```

The top five results from this query are listed in Table 2-4.

Table 2-4 Query Results When Using the *ROW_NUMBER* Function

Employee ID	Row Number	First Name	Last Name	Title
288	1	Syed	Abbas	Pacific Sales Manager
235	2	Kim	Abercrombie	Production Technician – WC60
200	3	Hazem	Abolrous	Quality Assurance Manager
85	4	Pilar	Ackerman	Shipping and Receiving Supervisor
208	5	Jay	Adams	Production Technician – WC60

Using the *COALESCE* and *ISNULL* Functions

The *COALESCE* function can be used to return the first non-null value for one or more expressions. For example, the address in the *AdventureWorks* database is split into two fields: *AddressLine1* and *AddressLine2*. If you wanted to return the address for all employees as one line instead, you could use the following Transact-SQL code:

```
SELECT ea.EmployeeID,
  COALESCE(addressline1 + ' ' + addressline2, addressline1, addressline2) as address
FROM Person.Address a
JOIN HumanResources.EmployeeAddress ea ON ea.addressid = a.AddressID
ORDER BY ea.EmployeeID
```

In the *AdventureWorks* database, employee number 100 has the following values set in *AddressLine1* and *AddressLine2*.

- AddressLine1: 3029 Pastime Dr.
- AddressLine2: #2

For this record, a column named address would be returned as "3029 Pastime Dr. #2." For all records in which *AddressLine2* was set with a NULL value, the address column would contain the value from *AddressLine1* only.

The *ISNULL* function is similar to the *COALESCE* function, and in some cases you cou *ISNULL* as a replacement for the *COALESCE* function. The *ISNULL* function is used to r NULL values with a specific replacement value. Unlike the *COALESCE* function, *ISNUL* only accept two arguments. The syntax for the function is as follows:

```
ISNULL (check_expression, replacement_value)
```

This function can be useful when there is only one column that contains a NULL valu example, assume you wanted to update the Production.Product table in the *Adventure* database. In this table, the color column contains several NULL values, because not all ucts are associated with a color. You might want to replace all NULL values with another "N/A," to indicate that the color is not applicable. The following query could be used to a plish this task:

```
UPDATE Production.Product
SET Color = ISNULL(Color, 'N/A')
```

IMPORTANT IS NULL vs. *ISNULL*

Be aware that the *ISNULL* function is not the same as using the IS NULL clause in a query. Th NULL clause is just used to detect whether the NULL value exists, whereas the *ISNULL* functic actually replace the NULL value with a replacement value.

When working with NULL values, be careful to distinguish between NULLs and e strings. You can easily identify NULL values in the query results window of SQL Server agement Studio. For example, the results window displayed in Figure 2-3 shows that th product contains an empty string. The next four products contain NULL values for the column. In this case, the UPDATE statement that used the *ISNULL* function would no updated the color for the first product.

	productid	name	productnumber	color
1	1	Adjustable Race	AR-5381	
2	2	Bearing Ball	BA-8327	NULL
3	3	BB Ball Bearing	BE-2349	NULL
4	4	Headset Ball Bearings	BE-2908	NULL
5	316	Blade	BL-2036	NULL
6	317	LL Crankarm	CA-5965	Black
7	318	ML Crankarm	CA-6738	Black
8	319	HL Crankarm	CA-7457	Black
9	320	Chainring Bolts	CB-2903	Silver

Figure 2-3 Portion of the results window that displays the query results, where the first record tains an empty string in the color column

Using Functions

SQL Server 2005 provides many built-in functions that can be used to accomplish various tasks. For example, Table 2-5 lists all the built-in functions that can be used to aggregate your data.

Table 2-5 Built-in Aggregate Functions

Function	Description
AVG	Returns the average of all values in the group, excluding NULL values.
CHECKSUM	Returns a hash value that is used for building hash indexes.
CHECKSUM_AGG	Returns the hash value for a group, ignoring any NULL values.
COUNT	Returns the number of items in a group.
COUNT_BIG	Also returns the number of items in a group, but the return data type is *bigint*.
GROUPING	When used in conjunction with the *CUBE* or *ROLLUP* operators, this returns a value of 1.
MAX	Returns the maximum value in an expression.
MIN	Returns the minimum value in an expression.
SUM	Returns the sum of all numeric values, excluding NULL values.
STDEV	Returns the standard deviation of all values in the expression. This is typically used on a sampling of the population.
STDEVP	Also returns the standard deviation of all values in the group, but this applies to the entire population and not just a sampling.
VAR	Returns the statistical variation of all values in the group.
VARP	Also returns the statistical variation, but it applies to the entire population of data and not just a sampling.

These functions are typically embedded inside of Transact-SQL statements, such as the following query, which is used to return the average list price for all products with a class of 'L':

```
SELECT avg(listprice)
FROM production.product
WHERE class = 'L'
```

In addition to using the built-in functions provided with SQL Server 2005, you can create and use your own user-defined functions. Typically, user-defined functions are used to perform a complex task on one or more values and then return a result. You have already seen a user-defined function in the section about using the *APPLY* operator. In that case, the function

returned a table as the result. This is known as a table-valued function. You can also cr
scalar function, which is used to return a single value such as a string or an integer.

The following is an example of a scalar function that accepts the Product ID as an input p
eter and returns a *smallint* data type. The function is used to determine the difference be
a products inventory and the reorder point.

```
-- Add this check to the beginning that will
-- drop the function if you are trying to replace it
IF OBJECT_ID(N'dbo.fnGetProductDiff', N'FN') IS NOT NULL
    DROP FUNCTION dbo.fnGetProductDiff;
GO

-- This is the part that actually creates the function
CREATE FUNCTION dbo.fnGetProductDiff       -- function name
(@ProdId int)                              -- input parameter name
RETURNS smallint                           -- data type returned
AS
BEGIN                                      -- begin function code

-- First get the current quantity
-- for this product, which may be in
-- multiple locations
DECLARE @qty smallint
SET @qty = (SELECT SUM(quantity)
FROM Production.ProductInventory
WHERE ProductID = @ProdId)

-- Now get the ReorderPoint for this Product
-- Return either the difference as:
-- negative, which means there is a shortage
-- positive, which means there is no shortage
-- zero, which indicates that the amounts are the same
-- NULL would indicate that the product has no inventory
DECLARE @point smallint
SELECT @point =
 CASE
  WHEN ReorderPoint = @qty
        THEN 0
  WHEN ReorderPoint <> @qty
        THEN @qty - ReorderPoint
 END
FROM Production.Product
WHERE ProductID = @ProdID

RETURN @point

END;                                       -- end function code
GO
```

Once the function has been created, you can reference the function in another query. For example, the following SELECT statement will return product numbers along with the difference between the inventory and reorder point:

```
SELECT ProductID, ProductNumber,
dbo.fnGetProductDiff(ProductID) As 'Quantity Diff'
FROM Production.Product
```

If the inventory level is equal to the reorder point, a value of zero will be returned. If the inventory level is below the reorder point, then a negative value reflecting the difference will be returned. If the inventory level is above the reorder point, then a positive value reflecting the difference will be returned. Finally, if no inventory exists for the product, then a NULL value will be returned.

ing Full-Text Queries

Full-text queries enable you to go beyond the traditional capabilities of a text-based search. These queries go beyond looking for an exact match or even using the *LIKE* operator to see whether a string matches a specified pattern. Full-text searching enables you to search a portion of the column and look for partial matches of text. This is not the same thing as using the *LIKE* operator and the wildcard character.

Full-text searching enables you to look for a word or phrase that is close to the search word or phrase. You can also look for two words that are next to each other or multiple words and then rank the results according to specific weightings. Full-text searching uses indexes, which enable it to perform quickly when querying against a large amount of data. It utilizes the new full-text searching engine service named Microsoft Full-Text Engine for SQL Server (MSFT-ESQL). This section will not cover full-text administration, which involves creating full-text catalogs and indexes. For more information about that topic, see the MSDN article "Administering a Full-Text Search" at *http://msdn2.microsoft.com/en-us/library/ms142557.aspx*.

The main predicates used in a full-text query are CONTAINS, FREETEXT, and CONTAINSTABLE. These predicates are used in the FROM portion of a Transact-SQL query. The CONTAINS predicate can be used to search a column for words, phrases, or prefixes that are near to the search word, derived from the search word, or a synonym of the search word. For example, each of the following SELECT statements will return results from the *AdventureWorks* database once a full-text catalog and index has been built:

```
-- Simple search that returns any comments that
-- contain the words easy or comfortable
SELECT comments
FROM Production.ProductReview
WHERE CONTAINS(comments, 'easy OR comfortable')
```

```
-- Proximity term example that returns any comments
-- that contain the word easy close to the word conditions
SELECT comments
FROM Production.ProductReview
WHERE CONTAINS(comments, 'easy NEAR conditions')
-- Generation term example that returns any comments
-- that can be derived from the word bike, which includes
-- biking, bicycle, etc. You could also replace the word
-- INFLECTIONAL with THESAURUS, but then you would only
-- return one record and not two
SELECT comments FROM Production.ProductReview
WHERE CONTAINS(comments, 'FORMSOF (INFLECTIONAL, bike)')
```

The FREETEXT predicate can be used to search a column by matching the meaning
word and not the exact wording. The results from this type of query are a little less precis
if you used the CONTAINS predicate, but such a query can still be useful when the user
sure what the exact wording will be. For example, each of the following SELECT state
can be used to return results:

```
-- FREETEXT example that returns any comments that contain
-- words similar to praise and recommended
SELECT comments
FROM Production.ProductReview
WHERE FREETEXT(comments, 'praise recommended')
```

The CONTAINSTABLE predicate is similar to the CONTAINS predicate, except that it r
a table that can be ranked according to weighted values. This can be useful if you n
return a result list to a user that is ranked accordingly. To return the ranking along wi
umns from the table that is being searched, you need to perform an INNER JOIN on the
that is returned. For example, the following query can be used to return not only the
ments, but their ranking according to the weighted values assigned:

```
-- Weighted term example that returns any comments
-- with the words easy or female, but will rank
-- the results with the word female higher than the result
-- with the word easy. This means you can display
-- the higher-ranking items first in a result list
SELECT pr.Comments, Results.RANK
FROM Production.Productreview pr
INNER JOIN CONTAINSTABLE(Production.ProductReview, comments,
  'ISABOUT (easy weight(.2), female weight(.6))')
AS Results ON pr.ProductReviewID = Results.[KEY]
ORDER BY Results.RANK DESC
```

Writing Database Queries

In this lab, you will experiment with writing database queries. In Exercise 1, you will create and modify a SELECT statement that performs a join on multiple tables. In Exercise 2, you will use the *APPLY* operator to return the average cost for products with a product cost history record.

The completed lab is available in the \Labs\Chapter 02\Lab1 folder on the companion CD.

IMPORTANT   Lab requirements

You will need to have SQL Server 2005 installed before you can complete this lab. Refer to the Introduction for setup instructions.

Exercise 1: Use the *JOIN* Operator

In this exercise, you will begin by executing a query that returns product information. To attain this information, it is necessary to join two other tables. You will execute the query and note the results. You will then modify the query, execute the query again, and compare the results to the first execution.

1. Open SQL Server Management Studio.
2. Connect to the instance of SQL Server 2005 that contains the *AdventureWorks* database.
3. Select New Query.
4. Add the following code to the query window:

    ```
    SELECT p.Name, p.ProductNumber, p.ListPrice,
      l.Name as Location, pin.Shelf, pin.Bin,
      pin.Quantity
    FROM Production.Product p
    JOIN Production.ProductInventory pin
      ON p.ProductID = pin.ProductID
    JOIN Production.Location l
      ON pin.LocationID = l.LocationID
    ```

5. Select the *AdventureWorks* database from the Available Databases drop-down list box, and then click Execute. The results window should display 1,069 records, which is the

exact number of records in the Production.ProductInventory table. The top 10 r
from this query are listed in Table 2-6.

Table 2-6   Partial Query Results After Executing First SELECT Statement

Name	ProductNumber	ListPrice	Location	Shelf	Bin	Qua
Adjustable Race	AR-5381	0.00	Tool Crib	A	1	408
Adjustable Race	AR-5381	0.00	Miscellaneous Storage	B	5	329
Adjustable Race	AR-5381	0.00	Subassembly	A	5	353
Bearing Ball	BA-8327	0.00	Tool Crib	A	2	427
Bearing Ball	BA-8327	0.00	Miscellaneous Storage	B	1	318
Bearing Ball	BA-8327	0.00	Subassembly	A	6	364
BB Ball Bearing	BE-2349	0.00	Tool Crib	A	7	585
BB Ball Bearing	BE-2349	0.00	Miscellaneous Storage	B	9	443
BB Ball Bearing	BE-2349	0.00	Subassembly	A	10	324
Headset Ball Bearings	BE-2908	0.00	Tool Crib	A	6	512

6. Return to the query window, and replace the previous SELECT statement with
   following:

```
SELECT p.Name, p.ProductNumber, p.ListPrice,
  l.Name as Location, pin.Shelf, pin.Bin,
  pin.Quantity
FROM Production.Product p
LEFT JOIN Production.ProductInventory pin
  ON p.ProductID = pin.ProductID
LEFT JOIN Production.Location l
  ON pin.LocationID = l.LocationID
```

7. Select the *AdventureWorks* database from the Available Databases drop-down lis
   and then click Execute. The only difference between this query and the previous
   that we are now performing left joins instead of inner joins. Inner joins, which is tl
   performed when no join type is specified, will return data that matches the join
   tion for both the left and right tables. Left joins can return records from the lef
   table that do not meet the join condition. If you were to execute this query, you
   have 1,141 records returned instead of 1,069. This is because there are some pro
   that have no product inventory associated with them.

8. This exercise demonstrates the importance of using the correct join type when joining multiple tables. Depending on what your query goals are, either query could be correct. If you wanted to return results for products with no inventory, then the second query would be correct. If you did not want to return records for products with no inventory, then the first query would be correct.

Exercise 2: Use the *APPLY* Operator

In this exercise, you will begin by creating a table-valued function that returns a table as the result. The table will contain the average cost for a particular product because there can be more than one record per product. You will then execute a query that uses the *APPLY* operator to join the results of the table-valued function.

1. Open SQL Server Management Studio.
2. Connect to the instance of SQL Server 2005 that contains the *AdventureWorks* database.
3. Select New Query.
4. Add the following code to the query window:

```
CREATE FUNCTION fnGetAvgCost(@ProdID int)
RETURNS @RetTable TABLE (AvgCost money)
AS

BEGIN

WITH Product(stdcost)
AS
(
  SELECT avg(standardcost) as AvgCost
  FROM Production.ProductCostHistory
  WHERE ProductID = @ProdID
)

INSERT INTO @RetTable
  SELECT * FROM Product

RETURN
END
```

5. Select the *AdventureWorks* database from the Available Databases drop-down list box, and then click Execute. Ensure that the command was executed successfully.
6. Replace the code in the query window with the following query and execute:

```
SELECT p.[Name], p.ProductNumber,
  CONVERT(varchar, cost.AvgCost,1) as 'Average Cost'
FROM Production.Product p
CROSS APPLY fnGetAvgCost(p.ProductID) as cost
```

```
WHERE cost.AvgCost IS NOT NULL
ORDER BY cost.AvgCost desc
```

7. The query should return 293 results, which represent each distinct record in the P⟩ tion.ProductCostHistory table.

Quick Check

1. Which join type will return matching rows from both the right and left tables?
2. How would you retrieve data from a data source other than SQL Server?
3. What new operator for SQL Server 2005 can be used to create cross-table repo⟩
4. What does the *APPLY* operator enable you to accomplish?
5. What operator(s), excluding a table join, can be used to combine and limit res sets?
6. What function can be used to return the first non-null values from more than ⟨ expression?
7. What is the difference between a table-valued function and a scalar function?
8. Which predicate can be used to search a column for words or phrases near to search word?

Quick Check Answers

1. An INNER join, which is the default join type if one is not specified, is used return data that matches the join condition from both the right and left tables.
2. If your data source is an OLE DB data source, then you can create a linked ser The linked server can then be referenced using a four-part name inside of a st dard Transact-SQL statement.
3. The *PIVOT* operator enables you to generate an output table. It can be used replace the need to utilize CASE statements and aggregate functions to accomp⟩ the same result.
4. When used in the FROM clause of a SELECT statement, the *APPLY* operator can used to apply a table-valued function to each row in an outer table. An *OUT* *APPLY* will return all rows that include NULL values, and the *CROSS APPLY* o⟩ ator will return rows from the outer table that provides a result set.
5. The *EXCEPT* and *INTERSECT* operators can be used to combine and limit res sets. The *EXCEPT* operator returns distinct values from the left side. The *INT* *SECT* operator returns distinct values from the left and right sides.

---

6. The *COALESCE* function can be used to return the first non-null value from more than one expression. Alternatively, the *ISNULL* function only accepts two arguments and can be used to replace NULL values with a replacement value.

7. A table-valued function is a user-defined function that returns a table, whereas a scalar function will return a single value, such as a string or an integer data type.

8. CONTAINS and CONTAINSTABLE can use a proximity term and the *NEAR* keyword to return a word that resides close to the other one.

Lesson 2: Improving Query Performance

Estimated lesson time: 45 minutes

One of the main reasons SQL Server has become popular is because of its self-tuning ca ities. Still, there might be situations where experienced database developers and admi tors want to alter the execution plan in an attempt to aid a poorly performing query Server 2005 offers several options for optimizing the performance of your queries. known as plan forcing, and it means you will force the query optimizer to use a specifi This is not a technique that should be used frequently or carelessly because the quer mizer will normally identify the optimal execution plan.

Showing the Execution Plan

For every query that is executed, you have the option of viewing how the database engi handle that query. For instance, the execution plan will show whether it needs to exe table scan or an index scan. To see what this query execution plan looks like, you can Display Estimated Execution Plan from the Query menu in SQL Server Management The Execution Plan tab will appear and give you a graphical representation of the exe plan. If you hover the mouse pointer over a node, it will show you the detail associate that node. (Refer to Figure 2-4.)

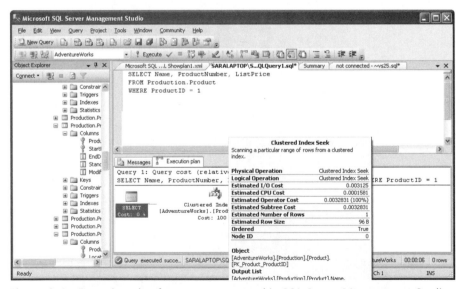

Figure 2-4 Execution plan for a query executed in SQL Server Management Studio

Alternatively, you can add the following Transact-SQL code before the query executes:

```
SET SHOWPLAN_XML ON
GO
```

When you add this Transact-SQL statement, it causes all statements that follow to not be executed. This condition will remain until you execute a statement that turns the SET SHOWPLAN option OFF. Instead of executing the query, you will be returned a formatted XML string that contains the query plan information.

g Query Hints

One method for optimizing queries is the query hint, which can be specified in the OPTION clause of a SELECT, UPDATE, DELETE, or INSERT statement. Although the concept of a query hint is not new to SQL Server 2005, the way it is implemented has improved.

One of the options available with the query hint is USE PLAN. The USE PLAN query hint takes an XML string as an argument. The XML string should be in the same format as the string displayed when you execute SET SHOWPLAN_XML ON. Keep in mind that if you use this method to modify an execution plan, you will need to replace all instances of single quotes with double quotes. The following is an XML string that was returned after executing a query against the *AdventureWorks* database:

```
<ShowPlanXML xmlns="http://schemas.microsoft.com/sqlserver/2004/07/showplan" Version="1.0"
Build="9.00.1399.06">
<BatchSequence>
  <Batch>
    <Statements>
      <StmtSimple StatementText="SELECT Name, ProductNumber, ListPrice&#xD;&#xA;FROM
Production.Product&#xD;&#xA;WHERE ProductID = 1&#xD;&#xA;" StatementId="1"
StatementCompId="1" StatementType="SELECT" StatementSubTreeCost="0.0032831"
StatementEstRows="1" StatementOptmLevel="TRIVIAL">
        <StatementSetOptions QUOTED_IDENTIFIER="false" ARITHABORT="true"
CONCAT_NULL_YIELDS_NULL="false" ANSI_NULLS="false" ANSI_PADDING="false" ANSI_WARNINGS="false"
NUMERIC_ROUNDABORT="false" />
        <QueryPlan CachedPlanSize="9">
        <RelOp NodeId="0" PhysicalOp="Clustered Index Seek" LogicalOp="Clustered Index Seek"
EstimateRows="1" EstimateIO="0.003125" EstimateCPU="0.0001581" AvgRowSize="96"
EstimatedTotalSubtreeCost="0.0032831" Parallel="0" EstimateRebinds="0" EstimateRewinds="0">
            <OutputList>
              <ColumnReference Database="[AdventureWorks]" Schema="[Production]"
Table="[Product]" Column="Name" />
              <ColumnReference Database="[AdventureWorks]" Schema="[Production]"
Table="[Product]" Column="ProductNumber" />
              <ColumnReference Database="[AdventureWorks]" Schema="[Production]"
Table="[Product]" Column="ListPrice" />
            </OutputList>
```

```
            <IndexScan Ordered="1" ScanDirection="FORWARD" ForcedIndex="0" NoExpandHint
              <DefinedValues>
                <DefinedValue>
                  <ColumnReference Database="[AdventureWorks]" Schema="[Production]"
Table="[Product]" Column="Name" />
                </DefinedValue>
                <DefinedValue>
                  <ColumnReference Database="[AdventureWorks]" Schema="[Production]"
Table="[Product]" Column="ProductNumber" />
                </DefinedValue>
                <DefinedValue>
                  <ColumnReference Database="[AdventureWorks]" Schema="[Production]"
Table="[Product]" Column="ListPrice" />
                </DefinedValue>
              </DefinedValues>
              <Object Database="[AdventureWorks]" Schema="[Production]" Table="[Product
Index="[PK_Product_ProductID]" />
              <SeekPredicates>
                <SeekPredicate>
                  <Prefix ScanType="EQ">
                    <RangeColumns>
                      <ColumnReference Database="[AdventureWorks]" Schema="[Production]
Table="[Product]" Column="ProductID" />
                    </RangeColumns>
                    <RangeExpressions>
                      <ScalarOperator ScalarString="CONVERT_IMPLICIT(int,[@1],0)">
                        <Convert DataType="int" Style="0" Implicit="1">
                          <ScalarOperator>
                            <Identifier>
                              <ColumnReference Column="@1" />
                            </Identifier>
                          </ScalarOperator>
                        </Convert>
                      </ScalarOperator>
                    </RangeExpressions>
                  </Prefix>
                </SeekPredicate>
              </SeekPredicates>
            </IndexScan>
          </RelOp>
          <ParameterList>
            <ColumnReference Column="@1" ParameterCompiledValue="(1)" />
          </ParameterList>
        </QueryPlan>
      </StmtSimple>
    </Statements>
  </Batch>
</BatchSequence>
</ShowPlanXML>
```

Notice that the *RelOp* node displays the physical and logical operations that will take place. For this query, a clustered index seek is utilized. For more information about what nodes can be altered, refer to the MSDN documentation titled "Using the USE PLAN Query Hint" at *http://msdn2.microsoft.com/en-us/library/ms186954.aspx.*

BEST PRACTICES   **Continually evaluate queries with altered execution plans**

It is likely that altering the execution plan will cause the query to perform even more slowly than it did previously. It is also possible that the query could perform differently after an upgrade or service pack is applied. Therefore, if you choose to alter the execution plan, be prepared to periodically evaluate the query to ensure that it is still performing adequately.

If you want to modify the current execution plan for a query, you will modify the XML string and then execute a query similar to the following instead (note that the entire XML string was not included and that ellipses represent the collapsed portion):

```
SELECT Name, ProductNumber, ListPrice
FROM Production.Product
WHERE ProductID = 1
(OPTION USE PLAN N'<ShowPlanXML xmlns="http://schemas.microsoft.com/sqlserver/2004/07/
showplan" Version="1.0" Build="9.00.1399.06">
  <BatchSequence>
    <Batch>
      <Statements>

      </Statements>
    </Batch>
  </BatchSequence>
</ShowPlanXML>')
```

ng Plan Guides

Plan guides are a new feature available with SQL Server 2005. This feature enables you to inject query hints into SQL statements without modifying the query itself. This can be useful when troubleshooting problems with third-party applications, and you do not have access to the code. Instead of modifying the query like we did with the USE PLAN query hint, plan guides use an internal system table to track whether plans are attached to certain queries.

You create a plan guide using the sp_create_plan_guide system stored procedure. This built-in stored procedure accepts the following parameters:

- **@name**   Plan guide name.
- **@stmt**   Actual SQL statement. You can use SQL Server Profiler to extract the text for the SQL: BatchStarting event. (See Figure 2-5.) You must replace all single quotes with double quotes.

- **@type**   Value this parameter as OBJECT if you are referring to a stored procedure, tion, or trigger. Use the value SQL if it is a standalone SQL statement. Use the TEMPLATE if it applies to any query that uses the same format as the SQL statem the @stmt parameter.
- **@module_or_batch**   If you set the @type parameter with a value of OBJECT, the should contain the schemaname.objectname of that object. If the @type paramete set with a value of SQL, then this should contain the same statement text specif @stmt. If the @type parameter was set with a value of TEMPLATE, then this must with a NULL.
- **@params**   Used to specify all parameters and their data types.
- **@hints**   Used to specify the query hint that applies to this query. You can us OPTION clause, which is the same clause used in the USE PLAN query hint.

Using Searchable Arguments

It is always best for queries to use a WHERE clause because this will restrict the num results returned and thus enable the query to perform faster. *Searchable arguments*, also k as SARGs, refer to a WHERE clause that compares a column to a constant value or a va This enables the query optimizer to take advantage of an index, which is better than exec a table scan. A table scan should be avoided whenever possible because it indicates th indexes will be utilized and the database engine will need to scan the entire table.

If you encounter a query that is performing poorly, take a look at whether it is using a s argument properly. If it is not, then determine whether the query can be rewritten. You c a quick check to see what type of operation will be performed by selecting Display Esti Execution Plan from the Query menu.

The query optimizer will attempt to resolve a query so that it utilizes a search argument ever possible. For example, if you were to display the execution plan for the following c you would see that it utilizes a clustered index seek:

```
SELECT Name, ProductNumber, ListPrice
FROM Production.Product
WHERE NOT Color IN ('Black', 'Silver', 'Red')
```

Other developers might tell you that this type of operation should be avoided becaus *NOT* keyword is not a valid search argument (SARG). However, the predicate column f execution plan indicates that the query optimizer knows the WHERE clause should be preted as the following:

```
[AdventureWorks].[Production].[Product].[Color] <> N'Black' AND
[AdventureWorks].[Production].[Product].[Color] <> N'Red' AND
[AdventureWorks].[Production].[Product].[Color] <> N'Silver'
```

Despite this, there are still some operations that can prevent the query optimizer from selecting the optimal execution plan. For example, you should not include a function on a searchable column because this can cause the query optimizer not to utilize an index properly. The following query would still utilize an index, but it would perform an index scan:

```
SELECT Name, ProductNumber, ListPrice
FROM Production.Product
WHERE SUBSTRING(name, 1,1) = 'b'
```

An index scan means that the database engine will need to scan the whole index page. A faster alternative would be to perform an index seek. The index seek will utilize a sort order, so it can access the index faster. The following query will return the same results but will utilize an index seek instead:

```
SELECT Name, ProductNumber, ListPrice
FROM Production.Product
WHERE name LIKE 'b%'
```

In some cases, you might need to join to another table in order to return the correct results. Typically, using a table join or subquery will accomplish this task. Both of the following queries return the same results, display a similar execution plan, and will have a similar resource cost:

```
SELECT Name, ProductNumber, ListPrice
FROM Production.Product
WHERE ProductSubCategoryID =
  (SELECT ProductSubCategoryID
    FROM Production.ProductSubCategory
    WHERE Name = 'Mountain Bikes')

SELECT p.Name, p.ProductNumber, p.ListPrice
FROM Production.Product p
JOIN Production.ProductSubCategory ps
  ON p.ProductSubCategoryID = ps.ProductSubCategoryID
WHERE ps.Name = 'Mountain Bikes'
```

Depending on the needs of your application, either query might be the only way you can accomplish your goal. However, the most efficient way to return the same results is with the following query:

```
SELECT Name, ProductNumber, ListPrice
FROM Production.Product
WHERE ProductSubCategoryID = 1
```

This version of the query only needs to perform one index scan to return the resul course, you might not be able to execute such a query if the ProductSubCategoryID known in advance. There are typically multiple methods to execute a query. If you dete that a query is performing poorly, consider alternative methods and display the exec plan to verify the results.

Lab: Tuning Queries

In this lab, you will experiment with tuning queries in order to improve query perform The first exercise will involve rewriting a query to speed the execution time for the quer second exercise will involve the creation of a plan guide to alter the way the query opti handles the query without altering the query itself.

The completed lab is available in the \Labs\Chapter 02\Lab2 folder on the companion

---

IMPORTANT   Lab requirements

You will need to have SQL Server 2005 installed before you can complete this lab. Refer to t Introduction for setup instructions.

Exercise 1: Rewrite a Query to Improve Performance

In this exercise, you will examine a poorly performing query by examining the estimate cution plan. You will then examine a replacement for the query and compare the exec plans for both queries.

1. Open SQL Server Management Studio.
2. Connect to the instance of SQL Server 2005 that contains the *AdventureWorks* data
3. Select New Query.
4. Add the following code to the query window:

```
DECLARE @Name nvarchar(50)
SET @Name = '11 Crankarm'

SELECT Name, ProductNumber,
       ListPrice, SafetyStockLevel
FROM Production.Product
WHERE SafetyStockLevel > 500
UNION ALL
SELECT Name, ProductNumber,
       ListPrice, SafetyStockLevel
FROM Production.Product
WHERE UPPER(Name) = UPPER(@Name)
```

5. Select the *AdventureWorks* database from the Available Databases drop-down list box, and then click Display Estimated Execution Plan from the Query menu. This will not execute the query but will provide a graphical representation of the execution plan. (See Figure 2-5.) Note that the query execution plan will first perform a clustered index scan to query the Production.Product table. It will also need to perform an index scan and clustered index seek against the same table.

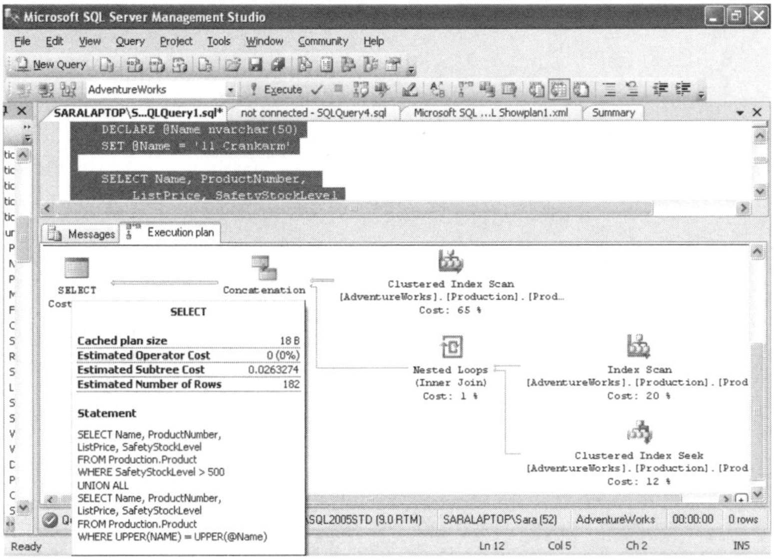

Figure 2-5   Execution plan for a poorly performing query executed in SQL Server Management Studio

6. The first query was identified as a poorly performing query, and a replacement query has been created. Paste the following code within the same query window (beneath the first query):

```
DECLARE @Name nvarchar(50)
SET @Name = '11 Crankarm'

SELECT Name, ProductNumber,
       ListPrice, SafetyStockLevel
FROM Production.Product
WHERE SafetyStockLevel > 500 OR
      [Name] = @Name
```

7. Highlight the new query, select the *AdventureWorks* database from the Available Databases drop-down list box, and then click Display Estimated Execution Plan from the Query menu. The main difference between this query and the first one is that this query does not perform a *UNION ALL*. The first query used the *UPPER* function to ensure that

a match was made against the input variable. The *UPPER* function is not necessary
are performing a query against a case-insensitive database.

8. The second query can utilize an execution plan that involves a single clustered
    scan on the Production Product table. Because only one of these scans is needed,
    resources are utilized.

Exercise 2: Create a Plan Guide

In this exercise, you will create a plan guide to change the way a query is ordered. The
guide is used because you are not able to modify the original query. The revised query r
one of the joins and then uses FORCE ORDER to force the query optimizer to use the
specified in the FROM clause. The end result is that the results are ordered differently.

1. Open SQL Server Management Studio.
2. Connect to the instance of SQL Server 2005 that contains the *AdventureWorks* data
3. Select New Query.
4. Add the following code to the query window:

```
-- Revised Query
SET STATISTICS XML ON;
GO
EXEC sp_executesql
@stmt = N'SELECT c.FirstName + '' '' + c.LastName,
   c.EmailAddress, a.city, jc.resume
FROM Person.Contact c
JOIN HumanResources.Employee e
   ON c.ContactID = e.ContactID
LEFT JOIN HumanResources.JobCandidate jc
   ON e.EmployeeID = jc.EmployeeID
JOIN HumanResources.EmployeeAddress ea
   ON e.EmployeeID = ea.EmployeeID
JOIN Person.Address a
   ON ea.AddressID = a.AddressID
OPTION (FORCE ORDER)';
GO
SET STATISTICS XML OFF;
GO
```

5. After executing the query, you will receive two sets of results. In the second set, th
    a column named Microsoft SQL Server 2005 XML Showplan. Click the link that ap
    here, and copy the results to the clipboard.
6. Return to the original query window, and replace the original query with the follo
    You will need to replace the section <*insert XML showplan for the revised query here*>
    the results you copied to the clipboard. You will also have to perform a find and re
    to replace all instances of single quotes (') with four quotes ('' '').

```
EXEC sp_create_plan_guide
  @name=N'TestPlanGuide',
  @stmt=N'SELECT c.FirstName + '' '' + c.LastName,
  c.EmailAddress, a.city, jc.resume
FROM Person.Contact c
JOIN HumanResources.Employee e
  ON c.ContactID = e.ContactID
JOIN HumanResources.EmployeeAddress ea
  ON e.EmployeeID = ea.EmployeeID
JOIN Person.Address a
  ON ea.AddressID = a.AddressID
LEFT JOIN HumanResources.JobCandidate jc
  ON e.EmployeeID = jc.EmployeeID',
  @type=N'SQL',
  @module_or_batch=NULL,
  @params=NULL,
  @hints=N'OPTION (USE PLAN
N'' <insert Show Plan XML for the revised query here> '')'
```

7. Execute the query, and ensure that the command is completed successfully.

Quick Check

1. What is the easiest way to display the execution plan designed by the query optimizer?
2. What Transact-SQL code can be used to represent the execution plan as an XML string?
3. What is the main advantage of using a plan guide versus the USE PLAN query hint?
4. What is the correct format for a searchable argument (SARG) that is needed by the query optimizer to determine the optimal execution plan?

Quick Check Answers

1. You can view a graphical representation of the execution plan without actually executing the code by selecting Display Estimated Execution Plan from the Query menu.
2. You can execute SET SHOWPLAN_XML ON from a query window. Until the option is turned off, all SQL statements will not execute and will instead return an XML string that represents the execution plan selected by the query optimizer.
3. Plan guides are useful when attempting to resolve problems with poorly performing queries from third-party applications or any application where the source code is not modifiable.
4. For a searchable argument to be valid, the left side of the operator should be a column, and the right side should be a constant or a variable.

Lesson 3: Retrieving Data from XML Sources

Estimated lesson time: 45 minutes

XML has become an integral part of many of today's database applications. This lightw
and extensible protocol offers many advantages to applications that need to store and
port dynamic data. This lesson covers the many ways that you can work with XML using
Server 2005. You will learn how to work with and query XML data as well as how to pro
XML from a relational query.

Working with XML Data

SQL Server 2005 introduced support for the *xml* data type, which enables you to store d
an XML document or a portion of an XML document within a relational table. The *Adve*
Works database contains several columns that are defined with the *xml* data type. To get a
at one of these, you can execute the following query from a new query window in SQL S
Management Studio:

```
USE AdventureWorks
GO
SELECT p.Name, p.ProductNumber, pm.Instructions
FROM Production.Product p
JOIN Production.ProductModel pm
  ON p.ProductModelID = pm.ProductModelID
WHERE pm.Instructions is not NULL
```

The query should return 25 rows, and the third column will contain product model ins
tions in the form of an XML document. You can click on the link for any of the rows retu
and view the expanded XML document in a separate window. You will see that the ins
tions contain several nodes, such as *step*, *material*, and *tool*, which are children nodes fo
or more locations.

You can optionally store XML schema information that is associated with a column, pa
ter, or variable. An XML column associated with a schema is said to be "typed." The sc
information provides information about what values are acceptable for nodes and attrib
When a schema is provided, there is automatic validation of the XML document.

Once the schema is created, you need to add it to the SQL Server repository by executin
Transact-SQL command CREATE XML SCHEMA COLLECTION. Once this is done, yo
reference the schema in SQL Server Management Studio. You can view a particular data
schema by expanding the *Programmability, Types, XML Schema Collections* node in O

Explorer. (See Figure 2-6.) The Universal Resource Identifier (URI) associated with each of these schema definitions will be needed in the next section when we query an XML column.

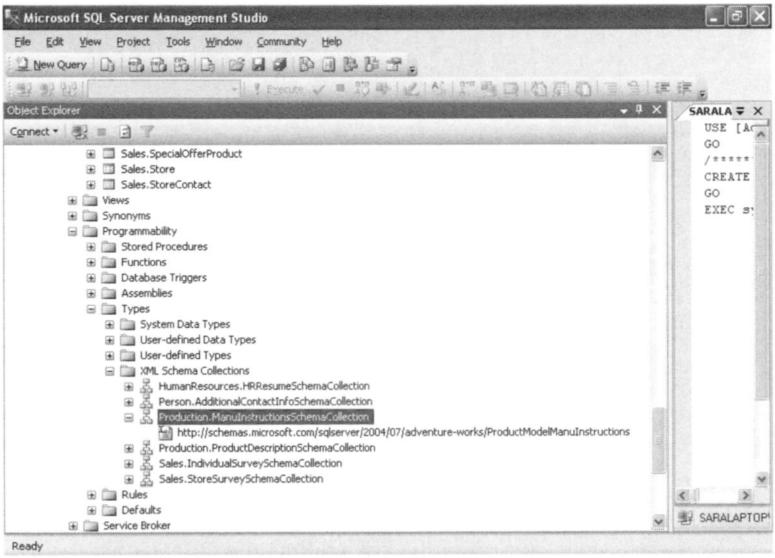

Figure 2-6   XML schemas available with the *AdventureWorks* database

Querying XML Data with XQuery

XQuery is an XML query language adopted by the World Wide Web Consortium (W3C). You can learn more about this language specification by going to *http://www.w3.org/TR/xquery/*. SQL Server 2005 provides a subset of this language in order to query the *xml* data type.

A query where you return the entire instructions column is fine if you want to return the entire XML document. However, if you want to just return a portion of the XML document, such as a particular node or attribute, then you will need to utilize one of the built-in methods for working with the *xml* data type.

The query method is used to query an *xml* data type using an XQuery expression. An XQuery expression is made up of the following:

- **Prolog**   This is typically a namespace declaration that includes a prefix. For the *AdventureWorks* database, we will use the prefix AW, which stands for Adventure Works. This prefix will be referenced in the body. The namespace points to a URI. The URI refers to the location of an XML schema (.xsd file) that is used to define the XML column. For the *AdventureWorks* database, several schemas have already been imported and will be used in subsequent examples.

- **Body** The body contains one or more expressions that specify what data needs returned. This expression is similar to an XPath expression.

If you were to use the query method to return instructions for those products where the ber of labor hours is greater than two and a half hours, the query would look like the follo

```
USE AdventureWorks
GO
SELECT p.Name, p.ProductNumber, pm.Instructions.query(
  'declare namespace AW="http://schemas.microsoft.com/sqlserver/2004/07/adventure-works
ProductModelManuInstructions";
  AW:root/AW:Location[@LaborHours>2.5]') As Locations
FROM Production.Product p
JOIN Production.ProductModel pm
  ON p.ProductModelID = pm.ProductModelID
WHERE pm.Instructions is not NULL
```

This query should return 25 results, just as the first query did. The only difference is th value in the third column will be different. In the second query, we are using the query me to limit the XML data returned in that column. The body portion of this query specifie XML from the *Location* node should be returned for locations where the *LaborHours* att is greater than two and a half hours. For example, after running this query, if you were to the XML link for the first product, you would see the following XML:

```
<AW:Location xmlns:AW="http://schemas.microsoft.com/sqlserver/2004/07/adventure-works/
ProductModelManuInstructions" LaborHours="3" LotSize="1" SetupHours="0.25" LocationID="
    Work Center 50 - SubAssembly. The following instructions pertain to Work
    Center 50. (Setup hours = .25, Labor Hours = 3, Machine Hours = 0, Lot Sizing
    = 1)
<AW:step>Add Seat Assembly. </AW:step>
<AW:step>Add Brake assembly. </AW:step>
<AW:step>Add Wheel Assembly. </AW:step>
<AW:step>Inspect Front Derailleur. </AW:step>
<AW:step>Inspect Rear Derailleur. </AW:step>
</AW:Location>
<AW:Location xmlns:AW="http://schemas.microsoft.com/sqlserver/2004/07/adventure-works/
ProductModelManuInstructions" LaborHours="4" LotSize="1" LocationID="60">
    Work Center 60 - Final Assembly. The following instructions pertain to Work
    Center 60. (Setup hours = 0, Labor Hours = 4, Machine Hours = 0, Lot Sizing
    = 1)
<AW:step>
        Perform final inspection per engineering specification <AW:specs>AWC-
            915</AW:specs>.
    </AW:step>
<AW:step>Complete all required certification forms.</AW:step>
<AW:step>Move to shipping.</AW:step>
</AW:Location>
```

Notice that the XML returned includes the prefix AW, which was specified in the prolog section of the query method. Also note that the XML includes all nodes beneath the *Locations* node, such as step and specs. For those products where the number of labor hours per location was less than or equal to two and a half hours, an empty string is returned.

IMPORTANT   XML is case-sensitive

Even though your instance of SQL Server 2005 might not be case-sensitive, XML is case-sensitive and so are the XQuery expressions. Make sure that any node and attribute names you specify in your expression match the XML document exactly. For example, if our query statement included an attribute named *Laborhours*, it would not be found. The attribute is correctly cased as *LaborHours*.

An alternative to declaring a namespace within the XQuery expression is to use an XML namespace. This is done using the XML NAMESPACES Transact-SQL statement. For example, you could replace the previous query with the following:

```
USE AdventureWorks
GO
WITH XMLNAMESPACES ('http://schemas.microsoft.com/sqlserver/2004/07/adventure-works/
ProductModelManuInstructions'
  As AW)
SELECT p.Name, p.ProductNumber, pm.Instructions.query(
   'AW:root/AW:Location[@LaborHours>2.5]') As Locations
FROM Production.Product p
JOIN Production.ProductModel pm
  ON p.ProductModelID = pm.ProductModelID
WHERE pm.Instructions is not NULL
```

Other methods available for the *xml* data type include the following:

- **value(XQuery expression, SQL type)**   Similar to the query method, this also performs an XQuery, but it returns the XML as a SQL type other than the *xml* data type.
- **exist(XQuery expression)**   Used to determine whether a query will return a nonempty result. If the method returns a value of 1, then there is at least one node to be returned. If the method returns a value of 0, then an empty result would be returned. If the method returns a value of NULL, then no XML document was found in that column.

   The *exist* method can be really useful in combining the results of an XQuery expression with a Transact-SQL query. For example, the second query in this section returned all records where the instructions were NOT NULL. Twenty-five records were returned, but not all of them contained XML due to the XQuery restriction. If you wanted to return records for those products that had locations in which the number of labor hours was greater than two and a half hours, you could use the following query instead and only return 22 results:

```
USE AdventureWorks
GO
WITH XMLNAMESPACES ('http://schemas.microsoft.com/sqlserver/2004/07/adventure-wor
ProductModelManuInstructions'
  As AW)

SELECT p.Name, p.ProductNumber, pm.Instructions.query(
   'AW:root/AW:Location[@LaborHours>2.5]') As Locations
FROM Production.Product p
JOIN Production.ProductModel pm
  ON p.ProductModelID = pm.ProductModelID
--WHERE pm.instructions is not null
WHERE pm.Instructions.exist('/AW:root/AW:Location[@LaborHours>2.5]') = 1
AND pm.instructions is not NULL
```

- **modify(XML DML)**   Used in conjunction with an UPDATE statement, this metho
  be used to insert, delete, or replace the XML using a Data Manipulation Lang
  (DML) statement.

- **nodes(XQuery expression)**   Used when you need to transform XML data into a rela
  format. The method returns the data as a column within a table. With this method
  can return multiple rows by using the *value* method with the *nodes* method. This c
  useful for retrieving a rowset view of the XML data.

Using Parameters

You need to query XML columns using parameters and not hard-coded values. The *sql:va*
function enables you to expose a variable to an XQuery statement. For example, you ca
this function together with the *query* method to return XML that contains locations wit
LocationID attribute set to a value of 50:

```
USE AdventureWorks
GO

DECLARE @LocID int;
SET @LocID = 50;

WITH XMLNAMESPACES ('http://schemas.microsoft.com/sqlserver/2004/07/adventure
-works/ProductModelManuInstructions'
  As AW)

SELECT p.Name, p.ProductNumber, pm.Instructions.query(
   'AW:root/AW:Location[@LocationID=(sql:variable("@LocID"))]') As Location
FROM Production.Product p
JOIN Production.ProductModel pm
  ON p.ProductModelID = pm.ProductModelID
WHERE pm.Instructions is not NULL
```

This query will return 25 records. If you were to click the link in the Location column for the first record, you should see the following:

```
<AW:Location xmlns:AW="http://schemas.microsoft.com/sqlserver/2004/07/adventure-works/
ProductModelManuInstructions" LaborHours="3" LotSize="1" SetupHours="0.25" LocationID="50">
Work Center 50 - SubAssembly. The following instructions pertain to Work Center 50. (Setup
hours = .25, Labor Hours = 3, Machine Hours = 0, Lot
Sizing = 1)
<AW:step>Add Seat Assembly. </AW:step>
<AW:step>Add Brake assembly.   </AW:step>
<AW:step>Add Wheel Assembly. </AW:step>
<AW:step>Inspect Front Derailleur. </AW:step>
<AW:step>Inspect Rear Derailleur. </AW:step>
</AW:Location>
```

Alternatively, you can use the *value* method to return a portion of the XML. The value that is returned can then be compared to a Transact-SQL variable in the WHERE clause. For example, the following query can also be used to return XML for a location with a location ID equal to 50:

```
USE AdventureWorks
GO

DECLARE @LocID int;
SET @LocID = 50;

WITH XMLNAMESPACES ('http://schemas.microsoft.com/sqlserver/2004/07/
adventure-works/ProductModelManuInstructions'
  As AW)

SELECT p.Name, p.ProductNumber, pm.Instructions.query(
   'AW:root/AW:Location') As Location
FROM Production.Product p
JOIN Production.ProductModel pm
  ON p.ProductModelID = pm.ProductModelID
WHERE pm.instructions.value('(AW:root/AW:Location/@LocationID
[1]', 'int') = @LocID
  AND pm.Instructions is not NULL
```

Note that this query still uses the *value* method to return the XML for the Location column. The WHERE clause uses the *value* method to specify that a singleton value should be returned as an integer. On the surface, this looks like the same result is being accomplished as in the previous query. However, the drawback to using this method is that you need to return a singleton value, which in this case is the first node. This means that the query will only return data where the Location ID is 50 in the first node. Due to this restriction, the query will only return five records instead of 25.

Returning Data as XML

There might be times when you need to return data from a relational database as XML. FOR XML clause can be used with a SELECT query to accomplish this. To use the FOR clause, you need to specify one of the following four modes:

- **RAW** The simplest form; this is used to return a single element for each row. For XML to be hierarchical, you would have to utilize nested FOR XML queries.
- **AUTO** This mode will return the data in a hierarchical format, but you have no co over how it is shaped. The shape is controlled by how the SELECT statement is wr
- **EXPLICIT** This mode enables you to control the shape of the XML by specifying mat. These types of queries can be difficult to write, and typically you can accomplis same result using nested FOR XML queries.
- **PATH** This mode is also an alternative to using the EXPLICIT mode. It enables ye specify attributes and elements as XPath expressions.

    The following query is an example of using the RAW mode and can be used to re XML for the Product ID with a value of 1:

```
Select Name, ProductNumber, ListPrice
FROM Production.Product
WHERE ProductID = 1
FOR XML RAW
The previous query should return the following XML string:
<row Name="Adjustable Race" ProductNumber="AR-5381" ListPrice="0.0000" />
```

If you preferred that the product columns were returned as elements and not attributes could alternatively use the following query:

```
Select Name, ProductNumber, ListPrice
FROM Production.Product
WHERE ProductID = 1
FOR XML RAW, ELEMENTS
```

The *ELEMENTS* keyword is an enhancement that forces the RAW mode to be element-ce and not attribute-centric. The results from the second query would be as follows:

```
<row>
  <Name>Adjustable Race</Name>
  <ProductNumber>AR-5381</ProductNumber>
  <ListPrice>0.0000</ListPrice>
</row>
```

If you were executing a complex SQL statement that included levels such as the detail as ated with an order, then using one of the other modes would be more appropriate. For e: ple, if you wanted to return information about purchase orders that included all deta orders with a status of 2, you could use the following query:

```
USE AdventureWorks
GO
Select [Order].PurchaseOrderID, [Order].Status,
  Vendor.Name as VendorName,
  ShipMethod.Name as ShipMethod,
  [Order].OrderDate, [Order].Shipdate, [Order].TotalDue,
  Detail.OrderQty, Detail.UnitPrice, Detail.LineTotal,
  Product.Name as ProductName
FROM Purchasing.PurchaseOrderHeader [Order]
JOIN Purchasing.Vendor Vendor
  ON [Order].VendorID = Vendor.VendorID
JOIN Purchasing.ShipMethod ShipMethod
  ON [Order].ShipMethodID = ShipMethod.ShipMethodID
JOIN Purchasing.PurchaseOrderDetail Detail
  ON [Order].PurchaseOrderID = Detail.PurchaseOrderID
JOIN Production.Product Product
  ON Detail.ProductID = Product.ProductID
WHERE [Order].Status = 2
FOR XML AUTO
```

By including the FOR XML AUTO clause, you will return XML in levels. However, you will have little control over how the XML is formatted. A portion of the XML returned from the previous query is as follows:

```
<Order PurchaseOrderID="4001" Status="2" OrderDate="2004-03-14T00:00:00" Shipdate="2004-04-
08T00:00:00" TotalDue="5036.1465">
<Vendor VendorName="G &amp; K Bicycle Corp.">
   <ShipMethod ShipMethod="OVERSEAS - DELUXE">
      <Detail OrderQty="25" UnitPrice="13.0863" LineTotal="327.1575">
        <Product ProductName="Sport-100 Helmet, Red" />
        <Product ProductName="Sport-100 Helmet, Black" />
      </Detail>
      <Detail OrderQty="300" UnitPrice="13.0800" LineTotal="3924.0000">
        <Product ProductName="Sport-100 Helmet, Blue" />
      </Detail>
   </ShipMethod>
 </Vendor>
</Order>
<Order PurchaseOrderID="4002" Status="2" OrderDate="2004-10-23T00:00:00" Shipdate="2004-11-
17T00:00:00" TotalDue="1122.0000">
<Vendor VendorName="Jeff's Sporting Goods">
  <ShipMethod ShipMethod="OVERSEAS - DELUXE">
      <Detail OrderQty="150" UnitPrice="3.4000" LineTotal="510.0000">
        <Product ProductName="Mountain Bike Socks, M" />
        <Product ProductName="Mountain Bike Socks, L" />
      </Detail>
  </ShipMethod>
 </Vendor>
</Order>
```

The element and attribute names derive from the alias names used in the SELECT query.
format created by the *AUTO* method is acceptable, then this is the easiest way to retur
matted XML data.

However, if you want more control over whether columns are assigned as attributes o
ments, you can use the *PATH* method. For example, assume you wanted to return the f
ing XML results:

```
<PurchaseOrders>
<Order PurchaseOrderID="4001" Status="2" VendorName="G &amp; K Bicycle Corp."
ShipMethodName="OVERSEAS - DELUXE" OrderDate="2004-03-14T00:00:00" ShipDate="2004-04-
08T00:00:00" TotalDue="5036.1465" />
  <Order PurchaseOrderID="4002" Status="2" VendorName="Jeff's Sporting Goods"
ShipMethodName="OVERSEAS - DELUXE" OrderDate="2004-10-23T00:00:00" ShipDate="2004-11-
17T00:00:00" TotalDue="1122.0000" />
  <Order PurchaseOrderID="4003" Status="2" VendorName="Integrated Sport Products"
ShipMethodName="OVERSEAS - DELUXE" OrderDate="2004-06-14T00:00:00" ShipDate="2004-07-
09T00:00:00" TotalDue="30198.9600" />
  <Order PurchaseOrderID="4004" Status="2" VendorName="Integrated Sport Products"
ShipMethodName="OVERSEAS - DELUXE" OrderDate="2003-12-05T00:00:00" ShipDate="2003-12-
30T00:00:00" TotalDue="51021.3000" />
  <Order PurchaseOrderID="4005" Status="2" VendorName="Integrated Sport Products"
ShipMethodName="OVERSEAS - DELUXE" OrderDate="2004-02-28T00:00:00" ShipDate="2004-03-
24T00:00:00" TotalDue="8167.5000" />
  <Order PurchaseOrderID="4006" Status="2" VendorName="International Trek Center"
ShipMethodName="OVERSEAS - DELUXE" OrderDate="2004-02-19T00:00:00" ShipDate="2004-03-
15T00:00:00" TotalDue="24070.7500" />
  <Order PurchaseOrderID="4007" Status="2" VendorName="Fitness Association"
ShipMethodName="OVERSEAS - DELUXE" OrderDate="2004-04-01T00:00:00" ShipDate="2004-04-
26T00:00:00" TotalDue="609422.0000" />
  <Order PurchaseOrderID="4008" Status="2" VendorName="Team Athletic Co."
ShipMethodName="OVERSEAS - DELUXE" OrderDate="2004-05-23T00:00:00" ShipDate="2004-06-
17T00:00:00" TotalDue="436401.9000" />
  <Order PurchaseOrderID="4009" Status="2" VendorName="Green Lake Bike Company"
ShipMethodName="OVERSEAS - DELUXE" OrderDate="2003-12-11T00:00:00" ShipDate="2004-01-
05T00:00:00" TotalDue="16406.5000" />
  <Order PurchaseOrderID="4010" Status="2" VendorName="Jeff's Sporting Goods"
ShipMethodName="OVERSEAS - DELUXE" OrderDate="2003-12-11T00:00:00" ShipDate="2004-01-
05T00:00:00" TotalDue="41536.0000" />
  <Order PurchaseOrderID="4011" Status="2" VendorName="Green Lake Bike Company"
ShipMethodName="OVERSEAS - DELUXE" OrderDate="2004-07-25T00:00:00" ShipDate="2004-08-
19T00:00:00" TotalDue="59941.7500" />
  <Order PurchaseOrderID="4012" Status="2" VendorName="Integrated Sport Products"
ShipMethodName="OVERSEAS - DELUXE" OrderDate="2004-07-25T00:00:00" ShipDate="2004-08-
19T00:00:00" TotalDue="1097448.0000" />
</PurchaseOrders>
You could use the following query to return the previous results:
USE AdventureWorks
GO
```

```
Select [Order].PurchaseOrderID "@PurchaseOrderID",
  [Order].Status "@Status",
  Vendor.Name "@VendorName",
  ShipMethod.Name "@ShipMethodName",
  [Order].OrderDate "@OrderDate", [Order].Shipdate "@ShipDate",
  [Order].TotalDue "@TotalDue"
FROM Purchasing.PurchaseOrderHeader [Order]
JOIN Purchasing.Vendor Vendor
  ON [Order].VendorID = Vendor.VendorID
JOIN Purchasing.ShipMethod ShipMethod
  ON [Order].ShipMethodID = ShipMethod.ShipMethodID
WHERE [Order].Status = 2
FOR XML PATH('Order'), ROOT('PurchaseOrders')
```

This query uses the PATH mode and passes in the name of the element to be used for each row returned. The query also uses the *ROOT* directive to pass in the name of the root element. Attributes are specified using the at (@) prefix. You can also specify element names using the name followed by the forward slash (/).

Updating Data Using XML

It might be necessary for you to update relational data based on some value in an XML document. Because SQL Server 2005 includes the *xml* data type, this can be accomplished by creating a stored procedure or user-defined function that accepts an XML document as an input parameter.

The body of the stored procedure or user-defined function would then contain Transact-SQL code that retrieved values from the XML document. This could be done using the methods shown in the preceding section, "Querying XML Data with XQuery."

For example, assume you had an XML document that contained updated contact information. The document might look similar to the following:

```
<UpdatedContactInfo ContactID="1">
  <Name>
    <FirstName>Gustavo</FirstName>
    <MiddleName>G.</MiddleName>
    <LastName>Achong</LastName>
  </Name>
</UpdatedContactInfo>
```

If you were to query the Person.Contact table for the *AdventureWorks* database, you would see that the middle name for the first contact is empty. The following stored procedure could be used to update the name columns in the Person.Contact table with the values from the XML document:

```
CREATE PROCEDURE spUpdateContactName(@xml xml)
AS

BEGIN
--Get the ID since we will use this in more than one
DECLARE @ID int
SET @ID = (SELECT @xml.value('/UpdatedContactInfo[1]/@ContactID', 'int'))

--Update the Names with the values in the XML Document
UPDATE Person.Contact
SET FirstName = (SELECT @xml.value('(/UpdatedContactInfo/Name/FirstName)
[1]', 'nvarchar(50)')),
  LastName = (SELECT @xml.value('(/UpdatedContactInfo/Name/LastName)
[1]', 'nvarchar(50)')),
  MiddleName = (SELECT @xml.value('(/UpdatedContactInfo/Name/MiddleName)
[1]', 'nvarchar(50)'))
WHERE ContactID = @ID


END
```

You would then execute the stored procedure and pass in the XML document using th
lowing Transact-SQL code:

```
DECLARE @xml xml
Set @xml = '<UpdatedContactInfo ContactID="1"><Name><FirstName>Gustavo</
FirstName><MiddleName>G.</MiddleName>
<LastName>Achong</LastName></Name></UpdatedContactInfo>'

EXEC spUpdateContactName @xml
```

The result of executing the previous Transact-SQL statements should be that one recor
updated. The middle name for the first contact would then be set with a value of "G."

Lab: Working with XML Data

In this lab, you will experiment with working with XML data. In the first exercise, you
write a query against an XML column using an XQuery expression. In the second exercise
will return data from a relational database as XML.

The completed lab is available in the \Labs\Chapter 02\Lab3 folder on the companion

---

IMPORTANT   Lab requirements

You will need to have SQL Server 2005 installed before you can complete this lab. Refer to th
Introduction for setup instructions.

Exercise 1: Write an XQuery Expression

In this exercise, you will create a query against an XML column in the Person.Contact table. The query returns data for all contacts with postal address information in the XML column AdditionalContactInfo.

Not all contacts have this information embedded in the XML column, so the query uses the *exist* method to test for this condition. If the postal address exists, then the *value* method is used to retrieve the street address, city, state, ZIP Code, and country for each contact.

Unlike the instructions column in the Production.ProductModel table, AdditionalContactInfo utilizes multiple schemas. For this reason, we use the WITH XMLNAMESPACES clause *and* declare namespace declarations to reference these schemas.

1. Open SQL Server Management Studio.
2. Connect to the instance of SQL Server 2005 that contains the *AdventureWorks* database.
3. Select New Query.
4. Add the following code to the query window:

```
USE AdventureWorks
GO

WITH XMLNAMESPACES ('http://schemas.microsoft.com/sqlserver/2004/07/adventure-works/
ContactInfo'
  As AW)

SELECT c.FirstName + ' ' + c.LastName as "Contact Name",
  ContactInfo.ref.value(
  'declare namespace act="http://schemas.microsoft.com/sqlserver/2004/07/a
dventure-works/ContactTypes";
  (act:homePostalAddress/act:Street)[1]', 'nvarchar(50)') As "Postal Street",
  ContactInfo.ref.value(
  'declare namespace act="http://schemas.microsoft.com/sqlserver/2004/07/adventure-
works/ContactTypes";
  (act:homePostalAddress/act:City)[1]', 'nvarchar(50)') As "Postal City",
  ContactInfo.ref.value(
  'declare namespace act="http://schemas.microsoft.com/sqlserver/2004/07/adventure-
works/ContactTypes";
  (act:homePostalAddress/act:StateProvince)[1]', 'nvarchar(50)')
 As "Postal State",
  ContactInfo.ref.value(
  'declare namespace act="http://schemas.microsoft.com/sqlserver/2004/07/adventure-
works/ContactTypes";
  (act:homePostalAddress/act:PostalCode)[1]', 'nvarchar(50)') As "Zip Code",
  ContactInfo.ref.value(
  'declare namespace act="http://schemas.microsoft.com/sqlserver/2004/07/adventure-
works/ContactTypes";
  (act:homePostalAddress/act:CountryRegion)[1]', 'nvarchar(50)')
```

```
 As "Postal Country"
FROM Person.Contact c
OUTER APPLY c.AdditionalContactInfo.nodes(
    '/AW:AdditionalContactInfo') AS ContactInfo(ref)
WHERE ContactInfo.ref.exist(
  'declare namespace act="http://schemas.microsoft.com/sqlserver/2004/07/
adventure-works/ContactTypes";
  act:homePostalAddress') = 1
AND c.AdditionalContactInfo is not NULL
```

5. Click the Execute button. The results window should display three records, whic
   the only records that contain the postal address information. The results from this
   are listed in Table 2-7.

Table 2-7   Query Results When Using the Query in Exercise 1

Contact Name	Postal Street	Postal City	Postal State	Zip Code	Cou
Gustavo Achong	123 Oak	Seattle	WA	98001	USA
Catherine Abel	P.O. Box 5	Edmonds	WA	98431	USA
Kim Abercrombie	990 5th Avenue	Redmond	WA	98052	USA

Exercise 2: Generate XML

In this exercise, you will generate raw XML by executing a query and using the FOR
clause. By default, this will use the RAW option to return the XML in the format t
implied.

1. Open SQL Server Management Studio.
2. Connect to the instance of SQL Server 2005 that contains the *AdventureWorks* data
3. Select New Query.
4. Add the following code to the query window:

```
USE AdventureWorks
GO
Select [Contact].FirstName, [Contact].LastName,
    [Contact].Title, [Contact].EmailAddress,
    [Address].AddressLine1, [Address].AddressLine2,
    [Address].City, [Address].StateProvinceID,
    [Address].PostalCode
FROM Person.Contact [Contact]
JOIN HumanResources.Employee [Employee]
    ON [Contact].ContactID = [Employee].ContactID
JOIN HumanResources.EmployeeAddress ea
    ON [Employee].EmployeeID = ea.EmployeeID
JOIN Person.Address [Address]
    ON ea.AddressID = [Address].AddressID
FOR XML AUTO
```

5. After executing the query, you should see a single result that displays the XML for all contacts returned by the query. You can click the link to see the XML that was generated.

Quick Check

1. What does it mean for an *xml* data type column to be "typed"?
2. What parts make up an XQuery expression?
3. What purpose does the *sql:variable* function provide?
4. When you are returning data as XML using the FOR XML clause, what mode enables you to easily return data in a hierarchical format?

Quick Check Answers

1. Typed XML columns are associated with one or more schema definitions. The schema is used to validate the XML document contained within the column and contains information about what data can reside within nodes and attributes.
2. An XQuery expression is composed of the prolog and the body. The prolog is the first part and is used to declare namespaces that refer to the location of the schema definition file.
3. The *sql:variable* function can be used to pass data to an XQuery expression. This enables you to pass parameters to your XQuery expression and makes the query more dynamic.
4. AUTO mode is the easiest way to return data in a hierarchical format. However, AUTO mode gives you the least control over how the data is shaped. You can use the PATH or EXPLICIT modes to control how the XML is shaped.

---

e Scenario: Creating a Plan Guide

You are a developer for a large retail company that uses software from several third-party vendors. All of the third-party applications use SQL Server 2005 as the database, and they typically use stored procedures as part of the data layer. The support contracts established with each of these vendors restricts you from modifying their databases directly. This means you are not allowed to modify any stored procedures that the applications utilize.

In recent months, you have been experiencing performance problems with one of the third-party applications. After extensive analysis using SQL Server Profiler and distributed management views, you have determined that several of the stored procedures contain poorly performing queries. Your manager has asked you if there is anything that can be done to

improve performance without violating the third-party vendors support contract. Wh
you suggest?

Suggested Practices

Objective 2.1: Write and modify queries

- **Practice 1**   Write a query using the *AdventureWorks* database that performs a tabl
  using the following tables:
    - ❏ Person.Contact
    - ❏ HumanResources.Employee
    - ❏ HumanResources.EmployeeDepartmentHistory
    - ❏ HumanResources.Department
    - ❏ HumanResources.Shift

The query should return at least one non-key column from each table and use a WI
clause to filter the results according to one of the shifts in HumanResources.ShiftID.

- **Practice 2**   Create a table-valued function that accepts the ContactID as an input p
  eter. The function should perform some operation to compute a value or append a
  to another string and return the result(s) in the output table. You will then write a
  that utilizes the *APPLY* operator and the table-valued function.

- **Practice 3**   Locate a test or production database utilized by your company. S
  through the stored procedures or user-defined functions for that database. Loc
  SELECT queries that do not utilize search arguments (SARGs). Determine if the
  way that the query could be rewritten to improve the performance. Remember
  make changes to the actual database, but instead, execute the queries in a separate
  window.

Objective 2.2: Design queries for retrieving data from XML sources

- **Practice 1**   Write a SELECT query using the *AdventureWorks* database. The
  should return both relational and XML data from the following tables:
    - ❏ Production.Product
    - ❏ Production.ProductModel

The query should use the *query* method and an XQuery expression to retrieve data
the CatalogDescription column using the Production.ProductDescriptionSchem
lection. If you wish, you can use the *exist* method to return data for those reco
which *AdventureWorks* is the name of the manufacturer.

■ **Practice 2** Write a SELECT query using the *AdventureWorks* database. The query should return at least one non-key column as XML from the following tables:

❑ Person.Contact

❑ HumanResources.Employee

❑ HumanResources.EmployeePayHistory

The query should use the FOR XML clause and the PATH mode to return data in a hierarchical format. Experiment with the XPath expressions, which are used to specify the shape of the XML. Return data both as attributes and then as elements. Once the query is finalized, you can attempt to return the same data using the EXPLICIT mode.

erences

■ Administering a Full-Text Search

http://msdn2.microsoft.com/en-us/library/ms142557.aspx

■ Overview of SQL Server 2005 for the Database Administrator

http://www.microsoft.com/technet/prodtechnol/sql/2005/sqlydba.mspx

■ Using the USE PLAN Query Hint

http://msdn2.microsoft.com/en-us/library/ms186954.aspx

■ Forcing Query Plans with SQL Server 2005

http://www.microsoft.com/technet/prodtechnol/sql/2005/frcqupln.mspx

■ Invoke UDFs That Accept Tables with SQL Server 2005's *APPLY* Operator

http://builder.com.com/5100-6388_14-6108869.html

■ New T-SQL Features in SQL Server 2005, Part 1

http://www.sqlservercentral.com/columnists/sramakrishnan/2734.asp

■ Returning Ranked Results with Microsoft SQL Server 2005

http://www.4guysfromrolla.com/webtech/010406-1.shtml

■ Optimizing Distributed Queries

http://msdn2.microsoft.com/en-us/library/ms180972.aspx

■ XQuery Specification

http://www.w3.org/TR/xquery/

■ Understanding SQL Server Full-Text Indexing

http://www.developer.com/db/article.php/3446891

■ XML Integration with SQL Server 2005

http://www.programmersheaven.com/2/SQL-server-2005-school-lesson-5

Chapter Summary

- Table joins enable you to return data from one or more related tables. Linked s‹ enable you to query data from heterogeneous data sources in the same way you ‹ query SQL Server.

- New operators include: the *PIVOT* operator, which enables you to generate an o‹ table that can then be used to create cross-tab reports by performing aggregations data. The *APPLY* operator is used in the FROM clause and enables you to apply a valued function to each row in the outer table. The *EXCEPT* operator can be us‹ combine and limit result sets by only returning distinct values from the left sid‹ *INTERSECT* operator does the same thing but returns distinct values from the le‹ right sides.

- Full-text searches enable you to perform partial searches of large columns .mor‹ ciently than traditional LIKE searches. Once a catalog and index are built, you c‹ the CONTAINS predicate to search columns for partial words or phrases. Other cates that can be used are CONTAINSTABLE and FREETEXT.

- The query optimizer for SQL Server 2005 will automatically search for the optim‹ cution plan. There might be specific instances where experienced developers or base administrators have the need to override this capability and use a specific exe‹ plan and a query hint. Plan guides enable you to apply a query hint to a query w‹ modifying the query itself.

- A searchable argument (SARG) is used by the query optimizer when determining t‹ rect execution plan and index to utilize. Therefore, it might be possible for you to im‹ the performance of an existing query by rewriting it to use a searchable argument

- You can query XML columns using an XQuery (an XML querying language) expr‹ and one of the following methods: *query, value, exist, nodes*. The *modify* method is to update the XML document in a column defined as such.

- The FOR XML clause enables you to return relational data as XML. You can use ‹ the following modes to affect the shape of the XML: RAW, EXPLICIT, PATH, or A‹

esigning a Cursor and Caching
rategy

ASP.NET and ADO.NET offer many ways to increase the performance of applications that access data from a data source. For data that is not updated frequently, you can consider caching, which involves the temporary storage of data outside of a database. Caching provides an opportunity to optimize network and server resources. ASP.NET offers three ways to implement caching; finding the right caching solution depends on the requirements of your application. Lesson 1 will cover considerations you need to make when designing a caching strategy. From there, the chapter moves on to discuss using cursors to efficiently handle row-by-row operations.

Cursors allow you to work with one row or a group of rows at the same time. When used properly, cursors can provide an opportunity to optimize server memory and improve application performance. When designing an application that uses cursors, it is important both to know where to implement cursors and to recognize when it is not appropriate to use cursors. This chapter will explore the considerations you need to make when designing a cursor strategy.

Exam objectives in this chapter:
- Design caching strategies.
  - Select ADO.NET caching.
  - Design custom caching functionality.
  - Design a refresh strategy for cached data.
- Design a cursor strategy for a data access component.
  - Decide when to use cursors.
  - Decide how to maximize cursor performance.
  - Decide which applications are using cursors and evaluate whether to remove them.
- Design a cursor strategy.
  - Design cursor logic.
  - Design cursors that work together with dynamic SQL execution.
  - Select an appropriate cursor type.
  - Design cursors that efficiently use server memory.

❑ Design cursors that minimize blocking.

❑ Design a strategy that minimizes or eliminates the use of cursors.

Before You Begin

To complete the lessons in this chapter, you must have:

■ A computer that meets or exceeds the minimum hardware requirements listed i
  Introduction.

■ Experience designing and executing queries in SQL Server Management Studio.

■ Experience creating Web-based applications using Microsoft Visual Studio 2005.

son 1: Designing Caching Strategies

Estimated lesson time: 60 minutes

Caching is the process of storing data in a cache until it is needed again. A cache is simply an in-memory representation of some data. The primary reason for caching data is to increase application performance. Caching is a good idea in cases where the data is expensive to retrieve and not likely to change. In many cases, you can achieve a significant performance advantage just by implementing the most basic caching.

One of the most common ways to use caching is in the population of large datagrid controls that need to be navigated with paging. In this case, it would be very costly to requery the database every time the user goes to the next page. Caching enables you to place the data returned from ADO.NET into a cache object. You can then use the cache object as the data source for the datagrid control.

at is Output Caching?

ASP.NET enables you to implement three types of caching. The first two, page level and user control level, are referred to as *output caching*; they are the easiest to implement. They involve adding a line of code to the top of the Web page or user control file. The third type of caching involves using the cache API to implement custom caching functionality.

Page-Level Output Caching

To implement page-level caching, you only need to specify the *OutputCache* directive at the top of the HTML for the Web page or .aspx file. This is used both for page-level caching and user control-level caching. Refer to Table 3-1 for the attributes that are used with the *OutputCache* directive.

The *OutputCache* directive will be placed at the top of the code file, before any other directives or HTML. The following is an example of a typical directive that would be placed in a file with an .aspx extension:

```
<%@ OutputCache Duration="15" VaryByParam="*" %>
```

In this example, the *Duration* and *VaryByParam* attributes were used. The *Duration* attribute specifies that the page will be cached for 15 seconds. The *VaryByParam* attribute specifies that the cache will be varied for all query string variables.

BEST PRACTICES   Avoid using asterisks

Only use an asterisk (*) for the *VaryByParam* attribute if you know the content is fairly static. O
wise, you are going to be consuming a lot of system resources, storing an exponentially large
ber of versions in the cache. This could cause you to get little or no performance advantage
caching.

Implementing page-level caching is a quick and easy way of gaining a performance adva
for your Web pages. However, you might have to modify the duration attribute and the
ByParam or *VaryByControl* attributes to find the optimum settings for your application. Yc
use a utility such as the Microsoft Web Application Stress Tool, which is free and availab
download at *http://www.microsoft.com/downloads/details.aspx?FamilyID=e2c0585a-062c
-a67d-75a89aa36495&DisplayLang=en*. This utility will simulate the execution of Web pa
multiple browsers, so you can evaluate the performance and scalability of your Web pa

User Control-Level Output Caching

User control-level output caching, also known as fragment caching, is similar to page
caching. The main difference is that the caching is restricted to the contents of the user co
and not the entire page in which it is hosted. This gives you finer control over what is
cached. You place the *OutputCache* directive at the top of the file, giving it the .ascx exten
Refer to Table 3-1 for the list of attributes that can be used with this directive. Notice that
of the attributes are used only for page-level caching. The *Shared* attribute, however, is
applicable for user control-level caching.

Table 3-1   Attributes of the *OutputCache* Directive

Attribute	Description
Duration	A required attribute; duration represents the time in seconds that the pa user control is cached.
Location	Only used for page-level caching; this specifies where the output cache be located. This can be set with a value of *Any, Client, Downstream, Ser None*, or *ServerAndClient*.
CacheProfile	Only used for page-level caching; this is a name that can be assigned to cache settings.
NoStore	Only used for page-level caching; this is a Boolean value that determine whether secondary storage can be used for sensitive information. Settir value to *true* signifies that secondary storage cannot be used.
SqlDependency	Specifies the name of a database and table that the output cache depen

Table 3-1 Attributes of the *OutputCache* Directive

Attribute	Description
VaryByCustom	Used when doing custom caching. Setting the value to Browser indicates that that cache will be varied by browser name and version. Setting the value to a custom string means you will have to add a *GetVaryByCustomString* method to your Global.asax file.
VaryByHeader	Only used for page-level caching; this can contain one or more header names separated by semicolons. If multiple header names are specified, the cache will contain a different version for each header.
VaryByParam	You need to include this attribute or the *VaryByControl* attribute. This will specify one or more query string values that are separated by semicolons. If multiple parameters are specified, the cache will contain a different version for each parameter. Setting this value with an * indicates that all parameters will be used to vary the cache.
VaryByControl	You need to include this attribute or the *VaryByParam* attribute. This will specify one or more control IDs that are separated by semicolons. If multiple control IDs are specified, the cache will contain a different version for each control.
Shared	Only used for user-level caching; this is a Boolean value that determines whether the output can be shared with multiple pages.

User control-level caching can be beneficial in cases where you have the contents of an application's header and footer stored in user controls. This is a common practice; in these cases, the content in the header and footer is not likely to change, so it is a perfect candidate for caching.

In addition to using the *OutputCache* directive in your page, you can use the *PartialCachingAttribute* class in the code for the user control. For example, the following code can be placed in the code-behind file for the user control, which enables it to be cached for 30 seconds:

```
//C#
[PartialCaching(30)]
public partial class WebUserControl : System.Web.UI.UserControl
{
    //Code for the class would go here
}

'VB
<PartialCaching(120)> _
Partial Class WebUserControl
    Inherits System.Web.UI.UserControl
    'Code for the class goes here
End Class
```

Designing Custom Caching Functionality

In some cases, even user-control level caching does not give you the level of granular c that you need from your caching strategy. Alternatively, you can use the cache API to stor cifically chosen data in a cache object. This is the most powerful method of caching ava but it also requires the most development time to implement.

The *System.Web.Caching* namespace contains a *Cache* class that can be used to add and items from the cache. This is only applicable to ASP.NET applications, although you ca implement caching with a Windows Forms application.

Exam Tip   For this exam, you only need to focus on using the *System.Web.Caching* namesp with an ASP.NET application. You do *not* need to know how to implement caching with a Win Forms application.

The first step in caching is to add an item to the cache. This is done using either the *In Add* methods. The *Insert* method will add the item, but if an item with the same name al exists, it will be replaced. The *Add* method will not replace a duplicate; instead, it will ra exception.

When the item is added, you will assign a key and value pair that is used to identify the The following code adds an item to the cache named "CacheKey"; this item is set with a of "Cache Value":

```
//C#
Cache["CacheKey"] = "Cache Value";
```

```
'VB
Cache("CacheKey") = "Cache Value"
```

In the previous example, the item was added directly to the cache without using the *In Add* method. Alternatively, you could use those methods as well. An example of usir *Insert* method is as follows:

```
//C#
//Use the Insert method to add an item to the cache
Cache.Insert("CacheKey", "Cache Value", null,
        System.Web.Caching.Cache.NoAbsoluteExpiration,
        System.Web.Caching.Cache.NoSlidingExpiration,
        System.Web.Caching.CacheItemPriority.Normal,
        null);
```

```
'VB
'Use the Insert method to add an item to the cache
Cache.Insert("CacheKey", "Cache Value", Nothing, _
        System.Web.Caching.Cache.NoAbsoluteExpiration, _
```

```
System.Web.Caching.Cache.NoSlidingExpiration, _
System.Web.Caching.CacheItemPriority.Normal, _
Nothing)
```

In the previous code example, the fourth parameter was set with a value of *NoAbsoluteExpiration*. This indicates that the item should never expire. The *NoSlidingExpiraton* value indicates that the item expiration will never be reset. Finally, the CacheItemPriority parameter with a value of *Normal* indicates that the item will not be removed until all BelowNormal and Low priority items are removed.

The *Add* method uses parameters similar to the *Insert* method. An example of using this method is as follows:

```
//C#
//Use the Add method to add an item to the cache
Cache.Add("CacheKey", "Cache Value", null,
          DateTime.Now.AddMinutes(2),
          System.Web.Caching.Cache.NoSlidingExpiration,
          System.Web.Caching.CacheItemPriority.High,
          null);
```

```
'VB
'Use the Add method to add an item to the cache
Cache.Add("CacheKey", "Cache Value", Nothing, _
          DateTime.Now.AddMinutes(2), _
          System.Web.Caching.Cache.NoSlidingExpiration, _
          System.Web.Caching.CacheItemPriority.High, _
          Nothing)
```

This code example specified an expiration date of two minutes. In addition, the priority value was set to high, which means that this is the last item that will be deleted from the cache.

To remove an item from the cache, you use the *Remove* method. This might be necessary when the item has no expiration date. Otherwise, an item will remain in the cache after it is no longer needed and will consume unnecessary system resources. A code example using the *Remove* method is as follows:

```
//C#
Cache.Remove("CacheKey");
```

```
'VB
Cache.Remove("CacheKey")
```

In some cases, you might want to store the results of a database query in the cache. Just as with a string value, you can store a *DataSet* in the cache. For example, the following code will first check to see whether the *DataSet* has been stored in the cache. If it has not, then it will retrieve the data using a command object. Otherwise, it will just use the *DataSet* that resides in the cache object named *dsProductsCache*.

```csharp
//C#
    DataSet dsProductsCache;

        //Look to see if the Dataset is already in the cache
        dsProductsCache = (DataSet)Cache["dsProducts"];

        if (dsProductsCache == null)
        {

            DataSet dsProducts = new DataSet("Products");
            SqlDataAdapter adapter = new SqlDataAdapter();

            //Initiate the connection to SQL Server
            String connString = @"server=.\SQL2005STD;" +
                                "Integrated Security=SSPI;" +
                                "Database=AdventureWorks";
            SqlConnection conn = new SqlConnection(connString);

            //Define the query that will be executed
            String queryString = "select * from production.product";
            //Define the query that will be executed
            SqlCommand cmd = new SqlCommand(queryString, conn);


            //Populate the adapter with results of the query
            adapter.SelectCommand = cmd;
            adapter.Fill(dsProducts);
            dsProductsCache = (DataSet)dsProducts;
        }

        try
        {
            //Set the datasource for the dataViewGrid control on the form
            grdProducts.DataSource = dsProductsCache.Tables[0];
            grdProducts.DataBind();
        }
        catch (Exception ex)
        {
            //Put exception handling here
        }
```

```vbnet
'VB
Dim dsProductsCache As New DataSet("dsProductsCache")

        dsProductsCache = Cache("dsProducts")

        If dsProductsCache Is Nothing Then


            Dim dsProducts As New DataSet("Products")
```

```
      Dim adapter As New SqlDataAdapter()

      'Initiate the connection to SQL Server
      Dim connString As String = "server=.\SQL2005STD;" & _
                                 "Integrated Security=SSPI;" & _
                                 "Database=AdventureWorks"
      Dim conn As New SqlConnection(connString)

      'Define the query that will be executed
      Dim queryString As String = "select * from production.product"
      'Define the query that will be executed
      Dim cmd As New SqlCommand(queryString, conn)

      'Populate the adapter with results of the query
      adapter.SelectCommand = cmd
      adapter.Fill(dsProducts)

      dsProductsCache = dsProducts
   End If

   Try

      'Set the datasource for the dataViewGrid control on the form
      grdProducts.DataSource = dsProductsCache.Tables(0)
      grdProducts.DataBind()

   Catch ex As Exception
      'Put exception handling code here
   End Try
```

ng Query Notifications

Query notifications is a new feature available with SQL Server 2005. It is available through the SQL Native Client provider. Query notifications allows applications to be notified when certain data has changed. Therefore, applications only need to refresh *DataSets* when the data is different and not every time the page is requested. This is particularly useful when establishing a caching strategy because you can control precisely when the cache is refreshed based on an actual need and not just when the cache expires.

The notifications are available because SQL Servers Service Broker is continually polling the server looking for updates. When the notification is established, a time-out period is assigned, and the notification stays active until that period has elapsed. You can cancel the notification prior to the time-out period by executing a notification using the same query but with a time-out period of zero.

To establish a query notification, you must first create a queue and a service. This can be accomplished with the following Transact-SQL code:

```
USE AdventureWorks
CREATE QUEUE myQueue
CREATE SERVICE myService ON QUEUE myQueue ([http://schemas.microsoft.com/SQL/Notificati(
PostQueryNotification]))
```

At this point, you can see the queue by going to SQL Server Management Studio and ex]
ing the *Service Broker* node for the *AdventureWorks* database. You should see a node na
Queues that, when expanded, looks like Figure 3-1.

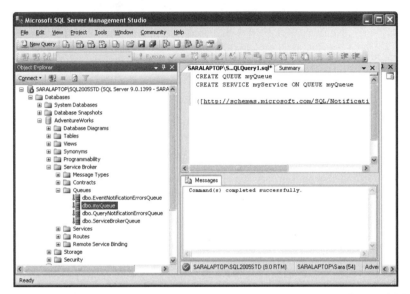

Figure 3-1   Expanding the Service Broker node and looking at the available queues for the *A
tureWorks* database

There is also a node for Services that enables you to see the service you just created. A
point, you instantiate a *SqlNotificationRequest* object to create your notification. You do
your Visual Studio application at the point that you are ready to query the database. Th
thing to do is add a reference to the *System.Data.Sql* namespace at the top of your cod
like so:

//C#
```
using System.Data.Sql;
```

'VB
```
Imports System.Data.Sql
```

You will also need to instantiate a *SqlNotificationRequest* object and set the *UserData* pro
with the value of a new Globally Unique IDentifier (GUID). You will set other properties

as the time for the request to be active and the name of the Service Broker service, as in the following code:

```
//C#
//Instantiate the Notification Request object
SqlNotificationRequest sqlNotify = new SqlNotificationRequest();

//Set a unique identifier for this request
sqlNotify.UserData = Guid.NewGuid().ToString;

//Specify the SQL Server Service Broker Name
sqlNotify.Options = "myService";

//Specify a timeout of 20 minutes or 1200 seconds
sqlNotify.Timeout = 1200;

'VB
'Instantiate the Notification Request object
Dim sqlNotify As New SqlNotificationRequest

'Set a unique identifier for this request
sqlNotify.UserData = Guid.NewGuid().ToString

'Specify the SQL Server Service Broker Name
sqlNotify.Options = "myService"

'Specify a timeout of 20 minutes or 1200 seconds
sqlNotify.Timeout = 1200
```

The last thing to do is to associate the *SqlNotificationRequest* object with a query or command object. This is done by setting the *Notification* property for a command object, as in the following example:

```
//C#
//Associate the SqlRequestNotification object
//with a command created earlier in the code
cmd.Notification = sqlNotify;

'VB
'Associate the SqlRequestNotification object
'with a command created earlier in the code
cmd.Notification = sqlNotify
```

At the point the command is executed and either a *DataReader* or a *DataSet* is populated with the query results, the notification will be registered. The next step is to create a secondary thread that watches the Service Broker queue and waits for changes.

Before you can use threading, you need to set a reference at the top of your code file to the *System.Threading* namespace. You can then add code that creates a thread and listens for

changes. In the following code, a reference is made to a method named *ListenMethod*, wh
where the code that listens for changes resides:

```C#
//C#
// A separate listener thread is needed to
// monitor the queue for notifications.
Thread listener = new Thread(ListenMethod);
listener.Name = "Query Notification Watcher";
listener.Start();
```

```VB
'VB
' A separate listener thread is needed to
' monitor the queue for notifications.
Dim listener As New Thread(AddressOf ListenMethod)
listener.Name = "Query Notification Watcher"
listener.Start()
```

The *ListenMethod* will contain code that executes a query against the Service Broker q
This will be done using an ordinary command object, and the query string for this com
will appear as follows:

```
WAITFOR ( RECEIVE * FROM myService);
```

Once the command object is executed and returned into a *DataReader* or a *DataSet* objec
can loop through the results and perform some additional processing. You can also regis
OnNotificationComplete method that performs some code after the notification is compl

Designing a Refresh Strategy

Once you have determined that you will use caching and have selected a caching methoc
need to determine how you will refresh the data. In the previous section, you saw how c
notifications could be used to notify an application when the data has changed. For dev
ers not willing or able to implement query notifications, you can alternatively refresh the
on a scheduled basis or on demand. When using the *Cache* object, you can set an expir
using either the *Add* or *Insert* method. *Add* includes the same options as the *Insert*; how
Add returns what you've added to the cache. Also, *Add* will not replace an existing cache

The *Add* method accepts an expiration as either an absolute datetime value or as a time
value. For example, the following code can be used to add an item to the cache, and that
will expire one day from the day it was created:

```C#
//C#
//Add an item to the cache that will expire in 1 day
Cache.Add("CacheKey", "Cache Value", null,
    null, System.TimeSpan.FromDays(1d),
    CacheItemPriority.Normal, null);
```

```vb
'VB
'Add an item to the cache that will expire in 1 day
Cache.Add("CacheKey", "Cache Value", Nothing, _
    Nothing, System.TimeSpan.FromDays(1.0), _
    CacheItemPriority.Normal, Nothing)
```

In some cases, it might be necessary to allow users the option of manually refreshing the cache. To accomplish this, provide a button to click that removes the appropriate value from the cache. You can do so using the *Remove* method. At this point, the *Cache* object would be empty and would be refilled the next time the object was accessed. For an example of this code, see the section titled "Designing Custom Caching Functionality."

Implementing Output Caching

In this lab, you implement output caching on a page-level basis. In Exercise 1, you will see the performance effects of changing certain attributes for the *OutputCache* directive. You will also see the effect of eliminating caching all together.

The completed code examples, in both Visual Basic and C#, are available in the \Labs\Chapter 03 folder on the companion CD.

IMPORTANT   Lab requirements

You will need to have both SQL Server and the Web Application Stress Tool installed before you can complete this lab. Refer to the Introduction for setup instructions.

▶ **Exercise 1: Use the *OutputCache* Directive**

In this exercise, you will create a simple ASP.NET application that connects to a SQL Server 2005 database and populates a *GridView* control with the results of a SQL query.

1. Open Microsoft Visual Studio 2005.
2. On the File menu, select New, Project.
3. In the New Project dialog box, expand the *Other Project Types* node, select Visual Studio Solutions, and then select Blank Solution.
4. For your blank solution, type the name **TK442Chapter3**, and place it into a directory of your choosing.

   A new solution file is created, and you can now add multiple projects to this solution. You will add one project for each lab included in this chapter.
5. On the File menu, select Add, New Web Site. Select ASP.NET Web Site as the template, and type ***http://localhost/TK442Chapter3*** as the project name. Set the language by selecting Visual Basic, Visual C#, or Visual J# from the language drop-down list box. By default, Visual Studio will select the language specified when it was first configured.

6. From the Toolbox, drag a label control onto the Default design surface. Use the fc ing property values for this control:

   Name = lblProducts

   Text = "Products:"

7. From the Toolbox, drag a *GridView* control onto the Default design surface. Use tl lowing property value for this control:

   Name: grdProducts

8. Right-click Default.aspx from Solution Explorer, and select View Code. At the top code file, add the following statement: Modify connection strings to match your ronment.

   ```
   //C#
   using System.Data.SqlClient;
   using System.Data;
   ```

   ```
   'VB
   Imports System.Data.SqlClient
   Imports System.Data
   ```

9. Add the following code to the Default class file:

   ```
   //C#
   protected void Page_Load(object sender, EventArgs e)
       {
           DataSet dsProducts = new DataSet("Products");
           SqlDataAdapter adapter = new SqlDataAdapter();

           //Initiate the connection to SQL Server
           String connString = @"server=.\SQL2005STD;" +
                               "Integrated Security=SSPI;" +
                               "Database=AdventureWorks";
           SqlConnection conn = new SqlConnection(connString);

           //Define the query that will be executed
           String queryString = "select * from production.product";
           //Define the query that will be executed
           SqlCommand cmd = new SqlCommand(queryString, conn);

           try
           {
               //Populate the adapter with results of the query
               adapter.SelectCommand = cmd;
               adapter.Fill(dsProducts);

               //Set the datasource for the dataViewGrid control on the form
               grdProducts.DataSource = dsProducts.Tables[0];
               grdProducts.DataBind();
   ```

```
        }
        catch (Exception ex)
        {
        }
        finally
        {
            if (adapter != null)
            {
                adapter.Dispose();
                adapter = null;
            }

            if (cmd != null)
            {
                cmd.Dispose();
                cmd = null;
            }

            if (conn != null)
            {
                if (conn.State == ConnectionState.Open)
                {
                    conn.Close();
                }
                conn = null;
            }
        }
    }
```

```vb
'VB
Protected Sub Page_Load(ByVal sender As Object, ByVal e As System.EventArgs) Handles
Me.Load
        Dim dsProducts As New DataSet("Products")
        Dim adapter As New SqlDataAdapter()

        'Initiate the connection to SQL Server
        Dim connString As String = "server=.\SQL2005STD;" & _
                                    "Integrated Security=SSPI;" & _
                                    "Database=AdventureWorks"
        Dim conn As New SqlConnection(connString)

        'Define the query that will be executed
        Dim queryString As String = "select * from production.product"
        'Define the query that will be executed
        Dim cmd As New SqlCommand(queryString, conn)

        Try
            'Populate the adapter with results of the query
            adapter.SelectCommand = cmd
            adapter.Fill(dsProducts)
```

```
                    'Set the datasource for the dataViewGrid control on the form
                    grdProducts.DataSource = dsProducts.Tables(0)
                    grdProducts.DataBind()


                Catch ex As Exception

                Finally
                    If Not (adapter Is Nothing) Then
                        adapter.Dispose()
                        adapter = Nothing
                    End If

                    If Not (cmd Is Nothing) Then
                        cmd.Dispose()
                        cmd = Nothing
                    End If

                    If Not (conn Is Nothing) Then
                        conn.Close()
                        conn = Nothing
                    End If
                End Try
            End Sub
```

10. Right-click the Default.aspx file from Solution Explorer, and select View Desi
    Select the Source tab, and add the following code to the top of the HTML (abov
    Page directive):

    ```
    <%@ OutputCache Duration="30" VaryByParam="*" %>
    ```

11. On the File menu, select Save All.

12. Click Build, click Build Web Site, and ensure that the build succeeded.

▶ **Exercise 2: Evaluate the Effects of Caching**

This exercise will show the effects of caching by running tests with the Microsoft Web A
cation Stress Tool and measuring the results in System Monitor.

1. Open the Microsoft Web Application Stress Tool. (Refer to the Introduction for
   instructions if you have not downloaded and installed this tool yet.) Select Record
   the Create New Script dialog box.

2. Click Next to proceed to step 2 of the Browser Recorder. Click Finish from step 2
   Browser Recorder. At this point, a browser window will open. Type the URL *http://*
   host/TK442Chapter3/Default.aspx.

3. Wait for the page to render, and ensure that you see a grid listing all the products
   the *AdventureWorks* database.

4. Return to the Web Application Stress Tool, and click Stop Recording.
5. Open System Monitor by clicking Start, Control Panel, Administrative Tools, Performance.
6. Click Add (the + icon on the Toolbar), and add the following counters for the ASP.NET Applications performance object:
   - ❑ **Cache Total Hits.**   The average for this counter should be high.
   - ❑ **Cache Total Misses.**   The average for this counter should be low.
   - ❑ **Cache Total Hit Ratio.**   The average for this counter should be high.
   - ❑ **Cache Total Turnover Rate.**   This counter might spike from time to time, but the average should be high.
7. Return to the Web Application Stress Tool, and make sure you have selected the *New Recorded Script* node that contains a GET for the URL entered in step 2.
8. Click Run from the Scripts menu. The script should take about a minute to complete. While it is running, you can switch back to System Monitor and watch the values of each of the counters added in step 6.
9. Once the script is complete, click View, and then Reports from the Web Application Stress Tool. A window should open, and you might have more than one recorded script node to select. You might have to expand all the nodes and look for the entry with the most recent time stamp. The results will vary, but you should see the number of hits and requests per second. When run on a test laptop, the following results were attained:

   ```
   Number of hits:            1897
   Requests per Second:       31.60
   ```

10. Return to Visual Studio 2005, and open the TK442Chapter3 solution if it is not already open.
11. Right-click the Default.aspx file from Solution Explorer, and select View Designer. Select the Source tab, and modify the *OutputCache* directive so it looks like this:

    ```
    <%@ OutputCache Duration="600" VaryByParam="*" %>
    ```

12. On the menu, click File, Save All.
13. Return to the Web Application Stress Tool, and on the Scripts menu, select Run. The script should take about a minute to complete. While it is running, you can switch back to System Monitor and watch the values of each of the counters added in step 6.
14. Once the script is complete, view the report by clicking View, Reports and selecting the entry with the latest time stamp value. When run on a test laptop, the following results were attained:

    ```
    Number of hits:            2733
    Requests per Second:       45.54
    ```

Notice that the number of hits increased because you increased the duration for the cache.

15. Return once more to Visual Studio 2005 and the Source tab for the Default.asp Remove the *OutputCache* directive entirely.

16. Click File and Save All.

17. For the last time, return to the Web Application Stress Tool, and click Run fror Scripts menu. While it is running, you can switch back to System Monitor and watc values of each of the counters added in step 6.

18. Once the script is complete, view the report by clicking View, then Reports, and the entry with the latest timestamp value. When run on a test laptop, the follc results were attained:

```
Number of hits:              455
Requests per Second:         7.58
```

Notice the significant drop in the number of hits. You can easily see the benefit of output caching.

Quick Check

1. Which caching methods are the easiest to implement?
2. Which method from the *Cache* class can be used to add an item to the cache rega less of whether a duplicate already exists?
3. What two SQL Server objects must be created in your database before you can c ate a query notification?
4. When using query notifications, what must be done to alert your application changes to the data?

Quick Check Answers

1. Page-level and user-control level caching are known as output caching; both met ods can be easily implemented using an *OutputCache* directive at the top of yo Web page or user control file.
2. Although the *Add* method will attempt to add an item if a duplicate exists, it w throw an exception. The *Insert* method will just replace the value for the cached ite
3. The *Queues* and *Services* objects, which are both visible from the *Service Broker* no in SQL Server Management Studio, must be created with Transact-SQL code befc you can create a query notification. The service will be referenced in the code establish the notification.
4. You must create code that instantiates a secondary thread, which is used to mo tor the Service Broker queue for items. At this point, you will need to also have co that does an update of the cached item.

son 2: **Designing a Cursor Strategy**

Estimated lesson time: 45 minutes

A *cursor* is a server-side object that is declared on the server hosting SQL Server. It represents the set of rows returned from a SELECT statement. Multiple rows are stored in a result set that can be accessed one row at a time. When used inside of a stored procedure or a user function, cursors allow you to access a specific row, manipulate and interpret the data in that row, and return whatever data is needed. The process of moving backward and forward through the cursor is known as *scrolling*.

In certain cases, using a cursor to process a set of data and return only a single value or a subset of the data can be an efficient way of handling data. It is not necessary to pass all of the data between SQL Server and the application. Instead, the processing remains in SQL Server, and only a small amount of data is returned across the network. However, it is possible for cursors to be used inefficiently, so care must be used when deciding whether to use cursors. Additionally, developers should consider alternatives to using cursors. This will be discussed further in the next section.

If you decide to use a cursor, you must first declare it. The following is an example of the Transact-SQL code used to declare a cursor:

```
DECLARE crsrProducts
    CURSOR FOR
SELECT ProductID, [Name], ProductNumber,
        StandardCost, ListPrice
FROM Production.Product
WHERE ListPrice > 0 and ListPrice < 50.00
```

Once the cursor is declared, it can be opened and then results will be fetched until there are no more results. For example, the following Transact-SQL code can be used to loop through the results of the crsrProducts cursor:

```
OPEN crsrProducts

FETCH NEXT FROM crsrProducts
WHILE @@FETCH_STATUS = 0
BEGIN
    --Add logic here that will perform operations
    --against the data in the cursor
    FETCH NEXT FROM crsrProducts
END
```

Because cursors require the use of server memory, it is very important that you rememl
close and deallocate the cursor. The following is an example of what this code would loo

```
CLOSE crsrProducts
DEALLOCATE crsrProducts
```

Considering Cursor Alternatives

Before you decide to use a cursor, you should consider whether there are any other alt
tives. SQL Server 2005 offers several methods for performing operations to multiple
This section highlights some of these alternatives.

Single SELECT Statements

In some cases, it might be possible to use a single SELECT statement in place of a cursor
might have to use operators such as *UNION* to combine multiple result sets, or *JOIN* to re
data from one or more tables. You might also have to use comparison operators such as
SOME, or *ALL*.

Very often, you can use a derived table inside a single SELECT statement instead of us
cursor. A derived table refers to a SELECT statement in the FROM clause of the outer SE
statement. For example, the following Transact-SQL uses a derived table to retriev
description for a product:

```
SELECT ProductID, [Name], ProductNumber, c.Description
FROM Production.Product a
INNER JOIN Production.ProductModelProductDescriptionCulture b ON a.ProductModelID =
b.ProductModelID
INNER JOIN (SELECT ProductDescriptionID, Description FROM Production.ProductDescription)
ON b.ProductDescriptionID = c.ProductDescriptionID
ORDER BY [Name]
```

Built-in functions such as *SUM*, *MAX*, and *AVG* can be used to perform calculations on a
values and return a single value. In many cases, this is the type of processing that a c
needs to perform. For example, consider the following cursor, which is used to get a
count and sum of all the products that start with the letter "S":

```
DECLARE @SumAmt money
DECLARE @Price money
DECLARE @Recs int
SET @Recs = 0
SET @SumAmt = 0
-- Get the ListPrice for all records
-- that have a name starting with A
DECLARE crsrProducts
  CURSOR
```

```
    READ_ONLY
FOR
SELECT ListPrice
FROM Production.Product
WHERE SUBSTRING([Name], 1, 1) = 'S'

OPEN crsrProducts

FETCH NEXT FROM crsrProducts INTO @Price
WHILE @@fetch_status = 0
BEGIN
    SET @SumAmt = @SumAmt + @Price
    SET @Recs = @Recs + 1

    FETCH NEXT FROM crsrProducts INTO @Price
END

SELECT @SumAmt, @Recs

CLOSE crsrProducts
DEALLOCATE crsrProducts
```

Alternatively, the same result can be obtained using a single SELECT statement. The following Transact-SQL query can be used to retrieve the total count and sum:

```
SELECT SUM(ListPrice), Count(ProductID)
FROM Production.Product
WHERE SUBSTRING([Name], 1, 1) = 'S'
```

Not only does the single SELECT statement take less code to implement, but it will execute significantly more quickly than the cursor alternative.

WHILE Loops

Although a WHILE loop is typically used when implementing a cursor, you can use a WHILE loop to perform operations against one or more rows without a cursor. For example, the following example uses a WHILE loop to increase the list price for products in the *Adventure-Works* database.

```
WHILE (SELECT AVG(ListPrice) FROM Production.Product) < $300
BEGIN
    UPDATE Production.Product
        SET ListPrice = ListPrice * 2
    SELECT MAX(ListPrice) FROM Production.Product
    IF (SELECT MAX(ListPrice) FROM Production.Product) > $800
        BREAK
    ELSE
        CONTINUE
END
```

The loop begins if the average list price is below $300.00. By using the BREAK and CONT keywords, the loop will continue to double the list price until the largest list price is g than $800.00. Although a cursor could have been used to accomplish this result, this exa demonstrates that a cursor is not always necessary.

CASE Functions

Case functions allow you to evaluate one or more conditions and return a result. Instead (ating a cursor that uses an IF statement to test for multiple conditions, it might be possi use a simple CASE function instead. For example, the following CASE function exists ins one of the table-valued functions for the AdventureWorks database:

```
SET @ContactType =
    CASE
    -- Check for employee
        WHEN EXISTS(SELECT * FROM [HumanResources].[Employee] e
            WHERE e.[ContactID] = @ContactID)
        THEN 'Employee'

    -- Check for vendor
        WHEN EXISTS(SELECT * FROM [Purchasing].[VendorContact] vc
            INNER JOIN [Person].[ContactType] ct
          ON vc.[ContactTypeID] = ct.[ContactTypeID]
            WHERE vc.[ContactID] = @ContactID)
        THEN 'Vendor Contact'

        -- Check for store
        WHEN EXISTS(SELECT * FROM [Sales].[StoreContact] sc
            INNER JOIN [Person].[ContactType] ct
        ON sc.[ContactTypeID] = ct.[ContactTypeID]
            WHERE sc.[ContactID] = @ContactID)
        THEN 'Store Contact'

    -- Check for individual consumer
        WHEN EXISTS(SELECT * FROM [Sales].[Individual] i
            WHERE i.[ContactID] = @ContactID)
        THEN 'Consumer'
    END;
```

The CASE function is used to determine the type of contact given a certain contact ID. It returns a string that identifies the contact type.

Recursive Queries

A common table expression (CTE) is a temporary result set that can be referenced mu times in the same query. It can also be used to self-reference the same query and therefor be used in what is known as a *recursive query*. Recursive queries involve a query that is executed multiple times until the desired result is obtained.

The *AdventureWorks* database comes with several stored procedures that utilize recursive queries. The uspGetWhereUsedProductID stored procedure can be used to generate a multilevel Bill of Material (BOM) statement. The first part of this stored procedure involves the invocation of the CTE and uses the *WITH* keyword to define the temporary result set. In this case, the CTE is named BOM_cte, and it contains eight different columns.

```
-- CTE name and columns
WITH [BOM_cte]([ProductAssemblyID], [ComponentID], [ComponentDesc],
    [PerAssemblyQty], [StandardCost], [ListPrice], [BOMLevel],
    [RecursionLevel])
```

The next part of the query uses the *AS* keyword to specify what data will initially fill the CTE columns. In this case, the data will come from more than one table and will use a UNION ALL statement to reference the CTE itself.

```
AS (
    SELECT b.[ProductAssemblyID], b.[ComponentID], p.[Name],
      b.[PerAssemblyQty], p.[StandardCost], p.[ListPrice], b.[BOMLevel], 0
    -- Get the initial list of components for the bike assembly
        FROM [Production].[BillOfMaterials] b
            INNER JOIN [Production].[Product] p
            ON b.[ProductAssemblyID] = p.[ProductID]
        WHERE b.[ComponentID] = @StartProductID
            AND @CheckDate >= b.[StartDate]
            AND @CheckDate <= ISNULL(b.[EndDate], @CheckDate)
    UNION ALL
    SELECT b.[ProductAssemblyID], b.[ComponentID], p.[Name],
      b.[PerAssemblyQty], p.[StandardCost], p.[ListPrice], b.[BOMLevel],
      [RecursionLevel] + 1
    -- Join recursive member to anchor
        FROM [BOM_cte] cte
            INNER JOIN [Production].[BillOfMaterials] b
            ON cte.[ProductAssemblyID] = b.[ComponentID]
            INNER JOIN [Production].[Product] p
            ON b.[ProductAssemblyID] = p.[ProductID]
        WHERE @CheckDate >= b.[StartDate]
            AND @CheckDate <= ISNULL(b.[EndDate], @CheckDate)
    )
```

The final part of the stored procedure will execute a SELECT statement against the CTE and represents the recursive invocation of the routine. In this case, the CTE routine will not be executed more than 25 times. This is specified using the *MAXRECURSION* keyword, as in the following example:

```
-- Outer select from the CTE
SELECT b.[ProductAssemblyID], b.[ComponentID], b.[ComponentDesc],
    SUM(b.[PerAssemblyQty]) AS [TotalQuantity] , b.[StandardCost],
    b.[ListPrice], b.[BOMLevel], b.[RecursionLevel]
  FROM [BOM_cte] b
  GROUP BY b.[ComponentID], b.[ComponentDesc], b.[ProductAssemblyID],
    b.[BOMLevel], b.[RecursionLevel], b.[StandardCost], b.[ListPrice]
  ORDER BY b.[BOMLevel], b.[ProductAssemblyID], b.[ComponentID]
  OPTION (MAXRECURSION 25)
```

Maximizing Cursor Performance

If at all possible, you should try to reduce the use of server-side cursors. For those cases v
a cursor is determined to be the best solution, you need to consider ways to maximize c
performance. This section highlights a few methods you can use to accomplish this goal

Reducing the Amount of Data in Your Cursor

Cursors consume server memory and can be costly in terms of application performance
this reason, you always want to reduce the amount of data held in the cursor. This appl
both the number of columns and rows. The easiest way to do this is to restrict the numl
columns returned from the SELECT statement. You would never want to declare a curso
returned all of the data from a table, as follows:

```
DECLARE crsrProducts
  CURSOR FOR
SELECT * FROM Production.Product
```

This cursor is inefficient because not only does it return all the columns in the table,
does not use a WHERE clause to restrict the number of rows returned. Limiting the amo
data processed by the cursor can significantly reduce the amount of server memory util

Using the READ_ONLY Concurrency Option

Concurrency control refers to the way SQL Server handles the updating of records by mu
users or processes. When declaring a cursor, SQL Server 2005 enables you to specify o
three different concurrency options. If you do not plan on updating any data values, the
best to use the READ_ONLY option. This indicates that no locking will occur, because no
tioned updating will occur.

It is not necessary to specify the concurrency option, and if one is not included, then th
sor is made updateable by default. Therefore, it is important for you to specify this opt
you know that no updating will take place. The following is an example of a READ_ONLY
sor declaration:

```
DECLARE crsrProducts
  CURSOR
    READ_ONLY
FOR SELECT ProductID, [Name], ProductNumber,
      StandardCost, ListPrice
FROM Production.Product
WHERE ListPrice > 0 and ListPrice < 50.00
```

If it is necessary to update data with your cursor, then the most efficient concurrency option is OPTIMISTIC. Try to avoid using the SCROLL_LOCK option, because this ensures all updates will succeed, but consumes the greatest amount of resources.

Using the FORWARD_ONLY or FAST_FORWARD Cursor Types

A cursor can be declared as FORWARD_ONLY and/or FAST_FOWARD. The FORWARD_ONLY type indicates that the cursor can only move forward and cannot be moved to a specific position in the cursor. This is the most efficient type because the other options, STATIC, KEYSET, and DYNAMIC, rely on temp tables and additional server memory. The following is an example of a cursor declared as FORWARD_ONLY and READ_ONLY:

```
DECLARE crsrProducts
  CURSOR
    FORWARD_ONLY READ_ONLY
FOR SELECT ProductID, [Name], ProductNumber,
      StandardCost, ListPrice
FROM Production.Product
WHERE ListPrice > 0 and ListPrice < 50.00
```

The FAST_FORWARD option is similar to the FORWARD_ONLY type in that it indicates that the cursor can only move in one direction. However, this option also implies that the cursor will be read-only. The FORWARD_ONLY option is not read-only by default. Instead, you have to specifically add the READ_ONLY option. The FAST_FORWARD option does not require you to add the READ_ONLY option. The following is an example of a cursor declared as FAST_FORWARD:

```
DECLARE crsrProducts
  CURSOR
    FAST_FORWARD
FOR SELECT ProductID, [Name], ProductNumber,
      StandardCost, ListPrice
FROM Production.Product
WHERE ListPrice > 0 and ListPrice < 50.00
```

Closing and Deallocating Your Cursors

A cursor consumes server memory as long as it is left open, but also until it is specifically deallocated using the *DEALLOCATE* keyword. Closing a cursor only releases any locks but

does not remove the cursor from memory. Therefore, you should *CLOSE* and *DEALLO*
your cursor as soon as possible. Typically, this is done within the stored procedure in '
the cursor is created.

Evaluating Use of Cursors

Because cursors are frequently used inefficiently, you will want to periodically eva
whether the use of cursors is warranted. It might be necessary to replace existing cursor
other alternatives or to move the data processing to the applications.

Your company might be utilizing cursors that were designed and implemented with an e
version of SQL Server. In these cases, new features such as recursive queries were not ava
so they would have not been considered. Now that you are using SQL Server 2005, you '
need to reconsider whether the cursor is the best alternative.

Comparing Execution Times

The easiest way to compare a cursor with another alternative is to execute the Transact-S(
both methods and compare the execution time. When you execute a query inside o
Server Management Studio, the execution time is displayed in the status bar of the query
dow, as shown in Figure 3-2.

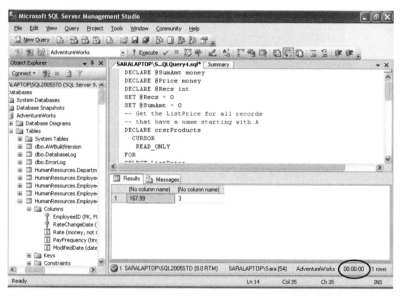

Figure 3-2   Execution time is displayed in the status bar of the new query window

In Figure 3-2, the execution time was 00:00:00, which means it took less than 1 second to execute. If you were evaluating a cursor that took less than 1 second to execute, it would hardly be worth it to investigate much further, because the execution time does not seem to be an issue. Before you waste any time rewriting an existing cursor, you might want to do a quick execution time check and make sure there is a potential savings to recover.

Using a Dynamic Management Function

Several dynamic management functions are included with SQL Server 2005. These functions allow you to monitor various SQL Server activities in real time. The function named *sys.dm_exec_cursors* enables you to monitor any currently allocated cursors. This means a cursor that has been created using the CREATE statement, but no corresponding DEALLOCATE statement has yet been issued.

The *sys.dm_exec_cursors* function provides a great way for you to determine whether you have any orphaned cursors on your SQL Server. Because cursors that are not released from memory continue to consume memory, it is important for you to know whether they exist. To use the cursors function, you would execute the following Transact-SQL command:

```
select * from sys.dm_exec_cursors(0)
```

If there are any allocated cursors, you will see records that contain useful information such as the following:

- **Session_id**   References the SQL Server session that was used to create the cursor
- **Name**   Refers to the name of the cursor
- **Properties**   Lists the options that were assigned to this cursor, such as whether it is FAST_FORWARD and/or READ_ONLY
- **Creation_Time**   Shows the DateTime stamp from when the cursor was created

Creating a Cursor

In this lab, you will create a cursor that is used to update certain records in the *AdventureWorks* database. The first exercise will deal with the basics of creating an updateable cursor. The second exercise will move on to comparing two methods to examine the same task. You will compare the execution of a cursor against a single UPDATE statement that uses a CASE statement.

The completed lab is available in the \Labs\Chapter 03 folder on the companion CD.

IMPORTANT   Lab requirements

You will need to have SQL Server installed before you can complete this lab. Refer to the Introduction for setup instructions.

▶ **Exercise 1: Create a Cursor**

In this exercise, you create a cursor that loops through all the records in the Production uct table for the *AdventureWorks* database. Within the cursor loop, the data will be printe to the messages window.

1. Open Microsoft SQL Server Management Studio.
2. Connect to the instance of SQL Server 2005 that contains the *AdventureWorks* data
3. Select New Query.
4. Add the following code to the query window:

```
USE AdventureWorks
GO

-- Declare variables that we will store fetch
-- results in
DECLARE @ProdName nvarchar(50)
DECLARE @ProdNum nvarchar(25)
DECLARE @StdCost money
DECLARE @LstPrice money

-- Allocate and define the cursor
DECLARE crsrProducts
  CURSOR
 FAST_FORWARD
FOR
  SELECT [Name], ProductNumber,
       StandardCost, ListPrice
   FROM Production.Product

-- Open the cursor and fetch the results
-- into the local variables
OPEN crsrProducts
FETCH NEXT FROM crsrProducts
  INTO @ProdName, @ProdNum,
        @StdCost, @LstPrice

-- Loop through the cursor while the fetch
-- is still successful
WHILE @@FETCH_STATUS = 0
BEGIN
    -- Print out the results to the messages window
    PRINT 'Product: ' + @ProdName + ' (' +  @ProdNum + ') '
        + 'Cost: ' + Cast(@StdCost as varchar(8))
        + ' Price: ' + Cast(@LstPrice as varchar(8))

    -- Get the next set of results
    FETCH NEXT FROM crsrProducts
      INTO @ProdName, @ProdNum,
```

```
                    @StdCost, @LstPrice
END
```

5. Select the *AdventureWorks* database from the Available Databases drop-down list box, and then click Execute.

   In the messages window, you should see results similar to the following:

```
Product: Adjustable Race (AR-5381) Cost: 0.00 Price: 0.00
Product: Bearing Ball (BA-8327) Cost: 0.00 Price: 0.00
Product: BB Ball Bearing (BE-2349) Cost: 0.00 Price: 0.00
Product: Headset Ball Bearings (BE-2908) Cost: 0.00 Price: 0.00
Product: Blade (BL-2036) Cost: 0.00 Price: 0.00
Product: LL Crankarm (CA-5965) Cost: 0.00 Price: 0.00
Product: ML Crankarm (CA-6738) Cost: 0.00 Price: 0.00
Product: HL Crankarm (CA-7457) Cost: 0.00 Price: 0.00
Product: Chainring Bolts (CB-2903) Cost: 0.00 Price: 0.00
```

6. At the bottom of the query window, add the following line of code:

```
select * from sys.dm_exec_cursors(0)
```

   Because the cursor code added in step 4 did not include a DEALLOCATE statement, the cursor is still allocated. You should see a single record with the name crsrProducts. Look at the data in all the fields for this record.

7. At the bottom of the query window, add the following code to close, and deallocate the cursor:

```
-- Close and release from memory the cursor
CLOSE crsrProducts
DEALLOCATE crsrProducts
```

▶ **Exercise 2: Compare Cursor Alternatives**

In this exercise, you create a cursor that loops through all the records in the Person.Contact table for the *AdventureWorks* database. Within the cursor loop, updates will be issued depending on the value of the EmailPromotion column. You then add the code for a replacement and compare the execution time results of both methods. This will allow you to see a situation in which the cursor is not the best alternative.

1. Open Microsoft SQL Server Management Studio.
2. Connect to the instance of SQL Server 2005 that contains the *AdventureWorks* database.
3. Select New Query.
4. Add the following code to the query window:

```
-- This cursor is used to update the EmailAddress in the
-- Person.contact table. There are three potential domain
-- names that can be used: adventure-works.net or
-- adventure-works.net or adventure-works.org. Which domain
-- is used depends on a field named EmailPromotion.
```

```
USE AdventureWorks
GO

DECLARE @ID int
DECLARE @Email nvarchar(50)
DECLARE @Promotion int

DECLARE crsrEmail
  CURSOR
 FORWARD_ONLY
FOR
  SELECT ContactID, EmailAddress, EmailPromotion
  FROM Person.Contact

-- Open the cursor and fetch the results
-- into the local variables
OPEN crsrEmail
FETCH NEXT FROM crsrEmail
  INTO @ID, @Email, @Promotion

-- Loop through the cursor while the fetch
-- is still successful
WHILE @@FETCH_STATUS = 0
BEGIN
   IF @Promotion = 0
    BEGIN
    UPDATE Person.Contact SET EmailAddress =
     REPLACE(@email, 'adventure-works.com', 'adventure-works.net')
     WHERE ContactID = @ID
    END

   IF @Promotion = 1
    BEGIN
    UPDATE Person.Contact SET EmailAddress =
     REPLACE(@email, 'adventure-works.com', 'adventure-works.biz')
     WHERE ContactID = @ID
    END

   IF @Promotion = 2
    BEGIN
    UPDATE Person.Contact SET EmailAddress =
     REPLACE(@email, 'adventure-works.com', 'adventure-works.org')
     WHERE ContactID = @ID
    END

    -- Get the next set of results
    FETCH NEXT FROM crsrEmail
      INTO @ID, @Email, @Promotion

  END
```

```
CLOSE crsrEmail
DEALLOCATE crsrEmail
```

5. Select the *AdventureWorks* database from the Available Databases drop-down list box, and then click Execute. On a test laptop, this code took 18 seconds to complete.

6. Open a New Query window by selecting New Query.

7. Paste the following code into the query window:

```
UPDATE Person.Contact
 SET EmailAddress =
  CASE
    WHEN EmailPromotion = 0
     THEN REPLACE(EmailAddress, 'adventure-works.com', 'adventure-works.net')
    WHEN EmailPromotion = 1
     THEN REPLACE(EmailAddress, 'adventure-works.com', 'adventure-works.biz')
   WHEN EmailPromotion = 2
     THEN REPLACE(EmailAddress, 'adventure-works.com', 'adventure-works.org')
   END
```

8. Select the *AdventureWorks* database from the Available Databases drop-down list box, and then click Execute. Note the amount of time it takes for the execution to complete. On a test laptop, it took only one second to complete. You can easily see how the cursor is not the most efficient alternative. Not only does it take more code to implement, but it takes 18 times longer to execute.

9. To reverse the update results and change the data back to its original value, execute the following query in a new query window:

```
UPDATE Person.Contact
 SET EmailAddress =
  CASE
    WHEN EmailPromotion = 0
     THEN REPLACE(EmailAddress, 'adventure-works.net', 'adventure-works.com')
    WHEN EmailPromotion = 1
     THEN REPLACE(EmailAddress, 'adventure-works.biz', 'adventure-works.com')
   WHEN EmailPromotion = 2
     THEN REPLACE(EmailAddress, 'adventure-works.org', 'adventure-works.com')
   END
```

Quick Check

1. How do you remove a cursor from server memory?
2. What are some commonly used alternatives to using a cursor?
3. Which concurrency option requires the least amount of resources?
4. Which cursor type also includes the READ_ONLY concurrency option?
5. What function enables you to monitor cursors in real time?

Quick Check Answers

1. You need to perform a CLOSE <cursorname> to release any locks associated w
   the cursor, but the DEALLOCATE <cursorname> command will actually rele
   the cursor from server memory.

2. In place of a cursor, you might want to consider using the built-in functiona
   available with SQL Server 2005 and combine the logic into a single SELECT sta
   ment. You might also be able to use a WHILE loop, *CASE* function, or even a rec
   sive query.

3. The READ_ONLY concurrency option indicates that no updates will occur wit
   the cursor. This is the fastest and most efficient concurrency option.

4. The FAST_FORWARD cursor type indicates that the cursor will scroll in only c
   direction, but it also indicates that the cursor will not include any updates a
   therefore utilizes the READ_ONLY concurrency option.

5. The *sys.dm_exec_cursors* dynamic management function enables you to moni
   currently allocated cursors. This enables you to easily identify any orphaned c
   sors in your SQL Server.

son 3: Designing Efficient Cursors

Estimated lesson time: 45 minutes

A quick Internet search will show you several articles and posts claiming that cursors are a bad thing. Developers who are unfamiliar with SQL Server tend to use many cursors because they are easy to write and follow. Because cursors perform operations one record at a time, looping through a cursor with a large set of records can take a long time to process. Many experienced developers avoid cursors because they can often find a set-based query that accomplishes the same result more quickly. While it is true that the logic in most cursors can be replaced with set-based logic, there are some cases where cursors are warranted and possibly faster than other alternatives. This section will highlight cases where cursors are a good choice and discuss the options that you can use when designing the logic.

ng Scrollable Cursors

Some application specifications might require you to scroll forward and backward among a set of results. For example, it might be necessary to retrieve a set of results, and then, based on the user input, scroll either forward or backward through the result set. This is a situation in which cursors might be the most efficient choice. By being able to scroll forward and backward through the results, you can eliminate the need to perform multiple queries.

The following fetch options can be used when working with a scrollable cursor:

- **Fetch First**   Retrieves the first row in the cursor.
- **Fetch Last**   Retrieves the last row in the cursor.
- **Fetch Next**   Retrieves the next row in the cursor.
- **Fetch Prior**   Retrieves the row before the last one fetched, unless you have just opened the cursor, or you are positioned at the first record.
- **Fetch Absolute n**   Retrieves the position specified with the n parameter, which can be set as a positive integer, negative integer, or a zero. If n is set with a positive value, then it will move that number of places from the first row. If n is set with a negative value, then it will move that number of places from the last row. If n is set with a zero, then no rows are fetched.
- **Fetch Relative n**   Retrieves the position specified, relative to the last row that was fetched. If n is set with a positive integer, then it will move that number of places after the last row is fetched. If n is set with a negative value, then it will move that number of places before the last row is fetched. If n is set with a zero, the same row is fetched again.

The scrollable cursor can be specified by using the SCROLL option instead o[f] FORWARD_ONLY option. For example, the following Transact-SQL can be used to cr[e] scrollable cursor named crsrScroll:

```
DECLARE crsrScroll
  CURSOR
 SCROLL
FOR
  SELECT [Name], ProductNumber,
       StandardCost, ListPrice
  FROM Production.Product
```

SQL Server 2005 offers a built-in function named *@@CURSOR_ROWS* that can be us[e] return the number of rows in a cursor. For example, the following Transact-SQL statemen[t] be used to return the product number along with the number of rows in the cursor:

```
SELECT ProductNumber, @@CURSOR_ROWS FROM Production.Product
```

Processing on a Row-by-Row Basis

When there is a need to perform processing, such as the execution of a stored procedur[e] row-by-row basis, it is possible for a cursor to perform more quickly than a set-based al[terna]tive. For example, the following stored procedure can be used to loop through all the pro[ducts] in the *AdventureWorks* database and, based on the value of an input variable, execut[e a] stored procedure sp_SomeStoredProcedure. The cursor will then perform an INSERT in[to the] Production.ProductCostHistory table if the stored procedure was executed successfully[:]

```
DECLARE crsrRowByRow
  CURSOR
 FAST_FORWARD
FOR
  SELECT ProductNumber, ListPrice,
   StandardCost
  FROM Production.Product

OPEN crsrRowByRow
FETCH NEXT FROM crsrProducts
  INTO @ProdNum, @Listprice,
       @StdCost

WHILE @@FETCH_STATUS = 0
BEGIN
   IF (@inVar = "Some Value")
   BEGIN
        EXEC @retcode = sp_SomeStoredProcedure
             @product_num = @ProdNum,
             @list_price = @Listprice,
```

```
                    @sp_var = @inVar
    END

    IF @retcode = <> 0
    BEGIN
          INSERT INTO Production.ProductCostHistory
                VALUES (@StartDate, @EndDate, @StdCost, GetDate())
    END

    FETCH NEXT FROM crsrProducts
      INTO @ProdNum, @LstPrice,
                @StdCost
END

CLOSE crsrRowByRow
DEALLOCATE crsrRowByRow
```

It is possible that the cursor named crsrRowByRow would execute more quickly than a set-based alternative. This would depend on various factors, such as the number of records to be processed and the efficiency of the code in the stored procedure. The only way to know for sure would be to compare execution times for both methods.

g Dynamic SQL

You can use dynamic SQL to build your cursors. This is done in the same way you would issue any SQL statement using dynamic SQL. You will need to include the DECLARE statement inside the dynamic SQL string. For example, the following Transact-SQL can be used to create a cursor named crsrProducts using dynamic SQL:

```
DECLARE @Color nvarchar(15)
SET @Color = 'Black'

DECLARE @sql nvarchar(255)
SELECT @sql = 'DECLARE crsrProducts CURSOR FAST_FORWARD FOR ' +
  'SELECT ProductNumber, ListPrice,StandardCost '+
  'FROM Production.Product ' +
  'WHERE Color = ''' + @Color + ''';' +
  'OPEN crsrProducts '
  'WHILE (@@FETCH_STATUS = 0) ' +
  'BEGIN ' +
  'FETCH NEXT FROM crsrProducts ' +
  'END; '
  'CLOSE crsrProducts ' +
  'DEALLOCATE crsrProducts'
EXEC sp_executesql @sql
```

IMPORTANT   **Security alert**

The use of dynamic SQL can make your application vulnerable to SQL injection attacks. This
enables malicious parties to gain control of your SQL Server by sending certain commands thr
the input parameters used to build the dynamic SQL.

When using dynamic SQL to create your cursors, you must take care to still close and d
cate these cursors. This also applies if you add any type of error handling. You want to e
that the cursor will be removed from memory, even if an error occurs.

Selecting a Cursor Type

As described in Lesson 2, you can improve cursor performance by using a FAST_FOWA
FORWARD_ONLY cursor type. In addition to these cursor types, there are others tha
might need to consider. This section highlights the things you need to consider when sel
a cursor type.

There are four types to consider when declaring your cursor. They are as follows:

- **Forward Only**   This is the fastest performing cursor; it moves in one direction o
  does not support scrolling. It is related to the FAST_FORWARD type, which is
  FORWARD_ONLY, READ_ONLY cursor.
- **Static**   Compared to dynamic and keyset-driven cursors, this one is the fastest. It
  snapshot of the data taken when it was opened and detects no changes since the
- **Keyset-driven**   This option uses a set of keys, known as a keyset, to uniquely ident
  rows in the result set. It can be used to detect most changes to the result set, s
  slightly more efficient than the dynamic cursor, but less efficient than a static one
- **Dynamic**   A dynamic cursor is the opposite of a static cursor, but it also consum
  most resources. This cursor can be used to detect changes made to the result set
  scrolling through the cursor. When dealing with a large result set, it can be faster to
  than a static or keyset-driven cursor.

It is possible for a cursor to be forward only and static, keyset, or dynamic. Alternatively,
be marked with the SCROLL option and be static, keyset, or dynamic. For example, you
have a cursor such as the following:

```
DECLARE crsrProducts
  CURSOR
 SCROLL STATIC
FOR
  SELECT ProductNumber, ListPrice,
   StandardCost
  FROM Production.Product
```

If the SCROLL option is used, then all of the fetching capabilities featured in the previous section are available. Alternatively, if the cursor is marked as FORWARD_ONLY SCROLL, then it will only be able to move from start to finish.

uating Cursor Efficiency

SQL Server 2005 is, first and foremost, a relational database, not a programming environment. Transact-SQL is a set-based language that was never designed to be an optimized object-oriented programming language. Cursors have their place in the SQL Server arsenal, but you need to be careful not to overuse them.

Utilizing Server Memory

A common mistake for new or inexperienced developers is to immediately create a cursor when another alternative would be more appropriate. Creating a cursor might be the easiest thing to do, but if you choose to use cursors all the time, you could be overtaxing the server's memory. Though you can simply choose to add more memory to the server, this is not always the best solution.

When faced with a situation where row-by-row processing needs to occur, do not immediately assume that a cursor is the best alternative. First, evaluate the other alternatives, such as a single SELECT statement or a WHILE loop. If you determine that a cursor is absolutely necessary, you need to design it so that it utilizes memory efficiently.

When designing your cursors, you should consider the following:

- The SELECT statement should return the least amount of data possible. Limit the number of columns returned and query from a temporary table if possible.
- Use a FAST_FORWARD or FORWARD_ONLY cursor if no updates will be performed.
- If you are using static or keyset-driven cursors, which build a temporary table, move the tempdb to a set of separate high-performance disk spindles in the form of a disk array.
- Break out of the cursor as soon as possible. If you accomplish your goal before the last record in the result set is reached, exit the cursor WHILE loop at that time to prevent unnecessary looping.
- If the cursor SELECT statement needs to perform JOINS, consider using static or keyset-driven cursors, as opposed to dynamic ones.
- Close and deallocate cursors as soon as possible.

Minimizing Blocking

The sensitivity of a cursor indicates that a change made to the cursors data is immediately visible. When declaring a cursor, you can use either the SQL-92 or Transact-SQL extended syntax.

The SQL-92 syntax uses the *INSENSITIVE* keyword to indicate sensitivity. By usin$
option, you can achieve slightly faster performance because SQL Server does not need t$
checking for updates to the data. You can also include the FOR READ_ONLY option to e$
that the cursor is not available for updates. For example, the following statement uses the
92 syntax to create a cursor that is not sensitive to changes:

```
DECLARE crsrProducts
 INSENSITIVE
  CURSOR
FOR
  SELECT ProductNumber, ListPrice,
   StandardCost
  FROM Production.Product
FOR READ_ONLY
```

Cursor concurrency is used to specify how locks are handled for the underlying data tal$
a cursor. The Transact-SQL extended syntax supports the following three concur$
options:

- **READ_ONLY**   This option specifies that no updates can be made to the underlyin$
  for that cursor. It is considered the most efficient option because it ensures that no$
  will be held on the rows that make up the result set.
- **OPTIMISTIC**   This option indicates that there is only a slight chance that an upda$
  take place while the cursor is being used. Instead of issuing a lock on the unde$
  table, this option indicates that if a user changes the data in the cursor, a check v$
  made against the data in the database first. If the data has changed since it was orig$
  retrieved, then an error will be issued.
- **SCROLL_LOCKS**   This is the most thorough option and the most expensive in ter$
  resource usage. Locks will be issued based on locking hints in the cursor SELECT$
  ment. This option should be used when you expect data to change before the curs$
  cessing ends.

The Transact-SQL extended syntax uses the SCROLL_LOCKS option to specify tha$
tioned updates can occur within the cursor. For example, the following statement us$
Transact-SQL extended syntax to create a cursor that is updateable:

```
DECLARE crsrProducts
  CURSOR
DYNAMIC SCROLL_LOCKS
FOR
  SELECT ProductNumber, ListPrice,
   StandardCost
  FROM Production.Product
FOR UPDATE OF StandardCost
```

These updates are guaranteed to succeed, which means that SQL Server will need to hold a lock on the table to ensure this. For this reason, you want to minimize the use of this option. This option cannot be used with the FAST_FORWARD cursor type. If you know that no updates need to occur, the cursor should be marked with the READ_ONLY concurrency option.

Minimizing or Eliminating Cursors

If your SQL Server responds slowly and applications start to experience performance problems, the best thing to do is to evaluate the Server's use of indexes. The next thing to do is to look at the Transact-SQL code running on your server. It is not uncommon to see cursors overused in stored procedures or user-defined functions.

If you see that cursors are being used too much, try to identify which are causing the most performance problems. This can be done by running a trace using SQL Server Profiler while the application is executing. SQL Server Profiler is accessible from the Tools menu in Microsoft SQL Server Management Studio. It enables you to select the events to be monitored by the trace. The trace can be configured to specifically monitor whether a cursor was opened, closed, or executed, as shown in Figure 3-3.

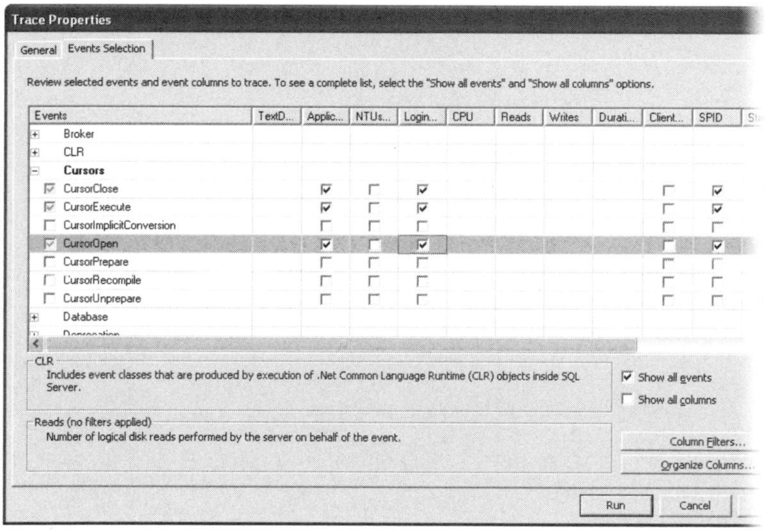

Figure 3-3 Configuring the SQL Server Profiler trace to monitor specific events

Once you have identified the longest executing cursors, you can start to analyze the Transact-SQL within those cursors. You might be able to speed up the cursor by making a few small changes, such as making it READ_ONLY and FORWARD_ONLY. At this point, you should consider whether there is an alternative for the cursor. If an alternative is found, make su execute both methods to determine which is the fastest.

Lab: Designing Cursors

In this lab, you will create a scrollable cursor and practice evaluating cursor efficiency. Th exercise will deal with creating a cursor that moves back and forth as it is looped. In the se exercise, you will use SQL Server Profiler to evaluate the cursor created in exercise 1.

The completed lab is available in the \Labs\Chapter 03 folder on the companion CD.

IMPORTANT   Lab requirements

You will need to have SQL Server installed before you can complete this lab. Refer to the Intr tion for setup instructions.

▶ **Exercise 1: Create a Scrollable Cursor**

In this exercise, you will create a scrollable cursor using the scroll option and one of the methods.

1. Open Microsoft SQL Server Management Studio.
2. Connect to the instance of SQL Server 2005 that contains the *AdventureWorks* data
3. Select New Query.
4. Add the following code to the query window:

```
SET ANSI_NULLS ON
GO
SET QUOTED_IDENTIFIER ON
GO

CREATE PROCEDURE spGetPriorProduct
  @InProdNum nvarchar(25)
AS

BEGIN
    -- Declare variables that we will store fetch
    -- results in
    DECLARE @ProdName nvarchar(50)
    DECLARE @ProdNum nvarchar(25)
    DECLARE @StdCost money
    DECLARE @ListPrice money

    SET NOCOUNT ON;

    -- Allocate and define the cursor
    DECLARE crsrProducts
```

```
            SCROLL CURSOR
FOR
            SELECT [Name], ProductNumber,
                   StandardCost, ListPrice
            FROM Production.Product
            ORDER BY ProductNumber

-- Open the cursor and fetch the results
-- into the local variables
 OPEN crsrProducts
 FETCH NEXT FROM crsrProducts
    INTO @ProdName, @ProdNum,
         @StdCost, @ListPrice

-- Loop through the cursor while the fetch
-- is still successful
WHILE @@FETCH_STATUS = 0
BEGIN
     IF @ProdNum = @InProdNum
       BEGIN
                --Get the previous record and
                --return the data for that record
                FETCH PRIOR FROM crsrProducts
                     INTO @ProdName, @ProdNum,
                  @StdCost, @ListPrice

                -- Print out the results to the messages window
                PRINT 'Product: ' + @ProdName + ' (' + @ProdNum + ') '
                     + 'Cost: ' + Cast(@StdCost as varchar(8))
                     + ' Price: ' + Cast(@ListPrice as varchar(8))

                --Exit the loop
                BREAK
         END

        -- Get the next set of results
        FETCH NEXT FROM crsrProducts
             INTO @ProdName, @ProdNum,
            @StdCost, @ListPrice
    END

    CLOSE crsrProducts
    DEALLOCATE crsrProducts


END
```

5. Select the *AdventureWorks* database from the Available Databases drop-down list, and then click Execute.

6. Add the following code to the bottom of the query window, highlight it, and click Ex

    ```
    exec spGetPriorProduct 'BB-7421'
    ```

    You should see the following result displayed in the messages box. This is the recor
    exists prior to the product with a product number of BB-7421.

    ```
    Product: Bearing Ball (BA-8327) Cost: 0.00 Price: 0.00
    ```

▶ **Exercise 2: Examine a Cursor**

In this exercise, you will use SQL Server Profiler to examine the execution of a cursor.

1. Open SQL Server Profiler by clicking Start, All Programs, Microsoft SQL Server
    Performance Tools, SQL Server Profiler.
2. Click File, New Trace.
3. Enter the connection information for the server that contains the *AdventureWorks*
    base, and then click Connect.
4. From the Trace Properties dialog box, enter a name for the trace, and select the F
    Selection tab.
5. Select the Show all events check box, and scroll to the Stored Procedures event cla
    expand that node. Select the check boxes for all stored procedure events.
6. Click Run to begin the trace. Do *not* close SQL Server Profiler or close the Trace P
    ties dialog box.
7. Open SQL Server Management Studio.
8. Connect to the instance of SQL Server 2005 that contains the *AdventureWorks* dat
9. Select New Query.
10. Add the following code to the query window:

    ```
    exec spGetPriorProduct 'BB-7421'
    ```

11. Select the *AdventureWorks* database from the Available Databases drop-down lis
    then click Execute.
12. Return to SQL Server Profiler, and stop the trace by clicking the Stop button c
    toolbar.
13. Scroll through the trace results and notice how many events were captured for th
    cution of the stored procedure. (See Figure 3-4.)

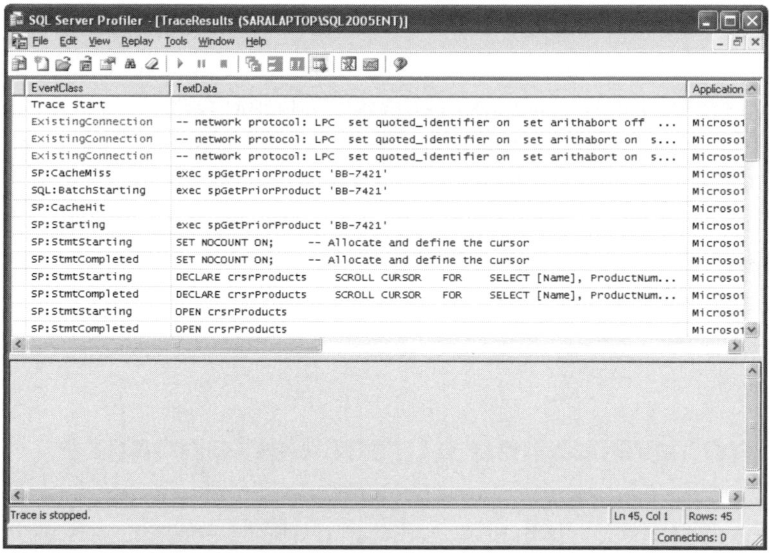

Figure 3-4   Trace results for a trace performed while executing the spGetPriorProduct stored procedure.

Quick Check

1. Which caching method is easy to implement but allows you the most control in how it is implemented?
2. What new feature with SQL Server 2005 enables you to receive notifications when the data in your cache has been updated?
3. What are some commonly used alternatives to using a server-side cursor?
4. Which two statements should be executed after all the rows in your cursor are fetched?
5. Which concurrency option should be avoided to minimize blocking?

Quick Check Answers

1. Control level-caching is easily implemented by adding the *OutputCache* directive to the top of the HTML. By using control level-caching as opposed to page level-caching, you have more control over what is cached in your Web page.
2. Query notifications allow you to receive notifications when the data in your cache has been updated. You can then execute a refresh of the cache and ensure that you have the latest version of the data.

3. Often, you can replace a cursor with a single SELECT statement. You can also c[
    sider using a WHILE loop, *CASE* function, and a recursive query.

4. You should always include the CLOSE and DEALLOCATE statements after all [
    data in your cursor has been fetched. This will release all locks and also remove [
    cursor from server memory.

5. The SCROLL_LOCKS option should be avoided, because it assumes upda[
    might occur to the data before the cursor has been closed. Depending on the l[
    hints specified in the SELECT statement, locks might be issued on the underly[
    tables by using this option.

Case Scenario: Evaluating Cursor Performance

In the this case scenario, you are a database developer for a large financial company tha[
vides mortgages to people with poor credit ratings. For the past three years, the compar[
been utilizing a complex ASP.NET application that retrieves data from a SQL 2000 dat[
As the amount of data in the database increased, company employees have noticed th[
application response time has decreased.

The company now intends to move the data to a SQL 2005 database. They would like f[
to analyze the solution and recommend ways that the application can be improved. [
reviewing the SQL code, you notice that a cursor is used in about half the stored proce[
What strategy might you recommend for improving database performance?

Suggested Practices

Objective 1.4: Design caching strategies

- **Practice 1**   Using the *AdventureWorks* database, you will design a solution using [
  notifications. To do this, you will need to perform the following steps:

    - Create a Service Queue using Transact-SQL code in Query Analyzer.
    - Create a Visual Studio application (Windows Forms or Web-based) that will [
      the notification and wait for changes. The application will need to create a [
      cation using the *SqlNotificationRequest* object. It will also need to create a t[
      that waits for changes. When changes are registered, an e-mail should b[
      directly to you.
    - Manually alter the data in the target table using Query Analyzer.
    - Ensure that the notification is triggered and the email is sent to your mailbo[

Objective 1.3: Design a cursor strategy for a data access component
Objective 2.3: Design a cursor strategy

■ **Practice 1**   Locate a production SQL Server in your organization (it can be one with an earlier version of SQL Server). Using Query Analyzer or SQL Server Management Studio, examine the stored procedures and user-defined functions and look for the use of cursors. If you locate any, see whether there is a way to rewrite the cursor using one of the alternatives suggested in this chapter.

erences

■ ASP.NET Caching

http://www.ondotnet.com/pub/a/dotnet/2002/12/30/cachingaspnet.html

■ .NET Data Caching

http://aspnet.4guysfromrolla.com/articles/100902-1.aspx

■ ASP.NET Caching: Techniques and Best Practices

http://msdn2.microsoft.com/en-us/library/aa478965.aspx

■ Working with Query Notifications

http://msdn2.microsoft.com/en-us/library/ms130764.aspx

■ Performance Tuning SQL Server Database Cursors

http://www.sql-server-performance.com/cursors.asp

■ Application Development Trends – The SQL Server 2005 Paradigm Shift

http://www.adtmag.com/article.aspx?id=11148&amp

■ SQL Server Query Design: 10 Mistakes to Avoid

*http://searchsqlserver.techtarget.com/loginMembersOnly/1,289498,sid87_gci1229788,00
.html?NextURL=http%3A//searchsqlserver.techtarget.com/tip/0%2C289483%2Csid87
_gci1229788%2C00.html*

■ The Curse and Blessings of Dynamic SQL

http://www.sommarskog.se/dynamic_sql.html

■ How to Perform SQL Server Row-by-Row Operations Without Cursors

http://www.sql-server-performance.com/dp_no_cursors.asp

■ Using SQL Server Cursors

http://www.mssqlcity.com/Articles/General/UseCursor.htm

■ SQL Server Clinic: T-SQL Performance Problems and Solutions

*http://searchsqlserver.techtarget.com/tip/1,289483,sid87_gci1170220_tax301334,00
.html?adg=301324&bucket=ETA?track=sy41*

Chapter Summary

- Page-level and user control-level caching are two output-caching methods that are e implement. Custom caching is done using the Cache API and the *System.Web.Cc* namespace. The *Insert* and *Add* methods are used to add items to the cache. Item added using a key and value pair and can be removed with the *Remove* method.

- Query notifications, new with SQL Server 2005, allow your applications to receive fications when the data in the cache has changed. Eventually, all caches will expire there must be a method in place for refreshing the cache. This can be done on de by the user or at the point the application attempts to access the expired cache.

- A cursor is a server-side object that can be used to access multiple rows one at a from a result set. Once the cursor is declared, it can be opened and then fetched on at a time.

- When using cursors, you should try to reduce the amount of server memory they sume so your applications will perform better. This can be accomplished by reducir amount of data in the cursor, using the READ_ONLY concurrency option, usin FAST_FORWARD or FORWARD_ONLY cursor type, and always remembering to and deallocate your cursors.

- You can evaluate the efficiency of your cursors by looking at the execution time. T done using the New Query window in Microsoft SQL Server Management Studic can also use the dynamic management function named *sys.dm_exec_cursors* to eva currently allocated cursors.

- Generally, you want to avoid the use of cursors whenever possible. Transact-SQ designed as a set-based language and not an object-oriented language. Try to use natives to the cursor. If you are able to, measure the execution times for the curso the alternative and use the fastest method.

dvanced Query Topics

Microsoft SQL Server 2005 offers many ways to administer a SQL Server service. Lesson 1 will examine SQL Server Management Objects (SMO), which is a replacement for SQL Distributed Management Objects (SQL-DMO) and enables programmatic access to any object in the SQL Server object model. Replication Management Objects (RMO) is used to programmatically control a replication topology by administrating the objects associated with replication. Analysis Management Objects (AMO) is a library that enables you to manage all the objects associated with your SQL Server Analysis Services (SSAS) objects.

Lesson 2 will move on to a new feature introduced with SQL Server 2005 called Multiple Active Result Sets (MARS). This offers developers an alternative way of executing multiple statements. With MARS, statements can all be processed within a single connection. Finally, Lesson 3 will focus on asynchronous processing, which enables you to perform database operations in parallel.

Exam objectives in this chapter:

- Design client libraries to write applications that administer a SQL Server service.
  - ❏ Design server management objects (SMO) applications.
  - ❏ Design replication management objects (RMO) applications.
  - ❏ Design automation management objects (AMO) applications.
  - ❏ Design SQL Server Networking Interface (SNI) for asynchronous queries.
- Design queries that use multiple active result sets (MARS).
  - ❏ Decide when MARS queries are appropriate.
  - ❏ Choose an appropriate transaction isolation level when you use MARS.
  - ❏ Choose when to use Asynchronous queries.

ore You Begin

To complete the lessons in this chapter, you must have:

- A computer that meets or exceeds the minimum hardware requirements listed in the Introduction at the beginning of this book.
- SQL Server 2005 installed as well as the SQL Server 2005 *AdventureWorks* sample database.

- Microsoft Visual Studio 2005 or Microsoft Visual Basic or Visual C# 2005 Ex Edition installed.
- Experience designing and executing queries in SQL Server Management Studio.
- Experience creating Microsoft Windows-based applications using Visual Studio

:son 1: Administering a SQL Server Service

Estimated lesson time: 90 minutes

SQL Server 2005 offers many ways to programmatically administer your SQL server. This includes not only the SQL Server service, but Analysis Services as well. This ability can be useful if you need to automate tasks or offer users a controlled interface. This lesson will review these options and identify key functions that you might wish to allow.

:igning Server Management Objects Applications

Server Management Objects enables you to administer a SQL Server service by controlling objects in the SQL Server object model. These objects include, but are not limited to, databases, tables, and columns. You can also access objects and properties that are new to SQL Server 2005, such as HTTP endpoints and the XML schema collection. *Data Definition Language (DDL)* is a component of SQL, and it can be used to create and delete databases and database objects. Essentially, any task that can be performed using DDL code in a SQL query window can also be performed with SMO and a Visual Studio .NET application.

SMO enables you to administer and automate many of the tasks that would normally have to be done with SQL Server Management Studio. Some of the more common tasks you can automate include backups, restores, index maintenance, and job management. You might also want to expose a limited subset of functionality to key people in your organization. SMO enables you to create a custom interface for your SQL Server service and automate certain functionality.

The main object in an SMO application is the *Server* object. This represents an instance of SQL Server and is the top-level object in the SMO hierarchy. There are collection items beneath this, such as a *DatabaseCollection*, *StoredProcedureCollection*, *TableCollection*, and *UserDefinedFunctionCollection*. There are several objects that reside within the hierarchy, but they will only be used if you need to perform a particular function.

SMO Assemblies and Namespaces

To begin programming with SMO, you need to set a reference to some of the key SMO assemblies. These assemblies are installed with the Client Tools option in the SQL Server 2005 installation program, as shown in Figure 4-1.

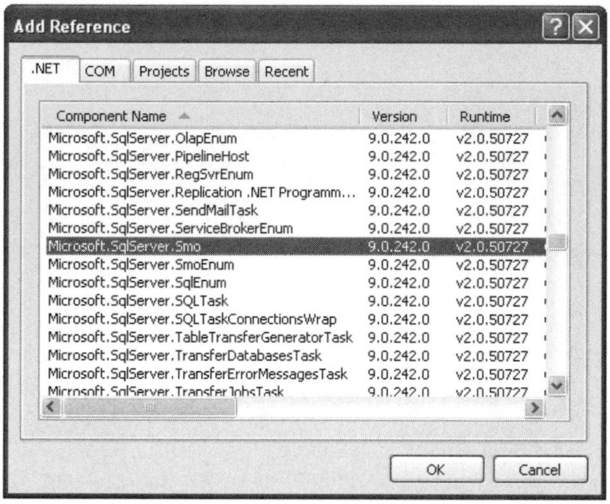

Figure 4-1 Add Reference to the *Microsoft.SqlServer.Smo* assembly, which is used in an SMO application

The following represent common assemblies you will need to reference in your Visual S 2005 application:

- **Microsoft.SqlServer.Smo** Contains the core classes for database engine objects a the main assembly used when building an SMO application

- **Microsoft.SqlServer.SmoEnum** Contains support for the SMO classes and many c enumeration classes

- **Microsoft.SqlServer.SqlEnum** Also contains enumerations used by your SMO applic

- **Microsoft.SqlServer.ConnectionInfo** Contains classes used to make a connection your SQL Server instance

Depending on what task you need to accomplish, you might need to add references to assemblies. For example, if you need to perform a task that involves the Service Broker will need to set a reference to the *Microsoft.SqlServer.ServiceBrokerEnum* assembly. The fo ing are the remaining assemblies that you might need to reference:

- **Microsoft.SqlServer.ServiceBrokerEnum** Contains support for programming ag Service Broker, which is a message-based communication platform that enables fea such as asynchronous programming.

- **Microsoft.SqlServer.WmiEnum** Contains support for the Windows Managen Instrumentation (WMI) provider, which is used to perform scripting tasks.

- **Microsoft.SqlServer.RegSvrEnum** Contains support for working with registered ers. It is used as support for the SMO infrastructure and contains only two classes

Each of the assemblies mentioned above support different namespaces that are needed for your SMO application. Table 4-1 lists the different SMO namespaces available.

Table 4-1   Server Management Object (SMO) Namespaces

Option	Description
Microsoft.SqlServer.Management.Common	Contains classes used to connect to SQL Server, run Transact-SQL statements, and manage transactions
Microsoft.SqlServer.Management.Nmo	Contains classes used when developing applications involving notification services
Microsoft.SqlServer.Management.Smo	The core namespace for the SMO library and used to represent all the core SMO objects
Microsoft.SqlServer.Management.Smo.Agent	Contains classes used to write applications that deal with the Microsoft SQL Server Agent
Microsoft.SqlServer.Management.Smo.Broker	Contains classes used when writing applications that deal with SQL Server Service Broker
Microsoft.SqlServer.Management.Smo.Mail	Contains classes used when writing applications that utilize the SQL Server Database Mail service
Microsoft.SqlServer.Management.Smo.RegisteredServers	Contains classes used when dealing with the Registered Servers service
Microsoft.SqlServer.Management.Smo.RegSvrEnum	Contains classes used by the SMO infrastructure to manage the Registered Servers service
Microsoft.SqlServer.Management.Smo.Wmi	Contains classes used to provide programmatic access to Windows Management Instrumentation (WMI)
Microsoft.SqlServer.Management.Trace	Contains the classes used to read trace data from files, tables, or rowsets

Exam Tip   For this exam, you should focus primarily on designing Server Management Objects applications. Even though other libraries, such as Replication Management Objects and Analysis Management Objects are important, they are not focused on as heavily as applications created with SMO.

Connecting to a Server

Once you have added references to the core SMO assemblies, you will need to make a connection to your SQL Server instance. You do so by first adding a reference to *Microsoft.SqlServer.Management.Smo* at the top of your code file, as in the following example.

```
//C#
using Microsoft.SqlServer.Management.Smo;
```

```
'VB
Imports Microsoft.SqlServer.Management.Smo
```

The next step is to make a connection to the SQL Server instance. If you are doing this
Windows authentication, then the following code could be used to connect to a SQL S
instance named ".\SQL2005STD" and display properties about that server in a message

```
//C#
Server svr = new Server(@".\SQL2005STD");
MessageBox.Show("Name:" + svr.Name
        + "; InstanceName:" + svr.InstanceName );
svr = null;
```

```
'VB
Dim svr As New Server(".\SQL2005STD")
MessageBox.Show("Name:" + svr.Name _
        + "; InstanceName:" + svr.InstanceName)
svr = Nothing
```

If you had to connect to a server using logon credentials, then you would need to use a S
Connection object to specify the logon credentials. To do this, you would need to add a
ence to the *Microsoft.SqlServer.ConnectionInfo* assembly and also include a directive t
Microsoft.SqlServer.Management.Common namespace. You could then use the following co
make the connection:

```
//C#
ServerConnection svrConn = new ServerConnection();
svrConn.LoginSecure = false;
svrConn.Login = "username";
svrConn.Password = "password";
svrConn.ServerInstance = @".\SQL2005STD";
Server svr = new Server(svrConn);
MessageBox.Show("Name:" + svr.Name
        + "; InstanceName:" + svr.InstanceName );
svrConn = null;
svr = null;
```

```
'VB
Dim svrConn As New ServerConnection
svrConn.LoginSecure = False
svrConn.Login = "username"
svrConn.Password = "password"
svrConn.ServerInstance = ".\SQL2005STD"
Dim svr As New Server(svrConn)
MessageBox.Show("Name:" + svr.Name + _
    "; InstanceName:" + svr.InstanceName)
```

```
svrConn = Nothing
svr = Nothing
```

After the connection has been established, you can perform various tasks, such as backing up the database, restoring the database, performing integrity checks, and other administrative tasks. You can also perform more complex tasks, such as creating and scheduling SQL Server Agent jobs. In the lab for this lesson, we will walk through how to create a new database using an SMO application.

IMPORTANT Additional sample code

SQL Server 2005 includes sample code as part of the Documentation and Tutorials. Several samples provided involve creating SMO applications. These samples are not installed by default, but you can install them later by executing Setup.exe on the first SQL Server 2005 CD. To learn how to do this, refer to *http://msdn2.microsoft.com/en-us/library/ms160898.aspx*. Once installed, you can locate the SMO samples in the \Microsoft SQL Server\90\Samples\Engine\Programmability\SMO directory.

---

igning Replication Management Objects Applications

Replication Management Objects enables you to programmatically configure your replication topology. *Replication* is the process of copying data and database objects from one database to another. You can also synchronize databases so that changes made to one database are reflected in the other database. This can be very useful for creating and maintaining a remote copy of your data. The primary database might be used for online transaction processing, and the remote copy can be used for reporting or some other use.

RMO objects can be used to create and configure publications, articles, and subscriptions. Normally, you would use Microsoft SQL Server Management Studio to accomplish these tasks, but with RMO objects, you can do it programmatically. Before RMO was available, replication was configured programmatically using SQL-DMO.

There are many steps that can be performed to configure your replication topology. Which steps you choose depends on the type of replication you are trying to configure. In all cases, you will need to configure replication, create an initial snapshot of the data, and then set up a way to synchronize and propagate data in the future.

The main objects involved with a replication are the Publisher and the Distributor. Once these are configured, you can create publications that specify the type of replication used and what data will be replicated. You can then create subscriptions that will either push or pull the data in order to keep the data up-to-date.

This section will not go into all the details associated with replication, because that is a huge topic in itself. For more information about the replication process, refer to the section titled

"SQL Server Replication" in SQL Server Books Online at *http://msdn2.microsoft.com/e*
library/ms151198.aspx.

RMO Assemblies and Namespaces

Replication is installed using the SQL Server 2005 Installation Wizard. To use RMO, yo▮
need to set references to key RMO assemblies. The two assemblies that provide replic
functionality include the following:

- **Microsoft.SqlServer.Rmo.dll**   This is the main assembly for RMO; it encapsulate▮
  functionality used to configure replication. When you add this reference in Visual S
  2005, the component will be named Microsoft.SqlServer.Replication.NET Program▮
  Interface, but it should still be pointing to the Microsoft.SqlServer.Rmo.dll file.
- **Microsoft.SqlServer.Replication.dll**   This assembly enables you to synchronize
  scriptions by controlling the replication agents. When you add this reference in V▮
  Studio 2005, the component will be named Replication Agent Library, but it shoul▮
  be pointing to the Microsoft.SqlServer.Replication.dll file.

IMPORTANT   **Namespace used in both RMO assemblies**

What can get a little confusing when working with the RMO objects is that the namespace use▮
replication is *Microsoft.SqlServer.Replication*. This is the case for classes that reside within the
Microsoft.SqlServer.Rmo assembly as well as the *Microsoft.SqlServer.Replication* assembly.

The RMO class library, which is represented by the *Microsoft.SqlServer.Rmo* assembly, con▮
dozens of classes that can be used to perform some of the following tasks:

- Specify the replication server, which can represent the distributor, publisher, subsc▮
  or all three.
- Create and edit profiles for certain agents that are used when an agent job is create
- Specify a distributor and distribution database.
- Specify a publisher and publication database.
- Create and define articles, and then add or remove columns from them.
- Create a subscription for transactional or merge replication.
- Define a pull or push subscription.
- Implement special business logic that handles events during the merge replication pr▮
- Set a schedule for a snapshot to be referenced.
- Monitor the replication process and get information about jobs.
- Specify an alternate publisher when creating a merge publication.

The Replication class library that is represented by the *Microsoft.SqlServer.Replication* assembly contains several classes that can be used to accomplish some of the following tasks:

- Create a snapshot agent that can be used to create the initial snapshot and generate a partitioned snapshot for a subscription.
- Create a merge synchronization agent that can be used to synchronize subscriptions and validate that the subscription has the correct data.
- For merge synchronizations, specify whether the upload, download, or both phases are performed.
- Specify an alternate snapshot folder for the subscription.
- Synchronize subscriptions to transactional or snapshot publications.
- Process exceptions specific to a certain replication task.
- Retrieve status information from the replication agent during synchronization.

Specifying a Publisher and a Distributor

Even though you might need to set references to both RMO assemblies, you will only reference one namespace in your code, *Microsoft.SqlServer.Replication*. You will need to establish a connection with SQL Server, so you will also add a reference to the *Microsoft.SqlServer.Connection-Info* assembly and add a directive to the *Microsoft.SqlServer.Management.Common* namespace in your code. The code reference would look like the following:

```
//C#
using Microsoft.SqlServer.Management.Common;
using Microsoft.SqlServer.Replication;\

'VB Imports Microsoft.SqlServer.Management.Common
Imports Microsoft.SqlServer.Replication
```

Regardless of the type of synchronization that is performed, you will need to specify a publisher and a distributor. It is possible that the publisher, distributor, and subscriber can exist on the same machine. The following code is used to specify the distributor, *distribution* database, publisher, and *publication* database:

```
//C#
ReplicationServer rSvr;
ReplicationDatabase rDb;
DistributionDatabase dDb;
DistributionPublisher dPub;

//Connect to the server
ServerConnection conn = new ServerConnection(@".\SQL2005STD");
conn.Connect;
```

```
//Specify the Distribution Database
dDb = new DistributionDatabase("DistributionDatabaseName", conn);
dDb.MaxDistributionRetention = 12;
dDb.HistoryRetention = 24;

//Specify the Distributor and create the
//Distribution database
rSvr = new ReplicationServer(conn);
rSvr.InstallDistributor((string)null, dDb);

//Specify the Publisher, which in this case is the
//same as the distributor
dPub = new DistributionPublisher(@".\SQL2005STD", conn);
dPub.DistributionDatabase = dDb.Name;
dPub.WorkingDirectory = "\\\\" + "SQL2005STD" + "\\repldata";
dPub.PublisherSecurity.WindowsAuthentication = true;
dPub.Create();

//Specify the Publication Database
rDb = new ReplicationDatabase("PublicationDatabaseName", conn);
rDb.EnabledTransPublishing = true;
rDb.EnabledMergePublishing = true;

//Disconnect
conn.Disconnect;
```

```
'VB
Dim rSvr As ReplicationServer
Dim rDB As ReplicationDatabase
Dim dDB As DistributionDatabase
Dim dPub As DistributionPublisher

'Connect to the server
Dim conn As New ServerConnection(".\SQL2005STD")
conn.Connect()

'Specify the Distribution Database
dDB = New DistributionDatabase("DistributionDatabaseName", conn)
dDB.MaxDistributionRetention = 12
dDB.HistoryRetention = 24

'Specify the Distributor and create the
'Distribution database
rSvr = New ReplicationServer(conn)
rSvr.InstallDistributor(CType(Nothing, String), dDB)

'Specify the Publisher, which in this case is the
'same as the distributor
dPub = New DistributionPublisher(".\SQL2005STD", conn)
dPub.DistributionDatabase = dDB.Name
```

```
dPub.WorkingDirectory = "\\\\" + "SQL2005STD" + "\\repldata"
dPub.PublisherSecurity.WindowsAuthentication = True
dPub.Create()

'Specify the Publication Database
rDB = New ReplicationDatabase("PublicationDatabaseName", conn)
rDB.EnabledTransPublishing = True
rDB.EnabledMergePublishing = True

'Disconnect
conn.Disconnect()
```

In the previous example, the *publication* and *distribution* database existed on the same machine. We also specified that the *publication* database would allow for both transactional and merge publishing. The next step from here would depend on what type of replication we wanted to perform. It would also depend on the type of subscription and whether it was a pull or push subscription. Microsoft Developer Network (MSDN) contains some useful how-to sections on the following topics:

- How To: Create a Publication (RMO Programming)
  http://msdn2.microsoft.com/fr-fr/library/ms146941.aspx
- How To: Creating, Modifying, and Deleting Subscriptions (RMO Programming)
  http://msdn2.microsoft.com/fr-fr/library/ms147918.aspx
- How To: Synchronize a Pull Subscription (RMO Programming)
  http://msdn2.microsoft.com /en-us/library/ms147890.aspx
- How To: Define an Article (RMO Programming)
  http://msdn2.microsoft.com/fr-fr/library/ms146883.aspx
- How to: Create a Push Subscription (RMO Programming)
  http://msdn2.microsoft.com/en-US/library/ms146863.aspx
- How to: Synchronize a Push Subscription (RMO Programming)
  http://msdn2.microsoft.com /en-us/library/ms146910.aspx

BEST PRACTICES **Secure your replication topology**

To prevent unauthorized access of your data, you should always encrypt data that is replicated to unsecured domains or across the Internet. This can be done using one of several methods, including Secure Sockets Layer (SSL), virtual private networks (VPNs), or IP Security (IPSec).

Designing Analysis Management Objects Applications

If you have wisely ventured into using SQL Server Analysis Services, you will be pleas
know that SQL Server 2005 offers a way to programmatically control your SSAS objects.
ysis Management Objects enables you to create, manage, and process cubes and dimens
You can also control data-mining objects by creating and processing mining models. All c
functionality you would normally need SQL Server Management Studio to perform ca
done programmatically using AMO.

Prior to AMO, programmatic communication with Analysis Services was done using XM
Analysis (XMLA). With AMO, XMLA is still being used, but AMO represents a layer betwee
XMLA message and the application. Just like with SMO and RMO, the classes are represent
a hierarchical structure. The main objects are the *Cube*, *Dimension*, and *MiningStructure*. W
of these objects is utilized depends on the type of operation that needs to be performed. I
are performing *Online Analytical Processing (OLAP)*, which is a process where large quan
of raw data are stored in a multidimensional format, then you will focus on cubes and di
sions. *Cubes* are multidimensional structures built from one or more tables in a relational
base. *Dimensions* are the attributes used to describe the data within a cube. If you
performing data-mining operations, then you will focus on the mining structure and m
model objects. A mining structure defines what data will be included in a mining m
which is the end result that will be processed and used to provide predictions about the

SSAS is a huge and complex topic. This book does not go into great detail regarding u
SSAS, but if you are interested in learning more about SSAS, refer to the section titled "
Server Analysis Services (SSAS)" in SQL Server Books Online at *http://msdn2.microsof
/en-us/library/ms175609.aspx*. If you are specifically interested in learning more about
mining, refer to "Data Mining with SQL Server 2005" by ZhaoHui Tang and Jamie MacLe
(Wiley, 2005). This well-written and thorough book guides you through everything you
to know about getting the most out of data mining with SQL Server 2005.

AMO Assemblies and Namespaces

Analysis Services is installed using the SQL Server 2005 Installation Wizard. The main ,
library uses only one assembly, *Microsoft.AnalysisServices*, and one namespace, *Microsoft.A
sisServices*. The AMO class library provides well over 100 classes that can be used to admin
all aspects of your SSAS. To reduce confusion, the classes can be divided into several categ

AMO Fundamental Objects   Regardless of whether you are performing OLAP or data
ing, you will need to utilize the *Server*, *Database*, *DataSource*, and *DataSourceView* objec
Database represents all the data objects that can be used in your application. This can repr
cubes, dimensions, and mining structures, and you can have more than one database i

databases collection. The *DataSourceView* object is built from the *DataSource* object; it can contain data from multiple *DataSource* objects or partial data from one *DataSource* object. The *DataSourceView* will be used as the data source for your OLAP cube, dimension, or mining model.

AMO OLAP Classes   These classes enable you to create, edit, and delete the objects for OLAP processing. Some of the key objects from this class can include the following:

- **Dimension**   Contains information used to represent a collection of data from one or more cubes.
- **Cube**   Represents a multidimensional database that can contain different dimensions and measures.
- **MeasureGroup**   A Measure is an expression used to evaluate some piece of data, and a *MeasureGroup* contains one or more related measure expressions.
- **Action**   This is a stored Multidimensional Expression (MDX) that can affect how a cube or dimension is processed.
- **KPI**   KPI is a Key Performance Indicator; it represents a collection of calculations that are used to evaluate data and determine if it meets a predetermined goal.
- **Perspective**   Can be used to controls what data from a cube the user sees.
- **ProactiveCaching**   Enables you to get the performance benefits of an OLAP data source, while still getting some of the real-time benefits from a relational data source.

AMO Data Mining Classes   These classes enable you to work with data-mining objects to create mining structures and mining models and then process the results. Without AMO, your only option for working with data mining is to use SQL Server Business Intelligence Development Studio. Data mining enables you to make predictions about the data that has been processed. This can be useful for finding patterns among a large set of data.

The data-mining structure identifies the data and columns that will be processed. Each column to be processed will be identified as Key, Input, Predictable, or InputPredictable. When defining the column, you will use one of two subclasses to identify the column structure:

- **ScalarMiningStructureColumn**   Columns that hold single values. For example, a column containing someone's age would only have one value.
- **TableMiningStructureColumn**   Columns that hold multiple values and actually embed a table inside the column. For example, a purchase detail column could contain multiple records for each item that was purchased.

The data itself will be assigned from a *DataSourceView*, which was one of the AMO fundamental objects. The data can come from either an OLAP data source or a relational data source.

One or more algorithms will be assigned to this structure. The algorithm is the piece that tells Analysis Services how to interpret the data that it processes. Once the algorithm has been applied to data from the mining structure, it becomes the mining model. You can then pr~~the mining model as many times as necessary with the *Process* method.

BEST PRACTICES   Use multiple algorithms

It is a good idea to assign multiple algorithms to your mining structure. This will enable you t~~compare the results from processing each algorithm and identify the algorithm that delivers t~~optimal results.

AMO Security Classes

Security for all SSAS objects is handled with roles and permissions. Multiple users are assi~~to a single role. One thing that can get confusing is that the terms *users* and *members* ~~essentially the same thing. Each role object will be assigned to multiple users or memb~~is this role object that determines what the user can do with the other SSAS objects.

There are several different permission objects, and one or more of these can be assigne~~role. Permissions can be assigned to a *Database*, *DataSource*, *Dimension*, *Cube*, *MiningStru~~and *MiningModel*. The action associated with the permission determines exactly what the~~can do with that object. The following is a list of possible actions:

- **Read**   Specifies whether the user can read the data or content of the object. This pe~~sion can be overridden by other permissions depending on the object. It can be set~~a value of *None* or *Allowed*.
- **ReadDefinition**   Specifies whether the user can read the data definition for the object~~is different than the Read permission, which is particular to content; this is particu~~structure or definition. The permission can be set with a value of *None*, *Basic*, or *Allo*~~
- **Write**   Specifies whether the user has write access to the data or content of the o~~This permission can be set with a value of *None* or *Allowed*.
- **Process**   A Boolean value determines whether the user can process that object an~~objects it contains.
- **Administer**   This permission only applies to the *Database* object, and it is a Boo~~value that determines whether the user can administer the database.

AMO Administrative Classes

A handful of classes are provided to help administer SSAS. These classes enable you to per~~the following functions:

- Back up and restore the SSAS database
- Monitor SSAS using Traces

- Add functionality by including external assemblies
- Script out objects and operations as XMLA
- Exception handling

Querying Data with ADOMD.NET

Having data reside in a *cube, dimension,* or *mining model* does you little good unless you can query the data inside these objects. ADOMD, which is Active Data Objects for Multidimensional objects, is a .NET Framework data provider that works specifically with SSAS.

ADOMD.NET is divided into two categories: client and server programming. Which one you use depends on where you want the processing to occur. When using this provider, you will need to add references to one of the following assemblies to your project:

- *Microsoft.AnalysisServices.AdomdClient.dll*
- *Microsoft.AnalysisServices.AdomdServer.dll*

You will then need to add one of the following directives to your code:

```
//C#
using Microsoft.AnalysisServices.AdomdClient;
using Microsoft.AnalysisServices.AdomdServer;
```

```
'VB
Imports Microsoft.AnalysisServices.AdomdClient
Imports Microsoft.AnalysisServices.AdomdServer
```

To query data from a multidimensional source, you first need to make a connection to the server. If you are creating an application for the client, you can use the *AdomdConnection* object with the *Microsoft.AnalysisServcices.AdomdClient* namespace to accomplish this. The following example could be used to make a connection to an OLAP database named "TestASDatabase":

```
//C#
//Make a connection to a fictional database named "TestASDatabase"
//for a user with the ID of "username" and a password of "password"
AdomdConnection conn = new AdomdConnection();
conn.ConnectionString = @"Data Source=.\SQL2005STD;" +
    @"Initial Catalog=TestASDatabase;" +
    @"UID=username;" +
    @"PWD=password;";
conn.Open();
```

```
'VB
'Make a connection to a fictional database named "TestASDatabase"
'for a user with the ID of "username" and a password of "password"
Dim conn As New AdomdConnection()
conn.ConnectionString = "Data Source=.\SQL2005STD;" + _
```

```
        "Initial Catalog=TestASDatabase;" + _
        "UID=username;" + _
        "PWD=password;"
conn.Open()
```

After the connection has been established, you can query data from the source and return one of the following objects:

■ *Cellset*   The *Cellset* provides a multidimensional view of the results and enables y drill down into the data. Of course, this method is the most resource intensive should only be used when necessary.

■ *DataSet*   This is the same *DataSet* object that is used with ADO. The difference i you will use a *AdomdDataAdapter* to populate the *DataSet*. Use this object whe there is a need for results to be stored in a *DataSet* object.

■ *AdomdDataReader*   Similar to the *DataReader* in ADO, this is a forward-only view query results. Care should be taken to close these objects so they do not con unnecessary resources.

■ *XmlReader*   The *XmlReader* retrieves the results as XML; it is the object that requir least amount of resources.

Creating a *DataSource* and *DataSourceView*

The *DataSource* and *DataSourceView* are key objects that will be used in all SSAS applica To create these objects, you will need to include a reference to the *Microsoft.AnalysisSe* namespace, because this will be used to get our *Server* and *Database* objects. The follc example can be used to create a *DataSource* and *DataSourceView* from the *AdventureWorks* base on the instance named ".\SQL2005STD". In this case, the *DataSourceView* will be on data coming from a single table. Typically, data might come from multiple related t and utilize named queries.

```
//C#
//Create the server object and connect using the DataSource keyword
Server svr = new Server();
Svr.Connect("DataSource=./SQL2005STD;");
svr.CaptureXml = false;

//Specify the SSAS database
Database db = svr.Databases.GetByName("TestASDatabase");

//Create the data source which will be named the same as the database
RelationalDataSource rDs = new RelationalDataSource("AdventureWorks",
        "AdventureWorks");

//Specify the connection string to the relational DB
rDs.ConnectionString = "Provider=SQLOLEDB; " +
```

```
    @"Data Source=.\SQL2005STD;" +
    @"Initial Catalog=AdventureWorks;" +
    @"Integrated Security=SSPI;";

//Add the new data source to the SSAS DB
db.DataSources.Add(rDs);

//Create a new DataSourceView
//We will name the view the same as the DB and the data source
DataSourceView dsV = new DataSourceView("AdventureWorksDV",
 "AdventureWorksDV");

//Create a dataset to populate the view
OleDbDataAdapter da = new OleDbDataAdapter("", rDs.ConnectionString);
DataSet ds = new DataSet();
da.SelectCommand.CommandText = "SELECT * FROM Person.Contact";
da.FillSchema(ds, SchemaType.Mapped, "Person.Contact");
db.DataSourceViews.Add(dsV.ID);
db.DataSourceViews["AdventureWorksDV"].DataSourceID = rDs.ID;
db.DataSourceViews["AdventureWorksDV"].Schema = ds;

//Update the database
db.Update(UpdateOptions.ExpandFull);
```

'VB
```
'Create the server object and connect using the DataSource keyword
Dim svr As New Server()
svr.Connect("Data Source=.\SQL2005STD")
svr.CaptureXml = False

'Specify the SSAS database
Dim db As Database
db = svr.Databases.GetByName("TestASDatabase")

'Create the data source which will be named the same as the database
Dim rDs As New RelationalDataSource("AdventureWorks", "AdventureWorks")

'Specify the connection string to the relational DB
rDs.ConnectionString = "Provider=SQLOLEDB; " + _
    "Data Source=.\SQL2005STD;" + _
    "Initial Catalog=AdventureWorks;" + _
    "Integrated Security=SSPI;"

'Create a new DataSourceView
'We will name the view the same as the DB and the data source
Dim dsV = New DataSourceView("AdventureWorksDV", "AdventureWorksDV")

'Create a dataset to populate the view
Dim da As New OleDbDataAdapter("", rDs.ConnectionString)
Dim ds As New DataSet()
da.SelectCommand.CommandText = "SELECT * FROM Person.Contact"
```

```
da.FillSchema(ds, SchemaType.Mapped, "Person.Contact")
db.DataSourceViews.Add(dsV.ID)
db.DataSourceViews("AdventureWorksDV").DataSourceID = rDs.ID
db.DataSourceViews("AdventureWorksDV").Schema = ds

'Add the new data source to the SSAS DB
db.DataSources.Add(rDs)

'Update the database
db.Update(UpdateOptions.ExpandFull)
```

Lab: Administrative Programming

In Lab 1, you will perform basic administrative tasks using some of the tools mentioned i
lesson. In Exercise 1, you will create a simple Windows-based application that can be us
create a new database on your SQL Server 2005. Exercise 2 will walk you through crea
data-mining structure using SQL Server Business Intelligence Studio.

The completed lab is available in the \Labs\Chapter 04 folder on the companion CD.

IMPORTANT   Lab requirements

You will need to have SQL Server 2005 installed before you can complete this lab. You will al
need to have administrative abilities for this instance of SQL Server. Refer to the Introduction
setup instructions.

▶ **Exercise 1: Create a Database by Using an SMO Application**

In this exercise, you create a simple Windows application that uses SMO to create a new
base on your SQL Server. The application will ask you to supply the SQL Server instance
and the name of the new database, and then it will create the database and display dat
property information in a list box.

1. Open Microsoft Visual Studio 2005.
2. Click File, New, and Project.
3. In the New Project dialog box, expand the Other Project Types node, and select V
    Studio Solutions. Type **TK442Chapter4** as the name of your blank solution, and
    it in a directory of your choosing. A new solution file will be created, and you ca
    multiple projects to this solution. You will add one project for each lab in included i
    chapter.
4. Select File, Add, and New Web Site. Select Windows Application as the template
    type **Lab1** as the project name. Set the language by selecting Visual Basic or Visu
    from the language drop-down list box. By default, Visual Studio will select the lan
    specified when it was first configured.

5. Select File, Add Reference. From the .NET tab, select the following assemblies:
    - ❑ *Microsoft.SqlServer.Smo*
    - ❑ *Microsoft.SqlServer.SmoEnum*
    - ❑ *Microsoft.SqlServer.SqlEnum*
    - ❑ *Microsoft.SqlServer.ConnectionInfo*

6. From the Toolbox, drag two label controls onto the Default design surface. Use the following property values for these controls:

    Control 1:

    ```
    Name = lblInstance
    Text = "Server Instance:"
    ```

    Control 2:

    ```
    Name = lblDatabase
    Text = "Database Name:"
    ```

7. From the Toolbox, drag two textbox controls onto the Default design surface. Use the following property values for these controls:

    Control 1:

    ```
    Name = txtInstance
    ```

    Control 2:

    ```
    Name = txtDatabase
    ```

8. From the Toolbox, drag one button control onto the Default design surface. Use the following property value for this control:

    ```
    Name = btnCreate
    Text = "Create a database"
    ```

9. The resulting design window should look similar to Figure 4-2.

Figure 4-2   Creating a new database

10. Right-click the Form1 file from Solution Explorer, and select View Code. At the top of the code file, add the following directives:

    ```
    //C#
    using Microsoft.SqlServer.Management.Smo;
    ```

```
using Microsoft.SqlServer.Management.Common;
```

```
'VB
Imports Microsoft.SqlServer.Management.Smo
Imports Microsoft.SqlServer.Management.Common
```

11. Within the same code window, add the following code beneath the *Form_Load* me

```c#
//C#
private void btnCreate_Click(object sender, EventArgs e)
{
    String strInstance;
    String strDatabase;
    Server svr;
    Database db;
    FileGroup fg;
    DataFile df;
    LogFile lf;
    try
    {
        //Get the Instance name and Database name from the textbox
        if (txtInstance.Text.Length > 0 && txtDatabase.Text.Length > 0)
        {
            strInstance = txtInstance.Text.Trim();

            strDatabase = txtDatabase.Text.Trim();

            //Change the cursor to a wait cursor
            this.Cursor = Cursors.WaitCursor;

            //Connect to the server
            svr = new Server(strInstance);

            //Get a list of the current databases on the server
            //and make sure it does not already exist
            if (svr.Databases.Contains(strDatabase))
            {
                MessageBox.Show("This database already exists. Please" +
                    " select a different name and try again");
                return;
            }

            //Create a new database object
            db = new Database(svr, strDatabase);

            //Create a new file group named PRIMARY
            //You can add one or more data files to this
            //group. In this example, we are only adding one
            fg = new FileGroup(db, @"PRIMARY");


            //Create a new data file and name it based on the master database
            //for the server. Then set properties for the data file
```

```
            df = new DataFile(fg, strDatabase + @"_Data",
                svr.Information.MasterDBPath + @"\"
                + strDatabase + @"_Data" + @".mdf");
            df.GrowthType = FileGrowthType.KB;
            df.Growth = 1024;  // In KB

            //Add the file to file group
            fg.Files.Add(df);

            //Add the filegroup to the database
            db.FileGroups.Add(fg);

            //Create the transaction log.
            lf = new LogFile(db, strDatabase + @"_Log",
                svr.Information.MasterDBPath + @"\" + strDatabase
                + @"_Log" + @".ldf");
            lf.GrowthType = FileGrowthType.KB;
            lf.Growth = 1024; // In KB

            //Add the logfile to the db
            db.LogFiles.Add(lf);

            //Create the DB
            db.Create();

            //Create a message that shows
            //the database was created successfully
            MessageBox.Show("A database named, " + db.Name +
                " was created on " + db.CreateDate +
                " with a size of " + db.Size + "MB" +
                " and " + db.SpaceAvailable + " MB of avaialble space." +
                " It currently has a status of " + db.Status);
        }
        else
        {
            MessageBox.Show("Please enter SQL Server instance name" +
                " and new database name before continuing");
        }
    }
    catch (Exception ex)
    {
        MessageBox.Show("The following error was encountered: " +
            ex.Message);
    }
    finally
    {
        //Release resources
        svr = null;
        db = null;
        fg = null;
```

```
        df = null;

        //Set the cursor back to the default
        this.Cursor = Cursors.Default;
    }
  }

'VB
Private Sub btnCreate_Click(ByVal sender As System.Object, ByVal e As System.Event
Handles btnCreate.Click
    Dim strInstance As String
    Dim strDatabase As String
    Dim svr As Server
    Dim db As Database
    Dim fg As FileGroup
    Dim df As DataFile
    Dim lf As LogFile

    Try

        'Get the Instance name and Database name from the textbox
        If txtInstance.Text.Length > 0 And txtDatabase.Text.Length > 0 Then
            strInstance = txtInstance.Text.Trim
            strDatabase = txtDatabase.Text.Trim

        'Change the cursor to a wait cursor
        Me.Cursor = Cursors.WaitCursor

        'Connect to the server
        svr = New Server(strInstance)

        'Get a list of the current databases on the server
        'and make sure it does not already exist
        If svr.Databases.Contains(strDatabase) Then
            MessageBox.Show("This database already exists. Please" + _
                    " select a different name and try again")
            Return
        End If

        'Create a new database object
        db = New Database(svr, strDatabase)

        'Create a new file group named PRIMARY
        'You can add one or more data files to this
        'group. In this example, we are only adding one
        fg = New FileGroup(db, "PRIMARY")

        'Create a new data file and name it based on the master database
        'for the server. Then set properties for the data file
        df = New DataFile(fg, strDatabase + "_Data", _
            svr.Information.MasterDBPath + "\" _
```

```vbnet
                + strDatabase + "_Data" + ".mdf")
            df.GrowthType = FileGrowthType.KB
            df.Growth = 1024   'In KB

            'Add the file to file group
            fg.Files.Add(df)

            'Add the filegroup to the database
            db.FileGroups.Add(fg)

            'Create the transaction log.
            lf = New LogFile(db, strDatabase + "_Log", _
                svr.Information.MasterDBPath + "\" + strDatabase _
                + "_Log" + ".ldf")
            lf.GrowthType = FileGrowthType.KB
            lf.Growth = 1024 'In KB

            'Add the logfile to the db
            db.LogFiles.Add(lf)

            'Create the DB
            db.Create()

            'Create a message that shows
            'the database was created successfully
            MessageBox.Show("A database named, " + db.Name.ToString + _
               " was created on " + db.CreateDate.ToString + _
               " with a size of " + db.Size.ToString + "MB" + _
               " and " + db.SpaceAvailable.ToString + _
   " MB of available space." + _
               " It currently has a status of " + db.Status.ToString)
        Else

            MessageBox.Show("Please enter SQL Server instance name" + _
                " and new database name before continuing")
        End If
    Catch ex As Exception
        MessageBox.Show("The following error was encountered: " + _
                ex.Message)
    Finally
        'Release resources
        svr = Nothing
        db = Nothing
        fg = Nothing
        df = Nothing

        'Set the cursor back to the default
        Me.Cursor = Cursors.Default
    End Try
End Sub
```

12. Click File, and then click Save All.

13. Click Build, and then click Build All, and ensure that the build succeeded.

14. Press Ctrl+F5 to start the project without debugging. When the form appears, en server instance name and the name of a database (*servername\instance*) that do already exist on your SQL Server. Click Create a database. The cursor should cha an hourglass, and within a few seconds, a message box should appear that inforr that the creation was successful.

15. Open Microsoft SQL Server Management Studio.

16. Connect to the instance of SQL Server that you specified when you created the dat Expand the *Databases* node and look for the new database you created earlier. Yo right-click the name of the database and select Properties. If you go to the Files pag will see the data file and log file that were created in the code. (See Figure 4-3.)

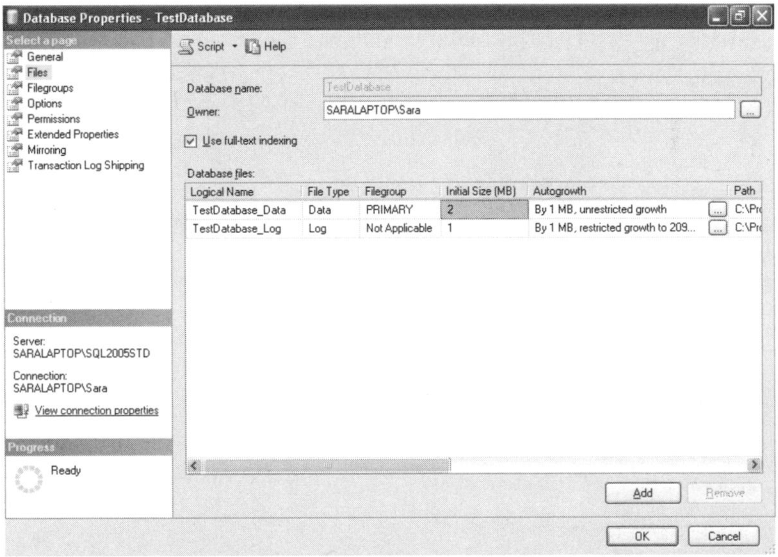

Figure 4-3 Files page for the properties of the newly created test database

▶ **Exercise 2: Create a Data-Mining Structure**

In this exercise, you create a data-mining structure using SQL Server Business Intelli Development Studio. You will walk through creating a *DataSource* and *DataSourceVie* uses data from the *AdventureWorks* database.

1. Open SQL Server Business Intelligence Development Studio. The application wi to the Start Page and will look just like the Start Page for Visual Studio 2005.

2. Click File, New Project.

3. Select Business Intelligence Projects as the Project type and Analysis Services Project as the template.

4. Type **TK442Chapter4Lab1Exercise2** as the project name, and choose a location on your local machine. Click OK to add the project, and create a new solution file. Note that this solution file will be separate from the one created in Exercise 1.

5. Right-click the Data Sources folder from Solution Explorer, and click New Data Source. This will start the Data Source Wizard. In the Welcome dialog box, click Next.

6. Click New to create a new data source. From the Connection Manager dialog box (see Figure 4-4), enter the SQL Server name in which the *AdventureWorks* database is installed. Select the type of authentication to use, and select the *AdventureWorks* database from the database drop-down list box. Click OK to return to the Data Source Wizard.

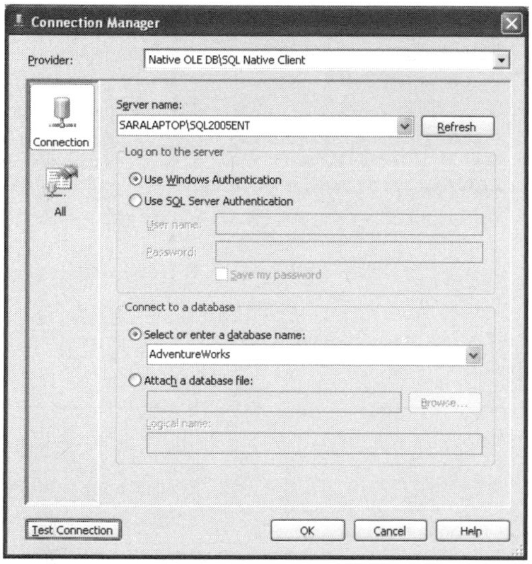

Figure 4-4 Connection Manager dialog box used when creating a new data source for an Analysis Services project

7. Click Finish twice to complete the wizard.

8. Right-click the Data Source Views folder from Solution Explorer, and click New Data Source View. This will start the New Data Source View Wizard. In the Welcome dialog box, click Next.

9. In the Select a Data Source dialog box, click Next to select the *AdventureWorks* relational data source.

10. Select the Person.Contact and Person.Address tables from the Available Objects list, and click the > arrow to move the tables to the list of Included Objects. (See Figure 4-5.) Click Next to continue.

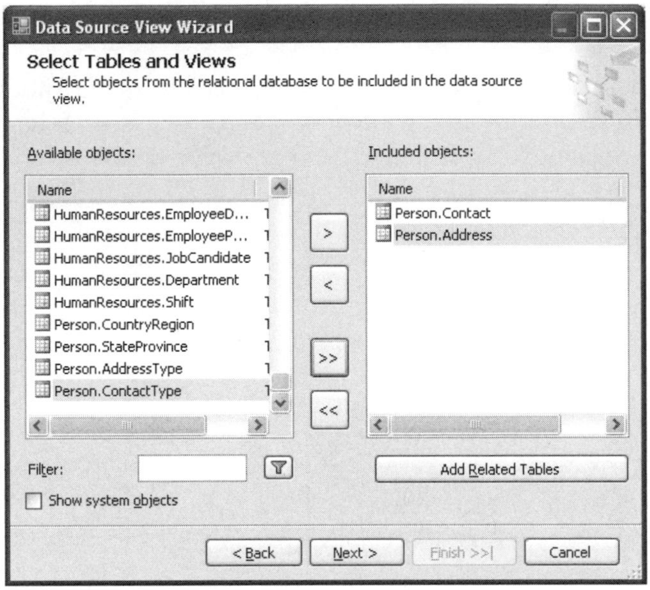

Figure 4-5   Select Table and Views dialog box, used when creating a new data source v▮ an Analysis Services project

11. Click Finish to complete the wizard.

12. On the Build menu, click Deploy to deploy your project to the localhost.

Quick Check

1. What are the key SMO assemblies that need to be referenced in an SMO app▮ tion?

2. How do you connect to a server using logon credentials?

3. What namespace is used by RMO to create an application that works with rep▮ tion objects?

4. What function must be performed regardless of the type of replication you ▮ using?

5. What are the main objects that can be used in an AMO application?

6. In an AMO application, what four objects are used to connect to a database?

7. What assembly enables you to connect to a client using ADOMD.NET?

Quick Check Answers

1. For most SMO applications, you will need to reference the following assemblies:
   - ❑ *Microsoft.SqlServer.Smo*
   - ❑ *Microsoft.SqlServer.SmoEnum*
   - ❑ *Microsoft.SqlServer.SqlEnum*
   - ❑ *Microsoft.SqlServer.ConnectionInfo*

2. To connect to a server using logon credentials, you will need to set a reference to the *Microsoft.SqlServer.ConnectionInfo* assembly and a directive to the *Microsoft.SqlServer.Management.Common* namespace. You then specify the logon credentials using the *ServerConnection* object.

3. Even though there are two assemblies used in RMO applications, *Microsoft.SqlServer.Replication* and *Microsoft.SqlServer.Rmo*, there is only one namespace directive that you need to add to your code: *Microsoft.SqlServer.Replication*.

4. Regardless of what type of replication you are performing, you need to specify a publisher and a distributor. You also need to specify the publisher and distributor databases.

5. The main objects in an AMO application are *Cube*, *Dimension*, and *MiningStructure*. You will need to use the *Server* and *Database* objects to get to these objects.

6. To connect to a database with an AMO application, you need the *Server* and *Database* objects mentioned in the previous answer. You will also need *DataSource* and *DataSourceView* objects.

7. To connect to a client using ADOMD.NET, you will set a reference to the *Microsoft.SqlServer.AdomdClient* assembly. For server-based applications, you will use the *Microsoft.SqlServer.AdomdServer* assembly.

Lesson 2: Querying with Multiple Active Result Sets

Estimated lesson time: 45 minutes

Multiple Active Result Sets is a new feature introduced with SQL Server 2005 that enabl to execute multiple statements through a single connection. MARS uses a connection att to indicate whether the connection can support this type of processing. Prior to this cap; you had to complete one batch before another one could be started. MARS enables you cute one or more statements as you loop through the results of a separate result set—all the same connection.

You might be thinking that MARS enables you to perform asynchronous or parallel p1 ing, but this is not true. MARS enables you to interleave multiple result sets while the c result set remains open. MARS addresses a specific concern among developers that receive transaction isolation level locks in their applications. MARS avoids this lock enabling you to have multiple *SqlDataReaders* open on a single connection. In situations transactions are used and multiple result sets must be processed, MARS can avoid the l(that might occur.

MARS is ideal for a situation where you need to perform some operation as a set of 1 being read. For example, consider the following *pseudo code*, which is code represented English:

```
Execute SELECT statement and return results to a DataReader
Loop through the DataReader
   Perform UPDATE to data from the table in the SELECT statement
End Loop
```

MARS is not a good idea when you have results that will be processed slowly. This can h when the processing is dependent on user interaction or the processing of some extern cess. It might take a long time for the processing to occur, and this could cause an unnec performance penalty when using MARS. In these cases, using a server-side cursor wou] better alternative.

Upon learning about MARS, do not be tempted to convert all existing server-side curs use MARS. It might be possible that the server-side cursor is still the faster alternative. T in this lesson will demonstrate that a server-side cursor is several times faster than the alternative. MARS was not intended to provide a performance advantage; it simply pr another option for developers and enables them to avoid problems with locking.

ng MARS

MARS can be utilized with the SQL Native Client Provider or with the SqlClient for the .NET Provider. For more information about the SQL Native Client Provider, refer to Lesson 1, "Designing Data Access Technologies" in Chapter 1, "Designing a Data Access Strategy." By default, MARS is not enabled, so you will have to enable it specifically. The following lists how it is enabled with each provider:

- **SQL Native Client using the OLEDB Provider** MARS is enabled through the SSPROP _INIT_MARSCONNECTION property from the DBPROPSET_SQLSERVERDBINIT property set. Alternatively, you can include the *MarsConn=yes/no* keyword in the connection string if you are using the SQL Native Client through ADO. The code that specifies the connection string would look similar to the following:

```
//C#
ADODB.Connection conn = new ADODB.Connection();
String connStr = "Provider=SQLNCLI;" +
            @"Server=.\SQL2005STD;" +
            "Database=AdventureWorks;" +
            "Integrated Security=SSPI;" +
            "DataTypeCompatibility=80;" +
            "MarsConn=yes;";
conn.Open(connStr, null, null, 0);
//Do some processing
conn.Close();
```

```
'VB
Dim conn As New ADODB.Connection
Dim connStr As String = "Provider=SQLNCLI;" + _
            "Server=.\SQL2005STD;" + _
            "Database=AdventureWorks;" + _
            "Integrated Security=SSPI;" + _
            "DataTypeCompatibility=80;" + _
            "MarsConn=Yes;"
conn.ConnectionString = connStr
conn.Open()
'Do some processing
conn.Close()
```

- **SQL Native Client using the ODBC Provider** MARS is enabled through the *SQLSetConnectAttr* and *SqlGetConnectAttr* functions. Alternatively, you can set include the *MARS CONNECTION=true/false* keyword in the connection string if you are using the SQL Native Client through ADO. The code that specifies the connection string would look similar to the following:

```
//C#
ADODB.Connection conn = new ADODB.Connection();
String connStr = "Provider=SQLNCLI;" +
            @"Server=.\SQL2005STD;" +
```

```
                "Database=AdventureWorks;" +
                "Integrated Security=SSPI;" +
                "DataTypeCompatibility=80;" +
                "MARS Connection=True;";
conn.Open(connStr, null, null, 0);
//Do some processing
conn.Close();
```

```
'VB
Dim conn As New ADODB.Connection
Dim connStr As String = "Provider=SQLNCLI;" + _
            "Server=.\SQL2005STD;" + _
            "Database=AdventureWorks;" + _
            "Integrated Security=SSPI;" + _
            "DataTypeCompatibility=80;" + _
            "MARS Connection=True;"
conn.ConnectionString = connStr
conn.Open()
'Do some processing
conn.Close()
```

- **SqlClient .NET Provider**   You can use the *System.Data.SqlClient* namespace with the
  Framework to specify whether MARS is enabled. To use this feature, you includ
  MultipleActiveResultSets = *True/False* keyword in the connection string. The follc
  code could be used to enable MARS for the *SqlClient*:

```
//C#
SqlConnection conn = new SqlConnection();
String connStr = @"Data Source=.\SQL2005STD;" +
        "Initial Catalog=AdventureWorks;" +
        "Integrated Security=SSPI;" +
        "MultipleActiveResultSets=True;";
conn.ConnectionString = connStr;
conn.Open();
//Do some processing
conn.Close();
```

```
'VB
   Dim conn As New SqlConnection
   Dim connStr As String = "Data Source=.\SQL2005STD;" + _
       "Initial Catalog=AdventureWorks;" + _
       "Integrated Security=SSPI;" + _
       "MultipleActiveResultSets=True;"
   conn.ConnectionString = connStr
   conn.Open()
   'Do some processing
   conn.Close()
```

g Transactions

The .NET Framework 2.0 provides a *TransactionScope* class, which is part of the *System.Transactions* namespace. This class enables you to easily wrap code that should execute within a single transaction inside a using statement. The code block will implicitly enlist all the commands within the block as part of a single transaction. You just have to call the *Complete* method at the end of the code block to signify that the transaction is finished.

For example, the following code can be used to wrap two commands within a single transaction:

```csharp
//C#
using (TransactionScope ts = new TransactionScope())
{
    //Connect to the Database and enable MARS
    SqlConnection conn = new SqlConnection();
    String connStr = @"Data Source=.\SQL2005STD;" +
        "Initial Catalog=AdventureWorks;" +
        "Integrated Security=SSPI;" +
        "MultipleActiveResultSets=True;";
    conn.ConnectionString = connStr;
    conn.Open();

    //Define our UPDATE statements
    SqlCommand cmd1 = new SqlCommand();
    SqlCommand cmd2 = new SqlCommand();
    cmd1.CommandText = "UPDATE Person.Contact SET MiddleName = 'G'" +
        " where contactid = 1";
    cmd1.Connection = conn;

    //This command will use the same connection
    cmd2.CommandText = "UPDATE Person.Contact SET MiddleName = 'F'" +
        " where contactid = 2";
    cmd2.Connection = conn;
    try
    {
        //Execute the commands
        cmd1.ExecuteNonQuery();
        cmd2.ExecuteNonQuery();
    }
    catch
    {
        //Do something with the exception
    }
    finally
    {
        conn.Close();
        ts.Complete();
        cmd1 = null;
        cmd2 = null;
```

```
            conn = null;
      }
   }
```

```
'VB
Using ts As New TransactionScope()
      'Connect to the Database and enable MARS
      Dim conn As New SqlConnection()
      Dim connStr As String = "Data Source=.\SQL2005STD;" + _
            "Initial Catalog=AdventureWorks;" + _
            "Integrated Security=SSPI;" + _
            "MultipleActiveResultSets=True;"
      conn.ConnectionString = connStr
      conn.Open()

      'Define our UPDATE statements
      Dim cmd1 As New SqlCommand()
      Dim cmd2 As New SqlCommand()
      cmd1.CommandText = "UPDATE Person.Contact SET MiddleName = 'G'" + _
            " where contactid = 1"
      cmd1.Connection = conn

      'This command will use the same connection
       cmd2.CommandText = "UPDATE Person.Contact SET MiddleName = 'F'" + _
            " where contactid = 2"
       cmd2.Connection = conn

      Try
          'Execute the commands
          cmd1.ExecuteNonQuery()
          cmd2.ExecuteNonQuery()
      Catch ex As Exception
          'Do something with the exception
      Finally
           conn.Close()
           ts.Complete()
           cmd1 = Nothing
           cmd2 = Nothing
           conn = Nothing
      End Try
End Using
```

IMPORTANT   Hotfix available

When working with transactions in SQL Server 2005 and the *SqlClient* class, it is possible you ᵒ receive the error "New request is not allowed to start because it should come with valid transaᵖ descriptor." The error occurs randomly, but there is a hotfix available to resolve this issue. The ᴴ is available at *http://support.microsoft.com/kb/916002*.

Creating MARS Connections

Lab 2 contains one exercise in which you create a Windows-based application that is used to query and perform updates on a SQL Server 2005 database. The application will enable you to compare the results of using a MARS connection and a single connection versus two connections.

The completed code examples, in both Visual Basic and C#, are available in the \Labs\Chapter 04 folder on the companion CD.

IMPORTANT   Lab requirements

You need to have SQL Server 2005 installed before you can complete this lab. Refer to the Introduction for setup instructions.

▶ **Exercise 1: Compare Execution of Queries With and Without MARS**

In this exercise, you create a simple Windows application that has two buttons. The first button will perform a query of all contacts and then loop through the results as it updates the e-mail address using the same connection. It is able to do this by using a MARS connection. The second button will perform the same function but will use two connections. You can then compare the execution time of both methods.

The code example for this exercise was borrowed from the cursor example used in Lesson 3 of Chapter 3. In that lesson, it was determined that the cursor was not the most efficient alternative. The example used in this exercise is also not the most efficient method of updating the records, but it demonstrates how to use a MARS connection and enables you to compare the execution times of using MARS and not using MARS.

1. Open Microsoft Visual Studio 2005.
2. If you completed the practice from Lesson 1, skip to step 5.
3. Click File, New, Project.
4. In the New Project dialog box, expand the Other Project Types node, and select Visual Studio Solutions. Type **TK442Chapter4** for the name of your blank solution, and place it in a directory of your choosing. A new solution file will be created, and you can add multiple projects to this solution. You will add one project for each lab included in this chapter.
5. Select File, Add, New Project. Select Windows Application as the template, and type **Lab2** as the project name. Set the language by selecting Visual Basic, Visual C#, or Visual J# from the language drop-down list box. By default, Visual Studio selects the language specified when it was first configured.
6. From the Toolbox, drag one label control onto the Default design surface. Use the following property value for this control:

```
Name = lblInstance
Text = "Server Instance: "
```

7. From the Toolbox, drag one textbox control onto the Default design surface. Use t lowing property value for this control:

```
Name = txtInstance
```

8. From the Toolbox, drag two button controls onto the Default design surface. Use t lowing property values for these controls:

Control 1:

```
Name = btnWithMARS
Text = "Run Query with MARS"
```

Control 2:

```
Name = btnWithoutMARS
Text = "Run Query without MARS"
```

9. Right-click the Form1 file from Solution Explorer, and select View Code. Paste tl lowing code at the top of the file:

```
//C#
using System.Data.SqlClient;
'VB
Imports System.Data.SqlClient
```

10. From the same code window, paste the following code beneath the *Form1_Load* me

```
//C#
private void btnWithMARS_Click(object sender, EventArgs e)
    {
            //Change the cursor to a wait cursor and get start time
            this.Cursor = Cursors.WaitCursor;
            DateTime startTime = DateTime.Now;

            //Connect to the Database and enable MARS
            SqlConnection conn = new SqlConnection();
            String connStr = @"Data Source=" + txtInstance.Text + ";" +
                "Initial Catalog=AdventureWorks;" +
                "Integrated Security=SSPI;" +
                "MultipleActiveResultSets=True;";
            conn.ConnectionString = connStr;
            conn.Open();

            //Get a SqlDataReader that contains contact records
            SqlCommand cmd1 = new SqlCommand("SELECT ContactID, " +
"EmailAddress, EmailPromotion " +
                    "FROM Person.Contact", conn);
            SqlDataReader dr = cmd1.ExecuteReader();

        //Define our UPDATE statements
```

```
SqlCommand cmd2 = new SqlCommand();
cmd2.Connection = conn;

try
{
  while (dr.Read())
  {
   if (dr.GetInt32(2) == 0)
   {
      cmd2.CommandText = "UPDATE Person.contact SET emailaddress = " +
          "REPLACE('" + dr.GetString(1) + "','adventure-works.com', " +
" +'adventure-works.net')" +
          "WHERE ContactID = " + dr.GetInt32(0);
    }

   if (dr.GetInt32(2) == 1)
   {
      cmd2.CommandText = "UPDATE Person.contact SET emailaddress = " +
          "REPLACE('" + dr.GetString(1) + "','adventure-works.com', " +
" +'adventure-works.biz')" +
          "WHERE ContactID = " + dr.GetInt32(0);
    }

   if (dr.GetInt32(2) == 2)
   {
      cmd2.CommandText = "UPDATE Person.contact SET emailaddress = " +
          "REPLACE('" + dr.GetString(1) + "','adventure-works.com', " +
" +'adventure-works.org')" +
          "WHERE ContactID = " + dr.GetInt32(0);
    }

    //Execute the command
    cmd2.ExecuteNonQuery();

  }
}
catch (Exception ex)
{
   MessageBox.Show("The following message was encountered: " +
ex.Message);
}
finally
{
      conn.Close();
      cmd1 = null;
      cmd2 = null;
      conn = null;
}
//Change the cursor back to default and get end time
this.Cursor = Cursors.Default;
```

```csharp
            DateTime endTime = DateTime.Now;
            TimeSpan ts = endTime.Subtract(startTime);
            MessageBox.Show("The queries took " +
                ts.Minutes + ":" + ts.Seconds + " to complete");

    }

    private void btnWithoutMARS_Click(object sender, EventArgs e)
    {
        //Change the cursor to a wait cursor and get start time
        this.Cursor = Cursors.WaitCursor;
        DateTime startTime = DateTime.Now;

        //Connect to the Database with the first connection
        SqlConnection conn1 = new SqlConnection();
        String connStr = @"Data Source=" + txtInstance.Text + ";" +
            "Initial Catalog=AdventureWorks;" +
            "Integrated Security=SSPI;";
        conn1.ConnectionString = connStr;
        conn1.Open();

            //Get a SqlDataReader that contains contact records
            SqlCommand cmd1 = new SqlCommand("SELECT ContactID, " +
"EmailAddress, EmailPromotion " +
                        "FROM Person.Contact", conn1);
        SqlDataReader dr = cmd1.ExecuteReader();

        //Define our UPDATE statements and create a second connection
        SqlConnection conn2 = new SqlConnection(connStr);
        conn2.Open();

        SqlCommand cmd2 = new SqlCommand();
        cmd2.Connection = conn2;

        try
        {
          while (dr.Read())
            {

                if (dr.GetInt32(2) == 0)
                {
                    cmd2.CommandText = "UPDATE Person.contact SET emailaddress = " +
                        "REPLACE('" + dr.GetString(1) + "','adventure-works.com', " +
" +'adventure-works.net')" +
                        "WHERE ContactID = " + dr.GetInt32(0);
                }

                if (dr.GetInt32(2) == 1)
                {
                    cmd2.CommandText = "UPDATE Person.contact SET emailaddress = " +
```

```
                "REPLACE('" + dr.GetString(1) + "','adventure-works.com', " +
 " +'adventure-works.biz')" +
                "WHERE ContactID = " + dr.GetInt32(0);
           }

           if (dr.GetInt32(2) == 2)
           {
             cmd2.CommandText = "UPDATE Person.contact SET emailaddress = " +
                "REPLACE('" + dr.GetString(1) + "','adventure-works.com', " +
 " +'adventure-works.org')" +
                "WHERE ContactID = " + dr.GetInt32(0);
           }


           //Execute the command
           cmd2.ExecuteNonQuery();


       }
     }
     catch (Exception ex)
     {
         MessageBox.Show("The following message was encountered: " +
ex.Message);
     }
     finally
     {
         conn1.Close();
         conn2.Close();
         cmd1 = null;
         cmd2 = null;
         conn1 = null;
         conn2 = null;
     }
     //Change the cursor back to default and get end time
     this.Cursor = Cursors.Default;
     DateTime endTime = DateTime.Now;
     TimeSpan ts = endTime.Subtract(startTime);
     MessageBox.Show("The queries took " +
         ts.Minutes + ":" + ts.Seconds + " to complete");
 }
'VB
Private Sub btnWithMars_Click(ByVal sender As System.Object, ByVal e As
System.EventArgs) Handles btnWithMars.Click

     'Change the cursor to a wait cursor and get start time
     Me.Cursor = Cursors.WaitCursor
     Dim startTime As System.DateTime
     startTime = Now()

     'Connect to the Database and enable MARS
```

```vb
Dim conn As New SqlConnection
Dim connStr As String = "Data Source=" + txtInstance.Text + ";" + _
    "Initial Catalog=AdventureWorks;" + _
    "Integrated Security=SSPI;" + _
    "MultipleActiveResultSets=True;"
conn.ConnectionString = connStr
conn.Open()

'Get a SqlDataReader that contains contact records
Dim cmd1 As New SqlCommand("SELECT ContactID, " + _
    "EmailAddress, EmailPromotion " + _
    " FROM Person.Contact", conn)

Dim dr As SqlDataReader = cmd1.ExecuteReader

'Define our UPDATE statements
Dim cmd2 As New SqlCommand
cmd2.Connection = conn

Try
 While dr.Read

    If dr.GetInt32(2) = 0 Then
     cmd2.CommandText = "UPDATE Person.contact SET emailaddress = " + _
       "REPLACE('" + dr.GetString(1) + "', 'adventure-works.com', " + _
       "'adventure-works.net')" + _
       "WHERE ContactID = " + dr.GetInt32(0)
    End If

    If dr.GetInt32(2) = 0 Then
     cmd2.CommandText = "UPDATE Person.contact SET emailaddress = " + _
       "REPLACE('" + dr.GetString(1) + "', 'adventure-works.com', " + _
       "'adventure-works.biz')" + _
       "WHERE ContactID = " + dr.GetInt32(0)
    End If

   If dr.GetInt32(2) = 0 Then
     cmd2.CommandText = "UPDATE Person.contact SET emailaddress = " + _
       "REPLACE('" + dr.GetString(1) + "', 'adventure-works.com', " + _
       "'adventure-works.org')" + _
       "WHERE ContactID = " + dr.GetInt32(0)
   End If
 End While


    'Execute the command
    cmd2.ExecuteNonQuery()

Catch ex As Exception
```

```
        MessageBox.Show("The following message was encountered: " + _
            ex.Message)
    Finally
        conn.Close()
        cmd1 = Nothing
        cmd2 = Nothing
        conn = Nothing
    End Try

    'Change the cursor back to default and get end time
    Me.Cursor = Cursors.Default
    Dim endTime As DateTime
    endTime = Now()
    Dim ts As TimeSpan = endTime.Subtract(startTime)
    MessageBox.Show("The queries took " + _
        ts.Minutes + ":" + ts.Seconds + " to complete")

End Sub

Private Sub btnWithoutMARS_Click(ByVal sender As System.Object, ByVal e As
System.EventArgs) Handles btnWithoutMARS.Click

    'Change the cursor to a wait cursor and get start time
    Me.Cursor = Cursors.WaitCursor
    Dim startTime As System.DateTime
    startTime = Now()

    'Connect to the Database with the first connection
    Dim conn1 As New SqlConnection
    Dim connStr As String = "Data Source=" + txtInstance.Text + ";" + _
        "Initial Catalog=AdventureWorks;" + _
        "Integrated Security=SSPI;"
    conn1.ConnectionString = connStr
    conn1.Open()

    'Get a SqlDataReader that contains contact records
    Dim cmd1 As New SqlCommand("SELECT ContactID, " + _
        "EmailAddress, EmailPromotion " + _
        " FROM Person.Contact", conn1)
    Dim dr As SqlDataReader = cmd1.ExecuteReader

    'Define our UPDATE statements and create a second connection
    Dim conn2 As New SqlConnection(connStr)
    conn2.Open()

    Dim cmd2 As New SqlCommand
    cmd2.Connection = conn2

    Try
```

```
    While dr.Read

      If dr.GetInt32(2) = 0 Then
        cmd2.CommandText = "UPDATE Person.contact SET emailaddress = " + _
          "REPLACE('" + dr.GetString(1) + "', 'adventure-works.com', " + _
          "'adventure-works.net')" + _
          "WHERE ContactID = " + dr.GetInt32(0)
      End If

      If dr.GetInt32(2) = 0 Then
        cmd2.CommandText = "UPDATE Person.contact SET emailaddress = " + _
          "REPLACE('" + dr.GetString(1) + "', 'adventure-works.com', " + _
          "'adventure-works.biz')" + _
          "WHERE ContactID = " + dr.GetInt32(0)
      End If

      If dr.GetInt32(2) = 0 Then
        cmd2.CommandText = "UPDATE Person.contact SET emailaddress = " + _
          "REPLACE('" + dr.GetString(1) + "', 'adventure-works.com', " + _
          "'adventure-works.org')" + _
          "WHERE ContactID = " + dr.GetInt32(0)
      End If
    End While

    'Execute the command
    cmd2.ExecuteNonQuery()

  Catch ex As Exception

    MessageBox.Show("The following message was encountered: " + _
        ex.Message)
  Finally
      conn1.Close()
      conn2.Close()
      cmd1 = Nothing
      cmd2 = Nothing
      conn1 = Nothing
      conn2 = Nothing
  End Try

    'Change the cursor back to default and get end time
    Me.Cursor = Cursors.Default
    Dim endTime As DateTime
    endTime = Now()
    Dim ts As TimeSpan = endTime.Subtract(startTime)
    MessageBox.Show("The queries took " + _
        ts.Minutes + ":" + ts.Seconds + " to complete")
  End Sub
```

11. Save the Lab2 project by going to File and clicking Save All.

12. Right-click the Lab2 project from Solution Explorer, and select Set As Startup Project.

13. Press Ctrl+F5 to build the project without debugging. Ensure that the project builds successfully. Form1 should appear after the project compiles and executes. You should see two buttons and a text box. Type the name of the instance of SQL Server 2005 in which you have the *AdventureWorks* database installed.

14. Click the Run Query With MARS button. The cursor should change to an hourglass, and the process might take over a minute to run. When complete, a message box displays the amount of time it took to execute. Make a note of this time. Keep in mind that the code for this test performs the same function that the inefficient cursor from Lab 3 of Chapter 3 used. In that lab, the cursor took approximately 18 seconds to complete. In one test, this code took over a minute to complete. In this case, the server-side cursor performed better than the MARS queries.

15. You can now click the Run Query Without MARS button. This set of code accomplishes the same task, but it uses two connections instead of one. The code should take approximately the same amount of time as the MARS alternative to execute. No performance advantage is achieved by using one connection versus two.

Quick Check

1. What problem does MARS attempt to resolve?
2. How is MARS enabled?
3. What method enables you to easily wrap code that should execute within a single transaction?

Quick Check Answers

1. MARS helps to resolve a problem developers would encounter with locking. This might occur when you perform updates and selects using different connections.
2. With SQL Native Client and OLEDB, you can add the *MarsConn* attribute to the connection string. With the SQL Native Client and ODBC, you can add the *MARS Connection* attribute to your connection string. With the *SqlClient*, add the *MultipleActiveResultSets* attribute to the connection string.
3. To easily utilize transactions, you can use the *TransactionScope*, which is part of the *System.Transactions* namespace.

Lesson 3: Performing Asynchronous Processing

Estimated lesson time: 30 minutes

Asynchronous processing enables you to perform operations in parallel. This means that operation can begin before the other has completed. ADO.NET enables you to execute commands asynchronously. This capability can be especially useful when you need to per operations against two different databases. It can also be effective in ASP.NET applicatio which one set of data can be rendered to the client before all the operations have comple

Asynchronous processing is supported through the SqlClient provider, but other prov could add the capabilities if warranted. This section will focus on executing commands chronously using the *System.Data.SqlClient* namespace. Implemented through the *Comr* object, it can be accomplished using any of the following command operations: *ExecuteRe ExecuteXmlReader*, *ExecuteScalar*, and *ExecuteNonQuery*.

Exam Tip   If you search on the MSDN Web site for "asynchronous processing," you might se papers that reference a new feature called Service Broker. Service Broker is a server-side platf that can be used to build asynchronous programs. For this exam, you only need to be aware how to use ADO.NET to execute commands asynchronously.

Asynchronous processing can provide a performance advantage for your applications. especially useful in situations where a long-running database operation would slow dowr processing of another operation. However, enabling asynchronous processing does resu additional overhead. Therefore, it should only be used if your application would benef allowing one operation to begin before another has completed.

Using Asynchronous Processing

Enabling asynchronous processing through ADO.NET requires that you first add directiv the *Microsoft.Data.SqlClient* namespace and potentially the *System.Threading* namespac well. You will also need to add the *Asynchronous Processing=True* keyword to your connec string. For example, the following connection string could be used to enable asynchron processing:

```
//C#
//Connect to the database and enable asynchronous processing
SqlConnection conn = new SqlConnection();
String connStr = @"Data Source=.\SQL2005STD;" +
    "Initial Catalog=AdventureWorks;" +
    "Integrated Security=SSPI;" +
    "Asynchronous Processing=True;";
```

```
conn.ConnectionString = connStr;
conn.Open();
```

```
'VB
'Connect to the database and enable asynchronous processing
Dim conn As New SqlConnection
Dim connStr As String = "Data Source=.\SQL2005STD;" + _
    "Initial Catalog=AdventureWorks;" + _
    "Integrated Security=SSPI;" + _
    "Asynchronous Processing=True;"
conn.ConnectionString = connStr
conn.Open()
```

Once asynchronous processing has been enabled, you can access certain asynchronous methods through the *Command* object. Each operation includes a *Begin* and *End* method. For example, if you want to use *ExecuteReader* to populate a *DataReader* object asynchronously, you would use the *BeginExecuteReader* and *EndExecuteReader* methods instead.

The *BeginExecuteReader* method will return an *IAsynchResult* object, which will be used to track the progress of the operation. You can then poll the *IsCompleted* property to determine when the operation has completed. Once complete, you can call the associated *End* method. For example, the following code can be used to execute a query asynchronously:

```
//C#
SqlCommand cmd = new SqlCommand("Select * from Person.Contact", conn);
IAsyncResult result = cmd.BeginExecuteReader;
while (! result.IsCompleted)
{
    //Perform additional processing
}
cmd.EndExecuteReader(result);
```

```
'VB
Dim cmd As New SqlCommand("Select * from Person.contact", conn)
Dim result As IAsyncResult = cmd.BeginExecuteReader
While Not result.IsCompleted
    'Perform additional processing
End While
cmd.EndExecuteReader(result)
```

There are several methods of handling the results of this type of processing. The *IAsynchResult* object has an *AsyncWaitHandle* property that enables you to issue a block until the operation completes. Finally, you could use a callback function that executes only when the operation is complete.

In some cases, it might be necessary to cancel an executing command. The *Command* object provides a *Cancel* method for accomplishing this. In terms of error handling, it is possible you could receive errors on both the *Begin* and *End* methods. You might have to make special considerations if certain operations are dependent on others, such as rolling back a prev transaction.

Lab: Performing Asynchronous Processing

Lab 3 contains one exercise in which you create a Windows-based application that is us perform asynchronous processing.

The completed code examples, in both Visual Basic and C#, are available in the \Labs\C ter 04 folder on the companion CD.

IMPORTANT Lab requirements

You will need to have SQL Server 2005 installed before you can complete this lab. Refer to th Introduction for setup instructions.

▶ **Exercise 1: Use the Callback Feature**

In this exercise, you create a simple Windows application that has one button. The buttor perform an asynchronous query using the callback feature. The code in the callback fea will simply return a message box that displays the amount of time the query took to exe

1. Open Microsoft Visual Studio 2005.
2. If you completed the practice from Lesson 1, skip to step 5.
3. Click File, New, Project.
4. In the New Project dialog box, expand the Other Project Types node, and select V Studio Solutions. Type **TK442Chapter4** for the name of your blank solution, and it in a directory of your choosing. A new solution file will be created, and you can add multiple projects to this solution. You will add one project for each lab include this chapter.
5. Select File, Add, New Project. Select Windows Application as the template, and Lab3 as the project name. Set the language by selecting Visual Basic or Visual C# the language drop-down list box. By default, Visual Studio will select the language ified when it was first configured.
6. From the Toolbox, drag one label control onto the Default design surface. Use th lowing property value for this control:
   ```
   Name = lblInstance
   Text = "Server Instance:"
   ```
7. From the Toolbox, drag one textbox control onto the Default design surface. Use th lowing property value for this control:
   ```
   Name = txtInstance
   ```

8. Right-click the Form1 file from Solution Explorer, and select View Code. Add the following directives to the top of the file:

```
//C#
using System.Data.SqlClient;
using System.Threading;
```

```
'VB
Imports System.Data.SqlClient
Imports System.Threading
```

9. Now add the following code before the constructor:

```
//C#
private int count;
private SqlCommand cmd;
```

```
'VB
Dim count As Int16
Dim cmd As SqlCommand
```

10. Now add the following code beneath the *Load* method for the Form1:

```
//C#
private void btnQuery_Click(object sender, EventArgs e)
{
    //Change the cursor to a wait cursor and get start time
    this.Cursor = Cursors.WaitCursor;
    DateTime startTime = DateTime.Now;

    //Connect to the database and enable asynchronous processing
    SqlConnection conn = new SqlConnection();
    String connStr = @"Data Source=" + txtInstance.Text + ";" +
      "Initial Catalog=AdventureWorks;" +
      "Integrated Security=SSPI;" +
      "Asynchronous Processing=True;";
    conn.ConnectionString = connStr;
    conn.Open();

    //Create our command
    cmd = new SqlCommand("SELECT Count(*) FROM Person.Contact", conn);

    //Reference the callback procedure
    IAsyncResult result = cmd.BeginExecuteReader(arCallBackMethod, null);
    while (!result.IsCompleted)
    {
        Thread.Sleep(1000);  //Pause the thread for a second
        count += count;
    }

    //Change the cursor back to default and get end time
    this.Cursor = Cursors.Default;

}
```

```csharp
private void arCallBackMethod(IAsyncResult ar)
{
    SqlDataReader dr = cmd.EndExecuteReader(ar);
    //We could display the results or process them at this point
    dr.Read();
    MessageBox.Show(dr[0].ToString() + " records were processed." +
        " The query took approximately " + count + " seconds to process");
}
```

```vb
'VB
Private Sub btnAsynch_Click(ByVal sender As System.Object, ByVal e As System.EventA
Handles btnAsynch.Click
        'Change the cursor to a wait cursor and get start time
        Me.Cursor = Cursors.WaitCursor
        Dim startTime As DateTime
        startTime = Now()

        'Connect to the Ddtabase and enable asynchronous processing
        Dim conn As New SqlConnection
        Dim connStr As String = "Data Source=" + txtInstance.Text + ";" + _
            "Initial Catalog=AdventureWorks;" + _
            "Integrated Security=SSPI;" + _
            "MultipleActiveResultSets=True;"
        conn.ConnectionString = connStr
        conn.Open()

        'Create our command
        cmd = New SqlCommand("SELECT Count(*) FROM Person.Contact", conn)

        'Reference the callback procedure
        Dim result As IAsyncResult = cmd.BeginExecuteReader(AddressOf arCallbackMet
Nothing)

        While Not result.IsCompleted
            Thread.Sleep(1000)   'Pause the thread for a second
            count += count
        End While

        'Change the cursor back to default and get end time
        Me.Cursor = Cursors.Default
    End Sub

    Private Sub arCallbackMethod(ByVal ar As IAsyncResult)
        Dim dr As SqlDataReader = cmd.EndExecuteReader(ar)
        'We could display the results or process them at this point
        dr.Read()
        MessageBox.Show(dr(0).ToString() + " records were processed." + _
            " The query took approximately " + count + " seconds to process")
    End Sub
```

11. Save the Lab3 project by clicking File, and then Save All.
12. Right-click the Lab3 project from Solution Explorer, and select Set As Startup project.
13. Press Ctrl+F5 to build the project without debugging. Ensure that the project builds successfully. Form1 should appear after the project compiles and executes. You should see one button and a text box. Type the name of the instance of SQL Server 2005 in which you have the *AdventureWorks* database installed. The cursor should change to an hourglass, and in a second or less, you should receive a message box with the results.

Quick Check

1. Which data provider supports asynchronous processing through the client?
2. How do you enable asynchronous processing?
3. What command methods are used to process a *DataReader* asynchronously?

Quick Check Answers

1. The SqlClient provider, which is part of ADO.NET and available through the *System.Data.SqlClient* namespace, is used to support asynchronous processing through the *Command* object.
2. You enable asynchronous processing by adding the *Asynchronous Processing* keyword to the connection string.
3. You will need to use both the *BeginDataReader* and *EndDataReader* methods to retrieve data asynchronously using the *Command* object.

---

e Scenario: Automating a Data-Mining Solution

You are a database developer for a large online retailer that has been in operation for several years. The retailer utilizes a customer specific ASP.NET application and maintains sales history records for each customer. The company plans to upgrade the Web site, and one feature they would like to add is the capability to make product recommendations to customers. The recommendations would be based on past sales history for that particular customer.

Your boss has asked you to evaluate ways to accomplish this and then make a recommendation for how the solution could be implemented. What strategy might you recommend to your boss?

Suggested Practices

Objective 1.5: Design client libraries to write applications that administer a SQL Server service

- **Practice 1:**   Expand on Exercise 2, "Create a Data-Mining Structure" from Less "Administering a SQL Server Service", and add a mining model to the mining stru This involves assigning an algorithm to the mining structure and then processin mining structure.

  To begin with, run the Data Mining Wizard. When specifying the tables, Person.C should be the case table and Person.Contact a nested table. Use the Suggest butt the Specify Column Usage page of the wizard to indicate which columns are likely t vide information. Use the Detect button on the to automatically assign the correc tent types. When assigning algorithms, use the following:

  - ❑ Microsoft Clustering
  - ❑ Microsoft Decision Trees
  - ❑ Microsoft Neural Network

Objective 1.6: Design queries that use multiple active results sets (M

- **Practice 1:**   Refer to Lesson 2, "Querying with Multiple Active Result Sets," Exer "Compare Execution of Queries With and Without MARS." Expand on the exerc enabling transactions for the code that uses a MARS connection. Intentionally an error and ensure that the transaction is rolled back and no updates are made database.

References

- "Data Mining with SQL Server 2005" by ZhaoHui Tang and Jamie MacLennan (V 2005)
- SQL Server Analysis Services

  http://msdn2.microsoft.com/en-us/library/ms175609.aspx
- FIX: Error message when you try to use the *SqlClient* class in an ADO.NET 2.0- application to connect to an instance of SQL Server 2005: "New request is not al to start because it should come with valid transaction descriptor"

  http://support.microsoft.com/kb/916002
- Installing Sample Integration Services Packages

  http://msdn2.microsoft.com/en-us/library/ms160898.aspx

- How To: Create a Publication (RMO Programming)
  http://msdn2.microsoft.com/fr-fr/library/ms146941.aspx
- How To: Creating, Modifying, and Deleting Subscriptions (RMO Programming)
  http://msdn2.microsoft.com/fr-fr/library/ms147918.aspx
- How To: Synchronize a Pull Subscription (RMO Programming)
  http://msdn2.microsoft.com/en-us/library/ms147890.aspx
- How To: Define an Article (RMO Programming)
  http://msdn2.microsoft.com/fr-fr/library/ms146883.aspx
- How to: Create a Push Subscription (RMO Programming)
  http://msdn2.microsoft.com/en-US/library/ms146863.aspx
- How to: Synchronize a Push Subscription (RMO Programming)
  http://msdn2.microsoft.com/en-us/library/ms146910.aspx
- Multiple Active Result Sets (MARS) in SQL Server 2005
  http://msdn2.microsoft.com/en-us/library/ms345109.aspx
- Asynchronous Command Execution in ADO.NET 2.0
  http://www.aspspider.net/resources/Resource244.aspx
- Asynchronous Command Execution in ADO.NET 2.0
  http://msdn2.microsoft.com/en-us/library/ms379553(VS.80).aspx

apter Summary

- Server Management Objects (SMO) enables you programmatic access to all objects in the SQL Server service hierarchy. SMO enables you to perform tasks such as backup and restore of databases, integrity checks, and creation and scheduling of agent jobs.
- Replication Management Objects (RMO) enables you to programmatically control your replication topology. Even though two assemblies need to be referenced: *Microsoft.SqlServer .Rmo* and *Microsoft.SqlServer.Replication*, only one namespace, *Microsoft.SqlServer.Replication* needs to be referenced in the code.
- Analysis Management Objects (AMO) enables you to programmatically control your SQL Server Analysis Server (SSAS) objects, which include *cubes*, *dimensions*, and *mining structures*.
- Multiple Active Result Sets (MARS) is a new feature that enables you to perform multiple database operations using the same connection. This helps to avoid locking that you might have encountered in the past.

ata Integrity and Error Handling
SQL Server 2005

Validating data is one of the most basic tasks in software development. As a result, validation routines tend to be spread all over the application architecture. You are likely to find data validation in the following technologies:

- Microsoft Windows Forms applications
- ASP.NET pages
- JavaScript embedded in HTML
- Business components (such as .NET library assemblies or COM components)
- Databases

Often, there are too few validation routines in the database because many developers trust the validation that is done before the data actually arrives in the database. This chapter covers what type of validation you can perform in the database and how you can implement it, as well as the key aspects of error handling and how to send messages back to the calling application. All examples in this chapter reference objects in a schema called Test. You can create this schema simply by executing the statement "CREATE SCHEMA Test;".

Exam objectives in this chapter:
- Design code that validates input data and permissions.
- Design code that detects and reacts to errors.
- Design user-defined messages to communicate application events.

Before You Begin

To complete the lessons in this chapter, you must have:

- A general understanding of Transact-SQL, stored procedures, user-defined func and triggers.
- Microsoft SQL Server 2005 installed, as well as the SQL Server 2005 *Adventure* sample database.
- Microsoft Visual Studio 2005 or Microsoft Visual Basic or Visual C# 2005 Expres tion installed. You can download Express Editions from *http://msdn.microso /vstudio/express*.

son 1: **Validating Data and Permissions**

Estimated lesson time: 60 minutes

There are several ways of validating data integrity in the database. These can be grouped into two categories:

- **Declarative data integrity**   Declarative data integrity is a set of rules that are applied to a table and its columns using the CREATE TABLE or ALTER TABLE statement. Examples of declarative data integrity include constraints (such as check, foreign key, unique, and primary key constraints) and rules.
- **Procedural data integrity**   Procedural data integrity is implemented either by having a stored procedure validate the data prior to inserting it into a table or by having a trigger check the data before or after a data manipulation language (DML) statement (such as INSERT, UPDATE, or DELETE) is issued.

In general, declarative data integrity is the simplest integrity check to integrate because it requires very little development effort. This also makes it less likely to produce bugs because it contains less code than procedural data integrity. On the other hand, procedural data integrity typically enables more advanced integrity checks. The typical database application will need to use both declarative and procedural data integrity.

In this lesson, you start with declarative data integrity and then look at procedural data integrity. This lesson ends with a look at using Transact-SQL (T-SQL) to verify permissions and protection methods that you can implement to help prevent damage from SQL injection attacks.

lementing Declarative Data Integrity

Declarative data integrity is implemented using either constraints or rules. *Rules* are objects that are similar in function to check constraints. However, you should not use rules in your database because rules are a deprecated feature in SQL Server and will most likely be removed in a future release of the product. This leaves you with constraints. There are five types of *constraints*: PRIMARY KEY, UNIQUE, FOREIGN KEY, CHECK, and DEFAULT. Default constraints are only used to provide default values for columns and, therefore, they are not covered in this chapter.

Primary Key and Unique Constraints

Both *primary keys* and *unique constraints* identify a column or combination of columns that uniquely identifies a row in a table. This is enforced through the creation of a unique index; for example, an index that does not allow duplicate values. Because of this, a primary key and

unique constraints have the same size limitations as the key of an index—that is, the key
not contain more than 16 columns or 900 bytes of data.

IMPORTANT   Index key

All columns that are part of an index, excluding included columns, are referred to as the index'
Included columns are covered in detail in Chapter 7, "Optimizing SQL Server 2005 Performan

---

If nothing else is specified, the index that is created for a primary key is a *clustered* inde
the index for a unique constraint is a *non-clustered* index. However, you can change this b
ior by specifying it in the following constraint definition:

```
-- Primary key as a clustered index.
ALTER TABLE MyTable
ADD PRIMARY KEY (MyTableID);

-- Primary key as a nonclustered index.
ALTER TABLE MyTable
ADD PRIMARY KEY NONCLUSTERED (MyTableID);
```

Because primary keys and unique constraints are both constraints and indexes, you can
information about them in both the *sys.key_constraints* and *sys.indexes* catalog views.

IMPORTANT   Computed columns

You can create both primary key and unique constraints on computed columns.

Foreign Key Constraints

Foreign key constraints identify a column or combination of columns whose values must
in another column or combination of columns in the same table or in another table
same database. Foreign key constraints manage referential integrity between tables or w
a single table. To implement a foreign key constraint, you must follow these rules:

- The columns being referenced must have exactly the same data type (and collatio
  string columns) as the local columns.
- The columns being referenced must have a unique index created on them. This i
  cally implemented using either a primary key or a unique constraint.
- Because the foreign key must reference a unique index, the foreign key columns ha
  same size limitations as that of the primary key and unique constraints.

A new feature of SQL Server 2005 is that you can create foreign key constraints on computed columns. You can find information about which foreign key constraints exist in your database by querying the *sys.foreign_keys* and *sys.foreign_key_columns* catalog views.

Foreign keys are usually queried frequently in user queries and in joins, as well as when SQL Server needs to verify referential integrity when deleting or updating primary key rows. This means that foreign keys usually greatly benefit from being indexed. Indexing is covered in greater detail in Chapter 7.

When a foreign key constraint raises an error because of a delete or an update of the row that it references, the default reaction is to raise an error message and roll back the statement that violated the constraint. If this is not the result you want, you can change the default action for the foreign key to delete the referenced row, update the referenced column, or both. There are four actions to choose from:

- NO ACTION (the default; also available in earlier versions of SQL Server)
- SET NULL
- SET DEFAULT
- CASCADE (also available in SQL Server 2000)

An example implementation is shown below:

```
CREATE TABLE Test.Customers (
    CustomerID INT PRIMARY KEY
);

CREATE TABLE Test.Orders (
    OrderID INT PRIMARY KEY
    ,CustomerID INT NULL
        REFERENCES Test.Customers
            ON DELETE SET NULL
            ON UPDATE CASCADE
);
```

The default behavior of the foreign key is NO ACTION. If the foreign key finds an error and NO ACTION is specified, SQL Server rolls back the statement that violated the constraint and raises an error message.

SET NULL and SET DEFAULT each cause all the referenced values to be set to either NULL (for SET NULL) or DEFAULT (for SET DEFAULT—that is, the default defined on the column) instead of raising an error and rolling back the statement. In the relationship between the Orders and Customers tables shown in the code sample, if a customer is deleted, the CustomerID column is set to NULL for all orders belonging to that customer and no error message is sent to the calling application.

The CASCADE action causes SQL Server to delete referenced rows for a delete statement
DELETE) and update the referenced values (ON UPDATE) for an update statement. Usin
same code sample, if the CustomerID column is changed for a row in the Customers tabl
corresponding rows in the Orders table are updated with the same CustomerID to reflec
change. If ON DELETE CASCADE is specified for the foreign key constraint and a row i
Customers table is deleted, all referencing rows in the Orders table are deleted. This n
sound reasonable, but it might not be possible to implement CASCADE for all foreign key
straints because cyclic references are not supported. For example, in the following scrip
error will be raised when you try to add the foreign key FKCustomersLastOrder because i
introduce a cyclic reference. If a customer is deleted, all referencing orders must be del
and all customers referencing those orders through the LastOrderID column must be del

```
CREATE TABLE Test.Customers (
    CustomerID INT PRIMARY KEY
    ,LastOrderID INT NULL
);

CREATE TABLE Test.Orders (
    OrderID INT PRIMARY KEY
    ,CustomerID INT NOT NULL
        REFERENCES Test.Customers
            ON DELETE CASCADE
            ON UPDATE NO ACTION
);

ALTER TABLE Test.Customers ADD
    CONSTRAINT FKCustomersLastOrder
    FOREIGN KEY (LastOrderID)
        REFERENCES Test.Orders (OrderID)
            ON DELETE CASCADE
            ON UPDATE NO ACTION
```

In the previous example, consider what happens if a customer is deleted—all of the custo
orders are also deleted. This might be fine, but consider the following example:

```
CREATE TABLE Test.Countries (
    CountryID INT PRIMARY KEY
);

CREATE TABLE Test.Cities (
    CityID INT PRIMARY KEY
    ,CountryID INT NOT NULL
        REFERENCES Test.Countries
            ON DELETE CASCADE
);

CREATE TABLE Test.Customers (
```

```
    CustomerID INT PRIMARY KEY
    ,CityID INT NOT NULL
        REFERENCES Test.Cities
            ON DELETE CASCADE
);

CREATE TABLE Test.Orders (
    OrderID INT PRIMARY KEY
    ,CustomerID INT NOT NULL
        REFERENCES Test.Customers
            ON DELETE CASCADE
);
```

In this example, if you delete a country, all cities in that country, all customers in those cities, and all orders belonging to those customers are also deleted. Be cautious—you might be deleting more than you think. Consider someone executing the query "DELETE Test.Countries WHERE CountryID = 1;" from SQL Server Management Studio. The person might think he is deleting only one row in the Countries table when he might actually be deleting millions of rows. The time it takes to execute this delete statement depends on how many rows are being deleted. When it finishes, SQL Server Management Studio will return the following message:

```
(1 row(s) affected)
```

This message is returned even if millions of rows were deleted because the message tells us only how many rows were directly deleted by the executed statement. If you check the return value of the @@ROWCOUNT function, you will find that it also returns the value 1. There is nothing wrong with this behavior, but it is definitely something you should be aware of.

IMPORTANT Triggers

If you have defined foreign keys with cascading actions, any AFTER triggers on the affected tables will still be executed, but they will be executed after the whole chain of cascading actions has completed. If an error occurs while the cascading action chain is being executed, the entire chain will be rolled back and no AFTER triggers will be executed for that chain.

Check Constraints

Check constraints are a set of rules that must be validated prior to data being allowed into a table. Advantages to using check constraints include:

- They are simple to implement. (They are very similar to a WHERE clause.)
- They are checked automatically.
- They can improve performance.

A sample check constraint that verifies that a Product must have a positive price is shown

```
ALTER TABLE Products
ADD CHECK(Price >= 0.0);
```

The simplicity is a great advantage over using triggers. However, there are some disadvan
as well, such as the following:

- Error messages from check constraints are system-generated and cannot be replace
  a more user-friendly error message.
- A check constraint cannot "see" the previous value of a column. This means that it
  not be used for some types of data integrity rules, such as "Updates to the price col
  cannot increase or decrease the price by more than ten percent."

One important aspect of check constraints is that they reject values that evaluate to
rather than accepting values that evaluate to True. That might seem like the same thing, b
SQL Server, it is not. It creates an issue related to NULL values that is important to ack
edge. For example, if you have a check constraint that states that "Price > 10.0," you car
insert a NULL value into the Price column. This value is allowed because any compa
made with NULL returns NULL—it is neither True nor False. If you don't want the check
straint to allow the null value, you can either disallow NULL in the Price column by speci
the NOT NULL constraint for the column or by changing the check constraint to read "
> 10.0 AND Price IS NOT NULL".

Extending Check Constraints with User-Defined Functions   The expression in a c
constraint can contain most of the logic that you can use in a WHERE clause (including
AND, and OR). It can call scalar functions and reference other columns in the same table;
ever, it is not allowed to directly contain subqueries. Because you can write your own s
functions in either T-SQL or managed code, you can apply advanced logic inside your c
constraints and, through them, even use subqueries.

The following example creates a user-defined function called *fnIsPhoneNumber* in mar
code to verify that a string contains a valid U.S. phone number by applying a regular ex
sion. It then creates a table that calls the function from a check constraint to validate the p
numbers entered into the table. Because the PhoneNumber column allows NULL va
inserts and updates of nulls are allowed.

```
//C#
[SqlFunction(IsDeterministic = true, DataAccess=DataAccessKind.None)]
static public SqlBoolean fnIsPhoneNumber(SqlString phoneNumber)
{
    if(phoneNumber.IsNull){
        return SqlBoolean.Null;
    }
    return System.Text.RegularExpressions.Regex
```

```
        .IsMatch(phoneNumber.Value, @"^\([1-9]\d{2}\)\s?\d{3}\-\d{4}$");
}
```

```
'VB
<Microsoft.SqlServer.Server.SqlFunction(IsDeterministic:=True,
DataAccess:=DataAccessKind.None)> _
Public Shared Function fnIsPhoneNumber(ByVal phoneNumber As SqlString) As
    SqlBoolean
    If (phoneNumber.IsNull) Then
        Return SqlBoolean.Null
    End If
    Return System.Text.RegularExpressions.Regex.IsMatch(phoneNumber.Value,
        "^\([1-9]\d{2}\)\s?\d{3}\-\d{4}$")
End Function
```

The following T-SQL statement creates a table and check constraint that references the user-defined function:

```
CREATE TABLE Test.Contacts (
        ContactID INT IDENTITY PRIMARY KEY
       ,Name NVARCHAR(50) NOT NULL
       ,PhoneNumber VARCHAR(20) NULL
       ,CONSTRAINT CKContactsPhoneNumber
        CHECK(dbo.fnIsPhoneNumber(PhoneNumber) = CAST(1 AS BIT))
);
-- Allowed:
INSERT Test.Contacts (Name, PhoneNumber)
        VALUES ('Tobias', '(425)555-1111');
INSERT Test.Contacts (Name, PhoneNumber)
        VALUES ('Sara', NULL);
-- Disallowed, will raise an error:
INSERT Test.Contacts (Name, PhoneNumber)
        VALUES ('Bill', '(42)555-2222');
```

When is the check constraint executed? Only when needed. The query optimizer will decide to run the check constraint only if columns referenced in the check constraints are referenced by the executed DML statement. For inserts, this is always true because an insert always affects all columns (even if you insert a null value). For updates, the check constraint is only executed if a column contained in the check constraint is referenced by the update. If you turn on the Actual Execution Plan in SQL Server Management Studio and run the two update statements in the following code sample, you will get the execution plan shown in Figure 5-1. Notice the Assert icon in Query 2 of the execution plan; this is the execution of the check constraint. It is not executed for Query 1.

```
UPDATE Test.Contacts SET Name = Name;
UPDATE Test.Contacts SET PhoneNumber = PhoneNumber;
```

```
Query 1: Query cost (relative to the batch): 50%
UPDATE Test.Contacts SET Name = Name;
```

```
   T-SQL     ←——         Clustered Index Update          ←—        Top        ←—      Clustered Index Scan
  UPDATE              [AdventureWorks].[Test].[Contacts]...        Top          [AdventureWorks].[Test].[Contacts]...
  Cost: 0 %                    Cost: 75 %                       Cost: 0 %                  Cost: 25 %
```

```
Query 2: Query cost (relative to the batch): 50%
UPDATE Test.Contacts SET PhoneNumber = PhoneNumber;
```

```
   T-SQL     ←——      Assert      ←—     Clustered Index Update          ←—       Top       ←—    Clustered Index Sc
  UPDATE           Cost: 0 %           [AdventureWorks].[Test].[Contacts]...      Top         [AdventureWorks].[Test].[C
  Cost: 0 %                                   Cost: 75 %                       Cost: 0 %                Cost: 25 %
```

Figure 5-1   Actual Execution Plan in SQL Server Management Studio

BEST PRACTICES   Performance

Adding a lot of logic to your check constraints can hurt performance. A good approach is to add
necessary constraints and then run a performance test to verify that the performance is sufficce

Here you can see a very simple test that can be used to indicate whether you have the
straint in place:

```
DECLARE @i INT;
SET @i = 1;
WHILE(@i < 100000)
    BEGIN
        UPDATE Test.Contacts SET PhoneNumber = PhoneNumber;
        SET @i = @i + 1;
    END
```

In one test, this sample script took about six seconds to run with the constraint in p
Remember that there are only two rows in the table. By turning off the check const
(ALTER TABLE Test.Contacts NOCHECK CONSTRAINT CKContactsPhoneNumber;
same batch took about three seconds to run, which is half the length of time.

Using a User-Defined Function with a Subquery   It is possible to include subqueri
check constraints by putting them inside a user-defined function. This pratice can resu
poor performance because the subquery will be executed once for each row affected k
update or insert statement against the table. Using the previous example, you can also val
telephone area codes using a subquery. Store the allowed area codes in a separate table.

The following code sample is a user-defined function:

```
//C#
[SqlFunction(IsDeterministic = true,
DataAccess=DataAccessKind.Read)]
static public SqlBoolean fnIsPhoneNumber(SqlString phoneNumber)
{    if(phoneNumber.IsNull)
        return SqlBoolean.Null;
```

```
        if(!System.Text.RegularExpressions.Regex
        .IsMatch(phoneNumber.Value, @"^\([1-9]\d{2}\)\s?\d{3}\-\d{4}$")){
        return false;
}else{
    string areaCode = phoneNumber.Value.Substring(1,3);
    using(SqlConnection conn = new
SqlConnection(@"context
                                                connection=true;"))
    {
        using(SqlCommand cmd = conn.CreateCommand())
{
                cmd.CommandText = @"IF EXISTS(SELECT * FROM Test.AreaCodes
WHERE AreaCode = @AreaCode)
                                        SELECT CAST(1 AS BIT) AS Found
                            ELSE
                                        SELECT CAST(0 AS BIT) AS Found";
cmd.Parameters.Add("@AreaCode", SqlDbType.Char, 3)
.Value = areaCode;
                conn.Open();
                return (bool)cmd.ExecuteScalar();
        }
    }
}
}
```

```
'VB
<Microsoft.SqlServer.Server.SqlFunction(IsDeterministic:=True,
DataAccess:=DataAccessKind.None)> _
Public Shared Function fnIsPhoneNumber(ByVal phoneNumber As SqlString) As SqlBoolean
  If (phoneNumber.IsNull) Then
    Return SqlBoolean.Null
  End If

  If Not System.Text.RegularExpressions.Regex.IsMatch(phoneNumber.Value, "^\([1-
9]\d{2}\)\s?\d{3}\-\d{4}$") Then
    Return False
  Else

    Dim areaCode As String = phoneNumber.Value.Substring(1, 3)

    Using conn As SqlConnection = New SqlConnection("context connection=true;")
      Using cmd As SqlCommand = conn.CreateCommand()
        cmd.CommandText = "IF EXISTS(SELECT * FROM Test.AreaCodes " & _
          "WHERE AreaCode = @AreaCode) " & _
          "SELECT CAST(1 AS BIT) AS Found " & _
          "ELSE " & _
          "SELECT CAST(0 AS BIT) AS Found"
        cmd.Parameters.Add("@AreaCode", SqlDbType.Char, 3).Value = areaCode
        conn.Open()
        Return CType(cmd.ExecuteScalar(), Boolean)
```

```
      End Using
    End Using
  End If
End Function
```

The following T-SQL statement is used to create the table and check constraint referencin
user-defined function:

```
CREATE TABLE Test.AreaCodes (
    AreaCode CHAR(3) NOT NULL PRIMARY KEY
);
INSERT Test.AreaCodes (AreaCode) VALUES ('425');

CREATE TABLE Test.Contacts (
   ContactID INT IDENTITY PRIMARY KEY
   ,Name NVARCHAR(50) NOT NULL
   ,PhoneNumber VARCHAR(20) NULL
   ,CONSTRAINT CKContactsPhoneNumber
CHECK(dbo.fnIsPhoneNumber(PhoneNumber) = CAST(1 AS BIT))
);
-- Allowed:
INSERT Test.Contacts (Name, PhoneNumber)
    VALUES ('Tobias', '(425)555-1111');
INSERT Test.Contacts (Name, PhoneNumber)
    VALUES ('Sara', NULL);
-- Disallowed because of invalid area code:
INSERT Test.Contacts (Name, PhoneNumber)
    VALUES ('Bill', '(111)555-2222');
```

Here is another imporant consideration: while the check constraint is verified for update
inserts to the table, it is not verified when deleting rows in the table that the subquery
ences. The data that the check constraint validated against on the insert or update c
deleted without raising an error. For example, the following delete statement would not
in an error:

```
DELETE Test.AreaCode WHERE AreaCode = '425';
```

However, after executing the delete statement, the following update statement would ra
error:

```
UPDATE Test.Contact SET PhoneNumber = PhoneNumber;
```

This behavior is highly undesirable because it leads you to think you have the same prote
that you have with foreign keys, which protect you against the delete statement as well.
happened to the performance with the new constraint in place? The test script that previ
ran in six seconds with the constraint in place now runs in 33 seconds! In SQL Server
you can implement this logic by using a foreign key.

Using a Foreign Key with a Subquery   Next, you'll implement the test of the phone number as a combination of a check constraint and a foreign key constraint. You will use the first version of the user-defined function (the one without the subquery) together with a foreign key. There are a couple of things that you need to do to make it possible to create the foreign key shown in the example.

- The result of the expression in the AreaCode column must be of the same data type as the column that the foreign key references: CHAR(3). You do this by adding the *CAST* function to the AreaCode expression.

- The column must also be marked as "persisted." *PERSISTED* means that SQL Server will physically store the result of the computed column's expression in the data row instead of calculating it each time it is referenced in a query. It will be recalculated every time the column is updated. One of the reasons for this requirement is performance; you don't want SQL Server to execute the *SUBSTRING* function each time the foreign key needs to be validated.

How can you implement the foreign key? You want it to check the area code only against the Test.AreaCodes table, not the entire phone number. You do this by implementing a computed column that returns only the area code portion of the phone number. The following script creates the new version of the Test.Contacts, including the added foreign key constraint table:

```
CREATE TABLE Test.Contacts (
    ContactID INT IDENTITY PRIMARY KEY
    ,Name NVARCHAR(50) NOT NULL
    ,PhoneNumber VARCHAR(20) NULL
    ,CONSTRAINT CKContactsPhoneNumber
        CHECK(dbo.fnIsPhoneNumber(PhoneNumber) = 1)
    ,AreaCode AS CAST(SUBSTRING(PhoneNumber, 2, 3) AS CHAR(3)) PERSISTED
    ,CONSTRAINT FKContactsAreaCodes
        FOREIGN KEY (AreaCode)
        REFERENCES Test.AreaCodes
);
```

As you can see, the AreaCode column in the Contacts table is just a subset of the PhoneNumber column.

What will happen if you insert a null value into the PhoneNumber column? The *SUBSTRING* function will return null, and null is accepted by the foreign key and interpreted as a value that does not reference the AreaCodes table. So, what happened with the performance this time? It took eight seconds, about two seconds slower than the first example that did not validate that the area code existed, but 25 seconds faster than the check constraint with the subquery. Remember that the foreign key now also protects from deleting area codes that are referenced by phone numbers.

Implementing Check and Foreign Key Constraints to Improve Query Performance
check and foreign key constraints improve query performance? Don't they just prote
against invalid data, and in doing so, somewhat degrade performance? The answers to
questions are: "Yes, they can" and "No, they don't."

Because foreign keys and check constraints are declared rules, the query optimizer ca
them to create more efficient query plans. This usually involves skipping some part o
query plan because the optmizer can see that, for example, because of a foreign key cons
it is unnecessary to execute that particular part of the plan. The following code sample is a
ple example of this behavior with a foreign key constraint. Consider the following two t
and the foreign key *FKOrdersCustomers*:

```
CREATE TABLE Test.Customers (
   CustomerID INT PRIMARY KEY
);

CREATE TABLE Test.Orders (
   OrderID INT PRIMARY KEY
   ,CustomerID INT NOT NULL
       CONSTRAINT FKOrdersCustomers
           REFERENCES Test.Customers (CustomerID)
);
```

If you execute the following query against the two tables, the query returns all orders tha
a valid customer reference.

```
SELECT o.* FROM Test.Orders AS o
WHERE EXISTS (SELECT * FROM Test.Customers AS c
                   WHERE c.CustomerID = o.CustomerID);
```

The execution plan used by SQL Server to execute this query is shown in Figure 5-2. I
execution plan, you can see the Test.Customers table is not accessed; the only table
accessed is Test.Orders. This is because the query optimizer knows that the *exists* opera
this query is unnecessery to execute because the foreign key constraint requires all ord
refer to an existing customer, which is what is checked in the where clause.

Figure 5-2   Actual Execution Plan in SQL Server Management Studio

Turn off the foreign key by executing the following statement:

```
ALTER TABLE Test.Orders NOCHECK CONSTRAINT FKOrdersCustomers;
```

After executing the same query again, you get a new execution plan, as shown in Figure 5-3. The query optimizer executes the *exists* operator (in this case, the Nested Loops icon in the execution plan) to return only those orders that actually have a valid reference to the Test.Customers table. Because you turned off the foreign key constraint, SQL Server could not be sure that all orders actually have valid customer references and, therefore, had to execute the *exists* operator. For a large table, this can make a huge difference in execution time and input/output.

```
Query 1: Query cost (relative to the batch): 100%
SELECT o.* FROM Test.Orders AS o WHERE EXISTS (SELECT * FROM Test.Customers AS c WHERE c.Custom
```

```
    SELECT              Nested Loops              Clustered Index Scan
    Cost: 0 %           (Inner Join)          [Test].[Test].[Orders].[PK__Orders__
                        Cost: 0 %                     Cost: 50 %

                                               Clustered Index Seek
                                     [Test].[Test].[Customers].[PK__Cust..
                                                Cost: 50 %
```

Figure 5-3 Actual Execution Plan in SQL Server Management Studio

Now turn on the foreign key again. Execute the statement below and rerun the query.

```
ALTER TABLE Test.Orders
    CHECK CONSTRAINT FKOrdersCustomers;
```

After running the query this time, you end up with the same plan again—the plan shown in Figure 5-3. How can this be? You turned the constraint back on, so now SQL Server should be sure that all orders have valid customer references. However, this is actually *not* the case. This is because the foreign key is considered not trusted. A constraint that is *not trusted* (which only applies to foreign key and check constraints) is not taken into account by the query optimizer. Your foreign key is not trusted because, while it was turned off, someone could have inserted or updated an order row with an invalid CustomerID. Turning the constraint back on does not verify existing data. You can verify that the foreign key is indeed not trusted by executing the following query:

```
SELECT name, is_not_trusted FROM sys.foreign_keys
    WHERE name = 'FKOrdersCustomers';
```

You will find that the is_not_trusted column contains the value 1, indicating that the constraint is not trusted. To make it trusted, you need to modify the earlier "turn on" statement by adding the WITH CHECK option to it, as shown in the following example:

```
ALTER TABLE Test.Orders
    WITH CHECK
    CHECK CONSTRAINT FKOrdersCustomers;
```

This option tells SQL Server to verify that all rows in the table comply with the constraint to turning it back on. If any rows do not comply with the constraint, an error messa returned and the ALTER TABLE statement is rolled back.

If you execute the query again, you will find that you are back to the first execution plan one shown in Figure 5-2) and, if you execute the query against sys.foriegn_keys again, you find that the is_not_trusted column now returns the value 0. It is once again trusted.

One last note on this implementation: you can change the script for the Test.Customers Test.Orders tables, as shown in the following example, so that the CustomerID colun the Test.Orders table allows for null values—that is, it is not declared with the NOT N constraint.

```
CREATE TABLE Test.Customers (
    CustomerID INT PRIMARY KEY
);

CREATE TABLE Test.Orders (
    OrderID INT PRIMARY KEY
    ,CustomerID INT NULL
        CONSTRAINT FKOrdersCustomers
            REFERENCES Test.Customers (CustomerID)
);
```

If you execute the same query against this table structure, you get the execution plan from ure 5-3. This means that the *exists* operator is being executed even if you have the trusted eign key constraint in place. To persuade the query optimizer to go back to the plan that d execute the *exists* operator, you need to change the query, as shown in the following exar

```
SELECT o.* FROM Test.Orders AS o
WHERE EXISTS (SELECT * FROM Test.Customers AS c
                    WHERE c.CustomerID = o.CustomerID)
    AND o.CustomerID IS NOT NULL;
```

This informs SQL Server that no orders with a CustomerID of NULL should be retur which brings you back to the plan from Figure 5-2.

Implementing Procedural Data Integrity

Procedural data integrity is implemented either using T-SQL or managed code by cre stored procedures or triggers. Of course, user-defined functions can be used in both s procedures and triggers to simplify integrity checks. Because procedural logic usually req more coding than declarative integrity checks, it should be used when it is most appropr

Stored Procedures

Using stored procedures for most data access is a good practice. Here, you only look at what type of validations to perform in the stored procedure rather than in a constraint. The main advantage to performing data validation in stored procedures is that the stored procecure can validate a rule prior to starting work. This is interesting because, for example, instead of performing 50 percent of the work up front and then finding an error and having to roll back this work, you have the option of first checking whether everything is okay and only then issuing the transaction.

IMPORTANT   **Error probability**

This practice is only good for performance if there is a high probability of an error in the execution. If there is no error 99 percent of the time, it is usually slower to perform data validation before issuing the transaction instead of just checking things as you procede (which is what the check constraint would do). For a typical system, because there are many validation checks done prior to executing a stored procedure, the number of times that a stored procedure finds an error is relatively low.

In stored procedures, you should check the flow of the stored procedure's transaction. For example, if you have a stored procedure that inserts an order into the Orders table, followed by some order detail rows being inserted into the OrderDetails table, you should check at least the following in the stored procedure's code:

- Did the insertion into the *Order* table actually insert anything? If you issue an INSERT...SELECT statement, the SELECT could have returned 0 rows, which would cause the INSERT statement to insert 0 rows. This check could easily be done using the *@@ROWCOUNT* function.
- Did the insertion into the OrderDetails table actually insert at least one row? Here you could again apply the same type of check using the *@@ROWCOUNT* function.

DML Triggers

Triggers are very powerful, but should usually be implemented only when they are absolutely necessary. Triggers are executed after an insert, update, or delete statement has been completed. The problem with this is that if the first row being updated contains an error according to the trigger, all other rows that are updated by the update statement will be updated prior to the trigger being called. When the trigger finds the error, the entire update that activated the trigger will have to be rolled back by the trigger. In this case, a check constraint would have stopped the update as soon as the first error was encountered and would only need to roll back the rows updated prior to that row.

You might think that using an INSTEAD OF trigger would solve this problem, becau would be executed prior to the insert, update, or delete statement that is actually being cuted. However, this is not the case. With this type of trigger, you have another perform penalty to pay. Because these triggers also provide you with the inserted and deleted t against which to do your validation checks, SQL Server must "pretend" to issue the ir update, or delete statement to populate these tables with the data touched by the state performed. Then, if your trigger doesn't find any errors, you will have to issue a DML ment in the trigger to apply the changes found in the inserted or deleted table to the a table. This type of trigger would only be better than an AFTER trigger if most executions tain errors.

In SQL Server 2005, triggers populate the inserted and deleted tables in tempdb. This n cause tempdb to require more space and have to handle more load than it would withou use of the trigger. Another common use for triggers is to maintain denormalized (th redundantly stored) data. Note that the query optimizer cannot use code found in trigg create better execution plans.

BEST PRACTICES   Data validation in triggers

For data validation checks, use triggers only if you can't do the same check using constraints your stored procedure. For example, if you need to compare the value found before an upda with the new value being inserted, you might use a trigger.

Exam Tip   For this exam, knowing when constraints, AFTER triggers, and INSTEAD OF trigg are executed is important.

Using T-SQL to Verify Permissions

Usually, you manage permissions by applying them to securables using the GRANT, D and REVOKE statements. However, sometimes you might need to verify certain securit tings inside a stored procedure. There are several functions available to help you with th

One example is the *IS_MEMBER* function. It can check whether the current user is a r ber of a specific database role or Windows group. If you issue the statement SEL IS_MEMBER('BUILTIN\Administrators'), it will return 1 if the current user is a memb the local Windows Administrators group and 0 if she is not. If the current user is not lo on using Windows authentication, the function will return NULL. There are several tions of this type that you can use. More information about them is available from Server 2005 Books Online under the topic "Security Functions (Transact-SQL)" at *ht msdn2.microsoft.com/en-us/library/ms186236.aspx*.

Be aware that this function might behave differently depending on whether a user is logged on using Windows or whether he is logged on using SQL Server authentication. Another thing to note is that some of these functions take into account the use of the EXECUTE AS option/statement.

SQL Injection Attacks

If a text is sent directly to SQL Server and then executed, it is potentially at risk for a SQL injection attack. SQL injection attacks occur if someone "injects" SQL code (such as a DELETE statement or the execution of a stored procedure) into an application or a Web site and the SQL code is then executed. This attack can occur either inside SQL Server when dynamic SQL is used or on the client side if a string containing SQL is created and then sent directly to SQL Server.

On the client side, there are some precautions you take to prevent SQL injection attacks:

- Always use the most restrictive data type to store user input before sending it to SQL Server. For example, put numbers into numeric variables rather than string variables.
- Verify the format of strings on the client side prior to sending them to the server. Disallow all characters that are not needed inside the string.
- If you are using ADO.NET, always use SqlParameter objects to send parameters to both stored procedures and DML statements. Avoid adding parameters to SQL statements using string concatenation.
- Never show detailed error messages to the user. He or she can use these to decide how to write his or her SQL injection code!

The following examples show inappropriate and appropriate ways to add parameters to SQL statements using ADO.NET.

In this inappropriate method for adding parameters, notice that the *SqlCommand.Parameters* collection is not used:

```
//C#
...
SqlCommand cmd = new SqlCommand();
cmd.CommandText = @"SELECT * FROM ATable
                   WHERE Name = '" + txtName.Text + "';";
...
```

```
'VB
...
Dim cmd As SqlCommand = New SqlCommand()
cmd.CommandText = "SELECT * FROM ATable " & _
                  "WHERE Name = '" & txtName.Text & "';"
...
```

Following is the appropriate method for adding parameters, this time using the *Sql(mand.Parameters* collection:

```
//C#
...
SqlCommand cmd = new SqlCommand();
cmd.CommandText = "SELECT * FROM ATable WHERE Name = @Name;";
cmd.Parameters.Add("@Name", SqlDbType.NVarChar, 20).Value = txtName.Text;
...
```

```
'VB
...
Dim cmd As SqlCommand = New SqlCommand()
cmd.CommandText = "SELECT * FROM ATable WHERE Name = @Name;"
cmd.Parameters.Add("@Name", SqlDbType.NVarChar, 20).Value = txtName.Text
...
```

Consider the inappropriate way. If someone enters the string " ' ; *DELETE ATable; –*" int txtName text box , the SQL statement sent to SQL Server would be as follows:

```
SELECT * FROM ATable WHERE Name = ' ';DELETE ATable;--';
```

This code could (depending on foreign keys, triggers, etc.) cause the deletion of all rows i table ATable. If you used the *SqlParameter* object, the code sent to SQL Server would look the following:

```
SELECT * FROM ATable WHERE Name = ' '';DELETE ATable;--';
```

Notice the two single quotes (' '). Because ADO.NET automatically replaces one single q with two, the entire text entered into the text box is used in the WHERE clause instead of f ing a new statement.

On the SQL Server side, you should take the same precautions as on the client side, but take the following into account:

- Avoid using dynamic SQL (EXECUTE and sp_executesql).
- If you must use dynamic SQL, use sp_executesql with parameters rather than EXEC and string concatenation (basically, the same as with ADO.NET).
- Consider the use of the EXECUTE AS option for stored procedures to avoid havir give elevated permissions to users who use stored procedures that contain dynamic

Following are examples of inappropriate as well as appropriate use of dynamic SQL. Fir: the example of inappropriate use of Dynamic SQL, notice that all parameters are concater into the *@SQL* variable to define the SELECT statement.

```
/*
@OrderDate, @CustomerType and @IncludeOrders are parameters to this "stored procedure".
*/
```

```
DECLARE @SQL NVARCHAR(max);
SET @SQL = N'SELECT * FROM Sales.Customer AS c ';
IF(@IncludeOrders = 1)
    SET @SQL = @SQL + N'INNER JOIN Sales.SalesOrderHeader AS soh ON
                        soh.CustomerID = c.CustomerID
                        AND soh.OrderDate = ''' + @OrderDate + ''' ';
SET @SQL = @SQL + N'WHERE c.CustomerType = ''' + @CustomerType + ''';';
EXECUTE(@SQL);
```

In the example of appropriate use of Dynamic SQL which follows, notice that the parameter values are added to the statement using the sp_executesql system stored procedure:

```
/*
@OrderDate, @CustomerType and @IncludeOrders are parameters to this "stored procedure".
*/
DECLARE @SQL NVARCHAR(max);
SET @SQL = N'SELECT * FROM Sales.Customer AS c ';
IF(@IncludeOrders = 1)
    SET @SQL = @SQL + N'INNER JOIN Sales.SalesOrderHeader AS soh ON
                        soh.CustomerID = c.CustomerID
                        AND soh.OrderDate = @OrderDate ';
SET @SQL = @SQL + N'WHERE c.CustomerType = @CustomerType;';
EXEC sp_executesql
    @stmt = @SQL
    ,@params = N'@OrderDate DATETIME, @CustomerType NCHAR(1)'
    ,@OrderDate = @OrderDate
    ,@CustomerType = @CustomerType
```

The difference between these statements is the same as was shown previously in the ADO.NET example. Here, sp_executesql adds the parameters correctly and, for example, replaces the single quotes with two single quotes. Because the INNER JOIN is an expression rather than a parameter, it has to be added using concatenation. However, the @OrderDate parameter that is used to filter the JOIN expression can be added as a parameter using sp_executesql. Note that sp_executesql will not raise an error if the join is not added to the query, even if the @OrderDate parameter would then be missing.

: Comparing Procedural and Declarative Data Validation
formance

In this lab, you create two similar tables with a specific data validation rule. You apply using a trigger in one table and a check constraint in the other table and compare results.

IMPORTANT Lab requirements

You will need to have SQL Server installed before you can complete this exercise. Refer to t Introduction for setup instructions.

▶ **Exercise 1: Apply a Data Validation Rule to Tables**

In this exercise, you create two tables. One table will use a trigger to validate the rule, ar other table will use a check constraint. You then compare the insert performance by ins 100,000 rows that adhere to the rule and 100,000 rows that do not adhere to the rule. Th is very simple: the column "Name" must contain more than five characters. You ins 100,000 rows in one insert statement by issuing an INSERT...SELECT. You can also try to each insert separately; the result will be very different!

1. Open Microsoft SQL Server Management Studio and connect to an instance o Server 2005.

2. In a new query window, type and execute the following SQL statements to crea *TestDB* database and the Test schema:

```
CREATE DATABASE TestDB;
GO
USE TestDB;
GO
CREATE SCHEMA Test;
GO
```

Note the results of the creation of the *TestDB* database in Figure 5-4.

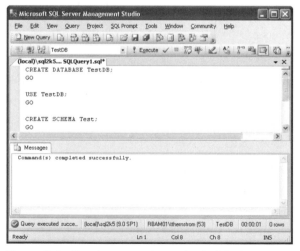

Figure 5-4 Database creation script in SQL Server Management Studio

3. In a new query window, type and execute the following SQL statements to create the Test.TableWithCheckConstraint (including its check constraint) and Test.TableWith-Trigger tables, as well as the trigger on Test.TableWithTrigger:

```
USE TestDB;
GO
CREATE TABLE Test.TableWithCheckConstraint (
    Name NVARCHAR(50) NOT NULL CHECK(LEN(Name) > 5)
);
CREATE TABLE Test.TableWithTrigger (
    Name NVARCHAR(50) NOT NULL
);
GO
CREATE TRIGGER TableWithTriggerTestTrigger ON Test.TableWithTrigger
AFTER INSERT, UPDATE
AS
BEGIN
    SET NOCOUNT ON;
    IF EXISTS (SELECT * FROM inserted
                    WHERE LEN(Name) <= 5)
        BEGIN
                RAISERROR('Too short name found, rolling back t.', 16, 1);
                ROLLBACK TRAN;
        END
END
```

4. Open a new query window and execute the following SQL statements to create a table containing 100,000 rows. This table will be used to issue the INSERT...SELECT statement against the previously created tables. This query might take several minutes to finish executing.

```
USE TestDB;
GO
CREATE TABLE Test.Rows100000 (
    Row INT NOT NULL
);
INSERT Test.Rows100000 (Row)
    SELECT TOP(100000)
            ROW_NUMBER() OVER (ORDER BY s1.message_id)
    FROM sys.messages AS s1
    CROSS JOIN sys.messages AS s2;
```

5. Open a new query window, execute the following INSERT...SELECT statement against the TableWithCheckConstraint table three times, and record the execution time of the last execution. In this step, you insert data that adheres to the rule—that is, is more than five characters long:

```
USE TestDB;
GO
DECLARE @Start DATETIME;
```

```
SET @Start = CURRENT_TIMESTAMP;
INSERT Test.TableWithCheckConstraint (Name)
   SELECT 'Name that is OK' FROM Test.Rows100000
SELECT DATEDIFF(ms, @Start, CURRENT_TIMESTAMP);
```

6. Clear the content of the query window, execute the following INSERT...SELECT
   ment against the TableWithTrigger table three times, and record the execution ti
   the last execution. In this step, you insert data that adheres to the rule—that is, is
   than five characters long:

```
DECLARE @Start DATETIME;
SET @Start = CURRENT_TIMESTAMP;
INSERT Test.TableWithTrigger (Name)
   SELECT 'Name that is OK' FROM Test.Rows100000
SELECT DATEDIFF(ms, @Start, CURRENT_TIMESTAMP);
```

   You should notice a small difference in execution time between steps 5 and 6.
   test machine, it was roughly 15 percent slower to insert the data into the table
   the trigger.

7. Try to insert data that does not adhere to the rule. Start by clearing the query wi
   and executing the following INSERT...SELECT statement against the Table
   CheckConstrain table only once. Because you get an error on the first inserted
   the check constraint stops the statement execution and rolls back the state
   immediately.

```
INSERT Test.TableWithCheckConstraint (Name)
   SELECT 'Short' FROM Test.Rows100000;
```

8. Finally, try to insert data that does not adhere to the rule against the table with th
   ger. Clear the query window and execute the following INSERT...SELECT state
   against the TableWithTrigger table only once. How does this differ from the res
   step 7?

```
INSERT Test.TableWithTrigger (Name)
   SELECT 'Short' FROM Test.Rows100000;
```

9. Type and execute the following SQL statement to clean up after this exercise:

```
USE master;
DROP DATABASE TestDB;
```

Quick Check

1. Which constraints can become "not trusted"?
2. Can the use of foreign key constraints result in increased performance for some SELECT statements?
3. Can the use of triggers result in increased performance for some SELECT statements?
4. Which type of data integrity results in more code needing to be written: declarative data integrity or procedural data integrity?

Quick Check Answers

1. Foreign key constraints and check constraints can become "not trusted."
2. Yes, for some SELECT statements, the use of foreign key constraints can result in increased performance. This is because the query optimizer can see the definition of the foreign key constraint and use it to optimize the produced execution plan.
3. No, the use of triggers will not result in increased performance for any SELECT statements. This is because triggers contain procedural code so the optimizer does not use them to optimize execution plans.
4. Procedural data integrity results in more code needing to be written.

Lesson 2: Detecting and Reacting to Errors

Estimated lesson time: 30 minutes

Implementing appropriate error handling is one of the most important tasks when devel
T-SQL scripts, stored procedures, and triggers. In this case, appropriate error handling r
that some routines (usually read-only) might not require the same error handling that
important transactional routines require.

Techniques for Detecting and Reacting to Errors

There are three ways to detect and react to errors in SQL Server 2005:

- Querying the @@ERROR function.
- Setting the XACT_ABORT session option.
- Implementing structured error handling using *TRY...CATCH* blocks.

The ability to use structured error handling is a new feature in SQL Server 2005 and m
less renders the first two ways obsolete. However, you will still find code that uses the fir
techniques.

Error Handling with @@ERROR

The @@ERROR function returns the ID (number) of the error message that was caused
previously executed statement. If the previous statement did not cause an error, the fur
will return 0. Because it only checks the previous statement, you will need to implen
check against this function after every statement that can cause an error to occur—that is
almost every statement. Below you can see an example of a transaction using the @@E
function to handle errors.

```
BEGIN TRAN;
    INSERT T1 (Col) VALUES (1);
    IF(@@ERROR <> 0)
        GOTO ErrorHandler;
    INSERT T1 (Col) VALUES (2);
    IF(@@ERROR <> 0)
        GOTO ErrorHandler;
    INSERT T1 (Col) VALUES (3);
    IF(@@ERROR <> 0)
        GOTO ErrorHandler;
COMMIT TRAN;
RETURN;

ErrorHandler:
```

```
ROLLBACK TRAN;
RETURN;
```

As you can see, the code gets polluted by all the checks against the *@@ERROR* function. This type of error handling renders code that is hard to read and maintain and is also prone to bugs. One problem is that it is easy to forget a check against the *@@ERROR* function and another problem is the use of GOTO statements to transfer control to the error handling part of our script. As you know, GOTO isn't exactly your friend if you want to develop maintainable code.

Error Handling with XACT_ABORT

The XACT_ABORT session option is another way to handle errors. Consider the following batch against the table "CREATE TABLE Test.ATable (ID INT PRIMARY KEY);" with the XACT_ABORT option set to OFF (the default setting).

```
SET XACT_ABORT OFF;
BEGIN TRAN;
   INSERT Test.ATable (ID) VALUES (1);
INSERT Test.ATable (ID) VALUES (1); -- Fails!
   INSERT Test.ATable (ID) VALUES (2); -- Execution continues.
COMMIT TRAN;
```

The result is:

- INSERT #1: Succeeds.
- INSERT #2: Fails with error 2627, primary key constraint violation, and the statement (that is, only the insert itself) is rolled back.
- INSERT #3: Succeeds.
- The transaction is committed.

After this batch has completed, the table will contain two rows, one with the value 1, and another one with the value 2. This is the default behavior in SQL Server: a statement that generates an error causes the statement itself to be rolled back, but any open user-defined transaction stays open and the batch continues execution.

Change the batch slightly by adding the SET XACT_ABORT ON; option at the beginning of the batch. (Note that this is a session-level option.)

```
SET XACT_ABORT ON;
BEGIN TRAN;
   INSERT Test.ATable (ID) VALUES (1);
   INSERT Test.ATable (ID) VALUES (1); -- Fails!
   INSERT Test.ATable (ID) VALUES (2); -- Not executed.
COMMIT TRAN;
```

When you execute this batch, the result is different:

- INSERT #1: Succeeds.
- INSERT #2: Fails with error 2627, primary key constraint violation, the entire tra
  tion is rolled back, and the execution of the batch is terminated.

Even though this behavior is simple and crude, it is actually very useful. Se
XACT_ABORT ON simply means: "If anything goes wrong, stop execution and roll bac
open transaction (in the current connection)." So, if you don't need to react to the erro
it to an error table, for example) in the database, you can make good use o
XACT_ABORT ON setting. The obvious advantage with this solution is ease of use. I
thing goes wrong, you know that the batch will be terminated and the transaction r
back. Note that you can turn off XACT_ABORT temporarily in, for example, a stored p
dure, and then turn it back on again.

The setting actually exists specifically for use with distributed transactions involving
database instances, such as through linked servers. These transactions requir
XACT_ABORT setting to be set to ON, basically because they have a higher risk of failing
to network problems, for example).

If you use XACT_ABORT ON with stored procedures, the entire batch, not only the store
cedure that caused the error, will still stop execution and the transaction will be rolled

Here is an example of XACT_ABORT ON with stored procedures against the same table
ture as in the previous examples. Note that the XACT_ABORT option is set to OFF and
turned on in the stored procedure:

```
CREATE PROC Test.sp1
AS
BEGIN
    SET XACT_ABORT ON;
    BEGIN TRAN;
        INSERT Test.ATable (ID) VALUES (1);
    COMMIT TRAN;
END
GO
TRUNCAT TABLE Test.ATable;
SET XACT_ABORT OFF;
BEGIN TRAN;
    EXEC Test.sp1;
    EXEC Test.sp1; -- Fails!
    EXEC Test.sp1; -- Not executed.
COMMIT TRAN;
```

The result of the previous batch is:

- Test.sp1 Execution #1: Succeeds.
- Test.sp1 Execution #2: Fails with error 2627, primary key constraint violation, the entire transaction is rolled back, and the execution of the batch is terminated.

Structured Error Handling Using TRY/CATCH

The ability to use *try/catch* type error handling in SQL Server 2005 is a great improvement to the product. This makes it simple to handle errors without polluting your code with lots of "IF @@ERROR" statements. This is brief explanation of the *try/catch*-block implementation in SQL Server 2005:

- Any error raised in the *try* block will cause control to jump to the associated catch block. The error will not be sent to the client application.
- An error raised in the *catch* block will cause the error to be sent to the calling application and the batch will continue execution. However, if the *try/catch* block is nested inside another *try* block, control will jump to the closest outer *catch* block. Note that the behavior relating to nested *try/catch* blocks is typical for nested stored procedures.

  This is dependent on the error's severity level. If the severity level is 20 or greater, SQL Server will terminate the connection, stop execution of the batch, and roll back any open transaction. Errors with severity levels of 20 or greater are referred to as fatal errors. This behavior is not new to SQL Server 2005; the same behavior can be found in earlier versions of the product.

- *Try/catch* blocks cannot be split into multiple batches; the *catch* block must directly follow the *try* block.
- In the *catch* block, the transaction can either be committed or rolled back (or left alone).
- Execution of a RAISERROR statement inside a *try* block transfers control to the *catch* block.

  Next, look at an example *try/catch* block (referring to the same Test.ATable table as before):

```
TRUNCATE TABLE Test.ATable;
BEGIN TRY
    BEGIN TRAN;
        INSERT Test.ATable (ID) VALUES (1);
        INSERT Test.ATable (ID) VALUES (1); -- Fails!
        INSERT Test.ATable (ID) VALUES (2);
    COMMIT TRAN;
END TRY
BEGIN CATCH
    ROLLBACK TRAN;
```

```
    RAISERROR('An error occurred! ', 16, 1);
END CATCH
```

The result of this batch is:

- INSERT #1: Succeeds.
- INSERT #2: Fails with error 2627, primary key constraint violation, and the state (that is, only the insert itself) is rolled back. No error message is sent to the ca application.
- Execution is transferred to the *catch* block.
- The transaction is rolled back.
- The RAISERROR statement is executed and the message is sent to the calling application.
- Any statements following the *catch* block are also executed.

One of the important aspects that you can see in the above sequence of events is that no sage is sent to the calling application until the RAISERROR statement is executed in the block. If you would remove the RAISERROR statement from the above batch, *no error w* be sent to the calling application. It would not be aware that an error was encountered. sider the following example:

```
TRUNCATE TABLE Test.ATable;
BEGIN TRY
    INSERT Test.ATable (ID) VALUES (1);
END TRY
BEGIN CATCH
    -- Doing nothing here :-)
END CATCH
```

If an error is encountered in the *try* block, no error message will be returned to the clier

How do you return the actual error message to the client when inside the *catch* block? L tunately, there isn't any command in SQL Server 2005 to raise exactly the same error a caught by the *catch* block. You can, however, fetch the information about the error usin following functions:

- *ERROR_NUMBER()*
- *ERROR_MESSAGE()*
- *ERROR_SEVERITY()*
- *ERROR_STATE()*

    This function can return a state of 0 for some system errors. If you want to raise the error again using RAISERROR, the 0 has to be replaced with a value between 1 and

- *ERROR_PROCEDURE()*

  Returns the name of the stored procedure, trigger, or function where the error was raised. This function returns NULL if the error was not raised inside of any of these object types.

- *ERROR_LINE()*

  These functions can be used anywhere inside of a *catch* block (outside of a *catch* block, all functions return NULL). You can also execute a stored procedure inside the *catch* block and use the functions inside of that stored procedure to raise the error again. To re-raise the original error, you will need to copy the return values from the above functions into variables and pass the variables to the RAISERROR statement.

One issue you will run into here is that you are not allowed to raise system error messages using RAISERROR. This means that you cannot specify the same error number as the original message; you can only specify the same message text. When executing RAISERROR without specifying an error number, the number will be set to 50000. This can be a problem if you have existing client-side code that checks the error number returned from a SQL execution and reacts to it. In the following example, you send the original error number at the end of the error message text. This is not a perfect solution, but at least it makes it possible to fetch the original error number on the client side if it is required.

```
TRUNCATE TABLE Test.ATable;
BEGIN TRY
    BEGIN TRAN;
        INSERT Test.ATable (ID) VALUES (1);
        INSERT Test.ATable (ID) VALUES (1); -- Fails!
    COMMIT TRAN;
END TRY
BEGIN CATCH
    -- Rollback the tran. and free locks held.
    ROLLBACK TRAN;

    -- Copy the error details to local variables.
    DECLARE @ErrMessage NVARCHAR(2047)
        ,@ErrNumber INT
        ,@ErrSeverity TINYINT
        ,@ErrState TINYINT;
    SELECT @ErrMessage = ERROR_MESSAGE() + N' #' +
            CAST(ERROR_NUMBER() AS NVARCHAR(10))
        ,@ErrNumber = ERROR_NUMBER()
        ,@ErrSeverity = ERROR_SEVERITY()
        ,@ErrState = ERROR_STATE();

    -- Re-raise the original error (or atlest something resembling it...)
    RAISERROR(@ErrMessage, @ErrSeverity, @ErrState);
END CATCH
```

There is one thing in particular to be aware of when executing this example. The error me returned from this execution will look like this in SQL Server Management Studio:

```
Msg 50000, Level 14, State 1, Line 25
Violation of PRIMARY KEY constraint 'PK__ATable__5AEE82B9'. Cannot insert duplicate key
object 'Test.ATable'. #2627
```

The original error number has been appended to the end of the error message. The line ber (Line) from which this message says the error originated is not the line which proc the original error, but rather the line in the *catch* block where you execute the RAISEI statement. You will run into this same issue if you use a stored procedure in the *catch* blc raise the error message again, in which case the line number would refer to the line ir stored procedure and the procedure part of the error message would be the name o stored procedure and not the stored procedure that you executed.

The SQL Server 2005 implementation of *try/catch* has some limitations compared to t *try/catch* implementations (as seen in C++, C#, J#, Java, JScript, Visual Basic .NET, and sc

- Only one *catch* block per *try* block is supported.
- There is no support for a *finally* block.
- There is no command to rethrow a caught error.

There are two more functions related to error handling and transactions. First, th *@@TRANCOUNT* function returns the current nesting level in terms of transactions. If ye not in a transaction, it returns 0; if you are nested in one, it returns 1; nested inside t returns 2, and so on. The second function is new to SQL Server 2005 and is c *XACT_STATE()*. This function returns -1, 0, or 1, which refer to the state of the current defined transaction.

- -1 (*uncommittable*) means that there is an open user-defined transaction. How because of the type of error that has occurred, this transaction cannot be commit must be rolled back. There are two other specific instances when *XACT_STATE(* return -1: one is inside of a trigger (which cannot commit a transaction) and the one is if you specified *SET XACT_ABORT ON*.
- 0 (no transaction) means that there is no open user-defined transaction.
- 1 (*committable*) means that there is an open user-defined transaction that can be committed or rolled back.

SET XACT_ABORT ON; behaves differently when you are inside a *try* block. The differe simply that, instead of terminating the batch and rolling back the transaction, control is ferred to the *catch* block, but the transaction is left uncommittable or doomed (tl *XACT_STATE()* returns -1). This means that if *XACT_ABORT* is turned on, you cannot cc transactions inside a *catch* block.

Exam Tip For this exam, it is important to understand the different reactions that SQL Server will have to errors depending on the setting of *SET XACT_ABORT*, as well as the use or non-use of *try/ catch* blocks.

ating User-Defined Messages

Previously in this lesson, you used the RAISERROR statement to send error messages back to the client application. When you used RAISERROR, you provided it with an error message in the form of a string, a severity level, and a state. If you issue the same error messages from different stored procedures or triggers, you might be interested in storing the messages in SQL Server to reuse them. You can create, modify, and delete error messages using the following three system-stored procedures:

- *sp_addmessage*
- *sp_altermessage*
- *sp_dropmessage*

The error messages that you create must have a message number of 50001 or higher. Messages are created using the sp_addmessage procedure. You can see which messages are already defined by querying the sys.messages catalog view.

IMPORTANT Storage of messages

These messages are stored in the *msdb* database. If you move a database to a new server, you must make sure that you create the messages used by this database on the new server.

The following is an example of creating a new user-defined message:

```
EXEC sp_addmessage @msgnum = 50001
,@severity = 16
  ,@msgtext = N'A customer named %s already exists with the ID %d.'
  ,@lang = 'us_english';
```

This message will get the message number 50001, severity level 16, and the text specified in the @msgtext parameter as its message text. The message is also specified to be in the language us_english. There are two placeholders, %s and %d. The placeholders can be populated by adding extra parameters to the end of the *RAISERROR* statement. Here is an example that raises the previous error and populates the placeholders:

```
RAISERROR(50001, 16, 1, 'Woodgrove Bank', 12902);
```

The message returned from the statement will look like this in SQL Server Manage
Studio:

```
Msg 50001, Level 16, State 1, Line 1
A customer named Woodgrove Bank already exists with the ID 12902.
```

The first placeholder is replaced by the first parameter, the second placeholder by th
ond parameter, and so on; a maximum of 20 placeholders is supported. The name
placeholder is not arbitrary; it specifies what type of parameter it can be replaced b
how it should be displayed. In this example, *%s* and *%d* are used, where *%s* means th
parameter must be a string and *%d* means that it must be an integer (signed). For more
mation about the definition of these placeholders, look up the RAISERROR statem
Books Online.

Creating Localized User-Defined Messages

In the previous example, the message was created for the *us_english* language. You can al
ate additional versions of this error message for other languages. The following examp
ates the same error message for the Swedish language:

```
EXEC sp_addmessage @msgnum = 50001
,@severity = 16
    ,@msgtext = N'Kunden %1! existerar redan med ID-nummer %2!.'
    ,@lang = 'Svenska';
```

The error message that is displayed depends on the current connection's language se
Consider the following batch:

```
SET LANGUAGE us_english;
RAISERROR(50001, 16, 1, 'Woodgrove Bank', 12902);

SET LANGUAGE Svenska;
RAISERROR(50001, 16, 1, 'Woodgrove Bank', 12902);

SET LANGUAGE Magyar;
RAISERROR(50001, 16, 1, 'Woodgrove Bank', 12902);
```

The first RAISERROR will display the English error message, and the second one will d
the Swedish error message. The last example changes the language to Magyar (Hung
but because there is no message defined for Hungarian, the *us_english* message will be s
A *us_english* version of the message is required as the base error message; you can only
messages in other languages after you first create a *us_english* version of the error mess
you look at the message texts specified for *us_english* and Swedish, you will see that the
holders are different.

- *us_english*: "A customer named *%s* already exists with the ID *%d*."
- Swedish: "Kunden *%1!* existerar redan med ID-nummer *%2!*"

In the localized version, the placeholders refer to the placeholders in the *us_english* message. The placeholder *%1!* refers to the first (1) placeholder in the English message (in this case, *%s*), and the placeholder *%2!* refers to the second one (*%d*). This is because the placeholders might need to be reordered when translating them to a language other than English (although we didn't need to do that for the Swedish version of this error message). You can find the available languages in the catalog view *sys.syslanguages*.

Writing Error Messages to the Windows Event Log

You can specify that error messages should be written to the Windows event log in three ways:

- By adding the parameter *@with_log* = *'true'* when creating a user-defined message using *sp_addmessage*.
- By adding the *WITH LOG* option at the end of a *RAISERROR* statement.
- By executing the *xp_logevent* extended stored procedure.

If you specify the *@with_log* = *'true'* parameter when you add the *us_english* version of an error message using *sp_addmessage*, the error message will always be written to the Windows event log when it is raised using the RAISERROR statement. If you add the WITH LOG option to the RAISERROR statement (as in the following example), only that specific execution of RAISERROR will be written to the Windows event log. See Figure 5-5 for an example.

```
RAISERROR(50001, 16, 1, 'Woodgrove Bank', 12902) WITH LOG;
```

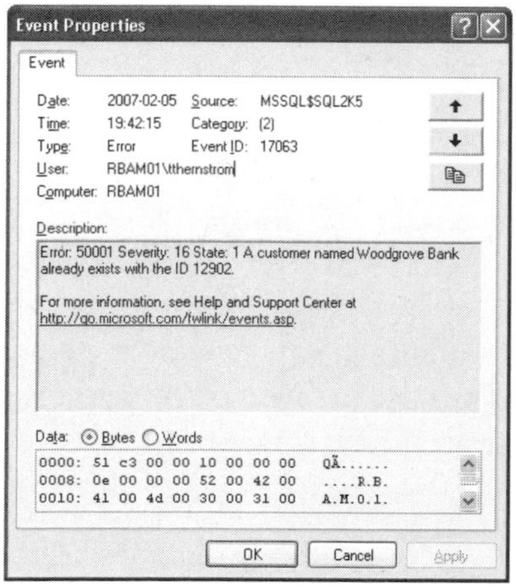

Figure 5-5 Error message from Windows Event Viewer

Another way to write messages to the Windows event log is by executing the *xp_log* extended stored procedure. The difference from using *RAISERROR ... WITH LOG* is *xp_logevent* does not send any error message back to the client application; it only write message to the Windows event log.

Lab: Using Try/Catch Blocks

In this lab, you create a stored procedure that uses a *try/catch* block to insert or update in a table. The first exercise will provide an example of unwanted behavior that can occu second exercise provides a fix to the problems found in the first exercise.

IMPORTANT   Lab requirements

You will need to have SQL Server installed before you can complete this exercise. Refer to 1 Introduction for setup instructions.

▶ **Exercise 1: Create an Initial Stored Procedure**

In this exercise, you will execute a batch to either insert or update a customer in the Tes tomers table, depending on whether the customer already exists.

1. Open SQL Server Management Studio and connect to an instance of SQL Server

2. In a new query window, type and execute the following SQL statements to crea *TestDB* database, the Test schema, and the Test.Customers table. (There is a chec straint on the Name column that specifies that the name must be at least five chan long.)

```
CREATE DATABASE TestDB;
GO
USE TestDB;
GO
CREATE SCHEMA Test;
GO
CREATE TABLE Test.Customers ( CustomerID INT PRIMARY KEY ,Name NVARCHAR(50) NOT N
CHECK(LEN(Name) > 5)
);
```

3. Open a new query window and execute the following SQL statements to create stored procedure. This stored procedure will be used to save a customer to the da by either inserting or updating data in the Test.Customers table.

```
USE TestDB;
GO
CREATE PROC Test.spCustomerSave
@CustomerID INT
,@Name NVARCHAR(50)
AS
```

```
BEGIN
    SET NOCOUNT ON;
    BEGIN TRAN;
        BEGIN TRY
            INSERT Test.Customers (CustomerID, Name)
                VALUES (@CustomerID, @Name);
        END TRY
        BEGIN CATCH
            UPDATE Test.Customers SET
                Name = @Name
            WHERE CustomerID = @CustomerID;
        END CATCH
    COMMIT TRAN;
END
```

4. Open a new query window and execute the following SQL statements to test the stored procedure.

```
USE TestDB;
GO
EXEC Test.spCustomerSave @CustomerID = 1, @Name = 'Woodgrove Bank';
SELECT * FROM Test.Customers;
GO
EXEC Test.spCustomerSave @CustomerID = 1, @Name = 'Contoso';
SELECT * FROM Test.Customers;
GO
EXEC Test.spCustomerSave @CustomerID = 1, @Name = '1';
SELECT * FROM Test.Customers;
GO
EXEC Test.spCustomerSave @CustomerID = 2, @Name = '2';
SELECT * FROM Test.Customers;
```

The last two executions try to update (the third one) and insert (the fourth one) a new customer with a name that is too short according to the check constraint on the Name column. The update will fail with an error message, but the insert will not; however, it will not be inserted.

► **Exercise 2: Create an Initial Try/Catch Block**

In this exercise, you will execute a batch to either insert or update a customer in the Test.Customers table depending on whether the customer already exists.

1. Open a new query window and execute the following SQL statements to alter the stored procedure created in Exercise 1, "Create an Initial Stored Procedure." Provide error checking for both the insert and the update. Also check whether the transaction should be committed or rolled back at the end of the stored procedure.

```
USE TestDB;
GO
ALTER PROC Test.spCustomerSave
```

```
@CustomerID INT
,@Name NVARCHAR(50)
AS
BEGIN
    SET NOCOUNT ON;
    SET XACT_ABORT OFF;
    BEGIN TRAN;
        BEGIN TRY
            INSERT Test.Customers (CustomerID, Name)
                VALUES (@CustomerID, @Name);
        END TRY
        BEGIN CATCH
            -- Only update if the error from the insert
            -- is a PK violation.
            IF(ERROR_NUMBER() = 2627)
                BEGIN
                    -- If the UPDATE fails, stop execution
                    -- and rollback tran.
                    SET XACT_ABORT ON;
                    UPDATE Test.Customers SET
                        Name = @Name
                    WHERE CustomerID = @CustomerID;
                    SET XACT_ABORT OFF;
                END
            ELSE
                BEGIN
                    ROLLBACK TRAN;
                    -- Reraise the orginal error message.
                    DECLARE @Msg NVARCHAR(2047)
                        ,@Severity INT
                        ,@State INT;
                    SET @Msg = ERROR_MESSAGE();
                    SET @Severity = ERROR_SEVERITY();
                    SET @State = CASE ERROR_STATE() WHEN 0 THEN 1
                            ELSE ERROR_STATE() END;

                    RAISERROR(@Msg, @Severity, @State);
                    -- Exit the stored procedure.
                    RETURN(1);
                END
        END CATCH
    COMMIT TRAN; END
```

2. Empty the Test.Customers table by executing the TRUNCATE TABLE statement b
    and then execute the stored procedure using the following four examples. Rur
    stored procedure execution separately.

```
USE TestDB;
TRUNCATE TABLE Test.Customers;
EXEC Test.spCustomerSave @CustomerID = 1, @Name = 'Woodgrove Bank';
```

```
SELECT * FROM Test.Customers;
EXEC Test.spCustomerSave @CustomerID = 1, @Name = 'Contoso';
SELECT * FROM Test.Customers;
EXEC Test.spCustomerSave @CustomerID = 1, @Name = '1';
EXEC Test.spCustomerSave @CustomerID = 2, @Name = '2';
```

The last two executions try to update (the third one) and insert (the fourth one) a new customer with a name that is too short according to the check constraint on the Name column, and both receive an error message.

3. To clean up after this exercise, close all open query windows in SQL Server Management Studio, open a new query window, and execute the SQL statements below:

```
USE master;
DROP DATABASE TestDB;
```

Quick Check

1. How can you tell SQL Server to roll back a transaction in case an error occurs?
2. What is the difference between the functions @@ERROR and ERROR_NUMBER()?
3. Can you commit a transaction in the *catch* block?

Quick Check Answers

1. In the event of an error that might keep a transaction from completing successfully, you can tell SQL Server to roll back a transaction by setting the XACT_ABORT session option to ON.
2. The function @@ERROR returns the error number of the previously executed statement and can be used outside of a *catch* block. The function ERROR_NUMBER() returns the error number that belongs to the error that caused control to be transferred to the current *catch* block. If not inside of a *catch* block, ERROR_NUMBER() returns NULL.
3. Yes, you can commit a transaction in the *catch* block if the transaction is committable. Use the XACT_STATE() function to find out if it is.

---

e Scenario: Validating Data Integrity

You are a database developer in your organization. Users are reporting that they find objects in the organization's customer relationship management (CRM) application whose parent objects have been deleted. One example is employees who work in a department that doesn't exist in the database. They also complain that prices for some products contain negative values, even though this should not be possible according to the documentation of the application. It is very important to find the source of these bugs as soon as possible, as well as to sure that these issues do not reappear. Design a solution to solve this problem.

Suggested Practices

Objective 3.1: Design code that validates input data and permission:

- **Practice 1**   Create a table called Customers, one called Orders that references the tomers table, and another called OrderRows that references the Orders table. Imple the foreign key constraints with cascading updates and deletes. Test the behav these constraints by inserting, updating, and deleting data in the tables.

Objective 3.2: Design code that detects and reacts to errors

- **Practice 1**   Create a stored procedure that includes a *try/catch* block. Test the bel of nested *try/catch* blocks by adding additional *try/catch* blocks both in the out block and in the outer *catch* block of the stored procedure.

Reference

- "Security Functions (Transact-SQL)," Microsoft SQL Server 2005 Books Online *http://msdn2.microsoft.com/en-us/library/ms186236.aspx*

Chapter Summary

- Data validation includes both procedural and declarative data integrity and can hurt and benefit performance.
- Error handling using @@ERROR should typically be replaced by structured erro dling using *try/catch* blocks.
- Consider how you handle transactions in your *try/catch* blocks. If you need to com continue a transaction in a *catch* block, use the *XACT_STATE()* function to verify th transaction is committable.
- If many error messages are sent from stored procedures and triggers, consider cr the messages inside SQL Server using the sp_addmessage procedure instead of p the actual error text in the stored procedure.
- SQL Server messages support localization of messages into other languages; you need to create your own table structure to manage these texts.

esigning Transactions and ansaction Isolation

Transactions are one of the most important aspects when working with a database system. Transactions are used to isolate database users from each other to make each executed query consistent. The use of transactions can both improve the performance of queries as well as degrade performance. It is important to understand how the use of transactions will affect a specific query.

When designing transactions, you will need to make decisions such as:

- When to start and end your transactions
- Which transaction isolation level to use
- Which locking hints you should consider supplying to the query optimizer

All examples in this chapter reference objects in a schema called "Test." You can create this schema simply by executing the statement CREATE SCHEMA TEST; in a database of your choice.

Exam objectives in this chapter:
- Manage concurrency by selecting the appropriate transaction isolation levels.
- Design the locking granularity level.
- Design transaction scopes.
- Design code that uses transactions.

fore You Begin

To complete the lessons in this chapter, you must have:

- A general understanding of Transact-SQL.
- A general understanding of database transactions.
- SQL Server 2005 as well as the SQL Server 2005 *AdventureWorks* sample database installed.

Lesson 1: Understanding the Available Transaction Isolation Levels

Estimated lesson time: 60 minutes

According to the SQL-99 standard, there are four transaction isolation levels:

- Read committed
- Read uncommitted
- Repeatable read
- Serializable

Each level protects against specific concurrency problems caused by access to the same by multiple connections. Besides these four isolation levels, SQL Server 2005 also provide following two additional isolation levels:

- Snapshot
- Read commited snapshot (which is a variation of the read committed isolation rather than an entirely different level)

To set the active transacton isolation level for a connection, execute the SET TRANSAC ISOLATION LEVEL statement. Note that the read committed snapshot isolation level ca be set by this statement. How to enable this isolation level is covered later in this chapt retreive the active isolation level for the current connection, execute the DBCC L OPTIONS statement and examine the row labeled "isolation level."

Types of Concurrency Problems

There are several concurrency problems that can occur in a database management sy when multiple users access the same data. The following is a short explanation of each currency problem.

Lost Update

A lost update can be interpreted in one of two ways. In the first scenario, a *lost update* i: sidered to have taken place when data that has been updated by one transaction is overw by another transaction, before the first transaction is either committed or rolled back type of lost update cannot occur in SQL Server 2005 because it is not allowed under any action isolation level.

The other interpretation of a lost update is when one transaction (Transaction #1) read: into its local memory, and then another transaction (Transaction #2) changes this dat commits its change. After this, Transaction #1 updates the same data based on what it read into memory before Transaction #2 was executed. In this case, the update performed by Transaction #2 can be considered a lost update.

Dirty Read

If data that has been changed by an open transaction is accessed by another transaction, a *dirty read* has taken place. A dirty read can cause problems because it means that a data manipulation language (DML) statement accessed data that logically does not exist yet or will never exist (if the open transaction is rolled back). All isolation levels except for read uncommitted protect against dirty reads.

Non-Repeatable Read

If a specific set of data is accessed more than once in the same transaction (such as when two different queries against the same table use the same WHERE clause) and the rows accessed between these accesses are updated or deleted by another transaction, a *non-repeatable read* has taken place. That is, if two queries against the same table with the same WHERE clause are executed in the same transaction, they return different results. The repeatable read, serializable, and snapshot isolation levels protect a transaction from non-repeatable reads.

Phantom Reads

Phantom reads are a variation of non-repeatable reads. A phantom read is when two queries in the same transaction, against the same table, use the same WHERE clause, and the query executed last returns more rows than the first query. Only the serializable and snapshot isolation levels protect a transaction from phantom reads.

g Locks to Solve Concurrency Problems

SQL Server uses *locks* stored in memory as a way to solve concurrency problems. There are several types of locks that are used. You can find more information about the available lock types in the article "Lock Compatibility" in SQL Server 2005 Books Online at *http://msdn2.microsoft.com/en-us/library/aa213041(SQL.80).aspx*. Following are the locks that you need to know about for this lesson:

- **Shared or S-locks** Shared locks are sometimes referred to as *read locks*. There can be several shared locks on any resource (such as a row or a page) at any one time. Shared locks are compatible with other shared locks.

- **Exclusive or X-locks**   Exclusive locks are also referred to as write locks. Only one
  sive lock can exist on a resource at any time. Exclusive locks are not compatible
  other locks, including shared locks.
- **Update or U-locks**   Update locks can be viewed as a combination of shared and
  sive locks. An update lock is used to lock rows when they are selected for update,
  they are actually updated. Update locks are compatible with shared locks, but no
  other update locks. Lesson 2, "Designing Transactions and Optimizing Locking
  cusses update locks further.

All isolation levels always issue exclusive locks for write operations and hold the locks f
entire duration of the transaction. In the next sections, you will look at how shared loc
handled by the different isolation levels. To see which locks are currently being held, yc
query the sys.dm_tran_locks dynamic management view or execute the sys.sp_lock s
stored procedure.

Choosing the Correct Isolation Level

Which lock types are acquired by SQL Server depends on the active transaction isolation
The type of isolation level used can significantly affect both the performance and the res
executed queries.

Read Committed Isolation Level

The read committed transaction isolation level is the default isolation level for new co
tions in SQL Server. This isolation level guarantees that dirty reads do not occur in your
action. A row is considered *dirty* when it has been deleted, updated, or inserted by an
transaction in another connection where the transaction has not yet been committed or
back. If your connection is using the read committed isolation level and SQL Server en
ters a dirty row while executing a DML statement, it will wait until the transaction tha
rently owns the row has been committed or rolled back before continuing execution.

By default, there is no timeout for these waits. However, you can specify a timeout by exe
the SET LOCK_TIMEOUT statement. This statement requires one parameter: the max
number of milliseconds to wait. Note that if you set it to 0, it will not wait at all. Instea
will immediately receive an error message, and the executing DML statement will be st
and rolled back.

In the read committed isolation level, shared locks are acquired for read operations, bu
are released as soon as they have been granted. The shared locks are not held for the du
of the transaction. The following is an example of the behavior of this isolation level. The
in the following table show the order in which the statements are executed. Note th

ALTER DATABASE statements are used to make sure that the correct settings are used for the database. These ALTER DATABASE statements require that no connections exist against the database.

```
ALTER DATABASE <current_database> SET ALLOW_SNAPSHOT_ISOLATION OFF;
ALTER DATABASE <current_database> SET READ_COMMITTED_SNAPSHOT OFF;

-- Table used in this example.
CREATE TABLE Test.TestTran (Col INT NOT NULL);
```

Connection 1	Connection 2

`BEGIN TRAN;`
`    INSERT Test.TestTran (Col)`
`        VALUES (1);`
	—

—	`SELECT * FROM Test.TestTran  WHERE Col = 1;`
	`/*`
	When this SELECT statement is executed, the connection will be blocked and wait for the transaction in connection 1 to complete.
	`*/`

`UPDATE Test.TestTran SET Col = 2` `    WHERE Col = 1;`	Still waiting...
`COMMIT TRAN;`	Because the transaction in connection 1 is now completed, this connection's SELECT statement now returns an empty result set (because the value of the Col-column is now 2 and it searched for Col = 1).

```
-- Drop the table used in this example.
DROP TABLE Test.TestTran;
```

The following code sample uses the SET LOCK_TIMEOUT setting together with a *try/catch* block to return only the rows found before the first dirty row is encountered by the SELECT statement.

```
ALTER DATABASE <current_database> SET ALLOW_SNAPSHOT_ISOLATION OFF;
ALTER DATABASE <current_database> SET READ_COMMITTED_SNAPSHOT OFF;

-- Table used in this example.
CREATE TABLE Test.TestTran (Col INT NOT NULL);
```

Connection 1	Connection 2

```INSERT Test.TestTran (Col)```
```   VALUES (1);```
```BEGIN TRAN;```
```   INSERT Test.TestTran (Col)```
```   VALUES (2);```
	—

—	```BEGIN TRY```
	``` SET LOCK_TIMEOUT 0;```
	``` SELECT * FROM Test.TestTran;```
	```END TRY```
	```BEGIN CATCH```
	```END CATCH```
	```/*```
	```Returns only Col = 1.```
	```*/```

```COMMIT TRAN;```	—

```
-- Drop the table used in this example.
DROP TABLE Test.TestTran;
```

Read Uncommitted Isolation Level

The read uncommitted isolation level is tempting to consider because it can provide grea formance benefits. Unfortunately, this is at the expense of returning valid results. This tion level only guarantees that a transaction does not experience lost updates. When exec a DML statement in the read uncommitted isolation level, SQL Server will allow dirty ro be returned. This might cause you to read data that has never existed because the data th read was inserted or updated by another transaction that was later rolled back.

You should consider using this isolation level only in routines where the issue of dirty re not a problem. Such routines usually return information that is not directly used as a ba decisions. A typical example where dirty reads might be allowed is for queries that return that are only used in lists in the application (such as a list of customers) or if the datab only used for read operations.

The read uncommitted isolation level is by far the best isolation level to use for perform as it does not wait for other connections to complete their transactions when it wants to data that these transactions have modified. In the read uncommitted isolation level, s locks are not acquired for read operations; this is what makes dirty reads possible. Th also reduces the work and memory required by the SQL Server lock manager. Because s locks are not acquired, it is no problem to read resources locked by exclusive locks. However, while a query is executing in the read uncommitted isolation level, another type of lock called a *schema stability lock* (Sch-S) is acquired to prevent Data Definition Language (DDL) statements from changing the table structure. Below is an example of the behavior of this isolation level. This example shows the behavior of the read uncommitted isolation level.

```
ALTER DATABASE <current_database> SET ALLOW_SNAPSHOT_ISOLATION OFF;
ALTER DATABASE <current_database> SET READ_COMMITTED_SNAPSHOT OFF;

-- Table used in this example.
CREATE TABLE Test.TestTran (Col INT NOT NULL);
```

Connection 1	Connection 2

BEGIN TRAN;
        INSERT Test.TestTran (Col)
            VALUES (1);
	—

—	SET TRANSACTION ISOLATION LEVEL READ UNCOMMITTED;
—	SELECT * FROM Test.TestTran; /* Returns Col = 1 which has not yet been committed, a dirty read. */
UPDATE Test.TestTran SET Col = 2 WHERE Col = 1;	—
—	SELECT * FROM Test.TestTran; /* Returns Col = 2 which has not yet been committed, another dirty read. */
ROLLBACK TRAN;	—
—	SELECT * FROM Test.TestTran; /* Returns an empty result set (which, in this case, is not a dirty read). This shows the problem with the read uncommitted isolation level. The previous 2 statements returned data that logically never existed! */

```
-- Drop the table used in this example.
DROP TABLE Test.TestTran;
```

Repeatable Read Isolation Level

In the repeatable read isolation level, SQL Server not only guarantees that dirty reads d happen in your transaction, but it also guarantees that if you issue two DML statem against the same table with the same WHERE clause (one query could be a select and the could be an update), both queries will return the same results. This is not entirely true be the latter queries might return more rows than the first query. A repeatable read pro against deletes and updates of accessed rows, but not against inserts that match the sp WHERE clause, which is the phantom rows concurrency problem. Note that phantom might also occur if you use aggregate functions, although it is not as easy to detect.

The first query might, for example, include the sum over four rows, while the second c includes the sum over five rows. One important thing to note is that, because the repea read isolation level is achieved using blocking of the other transaction, the use of this isol level greatly increases the number of locks held for the duration of the transaction. Th turn, can cause serious perfomance problems due to blocked transactions. It also gr increases the risk for *deadlocks*. A deadlock is encountered if different connections are wa for locks held by each other. In the repeatable read isolation level, shared locks are acq for read operations and are also held for the duration of the transaction, not allowing cha to the data by other transactions. The following example shows the behavior of the repea read isolation level:

```
ALTER DATABASE <current_database> SET ALLOW_SNAPSHOT_ISOLATION OFF;
ALTER DATABASE <current_database> SET READ_COMMITTED_SNAPSHOT OFF;

-- Table including some example rows used in this example.
CREATE TABLE Test.TestTran (Col1 INT NOT NULL, Col2 INT NOT NULL);
INSERT Test.TestTran (Col1, Col2) VALUES (1, 1);
INSERT Test.TestTran (Col1, Col2) VALUES (1, 2);
```

Connection 1	Connection 2

SET TRANSACTION ISOLATION LEVEL
    REPEATABLE READ;
	SET TRANSACTION ISOLATION LEVEL
	    READ COMMITTED;

BEGIN TRAN;
    SELECT * FROM Test.TestTran
    WHERE Col1 = 1;
    /* Returns 2 rows. */
	—

Connection 1	Connection 2

—	`SELECT * FROM Test.TestTran;`
	`/*`
	`Returns the 2 rows in the table. This state-`
	`ment is allowed because it does not change any`
	`rows that are included in the transaction in`
	`connection 1.`
	`*/`

—	`UPDATE Test.TestTran SET Col1 = 2`
	`    WHERE Col1 = 1;`
	`/*`
	`This statement is now blocked by connection 1`
	`because it would cause the transaction in`
	`connection 1 to experience a  non-repeatable`
	`read.`
	`*/`

`SELECT * FROM Test.TestTran WHERE Col1 = 1;`
`/*`
`Still returns 2 rows, i.e. a non-repeatable`
`read did not occur.`
`*/`
	Still blocked...

—	`/*`
	`Abort the above query and execute the`
	`following insert statement.`
	`*/`
	`INSERT Test.TestTran (Col1, Col2)`
	`    VALUES (1, 3);`

`SELECT * FROM Test.TestTran WHERE Col1 = 1;`
`/*`
`Now returns 3 rows. The rows with the values 1`
`& 2 for the column Col2 are unchanged. But the`
`row with Col2 = 3 is now included in the`
`result. That row is a phantom read!`
`*/`
	—

`COMMIT TRAN;`	—

```
-- Drop the table used in this example.
DROP TABLE Test.TestTran;
```

Serializable Isolation Level

The serializable isolation level guarantees that none of the concurrency problems menti
earlier can occur. Because this isolation level also protects from the occurrence of pha
reads through blocking, the use of the serializable isolation level increases the risk for blc
transactions and deadlocks even more than using the repeatable read isolation level. Th
lation level guarantees that if you issue two DML statements against the same table wit
same WHERE clause, both queries will return exactly the same results, including the
number of rows. To protect the transaction from inserts, SQL Server will need to lock a
of an index over a column that is included in the WHERE clause with shared locks. If su
index does not exist, SQL Server will need to lock the entire table. The following exa
shows the behavior of the serializable isolation level:

```
ALTER DATABASE <current_database> SET ALLOW_SNAPSHOT_ISOLATION OFF;
ALTER DATABASE <current_database> SET READ_COMMITTED_SNAPSHOT OFF;

-- Table including some example rows used in this example.
CREATE TABLE Test.TestTran (Col1 INT NOT NULL, Col2 INT NOT NULL);
INSERT Test.TestTran (Col1, Col2) VALUES (1, 1);
INSERT Test.TestTran (Col1, Col2) VALUES (1, 2);
```

Connection 1	Connection 2
`SET TRANSACTION ISOLATION LEVEL` `     SERIALIZABLE;`	`SET TRANSACTION ISOLATION LEVEL` `     READ COMMITTED;`

`BEGIN TRAN;`
`     SELECT * FROM Test.TestTran`
`     WHERE Col1 = 1;`
`     /* Returns 2 rows. */`
	—

—	`SELECT * FROM Test.TestTran;`
	`/*`
	`Returns the 2 rows in the table. This st`
	`ment is allowed because it does not change`
	`rows that are included in the transactior`
	`connection 1.`
	`*/`

—	`UPDATE Test.TestTran SET Col1 = 2`
	`     WHERE Col1 = 1;`
	`/*`
	`This statement is now blocked by connecti`
	`because it would cause the transaction i`
	`connection 1 to experience a non-repeata`
	`read.`
	`*/`

Connection 1	Connection 2

```SELECT * FROM Test.TestTran WHERE Col1 = 1;```
 ```/*```
 ```Still returns 2 rows, i.e. a non-repeatable```
 ```read did not occur.```
 ```*/```
	Still blocked...

—	```/*```
	 ```Abort the above query and execute the```
	 ```following insert statement.```
	 ```*/```
	 ```INSERT Test.TestTran (Col1, Col2)```
	 ``` VALUES (1, 3);```
	 ```/*```
	 ```This statement is also blocked, exactly as```
	 ```the update was, because it would cause the```
	 ```transaction in connection 1 to experience a```
	 ```phantom read.```
	 ```*/```

```SELECT * FROM Test.TestTran WHERE Col1 = 1;```
 ```/*```
 ```Still returns 2 rows, i.e. a phantom read did```
 ```not occur.```
 ```*/```
	—

—	```/*```
	 ```Abort the above query and execute the follow-```
	 ```ing insert statement.```
	 ```*/```
	 ```INSERT Test.TestTran (Col1, Col2)```
	 ``` VALUES (2, 1);```
	 ```/*```
	 ```This statement is also blocked, exactly as the```
	 ```previous insert was. This happened even```
	 ```though the row inserted by this statement```
	 ```would not be included in the query in connec-```
	 ```tion 1. This in turn is because SQL Server```
	 ```found no index to lock a range in, so it locked```
	 ```the entire table. */```

```COMMIT TRAN;```	—
—	The row from the above insert is now completed.

```
-- Drop the table used in this example.
DROP TABLE Test.TestTran;
```

Snapshot Isolation Level

SQL Server 2005 introduces the snapshot isolation level in addition to the four isolation l defined by the SQL-99 standard. This isolation level can be very useful because it pro against all of the previously mentioned concurrency problems, just as the serializable isol level does. However, it does not provide this protection by blocking access to rows by (transactions; it does so by storing versions of rows while the transaction is active as w tracking when a specific row was inserted. This means that while in a transaction in the s shot isolation level, depending on what has occurred since the transaction was started might not be looking at the current version of a row, but rather an older version of the row senting it as it looked when the transaction first accessed it. Because of this, when worki the snapshot isolation level, the transaction can be considered to be executing in an "alter reality." For more information on the snapshot isolation level, see the article "Using Snap Isolation" at *http://msdn2.microsoft.com/en-us/library/tcbchxcb.aspx.*

If a transaction is started by executing the BEGIN TRANSACTION statement (the transa is actually started when the first statement within it is executed) at 5:02 A.M., for examp will only return data from this exact point in time, independent of how many rows are b deleted, inserted, or updated while the transaction is active. The older row versions are st as a linked list of rows in the *tempdb* system database. There can be multiple versions of a gle row at any point in time in order to service multiple snapshot transactions starting a ferent points in time.

When snapshot transactions are being used, the *tempdb* database experiences additi activity and might require additional disk space. Because of storage of row versions, v operations will suffer some performance degradation. The snapshot isolation level ca particularly useful for read intensive databases and for databases that have perform problems caused by blocking. If you are looking for performance improvement only and accept dirty reads, remember that the read uncommitted isolation level provides the performance.

Using the Snapshot Isolation Level

To be able to use the snapshot isolation level in a database, the database op ALLOW_SNAPSHOT_ISOLATION must first be set to ON. This database option requires there are no connections to the database when it is set. It is the setting of this database op rather than the start of a transaction in the snapshot isolation level, that starts the proce generating and storing row versions. This is notable because it means that you pay the pe mance penalty of generating row versions for all transactions in the database, not just for t actions that use the snapshot isolation level. This occurs because the old version of a row i have been made available when the row was changed or deleted, even if the change was r by a transaction in an isolation level other than snapshot. In the snapshot isolation level, shared locks are not acquired for read operations because row versions are used instead. The following example shows the behavior of the snapshot isolation level:

```
ALTER DATABASE <current_database> SET ALLOW_SNAPSHOT_ISOLATION ON;
ALTER DATABASE <current_database> SET READ_COMMITTED_SNAPSHOT OFF;

-- Table including some example rows used in this example.
CREATE TABLE Test.TestTran (Col1 INT NOT NULL, Col2 INT NOT NULL);
INSERT Test.TestTran (Col1, Col2) VALUES (1, 1);
INSERT Test.TestTran (Col1, Col2) VALUES (1, 2);
INSERT Test.TestTran (Col1, Col2) VALUES (2, 1);
```

Connection 1	Connection 2
`SET TRANSACTION ISOLATION LEVEL` `    SNAPSHOT;`	`SET TRANSACTION ISOLATION LEVEL` `    READ COMMITTED;`

`BEGIN TRAN;`
`    SELECT * FROM Test.TestTran`
`    WHERE Col1 = 1;`
`    /* Returns 2 rows. */`
	—

—	`UPDATE Test.TestTran SET Col1 = 2  WHERE Col1` `= 1 AND Col2 = 1;`

`SELECT * FROM Test.TestTran`
`    WHERE Col1 = 1;`
`/*`
`Still returns the same 2 rows  with exactly the`
`same values.`
`*/`
	—

`SELECT * FROM Test.TestTran`
`    WHERE Col1 = 1;`
`/*`
`Still returns the same 2 rows  with exactly the`
`same values.`
`*/`
	`INSERT Test.TestTran (Col1, Col2)`
	`    VALUES (1, 3);`

—	`DELETE Test.TestTran;`
	`/*`
	`Deletes all rows in the table...`
	`*/`

`SELECT * FROM Test.TestTran  WHERE Col1 = 1;`
`/*`
`Still returns the same 2 rows  with exactly the`
`same values.`
`*/`
	—

Connection 1	Connection 2

`SELECT * FROM Test.TestTran;`
`/*`
`Returns the 3 rows that existed in the table`
`when the transaction  was started.`
`*/`
	—

`COMMIT TRAN;`	—

`SELECT * FROM Test.TestTran;`
`/*`
`Now returns an empty result set because the`
`alternate reality of the transaction has been`
`discarded.`
`*/`
	—

```
-- Drop the table used in this example.
DROP TABLE Test.TestTran;
```

To track snapshot transactions and row versions, you can query the dynamic manage views sys.dm_tran_active_snapshot_database_transactions (which shows the current snapshot transactions) and sys.dm_tran_version_store (which shows you the storage fo versions).

Update Conflicts   There is an additional concurrency problem not yet mentioned beca is specific to the snapshot isolation level. If a specific row (or version of a row) is read in shot isolation, SQL Server guarantees that you will get the same row if you issue the query in the transaction. What happens if the later query is an UPDATE or DELETE statemen the row has changed since it was read the first time? SQL Server can't use the current ve of the row as the base for the update because it would break the promise of the row not c ing while the snapshot transaction is active. And it can't use the row version used by the shot transaction as a base because the other transaction that updated or deleted the row w experience a lost update (which is not allowed or supported in SQL Server). Instead, the shot transaction is rolled back, and it receives the following error message:

```
Msg 3960, Level 16, State 4, Line 1
Snapshot isolation transaction aborted due to update conflict. You cannot use snapshot
isolation to access table 'Test.TestTran' directly or indirectly in database 'TestDatabase
update, delete, or insert the row that has been modified or deleted by another transact
Retry the transaction or change the isolation level for the update/delete statement.
```

Of course, this error can be caught in a *try/catch* block, but then the transaction (XACT_STATE()) will be set to uncommittable, meaning that the transaction must be r back. To find concurrent snapshot transactions that might experience update conflicts can query the sys.dm_tran_transactions_snapshot dynamic management view. Here is an example of an update conflict occurrence:

```
ALTER DATABASE <current_database> SET ALLOW_SNAPSHOT_ISOLATION ON;
ALTER DATABASE <current_database> SET READ_COMMITTED_SNAPSHOT OFF;

-- Table including some example rows used in this example.
CREATE TABLE Test.TestTran (Col1 INT NOT NULL, Col2 INT NOT NULL);
INSERT Test.TestTran (Col1, Col2) VALUES (1, 1);
```

Connection 1	Connection 2
SET TRANSACTION ISOLATION LEVEL SNAPSHOT;	SET TRANSACTION ISOLATION LEVEL READ COMMITTED;
BEGIN TRAN; SELECT * FROM Test.TestTran WHERE Col1 = 1; /* Returns the value 1 for the column Col2. */	—
—	UPDATE Test.TestTran SET Col2 = 10 WHERE Col1 = 1;
UPDATE Test.TestTran SET Col2 = Col2 + 1 WHERE Col1 = 1; /* Receives the update conflict error and the transaction is rolled back. According to the snapshot, the value of Col2 should become 2, but that would cause the transaction in connection 2 to be lost (or not durable according to ACID). */	—
SELECT * FROM Test.TestTran WHERE Col1 = 1; /* Now returns the value 10 for the Col2 column because the snapshot transaction was rolled back. */	—

```
-- Drop the table used in this example.
DROP TABLE Test.TestTran;
```

Apparently, because of update conflicts, the snapshot isolation level is not the best choice are reading and later updating a specific set of rows within a transaction. It is, however, esting to know that regardless of whether rows changed, you would not experience an u conflict if you execute an INSERT...SELECT statement within the snapshot transaction.

If you must issue an UPDATE or DELETE statement within a snapshot transaction, cor issuing it within a *try/catch* block. You can also consider switching back to the read comm isolation level before you issue the update. This will block the transaction if an open tra tion has updated or deleted the rows that need to be accessed and, if the transaction i blocked, the update will use the data from the current row version rather than the one in snapshot. Remember that the update might experience phantom rows, so you need to sp exactly which rows to update (by referencing the primary key column in your WHERE cla

You can also combine the two isolation levels by reading from the snapshot isolation leve writing to the read committed isolation level. If a transaction is implemented this way, transactions cannot be considered durable, because they can have their committed data written by old data. (This is also an alternative way of interpreting the lost update concur problem.) Here is an example of this scary but feasible implementation. In this case, the action isolation level is set for the UPDATE statement using a table locking hint.

```
ALTER DATABASE <current_database> SET ALLOW_SNAPSHOT_ISOLATION ON;
ALTER DATABASE <current_database> SET READ_COMMITTED_SNAPSHOT OFF;

-- Table including some example rows used in this example.
CREATE TABLE Test.TestTran (
    PKCol INT IDENTITY(1,1) PRIMARY KEY
    ,Col1 INT NOT NULL
    ,Col2 INT NOT NULL
);
INSERT Test.TestTran (Col1, Col2) VALUES (1, 1);
```

Connection 1	Connection 2

SET TRANSACTION ISOLATION LEVEL
        SNAPSHOT;
	SET TRANSACTION ISOLATION LEVEL
	        READ COMMITTED;

BEGIN TRAN;
        SELECT * FROM Test.TestTran
        WHERE Col1 = 1;
/*
Returns 1 row with the value 1 for the Col2
column.
*/
	—

Connection 1	Connection 2
| — | ```
INSERT Test.Testtran
      (Col1, Col2)
VALUES (1, 2);
``` |
| ```
SELECT * FROM Test.TestTran  WHERE Col1 = 1;
/*
Still returns the 1 row with the value 1 for
the Col2 column.  */
``` | — |
| — | ```
UPDATE Test.TestTran SET
       Col2 = 10
WHERE Col1 = 1;
/*
Sets the Col2 column of both rows to the value
10.
*/
``` |
| ```
SELECT * FROM Test.TestTran  WHERE Col1 = 1;
/*
Still returns the 1 row with the value 1 for
the Col2 column.
*/
``` | ```
SELECT * FROM Test.TestTran
WHERE Col1 = 1;
/*
Returns 2 rows with the value 10 for the Col2
column in both rows.
*/
``` |
| ```
UPDATE currRow SET
       Col2 = snapshotRow.Col2 + 1
FROM Test.TestTran AS currRow
     WITH(READCOMMITTED)
INNER JOIN Test.TestTran
       AS snapshotRow
       ON snapshotRow.PKCol
           = currRow.PKCol;
/*
This update is now executed in  read committed
isolation (because of the locking hint) but
reads the data from the snapshot isolation.
This causes the data  to be overwritten without an  update conflict being issued. If the
transaction in connection 2 was still open,
this query would have been blocked until it
finished. But when it is no longer blocked, it
will just overwrite whatever data had been
put in the row by the other transaction.
*/
``` | — |

Connection 1	Connection 2

`SELECT * FROM Test.TestTran  WHERE Col1 = 1;`
`/*`
Still returns the 1 row, but now with the value 2 for the Col2 column (because of the update above).
`*/`
	`SELECT * FROM Test.TestTran  WHERE Col1 =`
	`/*`
	This SELECT statement is now blocked bec it is being executed in read committed i tion and the transaction in connection 1 not been completed yet.
	`*/`

`COMMIT TRAN;`	The SELECT statement above now returns rows, but for the first row it returns the va for the Col2 column.

```
-- Drop the table used in this example.
DROP TABLE Test.TestTran;
```

Read Committed Snapshot Isolation Level

To the four isolation levels defined by the SQL-99 standard, SQL Server 2005 adds th committed snapshot isolation level. This isolation level is a bit different from the previou lation levels because it cannot be set using the SET TRANSACTION ISOLATION LEVEL ment; it is set by setting the database option READ_COMMITTED_SNAPSHOT to ON could also say that this isn't really its own transaction isolation level, but rather a variat the read committed isolation level. By changing this database option, the behavior of th committed isolation level is changed to read committed snapshot. The read committed tion level described earlier no longer exists for the specific database (although it can be using a table locking hint that we will describe later in this lesson). For more inform about the read committed snapshot isolation level, see the article "Using Snapshot Isola at *http://msdn2.microsoft.com/en-us/library/tcbchxcb.aspx.*

IMPORTANT   The READ_COMMITTED_SNAPSHOT database setting

Setting the database option READ_COMMITTED_SNAPSHOT to ON for an existing database changes the behavior of the read committed isolation level. It is very important to thoroughl the database after setting this option to avoid introducing bugs into your application.

The read committed snapshot isolation level is a combination of the isolation levels read mitted and snapshot. Because of this, the database option READ_COMMITTED_SNAPS will also cause SQL Server to start generating and storing row versions in the *tempdb* s database. As opposed to the read committed isolation level, in this isolation level, reade not blocked by writers, and vice versa. This is implemented through the reading of the available version of a row, in case the row is locked by another transaction that updated or deleted the row but had not yet completed.

Isn't this what snapshot isolation does? No, not exactly. In the read committed snapshot case, SQL Server always reads the latest version of the row; it doesn't care when the transaction was started. This means that it does not return dirty rows but can still encounter nonrepeatable and phantom reads. In the read committed snapshot isolation level, shared locks are not acquired for read operations because row versions are used instead.

So, if you already pay the price of generating row versions, why don't you just use the snapshot isolation level? First, in this isolation level, SQL Server doesn't need to find a particular version of a row; it just needs to find the last committed version. Also, update conflicts don't occur in the read committed snapshot isolation level. This is because SQL Server hasn't guaranteed that it will only return data that appears the way it did when the transaction started, so SQL Server will not break any guarantee if it uses the new committed version of a row. In this isolation level, instead of getting the update conflict error, SQL Server will just block the connection until the other connection releases its locks, and then it will execute the update. Here is an example:

```
ALTER DATABASE <current_database> SET ALLOW_SNAPSHOT_ISOLATION ON;
ALTER DATABASE <current_database> SET READ_COMMITTED_SNAPSHOT ON;

-- Table including some example rows used in this example.
CREATE TABLE Test.TestTran (Col1 INT NOT NULL, Col2 INT NOT NULL);
INSERT Test.TestTran (Col1, Col2) VALUES (1, 1);
```

Connection 1	Connection 2

SET TRANSACTION ISOLATION LEVEL
     READ COMMITTED;
	SET TRANSACTION ISOLATION LEVEL
	     READ COMMITTED;

BEGIN TRAN;
     SELECT * FROM Test.TestTran
     WHERE Col1 = 1;
/*
Returns 1 row.
*/
	—

—	BEGIN TRAN;
	     UPDATE Test.TestTran SET
	        Col2 = 10
	     WHERE Col1 = 1;
	     INSERT Test.TestTran
	        (Col1, Col2)
	     VALUES (1, 2);

Connection 1	Connection 2
SELECT * FROM Test.TestTran WHERE Col1 = 1; /* Returns the same row as above, still with the value 1 for the Col2 column. It does not return the row inserted by connection 2. */	—
—	COMMIT TRAN;
SELECT * FROM Test.TestTran WHERE Col1 = 1; /* Now returns both rows, including the row inserted by connection 2. The first row now includes the updated value of the Col2 column. */	—

UPDATE Test.TestTran SET
    Col2 = Col2 + 1 WHERE Col1 = 1;
/*
Does not encounter an update conflict. Rather,
it updates both rows' Col2 column and sets it
to the values 3 and 11.
*/
SELECT * FROM Test.TestTran
    WHERE Col1 = 1;
	—

COMMIT TRAN;	—

```
-- Drop the table used in this example.
DROP TABLE Test.TestTran;
```

Exam Tip   The difference in behavior between snapshot isolation and read committed snap
is an important part of this exam.

Avoiding Extensive Blocking

There are a few easy rules for reducing the risk of blocking issues caused by extensive loc

- Use the least-restrictive isolation level possible. Consider whether you can make u
  the read uncommitted isolation level.
- Avoid using the repeatable read and serializable isolation levels.

- Keep your transactions as short as possible (measured in execution time, not number of T-SQL code lines).
- If you mostly read data, consider using the snapshot and read committed snapshot isolation levels.

: Comparing Transaction Isolation Levels

This lab contains two exercises. In the first exercise, you investigate how locks are acquired in the read committed isolation level, which is the default isolation level. In the second exercise, you perform the same tests against the read committed snapshot isolation level.

IMPORTANT Lab requirements

You will need to have SQL Server 2005 and the *Adventure Works* database installed before you can complete this lab. Refer to the Introduction for setup instructions.

▶ **Exercise 1: Acquire Locks by Using the Read Committed Isolation Level**

1. Open Microsoft SQL Server Management Studio, and connect to an instance of SQL Server 2005.

2. In a new query window, which will be referred to as Connection 1, type and execute the following SQL statements to create the *TestDB* database, the Test schema, and the table that you will use in this exercise:

```
-- Connection 1 - Session ID: <put @@SPID result here>
/*  Leave the above line to easily see that this query window
belongs to Connection 1. */

SELECT @@SPID;
GO

CREATE DATABASE TestDB;
GO

USE TestDB;
GO

CREATE SCHEMA Test;
GO

CREATE TABLE Test.TestTable (
    Col1 INT NOT NULL
    ,Col2 INT NOT NULL
);
INSERT Test.TestTable (Col1, Col2) VALUES (1,10);
INSERT Test.TestTable (Col1, Col2) VALUES (2,20);
```

```
INSERT Test.TestTable (Col1, Col2) VALUES (3,30);
INSERT Test.TestTable (Col1, Col2) VALUES (4,40);
INSERT Test.TestTable (Col1, Col2) VALUES (5,50);
INSERT Test.TestTable (Col1, Col2) VALUES (6,60);
```

3. Open another query window, which will be referred to as Connection 2, and type execute the following SQL statement to prepare the connection:

```
-- Connection 2 - Session ID: <put @@SPID result here>
/* Leave the above line to easily see that this query window
belongs to Connection 2. */

SELECT @@SPID;
GO

USE TestDB;
```

4. Open a third query window, which will be referred to as Connection 3, and type an cute the following SQL statement to prepare the connection:

```
-- Connection 3
/* Leave the above line to easily see that this query window
belongs to Connection 3. */

USE TestDB;
```

5. In Connection 1, execute the following SQL statements to start a transaction in the committed transaction isolation level, and read a row from the test table (but d commit the transaction!).

```
-- Connection 1
SET TRANSACTION ISOLATION LEVEL READ COMMITTED;
BEGIN TRAN;
    SELECT * FROM Test.TestTable
    WHERE Col1 = 1;
```

6. To see which locks have been acquired by the transaction in Connection 1, open nection 3, and execute the following SELECT statement. In the line of code that con <@@SPID of Connection 1>, be sure to replace this with the ID value returned by the executed in step 2 of this exercise.

```
SELECT
    resource_type
    ,request_mode
    ,request_status
FROM sys.dm_tran_locks
WHERE resource_database_id = DB_ID('TestDB')
    AND request_session_id = <@@SPID of Connection 1>
    AND request_mode IN ('S', 'X')
    AND resource_type <> 'DATABASE';
```

Why doesn't Connection 1 have a shared lock on the row that it read using the SELECT statement?

7. In Connection 1, execute the following SQL statement to end the started transaction:

```
-- Connection 1
COMMIT TRAN;
```

8. In Connection 2, execute the following SQL statements to start a transaction, and acquire an exclusive lock on one row in the test table.

```
-- Connection 2
BEGIN TRAN;
    UPDATE Test.TestTable SET Col2 = Col2 + 1
    WHERE Col1 = 1;
```

9. In Connection 1, execute the following transaction to try to read the row that has been updated (but not committed) by Connection 2. After you execute the code in this step, move on to the next step, as this connection will now be blocked.

```
-- Connection 1
SET TRANSACTION ISOLATION LEVEL READ COMMITTED;

BEGIN TRAN;
    SELECT * FROM Test.TestTable
    WHERE Col1 = 1;
-- This SELECT statement will be blocked!
```

10. To see which locks have been acquired by the transaction in Connection 1, open Connection 3, and execute the following SELECT statement. In the line of code that contains *<@@SPID of Connection 1>*, be sure to replace this with the ID value returned by the code executed in step 2 of this exercise.

```
SELECT
    resource_type
    ,request_mode
    ,request_status
FROM sys.dm_tran_locks
WHERE resource_database_id = DB_ID('TestDB')
    AND request_session_id = <@@SPID of Connection 1>
    AND request_mode IN ('S', 'X')
    AND resource_type <> 'DATABASE';
```

Here you can see that Connection 1 tries to acquire a shared lock on the row.

11. In Connection 2, execute the following SQL statements to end the transaction started earlier.

```
-- Connection 2
COMMIT TRAN;
```

12. Now, first have a look in Connection 1 and note that the SELECT statement has completed. Switch to Connection 3, and execute its SELECT statement again which locks are now acquired by the transaction in Connection 1. In the line of cod contains *<@@SPID of Connection 1>*, be sure to replace this with the ID value returr the code executed in step 2 of this exercise.

```
SELECT
     resource_type
     ,request_mode
     ,request_status
FROM sys.dm_tran_locks
WHERE resource_database_id = DB_ID('TestDB')
     AND request_session_id = <@@SPID of Connection 1>
     AND request_mode IN ('S', 'X')
     AND resource_type <> 'DATABASE';
```

You should now see that no locks are acquired by Connection 1. This is because acquiring the lock on the row, Connection 1 released the lock.

13. Close the three query windows for Connections 1, 2, and 3. Open a new query wi and execute the following SQL statement to clean up after this exercise:

```
USE master;
DROP DATABASE TestDB;
```

▶ **Exercise 2: Acquire Locks by Using the Read Committed Snapshot Isolation Level**

In this exercise, you execute the same type of transactions as in the previous exercise, b the read committed snapshot transaction isolation level.

1. Open SQL Server Management Studio, and connect to an instance of SQL Server

2. In a new query window, which will be referred to as Connection 1, type and execu following SQL statements to create the *TestDB* database, the Test schema, and the that will be used in this exercise:

```
-- Connection 1
/*  Leave the above line to easily see that this query window
belongs to Connection 1. */

CREATE DATABASE TestDB;
GO

ALTER DATABASE TestDB SET READ_COMMITTED_SNAPSHOT ON;
GO

USE TestDB;
GO

CREATE SCHEMA Test;
GO
```

```
CREATE TABLE Test.TestTable (
    Col1 INT NOT NULL
    ,Col2 INT NOT NULL
);
INSERT Test.TestTable (Col1, Col2) VALUES (1,10);
INSERT Test.TestTable (Col1, Col2) VALUES (2,20);
INSERT Test.TestTable (Col1, Col2) VALUES (3,30);
INSERT Test.TestTable (Col1, Col2) VALUES (4,40);
INSERT Test.TestTable (Col1, Col2) VALUES (5,50);
INSERT Test.TestTable (Col1, Col2) VALUES (6,60);
```

3. Open another query window, which will be referred to as Connection 2, and type and execute the following SQL statement to prepare the connection:

```
-- Connection 2
/* Leave the above line to easily see that this query window
belongs to Connection 2. */

USE TestDB;
```

4. Open a third query window, which will be referred to as Connection 3, and type and execute the following SQL statement to prepare the connection:

```
-- Connection 3
/* Leave the above line to easily see that this query window
belongs to Connection 3. */

USE TestDB;
```

5. In Connection 2, execute the following SQL statements to start a transaction, and acquire an exclusive lock on one row in the test table.

```
-- Connection 2
BEGIN TRAN;
    UPDATE Test.TestTable SET Col2 = Col2 + 1
    WHERE Col1 = 1;
```

6. In Connection 1, execute the following transaction to try to read the row that has been updated (but not committed) by Connection 2.

```
-- Connection 1
SET TRANSACTION ISOLATION LEVEL READ COMMITTED;

BEGIN TRAN;
    SELECT * FROM Test.TestTable
    WHERE Col1 = 1;
```

Why wasn't the SELECT statement blocked by Connection 2?

Which values were returned by the query, the values that existed before or after the update?

7. To see which locks have been acquired by the transaction in Connections 1 and 2, Connection 3, and execute the following SELECT statement:

```
SELECT
      resource_type
     ,request_mode
     ,request_status
FROM sys.dm_tran_locks
WHERE resource_database_id = DB_ID('TestDB')
     AND request_mode IN ('S', 'X')
     AND resource_type <> 'DATABASE';
```

8. To see if any row versions are available for the *TestDB* database, execute the foll query in Connection 3:

```
SELECT * FROM sys.dm_tran_version_store
WHERE database_id = DB_ID('TestDB');
```

9. In Connection 2, execute the following SQL statements to end the transaction s earlier.

```
-- Connection 2
COMMIT TRAN;
```

10. In the open transaction in Connection 1, execute the SELECT statement again.

```
-- Connection 1
SELECT * FROM Test.TestTable
WHERE Col1 = 1;
```

Which values are now returned, the values that existed before or after the update

Did this SELECT statement return dirty reads?

Did the first SELECT statement in Connection 1 return dirty reads?

11. Close the three query windows for Connection 1, 2, and 3. Open a new query wi and execute the following SQL statement to clean up after this exercise:

```
USE master;
DROP DATABASE TestDB;
```

Quick Check

1. Which isolation level or levels protect against phantom rows?
2. Which isolation level or levels do not acquire shared locks?
3. Where are old versions of rows in snapshot isolation stored?
4. Which is the default isolation level?

Quick Check Answers

1. The serializable and snapshot isolation levels protect against phantom rows.
2. Snapshot, read committed snapshot, and the read uncommitted isolation level do not acquire shared locks.
3. Old versions of rows in snapshot isolation are stored in the *tempdb* system database.
4. The read committed isolation level is the default isolation level.

Lesson 2: Designing Transactions and Optimizing Lock

Estimated lesson time: 40 minutes

Always try to design a solution that minimizes both the amount of resources locked in a action and the risk of blocking and deadlocks. This lesson covers both using table l options and alternative ways of reducing and optimizing locking.

Optimizing Locking

In addition to using the correct transaction isolation level, you can take several other st reduce locking and still get the correct results in your transactions. You can use table l hints by applying the *WITH(<locking_hint>)* keyword after the table name in a DML state In this way, you can use a stricter transaction isolation level (such as serializable) or a isolation level (such as read uncommitted) for a specific table in a transaction. There a eral table locking hints available; the following are the most commonly used:

- **WITH (READUNCOMMITTED / READCOMMITTED / REPEATABLEREAD / SERIALIZAB** These hints specify an alternate isolation level to use for the specific table. Note th cannot specify the snapshot isolation level as a table locking hint.
- **WITH (NOLOCK)**   This hint is equal to specifying READUNCOMMITTED READUNCOMMITTED.
- **WITH (HOLDLOCK)**   This hint is equal to specifying SERIALIZABLE, but use SER ABLE. "Hold lock" sounds more like it should be translated to repeatable read; ho HOLDLOCK is translated to serializable because of the lack of row locks in SQL versions prior to 7.0. Because row locks were not available, HOLDLOCK could against phantom reads. Because of this backward-compatibility issue, HOLDLC translated to serializable.
- **WITH (READPAST)**   READPAST causes SQL Server to skip locked rows instead of w for the locks to be released. In SQL Server 2005, READPAST is also available for UF and DELETE statements. READPAST is usually used to mimic a queuing mechan this is what is needed, consider implementing a SQL Server 2005 Service Broke tion instead. Service Broker natively provides queues and is implemented using A great book about SQL Server 2005 Service Broker is *The Rational Guide to SQL 2005 Service Broker* by Roger Wolter (Rational Press, 2006).
- **WITH (XLOCK)**   This hint is used in DML statements to cause SQL Server to a exclusive locks instead of shared locks. The exclusive locks acquired will be held remainder of the transaction.

- **WITH (UPDLOCK)**   This hint is used in DML statements to cause SQL Server to acquire update locks instead of shared locks. The update locks acquired will be held for the remainder of the transaction. Update locks are compatible with shared locks but are not compatible with other update locks. Therefore, SELECT statements that acquire update locks will be blocked, while SELECT statements that only intend to read the data, and not change it, are allowed. WITH (UPDLOCK) is usually specified if data is to be read first and updated later. Because of this, it can be referred to as a "SELECT WITH INTENT TO UPDATE".

- **WITH (NOWAIT)**   This hint is equal to setting LOCK_TIMEOUT to 0. For example, SQL Server will return an error message and stop execution of the current statement if it encounters a lock that it would need to wait for—on the specific table!

For more information about table locking hints, see the SQL Server 2005 Books Online articles "Locking Hints" at *http://msdn2.microsoft.com/en-us/library/ms189857.aspx* or "Table Hint (Transact-SQL)" at *http://msdn2.microsoft.com/en-us/library/ms187373.aspx*.

Exam Tip   For this exam, it is recommended that you know and understand the behaviors of the different locking hints.

In addition to using locking hints, the *OUTPUT* keyword for INSERT, UPDATE, and DELETE statements can also be very helpful. This keyword makes it possible to know which rows were accessed (inserted, updated, or deleted) by a specific DML statement. Following is an example of how concurrency problems can be solved without increased locking. The example is a simplified account-withdrawal transaction. (The lab for this lesson includes a more complex example that uses an account transactions table instead of just storing the account balance in a column of the accounts table.)

Here's an example of the implementation in pseudo code:

```
If(Enough money in account)
    Withdraw the money
Else
    Return an error message
```

Here, this transaction is translated to T-SQL, and the test table used in the example is included.

```
CREATE TABLE Test.Accounts (
    AccountNumber INT PRIMARY KEY
    ,Balance DECIMAL(19,5) NOT NULL
);
GO
```

```
SET TRANSACTION ISOLATION LEVEL READ COMMITTED - Default...
BEGIN TRAN;
    IF EXISTS (SELECT * FROM Test.Accounts
                WHERE AccountNumber = @AccountNumber
                    AND Balance >= @AmountToWithdraw)
        UPDATE Test.Accounts SET
            Balance = Balance - @AmountToWithdraw
        WHERE AccountNumber = @AccountNumber;
    ELSE
        BEGIN
            RAISERROR('Not enough funds in account!', 16, 1);
            ROLLBACK TRAN;
            RETURN;
        END
COMMIT TRAN;
```

What is wrong with this transaction? There is one specific issue. There is a chance that th
ance of the account will be updated between the execution of the SELECT statement ar
execution of the UPDATE statement. This example shows the problem of two users (co
tions) trying to withdraw all the money in the account at the same time:

```
CREATE TABLE Test.Accounts (
    AccountNumber INT PRIMARY KEY
    ,Balance DECIMAL(19,5) NOT NULL
);
INSERT Test.Accounts (AccountNumber, Balance)
    VALUES (1001, 500);
```

Connection 1	Connection 2
`SET TRANSACTION ISOLATION LEVEL` `    READ COMMITTED;`	`SET TRANSACTION ISOLATION LEVEL` `    READ COMMITTED;`

`BEGIN TRAN;`
`    SELECT * FROM Test.Accounts`
`    WHERE AccountNumber = 1001`
`        AND Balance >= 500;`
`/*`
`If the above query returns 1 row (which it does),`
`continue with the next statement; otherwise,`
`roll back the transaction and exit.`
`*/`
	—

Connection 1	Connection 2
| — | ```
BEGIN TRAN;
IF EXISTS (
    SELECT *
    FROM Test.Accounts
      WHERE AccountNumber = 1001
          AND Balance >= 500
    )
    UPDATE Test.Accounts SET
        Balance = Balance - 500
    WHERE AccountNumber = 1001;
ELSE
    BEGIN
        RAISERROR('...', 16, 1);
        ROLLBACK TRAN;
        RETURN;
    END
COMMIT TRAN;
/*
Empties the account.
*/
``` |
| ```
UPDATE Test.Accounts SET
    Balance = Balance - 500
WHERE AccountNumber = 1001;
/*
Empties the account, again. That is, the account
is now at -500 instead of 0.
*/
``` | — |
| ```
COMMIT TRAN;
``` | — |

```
DROP TABLE Test.Accounts;
```

In this case, it is possible to withdraw more money from the account than what was available because the shared lock issued by the SELECT statement is not held for the duration of the transaction. This enables the update in Connection 2 to withdraw money from the account even though the transaction in Connection 1 has not yet completed. To solve this problem, you can change the transaction isolation level to repeatable read, which will cause Connection 1 to keep its lock on the row for the entire transaction, as follows:

```
CREATE TABLE Test.Accounts (
    AccountNumber INT PRIMARY KEY
    ,Balance DECIMAL(19,5) NOT NULL
);
INSERT Test.Accounts (AccountNumber, Balance)
    VALUES (1001, 500);
```
```

Connection 1	Connection 2

SET TRANSACTION ISOLATION LEVEL
    REPEATABLE READ;
	SET TRANSACTION ISOLATION LEVEL
	    REPEATABLE READ;

BEGIN TRAN;
    SELECT * FROM Test.Accounts
    WHERE AccountNumber = 1001
        AND Balance >= 500;
/*
If the above query returns 1 row (which it
does), continue with the next statement;
otherwise, roll back the transaction and
exit.
*/
	—

—	BEGIN TRAN;
	IF EXISTS (
	        SELECT *
	        FROM Test.Accounts
	        WHERE AccountNumber = 1001
	            AND Balance >= 500
	    )
	    UPDATE Test.Accounts SET
	        Balance = Balance - 500
	    WHERE AccountNumber = 1001;
	ELSE
	    BEGIN
	        RAISERROR('...', 16, 1);
	        ROLLBACK TRAN;
	        RETURN;
	    END
	COMMIT TRAN;
	/*
	The UPDATE statement in this transaction i
	blocked by connection 1. However, the SEL
	statement acquired an shared lock on the
	*/

UPDATE Test.Accounts SET Balance = Balance - 500 WHERE AccountNumber = 1001; /* This statement is now blocked by the shared lock held on the row by the SELECT statement in Connection */	—

Deadlock! Either Connection 1 or Connection 2 is allowed to continue, and the other conne is deemed the deadlock victim, its execution is cancelled, and the entire transaction is rolled

```
DROP TABLE Test.Accounts;
```

This solution solves the problem of two connections being able to overdraw the account if executed at the same time. However, it introduces a potential deadlock problem. Deadlocks seriously degrade performance and should be avoided if possible. Instead of using the repeatable read isolation level, you can use the UPDLOCK lock hint or XLOCK lock hint. If UPDLOCK is specified for the SELECT statement, only the first transaction would get the lock, because update locks are not compatible with other update locks. If UPDLOCK is used, it is important to use it wherever data is first read and then updated. If UPDLOCK is left out of some transactions, the solution won't work because those transactions will acquire shared locks instead of update locks and could cause deadlocks to occur. If you are not sure whether you are using UPDLOCK in all instances in which it is needed, consider implementing the XLOCK hint, because exclusive locks are not compatible with shared locks. Here is the updated transaction using update locks:

```
SET TRANSACTION ISOLATION LEVEL READ COMMITTED;
BEGIN TRAN;
    IF EXISTS (SELECT * FROM Test.Accounts WITH (UPDLOCK)
                WHERE AccountNumber = @AccountNumber
                    AND Balance >= @AmountToWithdraw)
        UPDATE Test.Accounts SET
            Balance = Balance - @AmountToWithdraw
        WHERE AccountNumber = @AccountNumber;
    ELSE
        BEGIN
            RAISERROR('Not enough funds in account!', 16, 1);
            ROLLBACK TRAN;
            RETURN;
        END
COMMIT TRAN;
```

However, there is an even simpler and better-performing solution: skip the IF and SELECT statements. Instead, execute the UPDATE statement, include the balance check in the WHERE clause, and check whether the UPDATE statement updated the account by querying the @@ROWCOUNT function. When possible, executing fewer statements is usually a better solution.

```
SET TRANSACTION ISOLATION LEVEL READ COMMITTED;
BEGIN TRAN;
    UPDATE Test.Accounts SET
        Balance = Balance - @AmountToWithdraw
    WHERE AccountNumber = @AccountNumber
        AND Balance >= @AmountToWithdraw;
    IF(@@ROWCOUNT <> 1)
    BEGIN
```

```
        RAISERROR('Not enough funds in account!', 16, 1);
        ROLLBACK TRAN;
    END
ELSE
    COMMIT TRAN;
```

This solution is very useful but works only if there is one row to be updated. If more rows to be updated, you need to use the OUTPUT clause. Typically, you would execute the UP statement and then OUTPUT the accessed rows into a table variable. You can then que table variable to find out which rows were updated. Below is a simple example of updati price of products in a specific category, and then returning the average price for the pro that were updated. To make sure that the SELECT statement that returns the average does not return phantom rows, either the snapshot transaction isolation level or the se able transaction isolation level would need to be used. In this case, the OUTPUT claus tects against phantom rows without added locking or use of row versions.

```
USE AdventureWorks;

SET TRANSACTION ISOLATION LEVEL READ COMMITTED;
BEGIN TRAN;
    DECLARE @tmp TABLE (ProductID INT PRIMARY KEY);

    UPDATE Production.Product SET
        ListPrice = ListPrice * 1.1
    OUTPUT INSERTED.ProductID INTO @tmp (ProductID)
    WHERE ProductSubcategoryID = 17;

    SELECT AVG(p.ListPrice) AS NewAvgPrice
    FROM Production.Product AS p
    WHERE p.ProductID IN (
        SELECT t.ProductID FROM @tmp AS t
    );
COMMIT TRAN;
```

Exam Tip   For this exam, knowledge of alternate solutions is important.

Minimizing Deadlocks

To minimize deadlocks, you should follow three guidelines:

- Minimize the time during which transactions are open by keeping transactions sh
- Minimize locking. Use the least-restrictive transaction isolation level, and impl more-restrictive locking by using table locking hints rather than the SET TRAI

TION ISOLATION LEVEL. The table locking hint only affects one table, while the SET statement affects all tables in the transaction.

■ Access tables in the same order in all transactions. This reduces the risk of deadlocks resulting from transactions crossing paths. Here is an example of two transactions that can potentially be deadlocked due to the tables not being accessed in the same order in each transaction.

Transaction 1	Transaction 2
❑ Start transaction	❑ Start transaction
❑ Update table A	❑ Update table B
❑ Update table B	❑ Update table A
❑ Commit transaction	❑ Commit transaction

The typical solution for avoiding these types of deadlocks is to always access tables in the order parent to child, such as Customer to Order. What if you first need to read the order (child) and then update the customer (parent) based on the previous select? First, you can probably do this by executing an UPDATE statement with a subquery. If not, you can start by executing a dummy statement to lock the parent row. (To avoid firing triggers, use a SELECT statement, rather than an UPDATE statement, as the dummy statement.) For example:

```
DECLARE @x INT;
BEGIN TRAN;
    -- Lock parent row.
    SET @x = (SELECT 1 FROM Customer WITH (XLOCK)
            WHERE CustomerID = @CustomerID)
    -- Now access the child rows...
...
```

rking with Distributed Transactions

Distributed transactions are needed when a transaction covers more than one resource manager. A SQL Server instance is a typical resource manager. When working with multiple resource managers, a transaction manager is used to manage the transaction. The transaction manager that is installed with Windows is the Distributed Transaction Coordinator (also known as MS DTC).

Server-Side Distributed Transactions in T-SQL

When T-SQL transactions contain write operations that affect both local and remote objects on linked servers, a distributed transaction is automatically started, and the Distributed Transaction Coordinator (DTC) service is engaged to manage the distributed transaction. If the DTC service is not started on all involved machines, an error message is thrown. A distributed ⬛ action can also be manually started by executing the BEGIN DISTRIBUTED TRANSAC⬛ statement. Note that the snapshot transaction isolation level is not supported for distri⬛ transactions.

Application-Side Distributed Transactions in .NET Framework 2.0

When developing applications using .NET Framework 2.0, the *System.Transac* namespace (which is found in the *System.Transactions.dll* assembly) can be used to ma⬛ transactions. If only one SQL Server instance is accessed in a transaction, *System.Transa*⬛ uses a local SQL Server transaction. However, if more resource managers are included ⬛ transaction, *System.Transactions* automatically promotes the local transaction to a distri⬛ transaction and involves the MS DTC to manage the transaction. This means that *System.*⬛ *actions* is ideal to use for all transactions that you want to manage from the client side, e⬛ they only involve one SQL Server instance. Following is an application sample implem⬛ tion of *System.Transactions*:

```csharp
//C#
using System.Transactions;
using System.Data.SqlClient;

//Start a new transaction.
using (TransactionScope tran = new TransactionScope())
{
    using (SqlConnection connSqlServer1 = new
        SqlConnection(connString1))
    {
        connSqlServer1.Open(); //Opens first connection.

        //The transaction is now local to the first SQL Server
        //instance.

        using(SqlConnection connSqlServer2 = new
            SqlConnection(connString2))
        {
            connSqlServer2.Open(); // Opens second connection.

            //The transaction is promoted to a distributed
            //transaction.
        }
    }

    //Commit the transaction.
    tran.Complete();
}
```

```vb
'VB
Imports System.Transactions
Imports System.Data.SqlClient

'Start a new transaction.
Using tran As New TransactionScope()
    Using connSqlServer1 As New SqlConnection(connString1)
        connSqlServer1.Open() 'Opens first connection.

        'The transaction is now local to the first SQL Server
        'instance.

        Using connSqlServer2 As New SqlConnection(connString2)
            connSqlServer2.Open() 'Opens second connection.

            'The transaction is promoted to a distributed
            'transaction.
        End Using
    End Using

    'Commit the transaction.
    tran.Complete()
End Using
```

Designing Code That Uses Transactions

In this lab, you create a stored procedure that will be used to withdraw money from a bank account. The stored procedure should make sure that no concurrency problems occur and that the account cannot be overdrawn.

IMPORTANT   Lab requirements

You will need to have SQL Server 2005 and the *Adventure Works* database installed before you can complete this lab. Refer to the Introduction for setup instructions.

▶ **Exercise 1: Use the Default Isolation Level**

In this exercise, you create the draft for the stored procedure and use the read committed transaction isolation level.

1. Open SQL Server Management Studio, and connect to an instance of SQL Server 2005.
2. Open a new query window, and type and execute the following SQL statements. This will create the *TestDB* database, the Test schema, and the tables that are used in this exercise: you will also create the Test.spAccountReset stored procedure. You can execute this procedure to reset the data in the tables if you need to restart the exercise.

```
CREATE DATABASE TestDB;
GO

USE TestDB;
GO

CREATE SCHEMA Test;
GO

CREATE TABLE Test.Accounts (
    AccountNumber INT PRIMARY KEY
);
CREATE TABLE Test.AccountTransactions (
    TransactionID INT IDENTITY PRIMARY KEY
    ,AccountNumber INT NOT NULL REFERENCES Test.Accounts
    ,CreatedDateTime DATETIME NOT NULL DEFAULT CURRENT_TIMESTAMP
    ,Amount DECIMAL(19, 5) NOT NULL
);
GO

CREATE PROC Test.spAccountReset
AS
BEGIN
    SET NOCOUNT ON;

    DELETE Test.AccountTransactions;
    DELETE Test.Accounts;

    INSERT Test.Accounts (AccountNumber) VALUES (1001);
    INSERT Test.AccountTransactions (AccountNumber, Amount)
    VALUES (1001, 100);
    INSERT Test.AccountTransactions (AccountNumber, Amount)
    VALUES (1001, 500);
    INSERT Test.AccountTransactions (AccountNumber, Amount)
    VALUES (1001, 1400);

    SELECT AccountNumber, SUM(Amount) AS Balance
    FROM Test.AccountTransactions
    GROUP BY AccountNumber;
END
```

3. Open another query window, and type and execute the following SQL statements t ate the Test.spAccountWithdraw stored procedure:

```
USE TestDB;
GO

CREATE PROC Test.spAccountWithdraw
@AccountNumber INT
,@AmountToWithdraw DECIMAL(19, 5)
AS
```

```
BEGIN
    SET TRANSACTION ISOLATION LEVEL READ COMMITTED;

    BEGIN TRY
        IF(@AmountToWithdraw <= 0)
            RAISERROR('@AmountToWithdraw must be > 0.', 16, 1);

        BEGIN TRAN;
            -- Verify that the account exists...
            IF NOT EXISTS(
                    SELECT *
                    FROM Test.Accounts
                    WHERE AccountNumber = @AccountNumber
                )
                RAISERROR('Account not found.', 16, 1);

            -- Verify that the account will not be overdrawn...
            IF (@AmountToWithdraw > (
                    SELECT SUM(Amount)
                    FROM Test.AccountTransactions
                    WHERE AccountNumber = @AccountNumber)
                )
                RAISERROR('Not enough funds in account.', 16, 1);

            -- ** USED TO TEST CONCURRENCY PROBLEMS **
            RAISERROR('Pausing procedure for 10 seconds...', 10, 1)
                WITH NOWAIT;
            WAITFOR DELAY '00:00:30';
            RAISERROR('Procedure continues...', 10, 1) WITH NOWAIT;

            -- Make the withdrawal...
            INSERT Test.AccountTransactions (AccountNumber, Amount)
                VALUES (@AccountNumber, -@AmountToWithdraw);

            -- Return the new balance of the account:
            SELECT SUM(Amount) AS BalanceAfterWithdrawal
            FROM Test.AccountTransactions
            WHERE AccountNumber = @AccountNumber;

        COMMIT TRAN;
    END TRY
    BEGIN CATCH
        DECLARE @ErrorMessage NVARCHAR(2047);
        SET @ErrorMessage = ERROR_MESSAGE();
        RAISERROR(@ErrorMessage, 16, 1);
        -- Should also use ERROR_SEVERITY() and ERROR_STATE()...
        IF(XACT_STATE() <> 0)
            ROLLBACK TRAN;
    END CATCH
END
```

4. Open another query window, which will be referred to as Connection 1, and typ
execute the following SQL statement to prepare the connection:

```
-- Connection 1
/*  Leave the above line to easily see that this query window
belongs to Connection 1. */

USE TestDB;
GO


-- Reset/generate the account data:
EXEC Test.spAccountReset;
```

5. Open another query window, which will be referred to as Connection 2, and typ
execute the following SQL statement to prepare the connection:

```
-- Connection 2
/*  Leave the above line to easily see that this query window
belongs to Connection 2. */

USE TestDB;
GO
```

6. In this step, you will execute two batches at the same time to try to test for concur
problems. In both the Connection 1 and Connection 2 query windows, type the f
ing SQL statements without executing them yet. The statements will first retrie
current account balance and then attempt to empty the account.

```
SELECT SUM(Amount) AS BalanceBeforeWithdrawal
FROM Test.AccountTransactions
WHERE AccountNumber = 1001;
GO

EXEC Test.spAccountWithdraw @AccountNumber = 1001,
                            @AmountToWithdraw = 2000;
```

To get a better view of what will happen, press Ctrl+T in SQL Server Management S
to set results to be returned as text instead of grids. Do this for both query win
Now, start the execution in both query windows simultaneously and wait for
batches to finish execution. (This should take approximately 30 seconds because
WAITFOR DELAY statement in the Test.spAccountWithdraw stored procedure.)
connections' batches should return two result sets; the first result set will conta
current account balance (which should be 2,000 for both batches), and the se
result set will contain the account balance after the withdrawal.

What was the result of the two withdrawals? Was the account overdrawn?

What kind of concurrency problem occurred (if any)?

7. Close all open query windows except one, and in that query window, type and execute the following SQL statements to clean up after this exercise:

```
USE master;
GO
DROP DATABASE TestDB;
```

▶ **Exercise 2: Use a Locking Hint**

In the previous exercise, you encountered the "phantom reads" concurrency problem. In this exercise, you re-create the stored procedure, but this time, you will use the serializable locking hint to protect against phantom reads.

1. Open SQL Server Management Studio, and connect to an instance of SQL Server 2005.

2. Open a new query window, and type and execute the following SQL statements. This will create the *TestDB* database, the Test schema, and the tables that you will use in this exercise. You will also create the Test.spAccountReset stored procedure. You can execute this procedure to reset the data in the tables if you need to restart the exercise.

```
CREATE DATABASE TestDB;
GO

USE TestDB;
GO

CREATE SCHEMA Test;
GO

CREATE TABLE Test.Accounts (
    AccountNumber INT PRIMARY KEY
);
CREATE TABLE Test.AccountTransactions (
    TransactionID INT IDENTITY PRIMARY KEY
    ,AccountNumber INT NOT NULL REFERENCES Test.Accounts
    ,CreatedDateTime DATETIME NOT NULL DEFAULT CURRENT_TIMESTAMP
    ,Amount DECIMAL(19, 5) NOT NULL
);
GO

CREATE PROC Test.spAccountReset
AS
BEGIN
    SET NOCOUNT ON;

    DELETE Test.AccountTransactions;
    DELETE Test.Accounts;

    INSERT Test.Accounts (AccountNumber) VALUES (1001);
    INSERT Test.AccountTransactions (AccountNumber, Amount)
    VALUES (1001, 100);
```

```
        INSERT Test.AccountTransactions (AccountNumber, Amount)
        VALUES (1001, 500);
        INSERT Test.AccountTransactions (AccountNumber, Amount)
        VALUES (1001, 1400);

        SELECT AccountNumber, SUM(Amount) AS Balance
        FROM Test.AccountTransactions
        GROUP BY AccountNumber;
    END
```

3. Open another query window, and type and execute the following SQL statements ▮ ate the Test.spAccountWithdraw stored procedure:

```
USE TestDB;
GO

CREATE PROC Test.spAccountWithdraw
@AccountNumber INT
,@AmountToWithdraw DECIMAL(19, 5)
AS
BEGIN
    SET TRANSACTION ISOLATION LEVEL READ COMMITTED;

    BEGIN TRY
        IF(@AmountToWithdraw <= 0)
            RAISERROR('@AmountToWithdraw must be > 0.', 16, 1);

        BEGIN TRAN;
            -- Verify that the account exists...
            IF NOT EXISTS(
                    SELECT *
                    FROM Test.Accounts
                    WHERE AccountNumber = @AccountNumber
                )
                RAISERROR('Account not found.', 16, 1);

            -- Verify that the account will not be overdrawn...
            IF (@AmountToWithdraw > (
                    SELECT SUM(Amount)
                    FROM Test.AccountTransactions WITH(SERIALIZABLE)
                    WHERE AccountNumber = @AccountNumber)
                )
                RAISERROR('Not enough funds in account.', 16, 1);

            -- ** USED TO TEST CONCURRENCY PROBLEMS **
            RAISERROR('Pausing procedure for 10 seconds...', 10, 1)
                WITH NOWAIT;
            WAITFOR DELAY '00:00:30';
            RAISERROR('Procedure continues...', 10, 1) WITH NOWAIT;

            -- Make the withdrawal...
```

```
        INSERT Test.AccountTransactions (AccountNumber, Amount)
            VALUES (@AccountNumber, -@AmountToWithdraw);

        -- Return the new balance of the account:
        SELECT SUM(Amount) AS BalanceAfterWithdrawal
        FROM Test.AccountTransactions
        WHERE AccountNumber = @AccountNumber;

        COMMIT TRAN;
    END TRY
    BEGIN CATCH
        DECLARE @ErrorMessage NVARCHAR(2047);
        SET @ErrorMessage = ERROR_MESSAGE();
        RAISERROR(@ErrorMessage, 16, 1);
        -- Should also use ERROR_SEVERITY() and ERROR_STATE()...
        IF(XACT_STATE() <> 0)
            ROLLBACK TRAN;
    END CATCH
END
```

4. Open another query window, which will be referred to as Connection 1, and type and execute the following SQL statement to prepare the connection:

```
-- Connection 1
/*  Leave the above line to easily see that this query window
belongs to Connection 1. */

USE TestDB;
GO

-- Reset/generate the account data:
EXEC Test.spAccountReset;
```

5. Open another query window, which will be referred to as Connection 2, and type and execute the following SQL statement to prepare the connection:

```
-- Connection 2
/*  Leave the above line to easily see that this query window
belongs to Connection 2. */

USE TestDB;
GO
```

6. In this step, you will execute two batches at the same time to try to test for concurrency problems. In both the Connection 1 and Connection 2 query windows, type the following SQL statements without executing them yet. The statements will first retrieve the current account balance and then attempt to empty the account.

```
SELECT SUM(Amount) AS BalanceBeforeWithdrawal
FROM Test.AccountTransactions
WHERE AccountNumber = 1001;
```

```
GO

EXEC Test.spAccountWithdraw @AccountNumber = 1001,
                           @AmountToWithdraw = 2000;
```

To get a better view of what will happen, press Ctrl+T in SQL Server Management S
to set results to be returned as text instead of grids. Do this for both query wind
Now, start the execution in both query windows simultaneously and wait for
batches to finish execution. (This should take approximately 30 seconds because c
WAITFOR DELAY statement in the Test.spAccountWithdraw stored procedure.)
connections' batches should return two result sets; the first result set will contai
current account balance (which should be 2,000 for both batches), and the se
result set will contain the account balance after the withdrawal.

What was the result of the two withdrawals? Was the account overdrawn?

What kind of concurrency problem occurred (if any)?

Was there any other problem with this implementation?

7. Close all open query windows except one, and in that query window, type and exe
the following SQL statements to clean up after this exercise:

```
USE master;
GO
DROP DATABASE TestDB;
```

▶ **Exercise 3: Use an Alternative Solution**

In Exercise 2, the account was not overdrawn, and you didn't experience any concurr
problems. The connections were instead deadlocked. In this exercise, you re-create the s
procedure to protect against both phantom reads and deadlocks by changing the imple
tation slightly.

1. Open SQL Server Management Studio, and connect to an instance of SQL Server 2

2. Open a new query window, and type and execute the following SQL statements.
   will create the *TestDB* database, the Test schema, and the tables that will be used ir
   exercise: you will also create the Test.spAccountReset stored procedure. You can exe
   this procedure to reset the data in the tables if you need to restart the exercise.

```
CREATE DATABASE TestDB;
GO

USE TestDB;
GO

CREATE SCHEMA Test;
GO
```

```
CREATE TABLE Test.Accounts (
    AccountNumber INT PRIMARY KEY
);
CREATE TABLE Test.AccountTransactions (
    TransactionID INT IDENTITY PRIMARY KEY
    ,AccountNumber INT NOT NULL REFERENCES Test.Accounts
    ,CreatedDateTime DATETIME NOT NULL DEFAULT CURRENT_TIMESTAMP
    ,Amount DECIMAL(19, 5) NOT NULL
);
GO

CREATE PROC Test.spAccountReset
AS
BEGIN
    SET NOCOUNT ON;

    DELETE Test.AccountTransactions;
    DELETE Test.Accounts;

    INSERT Test.Accounts (AccountNumber) VALUES (1001);
    INSERT Test.AccountTransactions (AccountNumber, Amount)
    VALUES (1001, 100);
    INSERT Test.AccountTransactions (AccountNumber, Amount)
    VALUES (1001, 500);
    INSERT Test.AccountTransactions (AccountNumber, Amount)
    VALUES (1001, 1400);

    SELECT AccountNumber, SUM(Amount) AS Balance
    FROM Test.AccountTransactions
    GROUP BY AccountNumber;
END
```

3. Open another query window, and type and execute the following SQL statements to create the Test.spAccountWithdraw stored procedure:

```
USE TestDB;
GO

CREATE PROC Test.spAccountWithdraw
@AccountNumber INT
,@AmountToWithdraw DECIMAL(19, 5)
AS
BEGIN
    SET TRANSACTION ISOLATION LEVEL READ COMMITTED;

    BEGIN TRY
        IF(@AmountToWithdraw <= 0)
            RAISERROR('@AmountToWithdraw must be > 0.', 16, 1);

        BEGIN TRAN;
```

```
        -- Verify that the account exists
        -- and LOCK the account from access by other queries
        -- that will write to the account or its transactions.
        -- Note that SELECT statements against the account
        -- will still be allowed.
        IF NOT EXISTS(
                SELECT *
                FROM Test.Accounts WITH (UPDLOCK)
                WHERE AccountNumber = @AccountNumber
            )
            RAISERROR('Account not found.', 16, 1);

        -- Verify that the account will not be overdrawn...
        IF (@AmountToWithdraw > (
                SELECT SUM(Amount)
                FROM Test.AccountTransactions /* NO LOCKING HINT */
                WHERE AccountNumber = @AccountNumber)
            )
            RAISERROR('Not enough funds in account.', 16, 1);

        -- ** USED TO TEST CONCURRENCY PROBLEMS **
        RAISERROR('Pausing procedure for 10 seconds...', 10, 1)
            WITH NOWAIT;
        WAITFOR DELAY '00:00:30';
        RAISERROR('Procedure continues...', 10, 1) WITH NOWAIT;

        -- Make the withdrawal...
        INSERT Test.AccountTransactions (AccountNumber, Amount)
            VALUES (@AccountNumber, -@AmountToWithdraw);

        -- Return the new balance of the account:
        SELECT SUM(Amount) AS BalanceAfterWithdrawal
        FROM Test.AccountTransactions
        WHERE AccountNumber = @AccountNumber;

    COMMIT TRAN;
END TRY
BEGIN CATCH
    DECLARE @ErrorMessage NVARCHAR(2047);
    SET @ErrorMessage = ERROR_MESSAGE();
    RAISERROR(@ErrorMessage, 16, 1);
    -- Should also use ERROR_SEVERITY() and ERROR_STATE()...
    IF(XACT_STATE() <> 0)
        ROLLBACK TRAN;
END CATCH
END
```

4. Open another query window, which will be referred to as Connection 1, and type and execute the following SQL statement to prepare the connection:

```
-- Connection 1
/*  Leave the above line to easily see that this query window
belongs to Connection 1. */

USE TestDB;
GO


-- Reset/generate the account data:
EXEC Test.spAccountReset;
```

5. Open another query window, which will be referred to as Connection 2, and type and execute the following SQL statement to prepare the connection:

```
-- Connection 2
/*  Leave the above line to easily see that this query window
belongs to Connection 2. */

USE TestDB;
GO
```

6. In this step, you will execute two batches at the same time to try to test for concurrency problems. In both the Connection 1 and Connection 2 query windows, type the following SQL statements without executing them yet. The statements will first retrieve the current account balance and will then attempt to empty the account.

```
SELECT SUM(Amount) AS BalanceBeforeWithdrawal
FROM Test.AccountTransactions
WHERE AccountNumber = 1001;
GO

EXEC Test.spAccountWithdraw @AccountNumber = 1001,
                            @AmountToWithdraw = 2000;
```

To get a better view of what will happen, press Ctrl+T in SQL Server Management Studio to set results to be returned as text instead of grids. Do this for both query windows. Now, start the execution in both query windows simultaneously and wait for both batches to finish execution. (This should take approximately 30 seconds because of the WAITFOR DELAY statement in the Test.spAccountWithdraw stored procedure.) Both connections' batches should return two result sets; the first result set will contain the current account balance (which should be 2,000 for both batches), and the second result set will contain the account balance after the withdrawal.

What was the result of the two withdrawals? Was the account overdrawn?

What kind of concurrency problem occurred (if any)?

Was there any other problem with this implementation?

7. Close all open query windows except one, and in that query window, type and ex
   the following SQL statements to clean up after this exercise:

```
USE master;
GO
DROP DATABASE TestDB;
```

Quick Check

1. What is the difference between the READPAST and READUNCOMMITTED tab
   locking hints?
2. Which transaction isolation level cannot be specified as a table locking hint?
3. What is the advantage of locking larger resources, such as tables, instead of row
4. What is the main advantage of locking smaller resources, such as rows, instead
   tables or pages?

Quick Check Answers

1. Both the READPAST and READUNCOMMITTED table locking hints will preve
   SELECT (and also UPDATE/DELETE for READPAST) statements from bei
   blocked by resources locked exclusively by other transactions. The difference
   that READUNCOMMITTED will return the dirty values for locked resourc
   while READPAST will simply skip them. (That is, it will not return them at all).
2. The snapshot isolation level cannot be specified as a table locking hint.
3. The advantage of locking larger resources is that it will reduce the work requir
   by the SQL Server lock manager to allocate locks (because far fewer locks are al
   cated), and it will also reduce the memory used to maintain locks.
4. The main advantage of locking smaller resources is that it greatly reduces the r
   of blocking and deadlocks.

Case Scenario: Optimizing Locking

In this scenario, you are a database developer in your organization. An order entry applic
contains various elements that list the database contents. During peak usage, the list
quently take longer than usual to display, even though they don't contain a lot of data
have noticed that these delays are caused by blocking. The order entry application also
tains several reports that display aggregated sales information. When these reports are do
checked by auditors, they are sometimes found to contain inconsistent data. The value
played at one place in a report might not be consistent with data in other places of the r

The application currently uses the default transaction isolation level and does not use locking hints. Design a solution for both problems by implementing the appropriate transaction isolation level.

ggested Practices

Objective 4.2: Design the locking granularity level

- **Practice 1**   Create a simple table with one column and no primary key. Insert two rows into the table. Start a transaction (without committing it), and update one of the rows in the table. In another connection, try to read the unaffected row, both rows, and the affected row, and watch the result. Do this for all different isolation levels (including read committed snapshot), and observe the differences in behavior.

Objective 4.4: Design code that uses transactions

- **Practice 1**   Create a simple table with one integer column, and declare it as the table's primary key. Within a user-defined transaction, insert the values 1, 1, and 2 into the table. Check whether any rows were persisted into the table (or if they were rolled back). Experiment with using the SET XACT_ABORT ON setting as well as using a *try/catch* block around the transaction. Also, always issue a SELECT XACT_STATE(); query at the end of each batch to see the state of the transaction.

ferences

- Lock Compatibility
  http://msdn2.microsoft.com/en-us/library/aa213041(SQL.80).aspx.
- Locking Hints
  http://msdn2.microsoft.com/en-us/library/ms189857.aspx
- Table Hint (Transact-SQL)
  http://msdn2.microsoft.com/en-us/library/ms187373.aspx.
- Using Snapshot Isolation
  http://msdn2.microsoft.com/en-us/library/tcbchxcb.aspx
- "The Rational Guide to SQL Server 2005 Service Broker" by Roger Wolter (Rational Press, 2006)

Chapter Summary

- The choice of transaction isolation level affects both query results and perform because of blocking and row versioning.

- Use the least restrictive transaction isolation level.

- When a more restrictive transaction isolation level is required, consider applying locking hints rather than specifying transaction isolation level on the session level the SET TRANSACTION ISOLATION LEVEL statement.

- Keep transactions short. Open the transaction as late as possible, and close it as ea possible.

- Design transactions to minimize deadlocks.

- Consider alternate solutions to locking by using the @@ROWCOUNT function an OUTPUT clause.

- When not rolling back a transaction in a *try/catch* block, always verify that the tra tion is not uncommittable by querying the *XACT_STATE()* function.

ptimizing SQL Server 2005
erformance

Database optimization is a compelling part of the database developer's job role. The difference in performance between a well-optimized database and a non-optimized database can be enormous. Working with optimization demands a keen eye for details and an interest in understanding how the database engine works. The more you learn about what Microsoft SQL Server actually needs to do to complete a task, the greater your chance will be to successfully optimize the database. In a sense, you must try to "become" SQL Server.

The task of optimizing a database can be broken down into subtasks, including: optimizing queries and database routines, creating appropriate indexes, and normalizing and de-normalizing the database. (Database normalization is beyond the scope of this training kit.)

Exam objectives in this chapter:
- Optimize and tune queries for performance.
  - Evaluate query performance.
- Analyze query plans.
- Modify queries to improve performance.
- Test queries for improved performance.
  - Detect locking problems.
  - Modify queries to optimize client and server performance.
  - Rewrite subqueries to joins.
  - Design queries that have search arguments (SARGs).
  - Convert single-row statements into set-based queries.
- Optimize indexing strategies.
  - Design an index strategy.
  - Analyze index use across an application.
  - Add, remove, or redesign indexes.
  - Optimize index-to-table-size ratio.

- Optimize data storage.
  - ❏ Choose column data types to reduce storage requirements across the enterp
  - ❏ Design appropriate use of varchar across the enterprise.
  - ❏ Denormalize entities to minimize page reads per query.
  - ❏ Optimize table width.

Before You Begin

To complete the lessons in this chapter, you must have:

- A thorough understanding of Transact-SQL, including inner joins, outer joins, a and subqueries.
- A good understanding of the indexes in SQL Server databases.
- SQL Server 2005 and the *AdventureWorks* sample database installed.

son 1: Optimizing and Tuning Queries

Estimated lesson time: 60 minutes

Optimizing and tuning queries is an important task for a database developer. Throughout this lesson, we will discuss several options for optimizing queries.

uating Query Performance

One of the most important aspects when measuring performance is what to actually measure, that is, what metric to use. In SQL Server, there are three main metrics to consider: query cost, page reads, and query execution time.

Exam Tip   In the exam, always consider the performance metric against which your solution to a specific problem is measured.

Query Cost

The query cost is typically the best metric to use when comparing query performance. It is an internal metric used in SQL Server that takes into account both CPU and input/output (IO) resources used by the query. The lower the query cost, the better the query performance. You can find it in the graphical execution plan of the query by moving the mouse pointer over the last (the leftmost) operation in the query and examining the value Estimated subtree cost. The query cost is not affected by things such as locking or resource contention. The cost is typically a good metric, but when certain items are used in a query, such as scalar user-defined functions and CLR routines, the cost for these items is not calculated, which renders the query cost lower than the accurate assessment. This is why it is called *estimated* query cost. The problem with query cost is discussed in greater detail later in this lesson.

Page Reads

Page reads represents the number of 8-kilobyte data pages accessed by the SQL Server storage engine while executing a query. You can retrieve this metric by executing SET STATISTICS IO ON. This will cause each query execution to output something similar to the following in the Messages tab of the query window:

```
Table 'Customer'. Scan count 2, logical reads 136, physical reads 0, read-ahead reads 0, lob
logical reads 0, lob physical reads 0, lob read-ahead reads 0.
Table 'SalesOrderHeader'. Scan count 121, logical reads 822, physical reads 5, read-ahead
reads 0, lob logical reads 0, lob physical reads 0, lob read-ahead reads 0.
```

The total page reads of this output is 136 + 822, which is the sum of the values labeled "l
reads." *Logical reads* are the number of pages read from memory. The logical reads repr
the total number of data pages read from any index on the SalesOrderHeader table. The
items tell you how many of the logical reads were read from the hard drive (physical and
ahead reads), the number of passes through an index or heap it took to respond to the
(scan count), and how many of the page reads were used to retrieve Large OBject (LOB
(data stored outside of the row for the data types *VARCHAR(max)*, *NVARCHAR(max)*, *V
NARY(max)*, *TEXT, NTEXT, IMAGE,* and *XML*). The metric page reads do not take into ac
the amount CPU resources used when executing the query. This is why page reads are
cally not as accurate a metric as the query cost. This metric also has the same problem
scalar used-defined functions and CLR routines as the query cost, which is that page
caused by these routines are not included in the output of STATISTICS IO.

Query Execution Time

The execution time of the query is the most volatile metric. It is affected by blocking as w
resource contention on the server. That said, it is particularly important always to inclu
query execution time metric in performance comparisons because it can help you spot
lems with the other performance metrics (page reads and query cost). By executing SE
TISTICS TIME ON, SQL Server will return the execution time in milliseconds for each
execution.

Examining the Theoretical Query Execution Order

It is vital to have a basic understanding of the theoretical execution order of a SELECT
working with query optimization. This helps in understanding what SQL Server ac
needs to do to produce the query results.

The theoretical execution order is referred to as such because the query optimizer
change the execution order to optimize performance. This is only done if the query r
would be the same were the theoretical execution order used.

The execution order needs to be split into two branches because it differs if the UNION
is included in the query. A simplified version of these two branches is described in Tab

Table 7-1 Theoretical Execution Order – Excluding the UNION Clause

	Commands	Results
1.	FROM, JOIN, APPLY and ON	Join execution and first query filter (th clause)
2.	WHERE	Second query filter; does not support a gate functions

Table 7-1   Theoretical Execution Order – Excluding the UNION Clause

	Commands	Results
3.	GROUP BY and aggregate functions (such as SUM, AVG etc.) that are included in the query	Grouping and aggregation calculations
4.	HAVING	Third query filter; only supports filtering on the results of aggregate functions
5.	SELECT	Determines which columns should be returned by the query
6.	ORDER BY	Result sorting
7.	TOP	Fourth (and last) query filter; causes the query to return only the first X rows from the previous clause
8.	FOR XML	Converts the tabular result returned by the SELECT statement to XML

The execution order shown in Table 7-1 holds true for all queries except those that contain the UNION clause. These queries will use the theoretical execution order shown in Table 7-2.

Table 7-2   Theoretical Execution Order – Including the UNION Clause

	Commands	Results
1.	FROM, JOIN, APPLY and ON	Join execution and first query filter (the ON clause).
2.	WHERE	Second query filter; does not support aggregate functions.
3.	GROUP BY and aggregate functions (such as SUM, AVG etc.) that are included in the query	Grouping and aggregation calculations.
4.	HAVING	Third query filter; only supports filtering on the results of aggregate functions.
5.	TOP	Fourth (and last) query filter; causes the query to return only the first X rows from the previous clause. (Note that, in this case, the TOP clause is executed *before* the ORDER BY clause.)

Table 7-2 Theoretical Execution Order – Including the UNION Clause

	Commands	Results
6.	UNION and SELECT	Concatenates the result of each SELECT statement included in the query; determi which columns should be returned by t query
7.	ORDER BY	Sorts the result of the UNION clause
8.	FOR XML	Converts the tabular result returned by UNION/SELECT clauses to XML

The cause of the difference in the execution order is the introduction of the TOP claus SQL Server 7.0), which is not part of the ANSI/ISO SQL standard. This makes the stan compliant behavior of the UNION clause (only allowing for one ORDER BY clause, v must be placed in the last SELECT statement of the query and must sort the entire (result) cause problems with the TOP clause. This isn't a huge issue, but it is important aware of. As an example, compare the result of the following two queries. Both queries ar posed to return the two most expensive "red" products and the two most expensive "t products. The first query will produce an incorrect result, as follows:

```
USE AdventureWorks;

SELECT TOP(2) ProductID, Name, Color, ListPrice
FROM Production.Product
WHERE Color = 'Black'
UNION
SELECT TOP(2) ProductID, Name, Color, ListPrice
FROM Production.Product
WHERE Color = 'Red'
ORDER BY ListPrice DESC;
```

Results:
```
ProductID   Name                            Color ListPrice
----------- ------------------------------- ----- ----------
706         HL Road Frame - Red, 58         Red   1431,50
707         Sport-100 Helmet, Red           Red   34,99
317         LL Crankarm                     Black 0,00
318         ML Crankarm                     Black 0,00
```

The second query will produce the correct result, as follows:

```
USE AdventureWorks;

WITH a AS (
    SELECT TOP(2) ProductID, Name, Color, ListPrice
    FROM Production.Product
```

```
    WHERE Color = 'Black'
    ORDER BY ListPrice DESC
), b AS (
    SELECT TOP(2) ProductID, Name, Color, ListPrice
    FROM Production.Product
    WHERE Color = 'Red'
    ORDER BY ListPrice DESC
)
SELECT * FROM a
UNION ALL
SELECT * FROM b;
```

Results:
```
ProductID    Name                        Color ListPrice
----------- ------------------------- ----- ----------
775          Mountain-100 Black, 38      Black 3374,99
776          Mountain-100 Black, 42      Black 3374,99
749          Road-150 Red, 62            Red   3578,27
750          Road-150 Red, 44            Red   3578,27
```

As you can see, the result of the first query does not return the correct values because the ORDER BY clause is executed after the TOP clause.

imizing Query Performance

There are several ways to optimize queries. Optimization consists of tasks such as rewriting the query, de-normalizing or normalizing tables, adding indexes, removing indexes, or a combination of these tasks.

The Graphical Execution Plan

The graphical execution plan is a great tool to use when optimizing queries. This chapter discusses several execution plans. Some of the items that you should look for in the execution plan are shown in Table 7-3.

Table 7-3   Items from the Graphical Execution Plan

"Thick arrows"	A "thick arrow" represents a large number of rows moving from one operation in the execution plan to another. The greater the number of rows transferred from one operation to another, the thicker the arrow.
Hash operations Hash Match	If a hash operation is used to handle clauses such as GROUP BY and JOIN, it often means that an appropriate index did not exist to optimize the query.

Table 7-3   Items from the Graphical Execution Plan

Sorts	A sort isn't necessarily bad, but if it is a high percentage of the query you should consider whether an index can be built to remove the nee the sort operation.
Sort	
"Large plans"	The plan with fewer operations is typically the better-optimized plar
Table scans or clustered index scans	A clustered index scan and a table scan indicate that no appropriate i can be used to optimize the query.
Clustered Index Scan	
Table Scan	

Using Search Arguments

A search argument (SARG) is a filter expression that is used to limit the number of returned by a query and that can utilize an index seek operation which will substar increase the performance of the query. Typically, a filter expression is not a SARG if the co from the table is changed in any way (such as LEFT(Name, 1) = 'A'). If the filter is not a and no other SARGs exist in the query, this will result in an index or table scan. A *scan* to the scan of the entire table or index. Instead of a scan, you want a seek to be perform *seek* implies the use of the index's balanced tree to find the values for which the c searched. For example, in the following query, the OrderDateIndex index will be sc: (rather than seeked). The execution plan for the following query is shown in Figure 7-1

```
USE AdventureWorks;

CREATE NONCLUSTERED INDEX OrderDateIndex
    ON Sales.SalesOrderHeader (OrderDate);

SELECT COUNT(*) FROM Sales.SalesOrderHeader
    WHERE YEAR(OrderDate) = 2004;
```

Query 1: Query cost (relative to the batch): 100%
SELECT COUNT(*) FROM Sales.SalesOrderHeader WHERE YEAR(OrderDate) = 2004;

Figure 7-1   An execution plan from SQL Server Management Studio showing an Index Scan operation

If the query is instead rewritten so that the OrderDate column is not changed, an index seek operation will be used instead of a scan. The execution plan for the following query is shown in Figure 7-2.

```
SELECT COUNT(*) FROM Sales.SalesOrderHeader
    WHERE OrderDate >= '20040101' AND OrderDate < '20050101';
```

```
Query 1: Query cost (relative to the batch): 100%
SELECT COUNT(*) FROM [Sales].[SalesOrderHeader] WHERE [OrderDate]>=@1 AND [OrderDate]<@2
```

SELECT	Compute Scalar	Stream Aggregate	Index Seek
Cost: 0 %	Cost: 0 %	(Aggregate)	[AdventureWorks].[Sales].[SalesOrde
		Cost: 18 %	Cost: 82 %

Figure 7-2 An execution plan from SQL Server Management Studio showing an Index Seek operation

Note that the use of the *COLLATE* operator in a filter expression also invalidates the use of an index on that column. We cover this in more detail in the next lesson.

Using Joins

To optimize queries, one of the first basic strategies is to minimize the number of join clauses used. Another consideration is that outer joins typically incur more cost than inner joins because of the extra work needed to find the unmatched rows. If only inner joins are used in a query, the behavior of the ON and WHERE clauses is the same; it does not matter if you put an expression in the ON or WHERE clause. Compare the following two queries; they both return the same results and will use equal execution plans.

```
-- Query #1
SELECT p.ProductID, p.Name, sod.SalesOrderID
FROM Production.Product AS p
INNER JOIN Sales.SalesOrderDetail AS sod
    ON sod.ProductID = p.ProductID
WHERE p.Color = 'Black';

-- Query #2
SELECT p.ProductID, p.Name, sod.SalesOrderID
FROM Production.Product AS p
INNER JOIN Sales.SalesOrderDetail AS sod
    ON sod.ProductID = p.ProductID
        AND p.Color = 'Black';
```

If these queries had been written with an outer join, they would not be syntactically equal and could have substantially different performances.

Subqueries Without Correlation to the Outer Query

An uncorrelated subquery is executed only once per query execution and returns on
value. These queries typically incur very little overhead. Note that this type of subquery c
have any reference (correlation) to the outer query. The following example uses a subqu
return all products that are cheaper than the average product price. The subquery calcu
the average product price is executed first (only once), and then the value returned by th
query is used as a parameter in the outer query.

```
USE AdventureWorks;

SELECT
    p.ProductID
    ,p.Name
    ,p.ListPrice
FROM Production.Product AS p
WHERE p.ListPrice > (
    SELECT AVG(p2.ListPrice)
    FROM Production.Product AS p2
);
```

Correlated Subqueries

Correlated subqueries include a reference to the outer query. Typically, this reference i
to filter the correlated subquery. A correlated subquery is typically good for perform
when used in combination with the *EXISTS* operator to filter the outer query. The fol
example query uses the *EXISTS* operator to return only products that have been sold:

```
USE AdventureWorks;

SELECT p.ProductID, p.Name
FROM Production.Product AS p
WHERE EXISTS (
    SELECT * FROM Sales.SalesOrderDetail AS sod
    WHERE sod.ProductID = p.ProductID)
```

While this type of correlated subquery is typically a good implementation, the use of
lated subqueries in the SELECT clause typically has a negative effect on performance. T
course, depends on the number of rows returned by the query; if a large number of
returned, each query in the SELECT clause would be executed for each row. The fol
query returns 6,224 rows and includes two correlated subqueries. Each of these queries
cuted once per row, resulting in a total of 12,448 subquery executions.

```
USE AdventureWorks;

SELECT
    soh.SalesOrderID
    ,soh.OrderDate
    ,(SELECT TOP(1) sod1.UnitPrice FROM Sales.SalesOrderDetail AS sod1
       WHERE sod1.SalesOrderID = soh.SalesOrderID
       ORDER BY sod1.OrderQty DESC) AS UnitPrice
    ,(SELECT TOP(1) sod2.OrderQty FROM Sales.SalesOrderDetail AS sod2
       WHERE sod2.SalesOrderID = soh.SalesOrderID
       ORDER BY sod2.OrderQty DESC) AS OrderQty
FROM Sales.SalesOrderHeader AS soh
WHERE soh.TerritoryID = 4;
```

There is also a potential bug in this query. Because each subquery is executed separately, they might end up using different indexes. This means that these queries might not return values from the same row (which they are probably intended to do) if the same value for OrderQty exists for multiple sales order details in any sales order.

There are several ways to rewrite this query; the most common one in SQL Server 2005 is probably to use the new APPLY clause. If the subquery is used in either one of the FROM, JOIN, or APPLY clauses, it might also be referred to as a derived table. The APPLY clause basically gives you the opportunity to combine the two subqueries in the previous query into one, splitting the number of subquery executions in half. For the new query to return the same results as the previous query, you must use an OUTER APPLY. (An OUTER APPLY works similarly to a left outer join, and its counterpart, the CROSS APPLY clause, behaves like an inner join.) This is because, in the previous query, the outer query will return a row even if the subqueries return nothing. The new query could be written as follows:

```
USE AdventureWorks;

SELECT
    soh.SalesOrderID
    ,soh.OrderDate
    ,a.*
FROM Sales.SalesOrderHeader AS soh
OUTER APPLY (
      SELECT TOP(1) sod.UnitPrice, sod.OrderQty
      FROM Sales.SalesOrderDetail AS sod
      WHERE sod.SalesOrderID = soh.SalesOrderID
      ORDER BY sod.OrderQty DESC
) AS a
WHERE soh.TerritoryID = 4;
```

This query has a cost of roughly 73, while the first query's cost was double that, at about 146.

Another solution to this type of problem is to make use of the *ROW_NUMBER* fun instead of a correlated subquery. By using the *ROW_NUMBER* function, you can find th cific number of rows that you need by filtering on the row number rather than using the clause. To be able to filter on the result of the *ROW_NUMBER* function, the query needs placed inside a derived table or a common table expression (CTE). The larger the resu the better this approach performs compared to the previous queries. The cost for the follc query drops from 73 to about 2.88!

```
WITH a AS ( -- Common table expression.
    SELECT
        soh.SalesOrderID
        ,soh.OrderDate
        ,sod.UnitPrice
        ,sod.OrderQty
        ,ROW_NUMBER() OVER (PARTITION BY soh.SalesOrderID
            ORDER BY sod.OrderQty DESC) AS RowNo
    FROM Sales.SalesOrderDetail AS sod
    INNER JOIN Sales.SalesOrderHeader AS soh
        ON sod.SalesOrderID = soh.SalesOrderID
    WHERE soh.TerritoryID = 4
)
SELECT
    a.SalesOrderID
    ,a.OrderDate
    ,a.UnitPrice
    ,a.OrderQty
FROM a
WHERE a.RowNo = 1;
```

Scalar User-Defined Functions

A scalar user-defined function (UDF) is a function that returns a single value (not a resu This type of function is frequently used in queries and can significantly degrade perform The reason for this is that these functions are not expanded and optimized into the query plan by the query optimizer, but they are rather just called from the executior (without any optimization based on the context into which it is inserted in the plan). Th means that the cost of whatever is done inside the function is not included in the cos mates found in the graphical execution plan for the query. This same problem occurs f output of the SET STATISTICS IO ON statement, which will contain no references to w done inside the UDF. The following performance comparison is between a query using a and another query using a correlated subquery. Because of the problem with the quer for these queries, the performance metric will be the execution time, which is returned the SET STATISTICS TIME ON statement.

BEST PRACTICES   Query execution time

When using query execution times as a performance metric, it is typically a good idea to execute each query a few times and use either the lowest or the last execution time as the metric.

The following is a query using a UDF. The execution plan produced for the query is shown in Figure 7-3.

```
USE AdventureWorks;
GO

CREATE FUNCTION dbo.fnGetCustomerAccountNumber(@CustomerID INT)
RETURNS VARCHAR(10)
AS
BEGIN
    RETURN ISNULL(
        (
        SELECT
            AccountNumber
        FROM Sales.Customer
        WHERE CustomerID = @CustomerID
    ), 'NOT FOUND');
END
GO

SET STATISTICS IO ON;
SET STATISTICS TIME ON;

SELECT
    soh.SalesOrderID
    ,soh.OrderDate
    ,dbo.fnGetCustomerAccountNumber(soh.CustomerID)
FROM Sales.SalesOrderHeader AS soh;
```

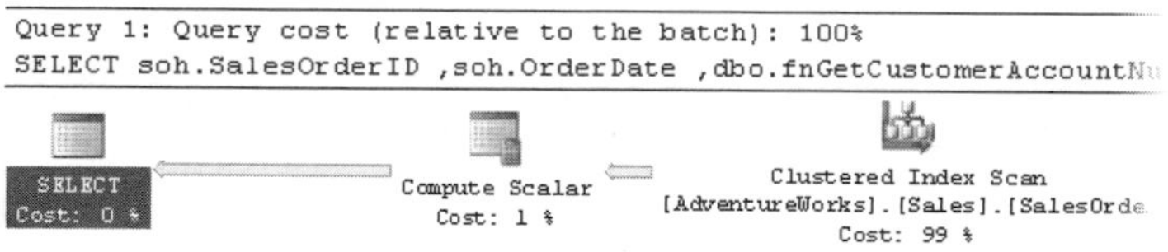

Query 1: Query cost (relative to the batch): 100%
SELECT soh.SalesOrderID ,soh.OrderDate ,dbo.fnGetCustomerAccountN⬚

SELECT		Compute Scalar		Clustered Index Scan
Cost: 0 %		Cost: 1 %		[AdventureWorks].[Sales].[SalesOrde⬚
				Cost: 99 %

Figure 7-3   An execution plan from SQL Server Management Studio

The cost of this query is 0.56 and the number of page reads is 703 (neither metric being useful for comparison), while the execution time on the test machine was 50 seconds. Examine the graphical execution plan and note that it contains no reference to the Sales.Customer table.

The following is an example query that uses a correlated subquery. The query's exec
plan is shown in Figure 7-4.

```
USE AdventureWorks;

SET STATISTICS IO ON;
SET STATISTICS TIME ON;

SELECT
    soh.SalesOrderID
    ,soh.OrderDate
    ,ISNULL(
      (
      SELECT
          AccountNumber
      FROM Sales.Customer
      WHERE CustomerID = soh.CustomerID
    ), 'NOT FOUND')
FROM Sales.SalesOrderHeader AS soh;
```

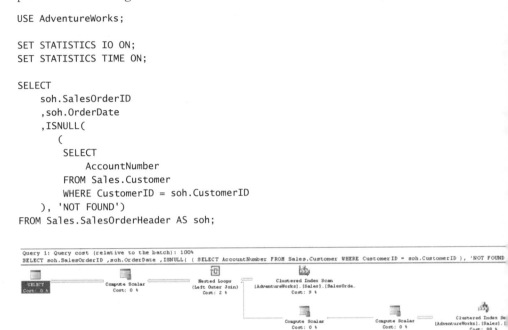

Figure 7-4   An execution plan from SQL Server Management Studio

The cost of the query without the UDF goes up to 5.99 and the number of page re
65,608 (both of which are "real" values). At the same time, the execution time drops to
seconds. As you can see, the first query using the UDF is over 700 percent slower than t
ter query because of the UDF use.

The use of inline table-valued user-defined functions or views does not incur the same
mance cost as the use of scalar user-defined functions. Both inline table-valued user-d
functions and views are optimized (expanded) into the query plan.

Table-Valued User-Defined Functions

There are three different types of table-valued functions; two of them can be develo
T-SQL and the other one can be developed in a CLR language such as C# .NET or
Basic .NET. They are as follows:

■ T-SQL inline table-valued function

- T-SQL multi-statement table-valued function
- CLR table-valued function

These different types of functions behave differently. A T-SQL inline table-valued function is actually just a view that can accept parameters. It is optimized in the same way as a view or any select statement would be. An advantage of using inline table-valued functions instead of views is that you can require the user (for example, a database developer) that uses the function to supply parameters. In this way, you can make sure that a filter is always used for the query inside the function (based on the parameters provided).

T-SQL multi-statement table-valued functions, on the other hand, can be considered to work like a stored procedure that populates a temporary table that is used by an outer stored procedure. If you include a multi-statement table-valued function in a query (for example, in a join), the function has to be fully executed (that is, finish execution) before the query can make use of its results. This means that if a multi-statement table-valued function needs to return 1,000,000 rows, all rows must be processed by the function before the function's results can be used by the query.

CLR table-valued functions, on the other hand, stream their results. This means that while the CLR table-valued function is executing, its results become available to the calling query. This difference can help performance because the outer query does not have to wait for the entire result from the function to be available before it can start processing the returned rows. A CLR table-valued function consists of two CLR methods: one method that manages the overall execution of the function and one method that is called for every row that is returned by the function. The method that is run for each row returned by the function is not first run until the method that manages the function execution first starts executing yield return commands. This is important to remember because any processing before the start of the yield return commands will have to be finished before any rows are returned from the the function. CLR table-valued functions are typically useful for querying objects other than tables, such as strings (by using regular expressions) or, for example, the file system. Note that the processing done by a CLR function is not accurately included in the cost or page reads of the query.

Cursors

You should generally avoid using cursors because of their negative effect on performance. They have such an effect partly because each execution of a FETCH statement in a cursor loop is similar in performance cost to executing a SELECT statement that returns one row. Another problem is that a DML statement is optimized as a single unit, while a cursor loop cannot be optimized in the same way. Instead, each item in the loop will be optimized and executed separately for each iteration of the loop.

You should try to rewrite cursor logic into one or more set-based statements (SEL
INSERT, UPDATE, DELETE). If you must use cursors, consider implementing the logic
a CLR stored procedure or a table-valued user-defined function instead (depending o
functionality you need).

Lab: Comparing Query Performance

In this lab, you will test the query performance of three different queries that should pro
the same result set. The query will return all customers in a specific territory and the last
received for those customers. If the customer does not have any orders, it must st
returned.

The completed lab is available in the \Labs\Chapter 07\Lab1 folder on the companion

---

IMPORTANT   Lab requirements

You will need to have SQL Server 2005 and the *AdventureWorks* database installed before you
complete this lab. Refer to the Introduction for setup instructions.

▶ **Exercise 1: Test Using a Small Result Set**

In this exercise, you will execute the three queries mentioned in the lab preface and re
each query's cost. In this case, the parameter supplied to all three queries (TerritoryID
yield a small result set of 64 rows.

1. Open SQL Server Management Studio and connect to an instance of SQL Server 2

2. In a new query window, type and execute the following SQL statements to crea
   TestDB database, the Test schema, and the two tables that will be used in this exer

   ```
   CREATE DATABASE TestDB;
   GO

   USE TestDB;
   GO

   CREATE SCHEMA Test;
   GO

   SELECT * INTO Test.SalesOrderHeader
   FROM AdventureWorks.Sales.SalesOrderHeader;
   GO

   SELECT * INTO Test.Customer
   FROM AdventureWorks.Sales.Customer;
   GO

   ALTER TABLE Test.SalesOrderHeader
   ```

```
    ADD CONSTRAINT PKSalesOrderHeader
    PRIMARY KEY(SalesOrderID);
GO

ALTER TABLE Test.Customer
    ADD CONSTRAINT PKCustomer
    PRIMARY KEY(CustomerID);
```

3. Turn on the Actual Execution Plan in SQL Server Management Studio by pressing Ctrl+M, or by selecting Include Actual Execution Plan from the Query menu.

4. Type and execute Query #1 to test its performance. (Because of the use of two separate correlated subqueries in this query, it is not guaranteed that both these subqueries return data from the same row in the Test.Customer table.)

```
-- Query #1
SELECT
    c.CustomerID
    ,c.AccountNumber
    ,(
        SELECT TOP(1) soh.SalesOrderID
        FROM Test.SalesOrderHeader AS soh
        WHERE soh.CustomerID = c.CustomerID
        ORDER BY OrderDate DESC
    ) AS SalesOrderID
    ,(
        SELECT TOP(1) soh.OrderDate
        FROM Test.SalesOrderHeader AS soh
        WHERE soh.CustomerID = c.CustomerID
        ORDER BY OrderDate DESC
    ) AS OrderDate
FROM Test.Customer AS c
WHERE c.TerritoryID = 2;
```

What was the total cost of Query #1?

(You can find the value in the Execution Plan tab by moving the mouse pointer over the *SELECT* operator and locating the value named Estimated Subtree Cost.)

5. Type and execute Query #2 to test its performance.

```
-- Query #2
SELECT
    c.CustomerID
    ,c.AccountNumber
    ,o.*
FROM Test.Customer AS c
OUTER APPLY (
    SELECT TOP(1) soh.SalesOrderID, soh.OrderDate
    FROM Test.SalesOrderHeader AS soh
    WHERE soh.CustomerID = c.CustomerID
    ORDER BY OrderDate DESC
```

```
) AS o
WHERE c.TerritoryID = 2;
```

What was the total cost of Query #2?

6. Type and execute Query #3 to test its performance.

```
-- Query #3
WITH a AS (
    SELECT
        c.CustomerID
        ,c.AccountNumber
        ,c.TerritoryID
        ,soh.SalesOrderID
        ,soh.OrderDate
        ,ROW_NUMBER() OVER (PARTITION BY c.CustomerID
                ORDER BY soh.OrderDate DESC) AS RowNo
    FROM Test.Customer AS c
    LEFT OUTER JOIN Test.SalesOrderHeader AS soh
        ON soh.CustomerID = c.CustomerID
)
SELECT
    a.CustomerID
    ,a.AccountNumber
    ,a.SalesOrderID
    ,a.OrderDate
FROM a
WHERE a.RowNo = 1 AND a.TerritoryID = 2;
```

What was the total cost of Query #3?

7. To clean up after this exercise, close all open query windows in SQL Server Manage
   Studio, open a new query window, and execute the following SQL statements:

```
USE master;
DROP DATABASE TestDB;
```

▶ **Exercise 2: Test Using a Large Result Set**

In this exercise, you will execute the three queries mentioned in the lab preface and re
each query's cost. In this case, the parameter supplied to all three queries (TerritoryID
yield a larger result set of 3,433 rows (compared to 64 rows in the previous exercise).

1. Open SQL Server Management Studio and connect to an instance of SQL Server 2

2. In a new query window, type and execute the following SQL statements to creat
   TestDB database, the Test schema, and the two tables that will be used in this exer

```
CREATE DATABASE TestDB;
GO

USE TestDB;
GO
```

```
CREATE SCHEMA Test;
GO

SELECT * INTO Test.SalesOrderHeader
FROM AdventureWorks.Sales.SalesOrderHeader;
GO

SELECT * INTO Test.Customer
FROM AdventureWorks.Sales.Customer;
GO

ALTER TABLE Test.SalesOrderHeader
    ADD CONSTRAINT PKSalesOrderHeader
    PRIMARY KEY(SalesOrderID);
GO

ALTER TABLE Test.Customer
    ADD CONSTRAINT PKCustomer
    PRIMARY KEY(CustomerID);
```

3. Turn on the Actual Execution Plan in SQL Server Management Studio by pressing Ctrl+M, or by selecting Include Actual Execution Plan from the Query menu.

4. Type and execute Query #1 to test its performance.

   (Because of the use of two separate correlated subqueries in this query, it is not guaranteed that both these subqueries return data from the same row in the Test.Customer table.)

```
-- Query #1
SELECT
    c.CustomerID
    ,c.AccountNumber
    ,(
        SELECT TOP(1) soh.SalesOrderID
        FROM Test.SalesOrderHeader AS soh
        WHERE soh.CustomerID = c.CustomerID
        ORDER BY OrderDate DESC
    ) AS SalesOrderID
    ,(
        SELECT TOP(1) soh.OrderDate
        FROM Test.SalesOrderHeader AS soh
        WHERE soh.CustomerID = c.CustomerID
        ORDER BY OrderDate DESC
    ) AS OrderDate
FROM Test.Customer AS c
WHERE c.TerritoryID = 1;
```

   What was the total cost of Query #1?

   (You can find the value in the Execution Plan tab by moving the mouse pointer over the *SELECT* operator and locating the value named Estimated Subtree Cost.)

5. Type and execute Query #2 to test its performance.

```
-- Query #2
SELECT
    c.CustomerID
    ,c.AccountNumber
    ,o.*
FROM Test.Customer AS c
OUTER APPLY (
    SELECT TOP(1) soh.SalesOrderID, soh.OrderDate
    FROM Test.SalesOrderHeader AS soh
    WHERE soh.CustomerID = c.CustomerID
    ORDER BY OrderDate DESC
) AS o
WHERE c.TerritoryID = 1;
```

What was the total cost of Query #2?

6. Type and execute Query #3 to test its performance.

```
-- Query #3
WITH a AS (
    SELECT
        c.CustomerID
        ,c.AccountNumber
        ,c.TerritoryID
        ,soh.SalesOrderID
        ,soh.OrderDate
        ,ROW_NUMBER() OVER (PARTITION BY c.CustomerID
                ORDER BY soh.OrderDate DESC) AS RowNo
    FROM Test.Customer AS c
    LEFT OUTER JOIN Test.SalesOrderHeader AS soh
        ON soh.CustomerID = c.CustomerID
)
SELECT
    a.CustomerID
    ,a.AccountNumber
    ,a.SalesOrderID
    ,a.OrderDate
FROM a
WHERE a.RowNo = 1 AND a.TerritoryID = 1;
```

What was the total cost of Query #3?

▶ **Exercise 3: Optimize Query #3**

In this exercise, you will make a small change to Query #3 to optimize it.

1. Open SQL Server Management Studio and connect to an instance of SQL Server 2

2. Turn on the Actual Execution Plan in SQL Server Management Studio by pre
   Ctrl+M.

3. Type and execute the new version of Query #3 with the small result set (TerritoryID = 2). (The difference from the previous version of the query appears in bold.)

```
USE TestDB;
GO

WITH a AS (
    SELECT
        c.CustomerID
        ,c.AccountNumber
        ,c.TerritoryID
        ,soh.SalesOrderID
        ,soh.OrderDate
        ,ROW_NUMBER() OVER (PARTITION BY c.CustomerID
                        ORDER BY soh.OrderDate DESC) AS RowNo
    FROM Test.Customer AS c
    LEFT OUTER JOIN Test.SalesOrderHeader AS soh
        ON soh.CustomerID = c.CustomerID
    WHERE c.TerritoryID = 2
)
SELECT
    a.CustomerID
    ,a.AccountNumber
    ,a.SalesOrderID
    ,a.OrderDate
FROM a
    WHERE a.RowNo = 1;
```

What was the total cost of this version of Query #3 for the small result set?

4. Type and execute the new version of Query #3 with the larger result set (TerritoryID = 1). (The difference from the previous version of the query appears in bold.)

```
USE TestDB;
GO

WITH a AS (
    SELECT
        c.CustomerID
        ,c.AccountNumber
        ,c.TerritoryID
        ,soh.SalesOrderID
        ,soh.OrderDate
        ,ROW_NUMBER() OVER (PARTITION BY c.CustomerID
                        ORDER BY soh.OrderDate DESC) AS RowNo
    FROM Test.Customer AS c
    LEFT OUTER JOIN Test.SalesOrderHeader AS soh
        ON soh.CustomerID = c.CustomerID
    WHERE c.TerritoryID = 2
)
SELECT
```

```
      a.CustomerID
     ,a.AccountNumber
     ,a.SalesOrderID
     ,a.OrderDate
FROM a
WHERE a.RowNo = 1;
```

What was the total cost of this version of Query #3 for the larger result set?

5. To clean up after this lab, close all open query windows in SQL Server Managemen dio, open a new query window, and execute the following SQL statements:

```
USE master;
DROP DATABASE TestDB;
```

Quick Check

1. Why should you avoid scalar user-defined functions in large result sets?
2. Why should you avoid query execution time as the primary metric when measu ing query performance?
3. Why should you avoid cursors?

Quick Check Answers

1. Avoid scalar user-defined functions because they are not optimized into the que and might therefore significantly degrade query performance.
2. Query execution time is a poor choice as primary metric because it is affected many things, such as locks and server load.
3. Avoid cursors because of their large impact on performance.

son 2: **Optimizing Index Strategies**

Estimated lesson time: 40 minutes

SQL Server 2005 supports two basic types of indexes: clustered and non-clustered. Both indexes are implemented as a balanced tree, where the so-called leaf level is the bottom level of the index structure. The difference between these index types is that the clustered index is the actual table, that is, the bottom level of a clustered index contains the actual rows, including all columns, of the table. A non-clustered index, on the other hand, only contains the columns included in its key, plus a pointer pointing to the actual data row. If a table does not have a clustered index defined on it, it is called a heap, or unsorted table. You could also say that a table can have one of two forms: It is either a heap (unsorted) or a clustered index (sorted).

roving Performance with Covered Indexes

The notion of a covered index is that SQL Server doesn't need to use lookups between the non-clustered index and the table to return the query results. Because a clustered index is the actual table, clustered indexes always cover queries.

To consider the index "covered," it must contain all columns referenced in the query (in any clause, SELECT, JOIN, WHERE, GROUP BY, HAVING, etc.). Consider the following SQL table and query:

Test TableA

Col1	Col2	Col3

```
SELECT Col1 FROM Test.TableA
WHERE Col2 = 1;
```

For an index to cover this query, it must contain at least the columns Col1 and Col2. You can do this in several ways. All of the following indexes would cover this query:

```
CREATE NONCLUSTERED INDEX TestIndex ON Test.TableA (Col1, Col2);
CREATE NONCLUSTERED INDEX TestIndex ON Test.TableA (Col2, Col1);
CREATE NONCLUSTERED INDEX TestIndex ON Test.TableA (Col1) INCLUDE (Col2);
CREATE NONCLUSTERED INDEX TestIndex ON Test.TableA (Col2) INCLUDE (Col1);
CREATE NONCLUSTERED INDEX TestIndex ON Test.TableA (Col1, Col2, Col3);
CREATE NONCLUSTERED INDEX TestIndex ON Test.TableA (Col3) INCLUDE (Col1, Col2);
```

As you can see, the columns only need to be found in the index; their position and whether they are found in the index key or are included columns (discussed in this lesson) does not matter. Of course, both the execution plan and the performance could differ greatly be‹ these indexes; however, they all cover the query.

The performance benefit gained by using a covered index is typically great for querie‹ return a large number of rows (a non-selective query) and small for queries that retur‹ rows (a selective query). Remember that a small number of rows could be 10 for a tabl‹ a couple of hundred rows and 1,000 for a table with millions of rows. Following is a p‹ mance comparison of four queries. The table that the queries are executed against has t‹ lowing schema and is populated with 1,000,000 rows:

```
CREATE TABLE Test.CoveredIndexTest (
    Col1 INT NOT NULL
    Col2 NVARCHAR(2047) NOT NULL
);
INSERT Test.CoveredIndexTest (Col1, Col2)
    VALUES (0, 'A lonely row...');
INSERT Test.CoveredIndexTest (Col1, Col2)
    SELECT TOP(999999) message_id, text FROM sys.messages AS sm
    CROSS JOIN (
        SELECT TOP(15) 1 AS Col FROM sys.messages
    ) AS x
```

On the test machine, the size of this table is 24,238 pages (roughly 193 MB); also note th‹ table is a heap, that is, it does not have a clustered index defined on it. The queries and in‹ used in this test have the following definitions; the performance metrics (measured in‹ reads) for the queries are shown in Table 7-4.

```
-- Query #1 -- Returns 1 row.
SELECT Col1, Col2 FROM Test.CoveredIndexTest
    WHERE Col1 = 0;

-- Query #2   -- Returns roughly 0.1% of the rows found in the table.
-- (1,056 rows)
SELECT Col1, Col2 FROM Test.CoveredIndexTest
    WHERE Col1 BETWEEN 1205 AND 1225;

-- Query #3 -- Returns roughly 0.5% of the rows found in the table.
-- (5,016 rows)
SELECT Col1, Col2 FROM Test.CoveredIndexTest
    WHERE Col1 BETWEEN 1205 AND 1426;   -- Query #4 (non-selective) -- Returns roughly 5‹
the rows found in the table.
-- (50,028 rows)
SELECT Col1, Col2 FROM Test.CoveredIndexTest
    WHERE Col1 BETWEEN 1205 AND 2298;

-- Non-covered index CREATE NONCLUSTERED INDEX NonCovered ON Test.CoveredIndexTest (Col‹

-- Covered index CREATE NONCLUSTERED INDEX Covered ON Test.CoveredIndexTest (Col1) INCL‹
(Col2);
```

Table 7-4   Query Performance Matrix

	Query #1 (1 row)	Query #2 (selective)	Query #3 (somewhat selective)	Query #4 (non-selective)
No index	24,237 pages	24,237 pages	24,237 pages	24,237 pages
Non-covered index	4 pages	1,062 pages	5,029 pages	50,125 pages
Covered index	3 pages	28 pages	139 pages	1,286 pages

```
-- Drop the table used in this example.
DROP TABLE Test.CoveredIndexTest;
```

The performance metric that is shown in the table is the number of data pages that SQL Server touched during the query execution (SET STATISTICS IO ON, logical reads).

Note that the so-called "selective" query (Query #2) returns 0.01 percent of the rows in the table. For a table of this size, that still amounts to 1,000 rows. If you are speaking to someone about the number of rows that will be affected by a query, and he or she says that number is "only a couple of percent of the table," this usually translates to a lot of rows.

Some conclusions that we can draw from the test are given here. (This is only with regard to read performance; write performance is discussed later in this lesson.)

- A covered index always performs better than a non-covered index.
- For queries that return a very limited number of rows, a non-covered index also performs very well.
- For the somewhat-selective query (Query #3), the covered index reads at least 36 times fewer pages than the non-covered index. In this case, a query was considered selective by the query optimizer when it matched less than roughly 0.77 percent of the table.

ng Included Columns and Index Depth

In earlier versions of SQL Server (before 2005), creating covered non-clustered indexes could often be impossible because an index could contain no more than 16 columns or be more than 900 bytes wide. The new "included column" feature makes it possible to add columns to an index without adding them to the index's key. Included columns cannot be used for tasks such as filtering or sorting; their sole benefit is reducing page reads through covering queries, thereby avoiding table lookups.

An index can have a maximum of 1,023 included columns (a table can have a maximum of 1,024 columns), making it possible to create a non-clustered index that covers the entire table, which is almost like having a second clustered index! In addition, columns that use one of the

large data types (*VARCHAR(max)*, *NVARCHAR(max)*, *VARBINARY(max)*, *XML*, *TEXT*, *NT*
and *IMAGE*) are allowed to be included in an index as an included column.

Only columns that are used for filtering, grouping, or sorting should be part of the index
all other columns included in the index should be included columns. Besides allowin
more columns in the index, included columns have other benefits. In the following
script, a table with 1,000,000 rows is created with two indexes. One index has all colum
the index key, while the other index only has one column in the key (the one that wou
filtered on), and the rest of the columns are included. The width of each row in the index w
a little over 300 bytes; this might sound like a very wide index row, but it not uncommon
also makes up for the fact that the test table only contains one million rows; for larger t
the width of the index does not need to be this big to make a performance difference. Th
lowing script defines (and populates) objects and indexes used in the following exampl

```
CREATE TABLE Test.IncludedColumnsTest(
    PKCol UNIQUEIDENTIFIER NOT NULL DEFAULT NEWSEQUENTIALID()
        PRIMARY KEY CLUSTERED
    ,Col1 INT IDENTITY NOT NULL
    ,Col2 CHAR(20) NOT NULL
    ,Col3 CHAR(20) NOT NULL
    ,Col4 CHAR(20) NOT NULL
    ,Col5 CHAR(20) NOT NULL
    ,Col6 CHAR(20) NOT NULL
    ,Col7 CHAR(20) NOT NULL
    ,Col8 CHAR(20) NOT NULL
    ,Col9 CHAR(20) NOT NULL
    ,Col10 CHAR(20) NOT NULL
    ,Col11 CHAR(20) NOT NULL
    ,Col12 CHAR(20) NOT NULL
    ,Col13 CHAR(20) NOT NULL
    ,Col14 CHAR(20) NOT NULL
    ,Col15 CHAR(20) NOT NULL
    ,Col16 CHAR(20) NOT NULL
);
INSERT Test.IncludedColumnsTest (Col2, Col3, Col4, Col5, Col6, Col7, Col8,
        Col9, Col10, Col11, Col12, Col13, Col14, Col15, Col16)
SELECT TOP(1000000)
    CAST(message_id AS CHAR(20)) AS Col2
    ,CAST(message_id AS CHAR(20)) AS Col3
    ,CAST(message_id AS CHAR(20)) AS Col4
    ,CAST(message_id AS CHAR(20)) AS Col5
    ,CAST(message_id AS CHAR(20)) AS Col6
    ,CAST(message_id AS CHAR(20)) AS Col7
    ,CAST(message_id AS CHAR(20)) AS Col8
    ,CAST(message_id AS CHAR(20)) AS Col9
    ,CAST(message_id AS CHAR(20)) AS Col10
    ,CAST(message_id AS CHAR(20)) AS Col11
```

```
        ,CAST(message_id AS CHAR(20)) AS Col12
        ,CAST(message_id AS CHAR(20)) AS Col13
        ,CAST(message_id AS CHAR(20)) AS Col14
        ,CAST(message_id AS CHAR(20)) AS Col15
        ,CAST(message_id AS CHAR(20)) AS Col16
FROM sys.messages AS sm
CROSS JOIN (
        SELECT TOP(15) 1 AS Col FROM sys.messages
) AS x;
CREATE NONCLUSTERED INDEX IncludedColumns ON Test.IncludedColumnsTest (Col1) INCLUDE (Col2,
Col3, Col4, Col5, Col6, Col7, Col8, Col9, Col10, Col11, Col12, Col13, Col14, Col15, Col16);
CREATE NONCLUSTERED INDEX NoIncludedColumns ON Test.IncludedColumnsTest (Col1, Col2, Col3,
Col4, Col5, Col6, Col7, Col8, Col9, Col10, Col11, Col12, Col13, Col14, Col15, Col16);
```

Table 7-5 shows some of the interesting differences between the index with and without included columns.

Table 7-5   Index Size Matrix

	IncludedColumns	NoIncludedColumns
Total size	40,147 pages	41,743 pages
Size of the non-leaf level of the index	146 pages	1,743 pages
Index depth	3 levels (root page + 1 intermediate level + leaf level)	5 levels (root page + 3 intermediate levels + leaf level)
Average size of rows in the non-leaf levels of the index	27 bytes	327 bytes
Average size of rows in the leaf level of the index	321 bytes	321 bytes

You can retrieve this information from the dynamic management function *sys.dm_db_index _physical_stats* by executing the following query:

```
SELECT * FROM sys.dm_db_index_physical_stats(DB_ID(),
OBJECT_ID('Test.IncludedColumnsTest'), NULL, NULL, 'DETAILED');
```

The total size of the index is not reduced by more than about four percent because the leaf levels of both indexes contain the same data. However, the non-leaf levels of the index with included columns only needs to contain the one column that is in the index's key (plus pointers to the next level), while, for the other index, all columns are part of the index key, making each row in the non-leaf level roughly the same size as that of the leaf level. Table 7-6 shows the layout of each level of a *NoIncludedColumns* index.

Table 7-6   Levels of the NoIncludedColumns Index

Root	1 page with 4 rows pointing to the next level
1st intermediate level	4 pages with a total of 70 rows pointing to the next level
2nd intermediate level	70 pages with a total of 1,668 rows pointing to the next level
3rd intermediate level	1,668 pages with a total of 40,000 rows pointing to the next level
Leaf level	40,000 pages containing all of the 1,000,000 rows of the index

Table 7-7 shows the layout of each level of an *IncludedColumns* index.

Table 7-7   Levels of the IncludedColumns Index

Root	1 page with 145 rows pointing to the next level
Intermediate level	145 pages with a total of 40,001 rows pointing to the next level
Leaf level	40,001 pages containing all of the 1,000,000 rows of the index

Due to the fact that the rows in the non-leaf level pages of the *NoIncludedColumns* inde substantially larger than those of the *IncludedColumns* index, more pages and therefore levels are needed to create the balanced tree for the index. Because the *NoIncludedCo* index is two levels (40 percent) deeper than the *IncludedColumns* index, each search th the *NoIncludedColumns* index will need two more page reads to get to the bottom of the i This might not sound like much, but if the index is used for repeated searches, such as fo or if it is heavily queried, this will cause performance degradation.

In Table 7-8, three example queries are shown that join a table called Test.OtherTable wi Test.IncludedColumnsTest using different indexes. Note that the index (WITH(INDEX)) are only used to force SQL Server to use the specified index instead optimal index (which would be the *IncludedColumns* index). A new index named *NotC* is added to show the performance of a non-clustered index that does not cover the quer following script defines additional objects and indexes required by the example:

```
-- Create the NotCovered index.
CREATE NONCLUSTERED INDEX NotCovered ON Test.IncludedColumnsTest
(Col1);

-- Create and populate the Test.OtherTable table.
CREATE TABLE Test.OtherTable (
    PKCol INT IDENTITY NOT NULL PRIMARY KEY
    ,Col1 INT NOT NULL
);
INSERT Test.OtherTable (Col1)
SELECT Col1 FROM Test.IncludedColumnsTest;
```

Table 7-8 **Levels of the *IncludedColumns* Index**

Query #	Definition	Page reads

Query #1 Index: *IncludedColumns* The execution plan is shown in Figure 7-5.	`SELECT o.PKCol, i.Col2`
	`FROM Test.OtherTable AS o INNER JOIN`
	`Test.IncludedColumnsTest AS i`
	`    WITH(INDEX(IncludedColumns))`
	`    ON o.Col1 = i.Col1`
	`WHERE o.PKCol BETWEEN 1`
	`    AND 10000;`
		32,726 pages

Query #2 Index: *NoIncludedColumns* The execution plan is shown in Figure 7-5.	`SELECT o.PKCol, i.Col2`
	`FROM Test.OtherTable AS o`
	`INNER JOIN`
	`    Test.IncludedColumnsTest AS i`
	`    WITH(INDEX(NoIncludedColumns))`
	`    ON o.Col1 = i.Col1`
	`WHERE o.PKCol BETWEEN 1`
	`    AND 10000;`
		53,994 pages

Query #3 Index: *NotCovered* The execution plan is shown in Figure 7-5.	`SELECT o.PKCol, i.Col2`
	`FROM Test.OtherTable AS o`
	`INNER JOIN`
	`    Test.IncludedColumnsTest AS i`
	`    WITH(INDEX(NotCovered))`
	`    ON o.Col1 = i.Col1`
	`WHERE o.PKCol BETWEEN 1`
	`    AND 10000;`
		62,617 pages

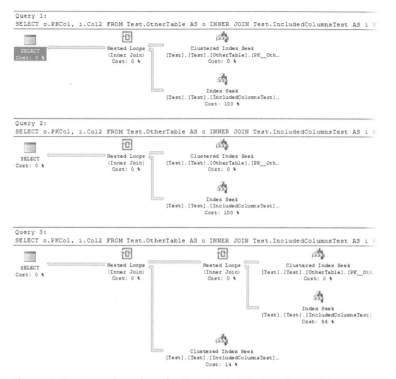

Figure 7-5   Execution plans for Queries 1–3 in SQL Server Management Studio

Query #1, with the *IncludedColumns* index, is the best-performing query with 32,726
reads. Query #2, with the *NoIncludedColumns* index, used 53,994 page reads. As you ca
the difference in the number of page reads between the two indexes is roughly the sai
the difference in index levels (40 percent). Query #3, with the *NotCovered* index, i
worst-performing query with 62,617 page reads because of the extra reads necessary to
the data that was not found in the index from the table. (Note the extra Nested Loops
in the execution plan of Query #3.)

Using Clustered Indexes

Because a clustered index is the actual table reading from the clustered index, it never re
in lookups. Therefore, the clustered index should generally be defined on columns tha
often queried and typically return a lot of data. This is because the problem of lookup
fetching a large number of rows doesn't exist. Two good candidates for the clustered inde
either the most frequently queried foreign key column of the table (a search on a foreigi

typically returns many rows) or the most frequently searched date column. (Date searches generally return a large number of rows as well.)

Another important consideration when selecting the column or columns on which to create the clustered index is that the key size of the clustered index should be as small as possible. If a clustered index exists on a table, all non-clustered indexes on that table will use the key of the clustered index as the row pointer from the non-clustered index to the table. If a clustered index does not exist, the Row Identifier is used, which takes up eight bytes of storage in each row of each non-clustered index. This can significantly increase size for larger tables. Consider the following:

- You have a table with 40,000,000 rows.
- The table has five non-clustered indexes.
- The clustered index key is 60 bytes wide. (This is not uncommon when you have clustered indexes that span a few columns.)

The total size of all row pointers from the non-clustered indexes on this table (*only* the pointers) would be:

40,000,000 * 5 * 60 = 12,000,000,000 bytes (close to 12 gigabytes)

If the clustered index was changed to be on only one column with a smaller data type, such as an integer for a foreign key, each row pointer would be only four bytes. Because four bytes is added to all duplicates of the clustered index key to keep it unique internally, the calculation uses eight bytes as the new clustered index key size.

40,000,000 * 5 * 8 = 1,600,000,000 bytes (close to 1.5 gigabytes)

The difference in storage needed is more than 10 gigabytes.

Exam Tip   For the exam, it's important to know the difference in non-clustered indexes depending on whether a clustered index exists on the table.

---

d Performance vs. Write Performance

The addition of indexes typically only helps boost read performance. Write performance is typically degraded because the indexes must be kept up-to-date with the data in the table. If a table has five non-clustered indexes defined on it, an insert into that table is really six inserts: one for the table and one for each index. The same goes for deletes. With update statements, only indexes that contain the columns that are updated by the update statement must be touched.

When index keys are updated, the row in the index must be moved to the appropriate po
in the index (which is not applicable for included columns). The result is that the up
split into a delete followed by an insert. Depending on the internal fragmentation of the
pages, this might also cause page splits.

Consider the following simple performance test on the Test.IndexInsertTest table cont
1,000,000 rows. 10,000 rows will be inserted in each test, and the table will be re-cr
between tests. First, the insert is performed against the table without any non-clus
indexes, then it is performed with one non-clustered index, and finally, with five non-clu
indexes.

```
CREATE TABLE Test.IndexInsertTest (
    PKCol UNIQUEIDENTIFIER NOT NULL DEFAULT NEWSEQUENTIALID()
        PRIMARY KEY CLUSTERED
    ,Col1 INT NOT NULL
);
INSERT Test.IndexInsertTest (Col1)
SELECT TOP(1000000)
    ROW_NUMBER() OVER (ORDER BY message_id) AS Col1
FROM sys.messages AS sm
CROSS JOIN (
SELECT TOP(15) 1 AS Col FROM sys.messages
) AS x;
-- Rebuild the table's clustered index.
ALTER INDEX ALL ON Test.OtherTable REBUILD;

-- Created table containing the rows used to perform the inserts.
CREATE TABLE Test.OtherTable (
    PKCol INT IDENTITY(100000,4) NOT NULL PRIMARY KEY
    ,OtherCol INT NOT NULL
)
INSERT Test.OtherTable (OtherCol)
SELECT Col1 FROM Test.IncludedColumnsTest
    WHERE Col1 BETWEEN 1 AND 10000;
```

Following is the first test, without any non-clustered indexes defined on the table. The
tion plan for this insert statement is shown in Figure 7-6.

```
INSERT Test.IndexInsertTest (Col1)
    SELECT PKCol FROM Test.OtherTable;
```

```
Query 1: Query cost (relative to the batch): 100%
INSERT Test.IndexInsertTest (Col1) SELECT PKCol FROM Test.OtherTable;
```

| INSERT | Index Insert | Sort | Clustered Index Insert | Sort | Compute Scalar | Top | Clustered Inde |
| Cost: 0 % | [TestDB].[Test].[IndexInsertTest].[… | Cost: 6 % | Cost: 39 % | [TestDB].[Test].[IndexInsertTest].[… | Cost: 39 % | Cost: 16 % | Cost: 0 % | Cost: 0 % | [TestDB].[Test].[Other | Cost: 2 % |

Figure 7-6   An execution plan from SQL Server Management Studio of the insert statement u
this test

The estimated query cost for the insert statement in this test was 0.74, and SQL Server touched 32,190 pages in the Test.IndexInsertTest table while performing the inserts.

Following is the second test with one non-clustered index defined on the table. The execution plan for this insert statement is shown in Figure 7-7.

```
-- 1. Drop and re-create the Test.IndexInsertTest table.
-- 2. Add one non-clustered index.
CREATE NONCLUSTERED INDEX NCIdx1 ON Test.IndexInsertTest (Col1);
-- 3. Execute the insert statement.
INSERT Test.IndexInsertTest (Col1)
    SELECT PKCol FROM Test.OtherTable;
```

Figure 7-7 An execution plan from SQL Server Management Studio of the insert statement used in this test

The estimated query cost for the insert statement in this test was 1.58, and SQL Server touched 65,125 pages in the Test.IndexInsertTest table while performing the inserts. This is roughly both twice the cost and number of pages compared with Test #1.

Following is the third test, with five non-clustered indexes defined on the table. The execution plan for this insert statement is shown in Figure 7-8.

```
-- 1. Drop and recreate the Test.IndexInsertTest table.
-- 2. Add five non-clustered indexes.
CREATE NONCLUSTERED INDEX NCIdx1 ON Test.IndexInsertTest (Col1);
CREATE NONCLUSTERED INDEX NCIdx2 ON Test.IndexInsertTest (Col1);
CREATE NONCLUSTERED INDEX NCIdx3 ON Test.IndexInsertTest (Col1);
CREATE NONCLUSTERED INDEX NCIdx4 ON Test.IndexInsertTest (Col1);
CREATE NONCLUSTERED INDEX NCIdx5 ON Test.IndexInsertTest (Col1);
-- 3. Execute the insert statement.
INSERT Test.IndexInsertTest (Col1)
    SELECT PKCol FROM Test.OtherTable;
```

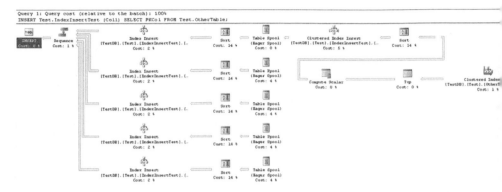

Figure 7-8 An execution plan from SQL Server Management Studio of the insert statement u this test

This time, the estimated query cost for the insert statement was 4.47, and SQL Server tou staggering 196,853 pages in the Test.IndexInsertTest table while performing the inserts. can see, the cost for performing the inserts is roughly doubled with each new non-clu index. However, in this case, each non-clustered index is roughly the same size (same as the table itself. For typical tables, the non-clustered indexes are narrower than the tab will not hurt performance (percentage-wise) to the same degree as in this test.

Because the ratio between read and write operations varies greatly between systems, an tables, it is a good idea to create indexes to optimize read performance and then test the that the created indexes has on write performance. As long as the write performance is able (and you have enough disk space to manage the created indexes), you can keep t ated indexes. It is also advisable to run such a test every so often to verify that the read write ratio for the table hasn't changed.

You should also note that both update and delete statements will benefit from certain ir to locate the rows in the table that they need to update or delete.

Using Computed Columns

A *computed column* is generally derived from other columns in the same table and car ence both system- and user-defined functions in its definition. To be able to create an in a computed column, it must adhere to a few requirements, which you can find in SQL 2005 Books Online under the topic "Creating Indexes on Computed Columns" at *msdn2.microsoft.com/en-us/library/ms189292.aspx.*

By defining a computed column and indexing it, it is possible to make queries that wou erally require an index or table scan to use a seek operation instead. Consider the foll query for sales orders in the *AdventureWorks* database. The query's execution plan is shown in Figure 7-9.

```
USE AdventureWorks;
-- First create an index on the OrderDate column
-- to support this query.
CREATE NONCLUSTERED INDEX OrderDateIndex ON
    Sales.SalesOrderHeader (OrderDate);
GO
SET STATISTICS IO ON;
SELECT COUNT(*) FROM Sales.SalesOrderHeader
WHERE MONTH(OrderDate) = 5;
```

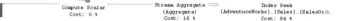

Query 1: Query cost (relative to the batch): 100%
SELECT COUNT(*) FROM Sales.SalesOrderHeader WHERE MONTH(OrderDate) = 5;

SELECT	Compute Scalar	Stream Aggregate	Index Scan
Cost: 0 %	Cost: 0 %	(Aggregate)	[AdventureWorks].[Sales].[SalesOrd
		Cost: 20 %	Cost: 80 %

Figure 7-9   An execution plan of the previous select statement from SQL Server Management Studio

Because the query did not use a valid search argument by modifying the column in the WHERE clause by applying a function to it, the *OrderDateIndex* index can only be used for scanning and not for seeking. To be able to produce an index seek, SQL Server must maintain an index of the result of the function call, in this case, *MONTH(OrderDate)*. You can do this by adding a computed column to the table and indexing that column as follows. The query's execution plan is shown in Figure 7-10.

```
-- Add the column.
ALTER TABLE Sales.SalesOrderHeader
    ADD OrderMonth AS MONTH(OrderDate);

-- Create an index on the computed column.
CREATE NONCLUSTERED INDEX OrderMonthIndex
    ON Sales.SalesOrderHeader (OrderMonth);
GO
SET STATISTICS IO ON;
-- Run the query and reference the new column.
SELECT COUNT(*) FROM Sales.SalesOrderHeader
WHERE OrderMonth = 5;
```

Query 1: Query cost (relative to the batch): 100%
SELECT COUNT(*) FROM Sales.SalesOrderHeader WHERE MONTH(OrderDate) = 5;

SELECT	Compute Scalar	Stream Aggregate	Index Seek
Cost: 0 %	Cost: 0 %	(Aggregate)	[AdventureWorks].[Sales].[SalesOrd
		Cost: 16 %	Cost: 84 %

Figure 7-10   An execution plan of the select using the computed column in the WHERE clause

This time, the query performs a seek operation on the index of the computed column, ~~~ing in only eight page reads. Depending on the complexity of your query and compute~ umn definition, the optimizer can automatically use the index of the computed cc~ without the computed column being referenced in the query, as follows. This query wi~ get the execution plan that was shown in Figure 7-10.

```
SET STATISTICS IO ON;
-- Run the query without referencing the computed column.
SELECT COUNT(*) FROM Sales.SalesOrderHeader
WHERE MONTH(OrderDate) = 5;
```

As you can see, SQL Server used the index of the computed column without having a ref~ to it in the query. This is a great feature because it makes it possible to add computed co~ and index them without having to change the queries in applications or stored proced~ use the new index.

Besides using computed columns with indexes with function calls, you can also use in~ computed columns to provide indexes in different collations. Consider that we have th~ Test.Person with the column Name using the Latin1_General_CI_AI collation. Now w~ to find all rows starting with the character "Ö." In Latin1_General, the dots over the O a~ considered accents, but in other languages, such as German and Swedish, Ö is a differen~ acter than O. Consider that the table is typically queried by English customers that will ~ to get both "O" and "Ö" back from a search such as LIKE 'Ö%' and occasionally by Sv~ customers who will expect to get only "Ö" back from the search. Because the table is ty~ queried by English customers, it makes sense to keep the Latin1_General_CI_AI collatio~ when Swedish customers query the table to use the *COLLATE* keyword to explicitly u~ Finnish_Swedish_CI_AI collation. Review the following script and queries. The exe~ plans for the two queries in the following script are shown in Figures 7-11 and 7-12.

```
-- Create and populate the table
CREATE TABLE Test.ProductNames (
    Name NVARCHAR(50) COLLATE Latin1_General_CI_AI
);
INSERT Test.ProductNames (Name) VALUES ('Öl');
INSERT Test.ProductNames (Name) VALUES ('Olja');
INSERT Test.ProductNames (Name) VALUES ('Beer');
INSERT Test.ProductNames (Name) VALUES ('Oil');
CREATE CLUSTERED INDEX NameIndex ON Test.ProductNames
    (Name);
GO

-- Query #1
-- Query for all product names that begin with the letter Ö
-- using the default collation.
SELECT Name FROM Test.ProductNames
```

```
    WHERE Name LIKE 'Ö%';
-- Result: Name
-------------
Oil
Öl
Olja

-- Query #2
-- Query for all product names that begin with the letter Ö
-- using the Finnish_Swedish_CI_AI collation.
SELECT Name FROM Test.ProductNames
    WHERE Name LIKE 'Ö%' COLLATE Finnish_Swedish_CI_AI;
-- Result: Name
-------------
Öl
```

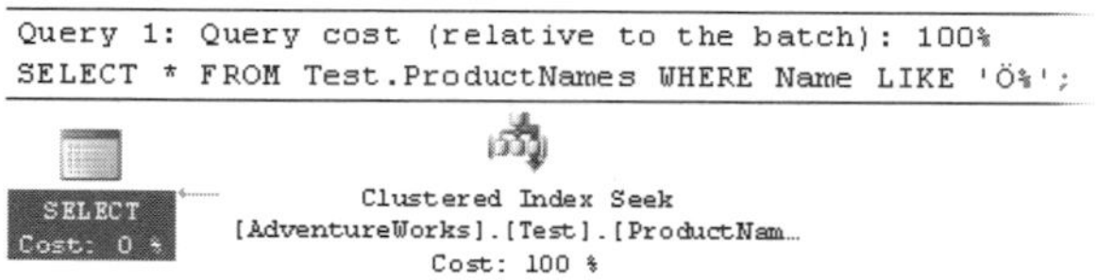

Figure 7-11   An execution plan of Query #1 in SQL Server Management Studio

Figure 7-12   An execution plan of Query #2 in SQL Server Management Studio

Comparing the execution plans of Query 1 (Figure 7-11) and Query 2 (Figure 7-12), we can see that, because the comparison in Query 2 needs to use a collation other than that of the column (and therefore, the index), a clustered index scan is used instead of an index seek, as in Query 1. By adding an indexed computed column to this table and specifying the Finnish_Swedish_CI_AS collation for this column, SQL Server can automatically use that index instead (which is shown below). Note that this is only a viable solution if you are using a relatively low number of collations because these indexes will need to be both stored and maintained like all other indexes. The execution plan for the query in the following script is shown in Figure 7-13.

```
-- Add a computed column with another collation.
ALTER TABLE Test.ProductNames
    ADD Name_Finnish_Swedish_CI_AI
        AS Name COLLATE Finnish_Swedish_CI_AI;
-- Create an index on the computed column.
CREATE NONCLUSTERED INDEX NameIndex2 ON Test.ProductNames
```

```
    (Name_Finnish_Swedish_CI_AI);
GO

-- Query for all product names that begin with the letter Ö
-- using the Finnish_Swedish_CI_AI collation without specifying
-- the computed column.
SELECT Name FROM Test.ProductNames
    WHERE Name LIKE 'Ö%' COLLATE Finnish_Swedish_CI_AI;
-- Result: Name
-------------
Ö1
```

```
Query 1: Query cost (relative to the batch): 100%
SELECT * FROM Test.ProductNames WHERE Name LIKE 'Ö%' COLLATE Finnish_Swedish_CI_A

    SELECT           Compute Scalar       Index Seek
   Cost: 0 %            Cost: 0 %    [AdventureWorks].[Test].[ProductNam...
                                          Cost: 100 %
```

Figure 7-13 An execution plan of the query in SQL Server Management Studio

Using Indexed Views

A normal database view is just a named select statement that can be used from other statements. These views have no particular impact on performance. Beginning wit Server 2000, you could create one or more indexes on a view because the view satisfi tain requirements. These requirements are quite extensive and can be found in Online under the heading "Creating Indexed Views" at *http://msdn2.microsoft.com/ library/ms191432.aspx*. By creating an index on a view, the view is materialized. This that, in the logical sense, it is still a view, but now that view actually stores the data fo the view. If the data is changed in the tables on which the view is based, the view is au ically updated to reflect those changes.

Creating indexed views can greatly improve read performance of queries. An imp aspect of indexed views is that the query optimizer can automatically detect that an in view that satisfies a certain query exists and can use it, even if the indexed view is refer in the query. This, however, is only true for SQL Server 2005 Enterprise Edition and oper Edition.

The following example shows a query and its execution plan (shown in Figure 7-14) w an indexed view:

```
USE AdventureWorks;

SELECT
    p.Name
    ,sod.OrderQty
    ,soh.OrderDate
```

```
FROM Production.Product AS p
INNER JOIN Sales.SalesOrderDetail AS sod
    ON sod.ProductID = p.ProductID
INNER JOIN Sales.SalesOrderHeader AS soh
    ON soh.SalesOrderID = sod.SalesOrderID
WHERE soh.TerritoryID = 1;
```

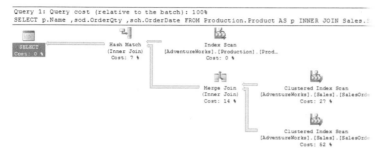

Figure 7-14   An execution plan of the query in SQL Server Management Studio

The cost of the previous query was 2.03. Next, an indexed view is created to optimize the query, and the same query is executed again. The execution plan for this query is shown in Figure 7-15. The first index created on a view must materialize the entire view, which means that it must be a clustered index. It is also a requirement that the first index be unique (which is why the column SalesOrderDetailID has been added to the example's indexed view).

```
CREATE VIEW Sales.ProductsSoldVw
WITH SCHEMABINDING
AS
SELECT
    soh.TerritoryID
    ,sod.SalesOrderDetailID
    ,p.Name
    ,sod.OrderQty
    ,soh.OrderDate
FROM Production.Product AS p
INNER JOIN Sales.SalesOrderDetail AS sod
    ON sod.ProductID = p.ProductID
INNER JOIN Sales.SalesOrderHeader AS soh
    ON soh.SalesOrderID = sod.SalesOrderID
GO

CREATE UNIQUE CLUSTERED INDEX ProductsSoldVwIdx
    ON Sales.ProductsSoldVw (TerritoryID, SalesOrderDetailID);
GO

SELECT
    p.Name
```

```
        ,sod.OrderQty
        ,soh.OrderDate
FROM Production.Product AS p
INNER JOIN Sales.SalesOrderDetail AS sod
    ON sod.ProductID = p.ProductID
INNER JOIN Sales.SalesOrderHeader AS soh
    ON soh.SalesOrderID = sod.SalesOrderID
WHERE soh.TerritoryID = 1;
```

```
Query 1: Query cost (relative to the batch): 100%
SELECT p.Name ,sod.OrderQty ,soh.OrderDate FROM P:
```

Figure 7-15   An execution plan of the query in SQL Server Management Studio

This time, the indexed view is used by the query (even though it is not referenced) an *query cost* drops to 0.14.

After you have created the unique clustered index on the view, it is possible to create addi non-clustered indexes on the same view. If you are using any edition of SQL Server othe Enterprise Edition or Developer Edition, your query must directly reference the view, an must add the optimizer hint WITH(NOEXPAND) to the query.

```
SELECT
    Name
    ,OrderQty
    ,OrderDate
FROM Sales.ProductsSoldVw WITH(NOEXPAND)
WHERE TerritoryID = 1;
```

Analyzing Index Usage

Because indexes incur a cost (for storage space and for keeping them up-to-date when statements are executed), it is important to keep track of which indexes are actually used. If an index is never used, it is likely that it can be dropped to both save storage spac reduce the cost of write operations. It is important to keep in mind that some indexes a ated for a specific purpose; for example, to optimize the monthly salary reports. Therefor should be careful when dropping unused or seldom-used indexes. When you drop an that is seldom used, you should document your actions so that the dropped index can created if it is needed later.

In earlier versions of SQL Server, there was no simple query that could be executed t out how frequently specific indexes were used. One possible method was to run a

Server Profiler trace and track the use of indexes. This trace could later be analyzed to find out which indexes were used, or rather, which indexes were not used.

In SQL Server 2005, you can query a dynamic management view called sys.dm_db_index _usage_stats to find the index-usage information. The columns from this view that are particularly interesting are shown in Table 7-9. (You can see the whole table at SQL Server 2005 Books Online at *http://msdn2.microsoft.com/en-us/library/ms188755.aspx.*)

Table 7-9   Subset of the sys.dm_db_index_usage_stats DMV

Column name	Data type	Description
database_id	*smallint*	ID of the database on which the table or view is defined
object_id	*int*	ID of the table or view on which the index is defined
index_id	*int*	ID of the index
user_seeks	*bigint*	Number of seeks by user queries
user_scans	*bigint*	Number of scans by user queries
user_lookups	*bigint*	Number of lookups by user queries
user_updates	*bigint*	Number of updates by user queries
last_user_seek	*datetime*	Time of last user seek
last_user_scan	*datetime*	Time of last user scan
last_user_lookup	*datetime*	Time of last user lookup

You should typically query this view for indexes that have low values in the user_seeks or user_scans column. All values in this view are reset whenever the SQL Server service is restarted. The values for a specific database are removed if the database is either detached or shut down. Note that indexes that have not been used since the view was reset are not included in the view.

Optimizing Queries Through Indexing

In this lab, you will use two different indexing techniques to optimize a specific query. The query returns the Customer ID and the total amount for all purchases for all customers (that have made purchases) in a specific territory. This lab only considers read performance and does not take write performance into account. The completed lab is available in the \Labs\Chapter 07\Lab2 folder on the companion CD.

Following is the query that you will try to optimize:

```
-- Query that will be optimized:
SELECT
    soh.CustomerID
    ,SUM(sod.OrderQty * sod.UnitPrice) AS TotalPurchases
FROM Test.SalesOrderHeader AS soh
INNER JOIN Test.SalesOrderDetail AS sod
    ON sod.SalesOrderID = soh.SalesOrderID
WHERE soh.TerritoryID = 1
GROUP BY soh.CustomerID;
```

▶ **Exercise 1: Create a Performance Base Line for the Query**

In this exercise, you will create the base line for the query that needs to be optimized b cuting it without adding any indexes.

1. Open SQL Server Management Studio and connect to an instance of SQL Server

2. In a new query window, type and execute the following SQL statements to crea *TestDB* database, the Test schema, and the two tables that will be used in this exe

   ```
   CREATE DATABASE TestDB;
   GO

   USE TestDB;
   GO

   CREATE SCHEMA Test;
   GO

   SELECT * INTO Test.SalesOrderHeader
   FROM AdventureWorks.Sales.SalesOrderHeader;
   GO

   SELECT * INTO Test.SalesOrderDetail
   FROM AdventureWorks.Sales.SalesOrderDetail;
   GO

   ALTER TABLE Test.SalesOrderHeader
       ADD CONSTRAINT PKSalesOrderHeader
       PRIMARY KEY(SalesOrderID);
   GO

   ALTER TABLE Test.SalesOrderDetail
       ADD CONSTRAINT PKSalesOrderDetail
       PRIMARY KEY(SalesOrderDetailID);
   ```

3. Turn on Include Actual Execution Plan in SQL Server Management Studio by pi Ctrl+M.

4. Type and execute the following SQL statement to turn on the reporting of page i

   ```
   SET STATISTICS IO ON;
   ```

5. Type and execute the query to test its performance:

```
SELECT
        soh.CustomerID
        ,SUM(sod.OrderQty * sod.UnitPrice) AS TotalPurchases
FROM Test.SalesOrderHeader AS soh
INNER JOIN Test.SalesOrderDetail AS sod ON sod.SalesOrderID = soh.SalesOrderID
WHERE soh.TerritoryID = 1
GROUP BY soh.CustomerID;
```

What was the total cost of the query?

(You can find the value in the Execution Plan tab by moving the mouse pointer over the *SELECT* operator and locating the value named Estimated Subtree Cost.)

What was the total number of page reads for the query?

(You can find this value by scrolling to the bottom of the Messages tab and summarizing the values for logical reads.)

6. Type and execute the following SQL statement to clean up after this exercise:

```
USE master;
DROP DATABASE TestDB;
```

▶ **Exercise 2: Optimize the Query by Using Clustered Indexes**

In this exercise, you will optimize the query by modifying the primary key constraints to be non-clustered indexes and then creating appropriate clustered indexes.

1. Open SQL Server Management Studio and connect to an instance of SQL Server 2005.

2. In a new query window, type and execute the following SQL statements to create the *TestDB* database, the Test schema, and the two tables that will be used in this exercise:

```
CREATE DATABASE TestDB;
GO

USE TestDB;
GO

CREATE SCHEMA Test;
GO

SELECT * INTO Test.SalesOrderHeader
FROM AdventureWorks.Sales.SalesOrderHeader;
GO

SELECT * INTO Test.SalesOrderDetail
FROM AdventureWorks.Sales.SalesOrderDetail;
GO

ALTER TABLE Test.SalesOrderHeader
    ADD CONSTRAINT PKSalesOrderHeader
```

```
    PRIMARY KEY(SalesOrderID);
GO

ALTER TABLE Test.SalesOrderDetail
    ADD CONSTRAINT PKSalesOrderDetail
    PRIMARY KEY(SalesOrderDetailID);
```

3. Type and execute the following SQL statements to modify the primary key constra the Test.SalesOrderHeader table to become a non-clustered index and then cre appropriate clustered index for the query:

```
-- Modify the PK to be a non-clustered index.
ALTER TABLE Test.SalesOrderHeader
    DROP CONSTRAINT PKSalesOrderHeader;
ALTER TABLE Test.SalesOrderHeader
    ADD CONSTRAINT PKSalesOrderHeader
    PRIMARY KEY NONCLUSTERED (SalesOrderID);

-- Create the clustered index.
CREATE CLUSTERED INDEX CluIdx ON Test.SalesOrderHeader
    (TerritoryID, CustomerID);
```

4. Type and execute the following SQL statements to modify the primary key constra the Test.SalesOrderDetail table to become a non-clustered index and then cre appropriate clustered index for the query:

```
-- Modify the PK to be a non-clustered index.
ALTER TABLE Test.SalesOrderDetail
    DROP CONSTRAINT PKSalesOrderDetail;
ALTER TABLE Test.SalesOrderDetail
    ADD CONSTRAINT PKSalesOrderDetail
    PRIMARY KEY NONCLUSTERED (SalesOrderDetailID);

-- Create the clustered index.
CREATE CLUSTERED INDEX CluIdx ON Test.SalesOrderDetail
    (SalesOrderID);
```

5. Turn on Include Actual Execution Plan in SQL Server Management Studio by p Ctrl+M.

6. Type and execute the following SQL statement to turn on the reporting of page r

```
SET STATISTICS IO ON;
```

7. Type and execute the query to test its performance:

```
SELECT
    soh.CustomerID
    ,SUM(sod.OrderQty * sod.UnitPrice) AS TotalPurchases
FROM Test.SalesOrderHeader AS soh
INNER JOIN Test.SalesOrderDetail AS sod
    ON sod.SalesOrderID = soh.SalesOrderID
```

```
WHERE soh.TerritoryID = 1
GROUP BY soh.CustomerID;
```

What was the total cost of the query?

What was the total number of page reads for the query?

8. Type and execute the following SQL statement to clean up after this exercise:

```
USE master;
DROP DATABASE TestDB;
```

▶ **Exercise 3: Optimize the Query by Using Covered Non-Clustered Indexes**

In this exercise, you will optimize the query by creating covered non-clustered indexes.

1. Open SQL Server Management Studio and connect to an instance of SQL Server 2005.

   In a new query window, type and execute the following SQL statements to create the *TestDB* database, the Test schema, and the two tables that will be used in this exercise:

```
CREATE DATABASE TestDB;
GO

USE TestDB;
GO

CREATE SCHEMA Test;
GO

SELECT * INTO Test.SalesOrderHeader
FROM AdventureWorks.Sales.SalesOrderHeader;
GO

SELECT * INTO Test.SalesOrderDetail
FROM AdventureWorks.Sales.SalesOrderDetail;
GO

ALTER TABLE Test.SalesOrderHeader
    ADD CONSTRAINT PKSalesOrderHeader
    PRIMARY KEY(SalesOrderID);
O
ALTER TABLE Test.SalesOrderDetail
    ADD CONSTRAINT PKSalesOrderDetail
    PRIMARY KEY(SalesOrderDetailID);
```

2. Type and execute the following SQL statement to create the covered non-clustered index that will be used by the query when accessing the Test.SalesOrderHeader table:

```
CREATE NONCLUSTERED INDEX TestIndex ON Test.SalesOrderHeader
(TerritoryID, SalesOrderID) INCLUDE (CustomerID);
```

3. Type and execute the following SQL statement to create the covered non-clustered that will be used by the query when accessing the Test.SalesOrderDetail table:

```
CREATE NONCLUSTERED INDEX TestIndex ON Test.SalesOrderDetail
(SalesOrderID) INCLUDE (OrderQty, UnitPrice);
```

4. Turn on Include Actual Execution Plan in SQL Server Management Studio by pre Ctrl+M.

5. Type and execute the following SQL statement to turn on the reporting of page re

```
SET STATISTICS IO ON;
```

6. Type and execute the query to test its performance:

```
SELECT
    soh.CustomerID
    ,SUM(sod.OrderQty * sod.UnitPrice) AS TotalPurchases
FROM Test.SalesOrderHeader AS soh
INNER JOIN Test.SalesOrderDetail AS sod
    ON sod.SalesOrderID = soh.SalesOrderID
WHERE soh.TerritoryID = 1
GROUP BY soh.CustomerID;
```

What was the total cost of the query?

(You can find the value in the Execution Plan tab by moving the mouse pointer ov *SELECT* operator and locating the value named Estimated Subtree Cost.)

What was the total number of page reads for the query?

(You can find this value by scrolling to the bottom of the Messages tab and summa the values for logical reads.)

7. Type and execute the following SQL statement to clean up after this exercise:

```
USE master;
DROP DATABASE TestDB;
```

▶ **Exercise 4: Optimize the Query by Implementing an Indexed View**

In this exercise, you will optimize the query by creating an indexed view to cover the q

1. Open SQL Server Management Studio and connect to an instance of SQL Server

2. In a new query window, type and execute the following SQL statements to crea *TestDB* database, the Test schema, and the two tables that will be used in this ex

```
CREATE DATABASE TestDB;
GO

USE TestDB;
GO

CREATE SCHEMA Test;
GO
```

```
SELECT * INTO Test.SalesOrderHeader
FROM AdventureWorks.Sales.SalesOrderHeader;
GO

SELECT * INTO Test.SalesOrderDetail
FROM AdventureWorks.Sales.SalesOrderDetail;
GO

ALTER TABLE Test.SalesOrderHeader
    ADD CONSTRAINT PKSalesOrderHeader
    PRIMARY KEY(SalesOrderID);
GO

ALTER TABLE Test.SalesOrderDetail
    ADD CONSTRAINT PKSalesOrderDetail
    PRIMARY KEY(SalesOrderDetailID);
```

3. Type and execute the following SQL statement to create the view:

```
CREATE VIEW Test.SalesByCustomerVw
WITH SCHEMABINDING
AS
SELECT
    soh.TerritoryID
    ,soh.CustomerID
    ,SUM(sod.OrderQty * sod.UnitPrice) AS TotalPurchases
    ,COUNT_BIG(*) AS NumberOfRows
FROM Test.SalesOrderHeader AS soh
INNER JOIN Test.SalesOrderDetail AS sod
    ON sod.SalesOrderID = soh.SalesOrderID
GROUP BY soh.TerritoryID, soh.CustomerID;
```

4. Type and execute the following SQL statement to index the view:

```
CREATE UNIQUE CLUSTERED INDEX SalesByCustomerVwIdx
ON Test.SalesByCustomerVw (TerritoryID, CustomerID);
```

5. Turn on Include Actual Execution Plan in SQL Server Management Studio by pressing Ctrl+M.

6. Type and execute the following SQL statement to turn on the reporting of page reads:

```
SET STATISTICS IO ON;
```

7. Type and execute the query to test its performance:

```
SELECT
    soh.CustomerID
    ,SUM(sod.OrderQty * sod.UnitPrice) AS TotalPurchases
FROM Test.SalesOrderHeader AS soh
INNER JOIN Test.SalesOrderDetail AS sod
    ON sod.SalesOrderID = soh.SalesOrderID
WHERE soh.TerritoryID = 1
GROUP BY soh.CustomerID;
```

IMPORTANT Verify that the indexed view is used

Verify that the indexed view is used to execute the query by examining the query exec plan. If the indexed view is not used (which is probably because you are running neither Server 2005 Developer Edition nor Enterprise Edition), execute the following query to the use of the indexed view:

```
SELECT CustomerID, TotalPurchases
FROM Test.SalesByCustomerVw WITH(NOEXPAND)
WHERE TerritoryID = 1;
```

What was the total cost of the query?

What was the total number of page reads for the query?

8. Type and execute the following SQL statement to clean up after this exercise:

```
USE master;
DROP DATABASE TestDB;
```

▶ **Exercise 5: Compare the Test Results**

In this exercise, you will compare the results from the earlier exercises.

Enter the cost and page read count for each index technique in the following table.

Index technique	Cost	Pages
Base line		
Clustered indexes		
Covered non-clustered indexes		
Indexed view		

Which of these techniques provided the lowest (best) cost?

Which of these techniques provided the lowest (best) page count?

Quick Check

1. Why should the size of the clustered index key be kept low?
2. What is the maximum number of included columns allowed in a non-clustered index?
3. What is the maximum number of columns that can make up an index key?

Quick Check Answers

1. Keep the clustered index small because it is copied into each row in each non-clustered index on the same table.
2. 1,023 columns is the maximum number of included columns allowed in a non-clustered index.
3. 16 columns (or a width of 900 bytes) is the maximum number of columns that can make up an index key.

Lesson 3: Optimizing Data Storage

Estimated lesson time: 25 minutes

The optimization of data storage is dependent on why you are optimizing as well as wha users' requirements are. Sometimes, you might be optimizing data storage to save disk (which is typical for data warehouses), and other times, you might want to save mem optimize query performance.

Optimizing Row Width

One of the ways to optimize a database to save disk space is simply to remove seldom indexes that allocate a lot of disk space. In Lesson 2, the section titled "Analyzing Index L covered the details regarding which indexes to remove. Another important task is to op the row width of large indexes and tables. SQL Server stores data on 8-kilobyte pages, is important to have as little unused space as possible in each data page. Note that this t optimization is typically only useful on tables that contain wide rows—that is, those that least over 400 bytes per row. Each data page has a 96-byte header and 8,096 bytes availa rows (data) and row offsets (the pointers stored at the end of each page telling where eac begins). If a row cannot fit into the free space of a data page, it will need to be stored in data page. This means that, for some tables and indexes, the size of the rows might caus pages not to be filled. The less that each data page is filled, the more disk space is wasted. table isn't very big (1 GB, for example), you might not care so much about the price o space, but consider that everything located on the disk will be placed in memory whe accessed. If the page space is poorly used, it will use more memory than necessary, and ory is far more expensive than disk space.

Data stored using variable-length data types (*VARCHAR*, *NVARCHAR*, and *VARBINARY*) moved to overflow pages if they cannot fit into the row's original data page.

The following is an example of one table (Test.BigWaste) with a row width that causes amount of unused space in each data page and another table (Test.OnlyALittleWaste almost fills each data page completely. Each table is populated with 10,000 rows.

```
CREATE TABLE Test.BigWaste (
    Txt CHAR(3000) NOT NULL
);
INSERT Test.BigWaste (Txt)
    SELECT TOP(10000) text
    FROM sys.messages;

CREATE TABLE Test.OnlyALittleWaste (
```

```
    Txt CHAR(4000) NOT NULL
);
INSERT Test.OnlyALittleWaste (Txt)
    SELECT TOP(10000) text
    FROM sys.messages;
```

Note that, for the purpose of this example, the empty space caused by a column using a large char data type is not considered to be waste. Now, the *sys.dm_db_index_physical_stats* database management function is used to retrieve information on the storage of these two tables:

```
SELECT
    OBJECT_NAME(object_id) AS TableName
    ,page_count
    ,ROUND(avg_page_space_used_in_percent, 2) AS avg_page_space_used_in_percent
FROM sys.dm_db_index_physical_stats (DB_ID(),
OBJECT_ID('Test.BigWaste'), NULL, NULL, 'DETAILED')
UNION ALL
SELECT
    OBJECT_NAME(object_id) AS TableName
    ,page_count
    ,ROUND(avg_page_space_used_in_percent, 2) AS avg_page_space_used_in_percent
FROM sys.dm_db_index_physical_stats (DB_ID(),
OBJECT_ID('Test.OnlyALittleWaste'), NULL, NULL, 'DETAILED')
ORDER BY TableName;
```

The output of the previous query is shown in the following table.

TableName	page_count	avg_page_space_used_ in_percent
BigWaste	5,000	74.33
OnlyALittleWaste	5,000	99.04

Note that both tables use exactly the same number of pages to store their data, even though each row in the OnlyALittleWaste table is 1,000 bytes wider than in the BigWaste table. As you can see, in this example, almost 26 percent of the BigWaste table's size is wasted on empty page space. If this table was 10 GB in size, 26 percent would amount to 2.6 GB.

Normalizing

De-normalizing a database design implies storing data redundantly. The benefit of this is typically less work for the database engine when reading data, while it means more work when writing data because of the need to update more places than one. De-normalizing can also result in bugs when redundant data is not updated accordingly.

De-normalizing a database design should typically be used as a last resort. That said, de-normalization can increase performance dramatically. In fact, you could say that indexing,

and especially indexed views, is de-normalizing at the physical level. The great benefit
de-normalizing at the physical level is that the database engine will maintain the re
dant data for you.

An example of de-normalization is to store the finished result of certain queries in a table
instead of executing these queries again, to just read the result directly from that table. I
is what you need, you should probably first look at the possibility of caching the result of
queries in the application. Another use of de-normalization is to redundantly store col
from a parent table in a child table, for example:

```
USE AdventureWorks;
-- Add the column to the child table.
ALTER TABLE Sales.SalesOrderHeader
    ADD CustomerAccountNumber VARCHAR(10) NULL;
GO

-- Update the child table's column with values from the
-- parent table.
UPDATE soh SET
    CustomerAccountNumber = c.AccountNumber
FROM Sales.SalesOrderHeader AS soh
INNER JOIN Sales.Customer AS c ON soh.CustomerID = c.CustomerID;
```

Now the following query can be executed without joining to the parent table:

```
SELECT
    CustomerAccountNumber
    ,SalesOrderID
    ,OrderDate
FROM Sales.SalesOrderHeader;
```

To keep the values in the CustomerAccountNumber column up-to-date, you will need
an update trigger on the Sales.Customer table or, at certain intervals, execute the pre
update statement.

You should generally use de-normalization when the redundant data (the CustomerAcc
Number column in the previous example) does not always need to be synchronized wit
source data. That is, that the redundant data is updated periodically, such as once a c
every 30 minutes.

Data Types

You can think of selecting data types as a two-step process. The first step is deciding v
data type is appropriate, and the second step is making sure that the usage of the data tyr
the specific purpose, is consistent throughout the organization or at least throughout the
base. The second step is usually the most difficult of the two.

Deciding on the Appropriate Data Type

When you decide on the appropriate data type to implement, you should typically at least consider the following:

- What needs to be stored in the column?

  The data type must support the data that it needs to store. For example, the *nvarchar* data type requires more space than the *varchar* data type, but if you need to store Unicode data, you must use the *nvarchar* data type.

- How much storage space does the data type use?

  The less storage space needed, the less disk space and memory will be required by the table in which the data type is used.

- Will the column be indexed?

  If the column will be indexed, it is important that the data type be as small as possible to allow for effective indexes.

Using Data Types Consistently

Selecting data types is a time-consuming process when implementing and designing databases. Also, inconsistent use of data types throughout a database can amount to big problems. To facilitate the consistent use of data types, you should consider the use of alias types (also known as user-defined data types). An alias data type is just what it sounds like: an alias for a system data type. You can create one data type for each type of data in your tables at a more granular level than merely text or numbers. The following example illustrates the use of alias data types:

```
CREATE TYPE Test.PHONE_NUMBER FROM VARCHAR(20);
CREATE TYPE Test.PERSON_NAME FROM NVARCHAR(50);
GO

CREATE TABLE Test.Employees (
    Firstname Test.PERSON_NAME NOT NULL
    ,Lastname Test.PERSON_NAME NOT NULL
    ,HomePhoneNumber Test.PHONE_NUMBER NULL
    ,FaxNumber Test.PHONE_NUMBER NULL
)
```

De-Normalizing an Aggregation

In this lab, you will de-normalize the Sales.Customer table to include a column with the sum of purchases for each customer. You will then create a trigger to maintain the redundant data stored in this column. This lab is intended to show the expense of automatically updating redundant columns, especially if these columns contain aggregated data. Instead of us trigger, for example, this column could have been updated by a SQL Server Agent Job per day. The completed lab is available in the \Labs\Chapter 07\Lab3 folder on the panion CD.

1. Open SQL Server Management Studio and connect to an instance of SQL Server 2

2. Open a new query window and type and execute the following data definition lang (DDL) statement to disable an existing trigger on the Sales.SalesOrderDetail table

```
USE AdventureWorks;

ALTER TABLE Sales.SalesOrderDetail
    DISABLE TRIGGER iduSalesOrderDetail;

IF(OBJECT_ID('Sales.Customer') IS NOT NULL)
    ALTER TABLE Sales.Customer
        DISABLE TRIGGER uCustomer;
```

3. Turn on Include Actual Execution Plan in SQL Server Management Studio by pre Ctrl+M.

4. Type and execute the following dummy update statement to test its performance. update statement is executed to check the query cost of updating an order detai prior to the implementation of the de-normalization:

```
UPDATE Sales.SalesOrderDetail SET
    OrderQty = OrderQty
WHERE SalesOrderDetailID BETWEEN 1 AND 1000;
```

Note the cost of the update from the graphical execution plan.

5. Type and execute the following DDL statement to add the column that will stor total sales for each customer:

```
ALTER TABLE Sales.Customer
    ADD TotalSales MONEY NULL;
```

6. Type and execute the following statement to create the trigger that will maintai TotalSales column on the Customer table. This trigger is created on the Sales.! OrderDetail table because it is changes to that table that will affect a customer's tota chases. The trigger will recalculate the entire TotalSales figure for each customer v order details have been updated; it does not add or subtract from the TotalSales co because of the risk for inconsistencies (which, for example, could be caused by th ger being turned off for a period).

```
CREATE TRIGGER trgSalesOrderDetailDenorm
ON Sales.SalesOrderDetail
AFTER INSERT, UPDATE, DELETE
AS
BEGIN
```

```
SET NOCOUNT ON;

UPDATE c SET
    TotalSales = (
                    SELECT ISNULL(SUM(sod.LineTotal), 0)
                    FROM Sales.SalesOrderDetail AS sod
                    INNER JOIN Sales.SalesOrderHeader AS soh
                        ON soh.SalesOrderID = sod.SalesOrderID
                    WHERE soh.CustomerID = c.CustomerID
                 )
FROM Sales.Customer AS c
-- Only update customers whose order details have been updated.
INNER JOIN Sales.SalesOrderHeader AS soh
    ON soh.CustomerID = c.CustomerID
WHERE
    EXISTS (SELECT * FROM inserted AS i
            WHERE i.SalesOrderID = soh.SalesOrderID)
    OR
    EXISTS (SELECT * FROM deleted AS d
            WHERE d.SalesOrderID = soh.SalesOrderID);
END
```

7. Type and execute the dummy update statement again to test its performance after the implementation of the trigger:

```
UPDATE Sales.SalesOrderDetail SET
    OrderQty = OrderQty
WHERE SalesOrderDetailID BETWEEN 1 AND 1000;
```

Note the cost of the update from the Execution Plan tab.

Because there are two separate plans displayed in the Execution Plan tab, one for the update statement, and one for the update statement executed by the trigger, the new cost of the update will be the sum of the cost of these updates.

8. Test the accuracy of the trigger by inserting, deleting and updating rows in the Sales.OrderDetail table and validating the changes to the TotalSales column in the Sales.Customer table for the affected customer or customers.

9. To clean up after this lab, close all open query windows in SQL Server Management Studio, open a new query window, and execute the following SQL statements:

```
USE AdventureWorks;

ALTER TABLE Sales.SalesOrderDetail
    ENABLE TRIGGER iduSalesOrderDetail;

IF(OBJECT_ID('Sales.Customer') IS NOT NULL)
    ALTER TABLE Sales.Customer
        ENABLE TRIGGER uCustomer;
```

```
DROP TRIGGER trgSalesOrderDetailDenorm;

ALTER TABLE Sales.Customer DROP COLUMN TotalSales;
```

Quick Check

1. Why is the width of rows important?
2. What does de-normalization imply?
3. Why should you avoid de-normalizing data that is frequently updated?

Quick Check Answers

1. The width of rows is important because wide rows take up more space and c
   cause a waste of both memory and disk space.
2. De-normalization implies the storage of specific data redundantly.
3. You should avoid de-normalizing data that is frequently updated because of t
   cost of maintaining the redundant data.

Case Scenario: Optimizing Query Performance

In this scenario, you are a database developer in your organization. You have been assigne
task of optimizing the database used by the popular community Web site that your orga
tion owns. Because of the high user activity on the community Web site, there are two p
mance problems. First, the user response time for the community chat forums is very
The Web site developers have narrowed this problem down to slow response times fror
forum stored procedures in the SQL Server instance hosting the forums. You need to fin
poorly performing stored procedures and optimize them. Second, employees in the fir
department use database queries from Microsoft Office Excel to retreive usage statistics fc
community Web site. These queries currently take up to 30 minutes to execute dependi
what statistics are being retrieved. The CFO has stated that the execution time for these
ries must be reduced to a couple of seconds.

Suggested Practices

Objective 5.1: Optimize and tune queries for performance

- **Practice 1**   Create a simple table without indexes, insert 1,000,000 rows into the
  and write down the query cost and execution time. Add one non-clustered index I
  table, truncate the table, re-insert the 1,000,000 rows, and write down the query

and execution time again. Do this for a few more non-clustered indexes and review the performance difference.

Objective 5.2: Optimize indexing strategies

- **Practice 1**   Create a simple table (with a row width of at least 50 bytes) without indexes and insert 1,000,000 rows into the table. Execute queries that retrieve 10, 100, 1,000, 10,000 and 100,000 rows (for example, use a BETWEEN filter on an identity column in the table) against the table without indexes and write down the query cost and number of page reads for each query. Create a clustered index on the column being searched, re-execute the queries, and write down the performance metrics again. Do the same thing for a covered and uncovered non-clustered index.

erences

- Creating Indexes on Computed Columns
  http://msdn2.microsoft.com/en-us/library/ms189292.aspx
- Creating Indexed Views
  http://msdn2.microsoft.com/en-us/library/ms191432.aspx
- sys.dm_db_index_usage_stats
  http://msdn2.microsoft.com/en-us/library/ms188755.aspx

pter Summary

- Always evaluate different ways of implementing costly queries.
- Drop unused indexes.
- Typically, only de-normalize data that is not updated frequently.
- When measuring query performance, always include the query execution time as a secondary metric.
- Minimize the size of rows in tables and indexes.
- Create covered indexes for the most frequently executed queries.
- Don't forget to index foreign keys.
- Evaluate creating indexed views to cover entire queries or parts of queries.

Improving Database Application Performance

Microsoft SQL Server 2005 is designed to handle databases of all sizes, but unless you are careful about how you design, develop, and maintain your database applications, they might not perform as expected. It is critical that you know what considerations need to be made so your applications perform optimally.

Lesson 1 will cover the topic of scalability and the different technologies you should consider. You must take several factors into consideration when determining what scaling methods to use. Lesson 2 will move on to resolving performance problems. Not only do you need to know how to identify problems, but you should be prepared to suggest resolutions.

Exam objectives in this chapter:

- Scale database applications.
    - Specify a data-partitioning model.
    - Design queries that target multiple servers.
    - Implement scale-out techniques like federated database, service broker, distributed partitioned views.
    - Design applications to distribute data and workload transparently.
    - Identify code or processes that can be moved to a different tier to improve performance.
    - Rewrite algorithms to improve efficiency.
- Resolve performance problems.
    - Analyze application performance across multiple users.
    - Capture workload information.
    - Find out the causes of performance problems.
    - Specify resolutions such as: changing algorithms, scaling up, and scaling out, terminating a session.

Before You Begin

To complete the lessons in this chapter, you must have:

- A computer that meets or exceeds the minimum hardware requirements listed in Introduction at the beginning of this book.
- SQL Server 2005 installed, as well as the SQL Server 2005 *AdventureWorks* sample database.
- Microsoft Visual Studio 2005 or Microsoft Visual C# or Visual Basic 2005 Express tion installed.
- Experience designing and executing queries in SQL Server Management Studio.
- Experience creating Web-based applications using Visual Studio 2005.

son 1: Scale Database Applications

Estimated lesson time: 120 minutes

Scalability refers to the ability of an application to efficiently utilize resources to accommodate an increased workload. In other words, your application should be able to grow along with the number of users. Even though your application might have a limit to the number of concurrent users it can handle, you should be able to make a change to either the application or the environment that allows it to increase that limit.

Typically, scalability is accomplished by increasing the capacity of the server. This is referred to as scaling up; it usually involves adding more processing power or memory to the server. Because no application changes are required when scaling up, this tends to be a preferred method.

Another method for scaling your application involves adding additional servers to handle database workload. SQL Server 2005 provides several ways for you to scale out a database application. Which methods you use depends on factors such as the degree of data coupling, the number of application changes, and the maintainability requirements.

Application scalability should not be an afterthought in the design and development process. Even if there is only a remote chance that your application will need to accommodate a larger number of users, it should be designed to be scalable from the very beginning. Depending on the technique chosen, implementing application scalability can involve quite a few changes.

This lesson will cover several techniques you can use to scale your application. Table 8-1 lists each of these techniques along with their advantages and disadvantages. As you read through the lesson, you can refer to this table and determine which technique is best suited to your application. Keep in mind that it might be necessary to utilize more than one of these techniques.

Table 8-1   Advantages and Disadvantages of Scale-Out Techniques

Scale-Out Technique	Description	Advantage	Disadvantage
Scalable shared database	Represents a read-only database located on a storage area network. It can have up to eight different instances executing queries against the database.	Simple to implement and no application changes are required.	Database must be set as read-only, so it needs to be a database that is rarely updated.

Table 8-1   Advantages and Disadvantages of Scale-Out Techniques

Scale-Out Technique	Description	Advantage	Disadvantage
Peer-to-peer replication	Type of replication in which changes made to one database are copied to all other peer databases.	Easy to implement and allows for updates.	Does not provide cor resolution, so only o member can update database at a time.
Linked servers	Allows you to execute queries against remote data sources as if they were local.	Allows for updates and requires minimal application changes.	Not effective when d coupling is high.
Distributed partition views	Allows you to partition data using a partition key.	Provides good performance even if data updates are required.	Application changes needed, and it is not easy to implement a maintain.
Data-dependent routing	Middleware services or the application is used to route queries for a partitioned database.	Good for handling a large number of servers with many updates.	Not easy to impleme and maintain and ca cumbersome if you r to search for all data
Service-oriented data architecture	Represents a database application that uses autonomous and reusable services that are implemented by the database itself using Service Broker.	Flexible solution that allows you to easily move services to another server if necessary.	Requires a lot of app tion changes.

Specifying a Data-Partitioning Model

Data partitioning involves moving data from a single database server into more than one r itory. It is not uncommon for applications to perform fine when they are moved into pr tion and then start to slow as more data is added to the database. In some cases, changes to the application or the database, such as applying indexes, allow the application to retu acceptable performance. In cases where this is no longer possible, you might need to con implementing a data-partitioning model.

There are two kinds of data partitioning: vertical and horizontal. Vertical partitioning inv splitting a table into multiple tables. Typically, this is done to reduce data redundancy, a database has gone through the normalization process, this type of partitioning might r necessary. Horizontal partitioning is used to restrict the number of rows within each table. This is a more commonly used form of data partitioning. The table is partitioned by values in one or more of the columns. For example, you could partition the Person.Contacts table based on the Contact ID. In some cases, it might be necessary to combine both types of partitioning to achieve the desired results.

How data is partitioned and what data is affected depends on the type of data involved. It also depends on the amount of data coupling that exists between tables. For example, if you have a database that contains several years of customer account data, you might need to move some of that customer data to another database. Typically, all this data will not reside within a single table. It might be spread out among several related tables. Even though you might have a table named Customer, you will need to move data as it relates to a customer entity and not just the single customer record from the Customers table. By moving the data as an entity, you will reduce the need to execute distributed queries and allow queries to be executed faster.

Data partitioning is typically just one step in implementing a scale-out solution. It is important to identify the type and amount of data to be partitioned early on. This will help you to select a scale-out technique most appropriate for your application.

Partition Functions

Once you have determined what data needs to be moved, you will need to create the additional repositories. This might involve creating databases on separate servers or creating additional filegroups on the same server. If you are creating additional file groups, you will need to use a partition function and partition scheme to specify how tables and indexes are partitioned.

IMPORTANT   SQL Server 2005 Enterprise Edition required

Partition functions can only be created using SQL Server 2005 Enterprise Edition. See the Introduction for instructions on how to install the free 180-day evaluation edition of SQL Server 2005 Enterprise Edition from the companion DVD, if you do not already have a copy installed.

To demonstrate how partitioning works, assume that you wish to partition the Production.Product table in the *AdventureWorks* database. The *AdventureWorks* database includes one file group named PRIMARY that contains one data file and one transaction log file. To partition this database, you could add two filegroups named FG2 and FG3, which contain additional data files. This could be accomplished by using the interface in SQL Server Management Studio or by issuing the following Transact-SQL statements. The path to your database may be different than the following.

```
USE [master]
GO
ALTER DATABASE [AdventureWorks] ADD FILEGROUP [FG2]
GO
ALTER DATABASE [AdventureWorks] ADD FILE ( NAME = N'AdventureWorks_Data_FG2',
FILENAME = N'C:\Program Files\Microsoft SQL
Server\MSSQL.8\MSSQL\DATA\AdventureWorks_Data_FG2.ndf' , SIZE = 5120KB ,
FILEGROWTH = 1024KB ) TO FILEGROUP [FG2]
GO
ALTER DATABASE [AdventureWorks] ADD FILEGROUP [FG3]
GO
ALTER DATABASE [AdventureWorks] ADD FILE ( NAME = N'AdventureWorks_Data_FG3',
FILENAME = N'C:\Program Files\Microsoft SQL
Server\MSSQL.8\MSSQL\DATA\AdventureWorks_Data_FG3.ndf' , SIZE = 5120KB ,
FILEGROWTH = 1024KB ) TO FILEGROUP [FG3]
GO
```

The partition function is used to define a range of records that will be included in the tion(s). By default, all tables and indexes in SQL Server 2005 are assigned to at least on tition. You can view these partitions by executing a query using the sys.partitions catalog

The partition function accepts an input parameter type, which in this case will be an ir because you wish to partition the table by Product ID. The function also accepts a range of v that will be used to separate the table into groups. In the following Transact-SQL statemer partition function is named *pfnProduct*, and it is used to separate an integer value into groups. In this case, the ranges will be: less than or equal to 450, 451 to 800, and 801 or gr

```
CREATE PARTITION FUNCTION
    pfnProduct (int)
AS RANGE LEFT FOR VALUES (450, 800)
```

Partition Schemes

The next step is to create a partition scheme. The partition scheme is used to assign a par to certain filegroups. In the following example, the partition scheme named pscPr assigns the partition to the filegroups named Primary, FG2, and FG3:

```
CREATE PARTITION SCHEME
    pscProduct
AS PARTITION pfnProduct
    TO ('Primary', 'FG2', 'FG3')
```

The last thing to do is associate a particular index with the new partition scheme. Prod is the column you will partition on, but this column is defined as a primary key for th duction.Product table. To associate an index with a partition scheme, you need to execu DROP INDEX Transact-SQL statement against that index.

You cannot execute the DROP INDEX statement on a primary key. To get around this, you would first need to remove the primary key by using the interface in SQL Server Enterprise Manager or by using the ALTER TABLE statement. Before you do this, be aware that doing so will also remove all foreign key relationships. For the *AdventureWorks* database, this change will affect several tables.

Once the primary key is removed, you can re-create the index as a unique and clustered index and execute the following Transact-SQL code:

```
IF  EXISTS (SELECT * FROM sys.indexes
WHERE object_id = OBJECT_ID(N'[Production].[Product]')
AND name = N'PK_Product_ProductID')

DROP INDEX PK_Product_ProductID
   ON Production.Product
WITH (MOVE TO pscProduct (ProductID), ONLINE = OFF )
```

The DROP INDEX statement will move the index from the primary filegroup to the partition defined by the partition scheme. An alternative to executing the DROP INDEX statement is to use the Storage page for the index properties. (Refer to Figure 8-1.)

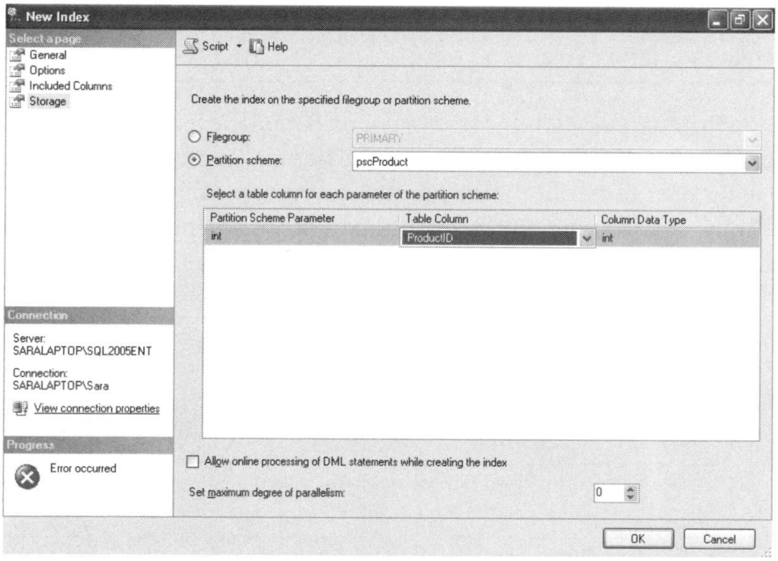

Figure 8-1 Storage page within the properties for the ProductID index

Object Catalog Views

Once the partition is created, you can see the new partition records using the sys.parti
object catalog view. For example, the following Transact-SQL statement can be used to vie
partitions for the object named "*Product*":

```
select * from sys.partitions
where object_name(object_id) = 'Product'
```

Before the partition scheme was added, the previous query would have returned four rec
Each record represented one of the four indexes for the Production.Product table. Now
the partition has been created, the query will return six records, as follows:

Partition ID	Object ID	Index ID	Partition Number	Hobt ID	Rov
72057594056278016	1429580131	0	1	72057594056278016	129
72057594056343552	1429580131	0	2	72057594056343552	176
72057594056409088	1429580131	0	3	72057594056409088	199
72057594056474624	1429580131	2	1	72057594056474624	504
72057594056540160	1429580131	3	1	72057594056540160	504
72057594056605696	1429580131	4	1	72057594056605696	504

The last column in the query result is the number of rows, and the first three records repr
the partition for the Product ID index. Notice that the number of rows for these records
504, which is the number of records in the Production.Product table. You can see how
records exist within each partition. If the distribution is not acceptable, you would ne
drop and re-create the partition function to specify a different range.

As shown in Table 8-2, in addition to the sys.partitions view, SQL Server 2005 include
other views that can be used to query partition information.

Table 8-2   Partition Function Catalog Views

View Name	Description
sys.partitions	Returns information about partitions assigned to objects in a database.
sys.partition_functions	Returns information about any partition functions created fo database.
sys.partition_parameters	Returns information about parameters used in partition funct This view could be joined to the sys.partition_functions view the function_id column.

Table 8-2 Partition Function Catalog Views

View Name	Description
sys.partition_schemes	Returns information about partition schemes created for the database. This view can be joined to the sys.partition_functions on the function_id column.
sys.partition_range_values	Returns the ranges allowed for parameters in a partition function. This was specified when creating the partition scheme.

ʝeting Multiple Servers

In the previous section, we examined a partitioning model that involved adding filegroups to a single server. While this can help an application to scale, it might be necessary to target multiple servers to achieve the desired results. For many of today's Web sites and enterprise-wide applications, targeting multiple servers is the only way these applications can accommodate the high demand.

In cases where data is partitioned across multiple servers, those servers will need to cooperate to balance the load of the application. A group of servers joined together in this way is known as a *federation*. How these federated servers cooperate depends on the technique chosen. This section will present several techniques that can be used to target multiple servers.

Using Linked Servers

Linked servers (which were introduced in Chapter 2, "Designing Database Queries") provide a way to issue queries against remote data sources as if they were local. If you were to partition data so that it resided on more than one server, linked servers could be used to query the remote data. The advantage to linked servers is that as far as the application is concerned, the remote data source exists on the local database server.

Only small application changes are needed to make this scenario work. The drawback is that the remote query consumes more resources than a local query. For a partitioning model that targets multiple servers to be effective, the performance benefit from partitioning the data has to outweigh the cost of querying the remote data.

To demonstrate a scenario involving partitioned data and linked servers, let's assume that you needed to partition data in the *AdventureWorks* database. You have decided to move product history information to another server, a method known as data archiving.

BEST PRACTICES   **Partition large databases only**

The *AdventureWorks* database would not be considered a large database and typically, there w
be no need to partition data from tables that contained only a few hundred records. A table
did need to be partitioned might contain millions or even billions of records. Keep this in mir
you are selecting a scale-out technique for your real-world application.

In many cases, there are legal and/or company policy restrictions that force you to main
certain number of years of historical data. Even though users rarely access historical
beyond three years, assume you have to maintain history for up to seven years.

The product history information is stored in two tables: Production.ProductListPriceH
and Production.ProductCostHistory. Both these tables have a start and end date. The end
could be used to partition the data and move data older than three years but less than
years into a separate database. You could also move data older than seven years into a dat
that would only be accessible through backups.

The data residing in a separate database would need to be accessible to the database ap
tion. A linked server could be created which points to this database. The database applic
allows users to optionally select a date range when requesting product history. Assum
the following stored procedure was originally used to access the historical data:

```
CREATE PROCEDURE spGetProductListPriceHistory
      @ProdID int,
      @EndDate datetime = NULL
AS
BEGIN

      SET NOCOUNT ON;

      IF @EndDate IS NULL
        BEGIN
            SELECT StartDate, EndDate, ListPrice
            FROM Production.ProductListPriceHistory
            WHERE ProductID = @ProdID
            AND EndDate IS NULL
            ORDER BY EndDate
        END
      ELSE
        BEGIN
            SELECT StartDate, EndDate, ListPrice
            FROM Production.ProductListPriceHistory
            WHERE ProductID = @ProdID
            AND EndDate IS NOT NULL
```

```
            AND EndDate <= @EndDate
            ORDER BY EndDate
      END

END
```

The spGetProductListPriceHistory stored procedure accepts two input parameters: product ID and end date. If an end date is not provided, a default value of NULL is assigned, and the stored procedure returns history records where the end date is set with a value of NULL. Otherwise, the stored procedure will return all history records that fall before or on the end date passed in as a parameter.

Once the history records have been moved to a new database, we will need to alter the previous stored procedure. Assume that a linked server named svrProductHistory was created. We could then use the following Transact-SQL to alter the stored procedure:

```
ALTER PROCEDURE spGetProductListPriceHistory
      @ProdID int,
      @EndDate datetime = NULL
AS
BEGIN

      SET NOCOUNT ON;

      IF @EndDate IS NULL
        BEGIN
            SELECT StartDate, EndDate, ListPrice
            FROM Production.ProductListPriceHistory
            WHERE ProductID = @ProdID
            AND EndDate IS NULL
            ORDER BY EndDate
        END
      ELSE IF DateDiff(dd, GetDate(), @EndDate) > 1095 --3 * 365 = 1095
        BEGIN
            SELECT StartDate, EndDate, ListPrice
            FROM Production.ProductListPriceHistory
            WHERE ProductID = @ProdID
            AND EndDate IS NOT NULL
            AND EndDate <= @EndDate
            UNION
            SELECT StartDate, EndDate, ListPrice
          FROM OPENDATASOURCE('SQLNCLI',
              'Data Source=svrProductHistory\sql2005ent;
              Integrated Security=SSPI')
             .AdventureWorks.Production.ProductListPriceHistory
            WHERE ProductID = @ProdID
```

```
                    AND EndDate IS NOT NULL
                    AND EndDate <= @EndDate
                    Order BY EndDate
              END

      END
```

The new version of the stored procedure would check to see whether the end date pass
as a parameter exceeded three years. If it did, then it would use a UNION clause to r
records from both the original database and the newly created linked server. The *OPEN*
SOURCE function is used to execute an ad hoc query against the server named svrProdu
tory. The *OPENDATASOURCE* function provides an alternative to using a four-part na
query the linked server. For more information about using a four-part name to query a l
server, refer to Lesson 1, "Writing Database Queries," in Chapter 2.

By default, SQL Server 2005 does not allow you to execute ad hoc queries. Therefore, you
enable this option using the sp_configure system stored procedure. Because it is an adv
option, you will also need to first show the advanced options. You could use the foll
Transact-SQL code to enable ad hoc queries:

```
sp_configure 'show advanced options', 1;
GO
RECONFIGURE;
GO
sp_configure 'Ad Hoc Distributed Queries', 1;
GO
RECONFIGURE;
GO
```

The last thing to consider is that as time passes, more history records will be added the
base. You will need to create a process that moves records older than three years to the s
database. Although you could do this using a custom application, it would be easier to s
create a SQL Server Integration Services (SSIS) package that can be scheduled to run (
day. The package would execute code that queried the database for records older than
years. If any are found, it can delete the records from the original database and insert the
the second database.

Implementing Scale-Out Techniques

Implementing a successful scale-out technique involves consideration of all potentia
tions. It is possible that you might need to implement a combination of one or mor
niques to accomplish your goal. This section presents techniques that can be used to
multiple servers and thus scale out your application.

Using a Distributed Partition View

A Distributed Partition View (DPV) is a technique in which data partitioned horizontally across multiple servers is joined together to make it appear as if it comes from one table. The data is partitioned by a key value from each table. For example, the Product ID column could be used to partition the product tables in the *AdventureWorks* database.

The goal of a DPV is to transparently distribute the load of a database application across multiple servers. This is different from the partition we created earlier, in which a table was assigned to multiple filegroups on the same server. In the case of a DPV, the data is partitioned across two or more servers.

To create a DPV, you will first need to horizontally partition your table or tables. The considerations that apply to this task are the same as those discussed in the section of this chapter titled "Specifying a Data-Partitioning Model." Once the data has been moved to its respective servers, you will need to utilize check constraints to ensure the range of values for each partition.

For example, assume we want to create three partitions for the Person.Contact table in the *AdventureWorks* database. The partitions will reside on three separate servers named ServerA, ServerB, and ServerC. The Person.Contact table contains 19,972 records. If this table is partitioned on the column ContactID, we can split it so that 6,657 records reside in the partition on ServerA, 6,657 records in the partition on ServerB, and 6,658 records in the partition on ServerC (6,657 + 6,657 + 6,658 = 19,972).

The partitioned tables will need to include a check constraint that enforces the rule that each server will contain a certain range of ContactID records. You can add check constraints with the ALTER TABLE statement or by using the Check Constraints dialog box in SQL Server Management Studio (refer to Figure 8-2). The Transact-SQL statement used to create a check constraint on ServerA would appear as follows:

```
ALTER TABLE Person.Contact ADD CONSTRAINT
    CK_Contact_ContactID CHECK (ContactID BETWEEN 1 AND 6657)
GO
```

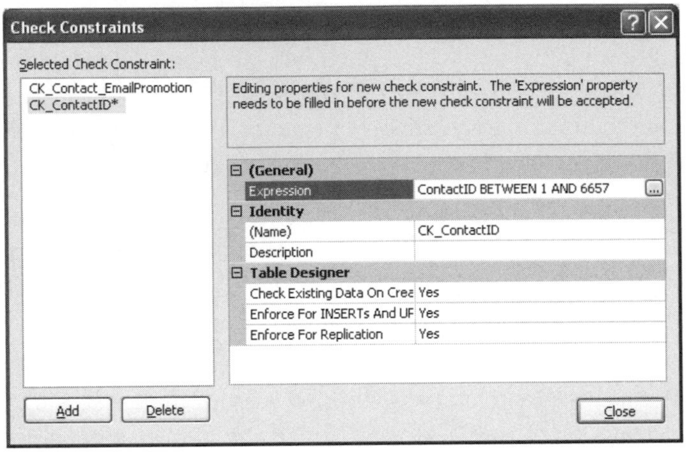

Figure 8-2   The Check Constraints dialog box used to add a new constraint to the Person.Co▮ table

Now, we can create linked servers to reference the additional servers. Once the linked s▮ are created, we can create the DPV using the following Transact-SQL statement:

```
CREATE VIEW tblContact AS
    SELECT * FROM ServerA.AdventureWorks.Person.Contact
UNION
    SELECT * FROM ServerB.AdventureWorks.Person.Contact
UNION
    SELECT * FROM ServerC.AdventureWorks.Person.Contact
```

The CREATE VIEW statement will need to be executed on all three servers. The view w▮ the records from all three tables. When the application needs to search for contacts, y▮ execute a SELECT query using the view named tblContact.

IMPORTANT   A loopback linked server is not allowed

You might be tempted to create a linked server definition that points back to the same insta▮ SQL Server. This is known as a loopback linked server, and it is not allowed. If you want to e▮ ment with creating a distributed partition view, you will have to use separate instances of S▮ Server 2005.

You will need to set the LazySchemaValidation property for each linked server. This ▮ specifies whether the schema used by the linked server is validated when the local SQL instance is idle. Setting this option provides a performance advantage for queries agai▮ linked server. You can set this option by using the sp_serveroption system stored proc▮ The Transact-SQL code needed to set this option is as follows:

```
USE master;
EXEC sp_serveroption 'ServerB', 'lazy schema validation', 'true';
GO
```

For your view to be updateable, you will need to ensure that no triggers are enabled on any of the partitioned tables. You will also need to remove any indexes for computed columns, and the view cannot be created using the EXCEPT or INTERCEPT clauses. In addition, each partitioned table must be referenced only once. Because a distributed transaction will be created during an update, you need to set the XACT_ABORT_OPTION to ON. This ensures that the transaction will be rolled back if a run-time error is encountered.

Using Data-Dependent Routing

Data-Dependent Routing (DDR) is a technique in which data is partitioned horizontally and then middleware or the application itself is used to route requests to the appropriate database. If middleware is used to accomplish this task, then the process is considered somewhat transparent. If the routing is done by the application, then changes to accommodate this type of routing will need to be made.

Because DDR requires a good deal of application changes to implement, it is generally only utilized by high-performing Web applications that require a lot of updates. Typically, routing will occur within the data access layer and will require that a table containing the server names, table names, and value ranges is created. This table will be used to route requests based on a key value to the appropriate server.

To demonstrate how DDR works, assume that you want to partition the *AdventureWorks* database. The data will be partitioned across 10 servers, although, in a real-world situation, this could potentially be hundreds or even thousands of servers. The first step is to partition the data. The considerations to assess are featured in the section of this chapter titled "Specifying a Data-Partitioning Model."

Assume that you have decided to partition the customer tables according to CustomerID. The data will be partitioned as an entity, and all of the data for a customer will be moved to a single server. When there is a need to return customer information, it can be retrieved from one server and thereby reduce the need for costly distributed queries.

Once the data has been moved to separate tables, you will need to create lookup tables that store the routing information. One lookup table will contain a single record for each partitioned server, along with the linked server name used to query that server. For example, the following records would reside in a server lookup table:

ServerID	ServerName	Description
1	Server1	Customers 1 – 2000
2	Server2	Customers 2001 – 4000
3	Server3	Customers 4001 – 6000
4	Server4	Customers 6001 – 8000
5	Server5	Customers 8001 – 10000
6	Server6	Customers 10001 – 12000
7	Server7	Customers 12001 – 14000
8	Server8	Customers 14001 – 16000
9	Server9	Customers 16001 – 18000
10	Server10	Customers 18001 – 19185

Another table would contain the partition key, which in this case is the CustomerID, with the ServerID. For example, the following is a partial result set for a customer lookup

CustomerID	ServerID
1	1
2	1
2557	2
2634	2
8999	5
12455	7

The challenge with DDR involves searching for data across all partitions. You definitely want to execute distributed queries against hundreds of servers. Typically, the solution problem lies with the creation of summary data. For example, you could create a table contained summary data for each customer and all orders for that customer. This same would be located on all the servers. When there was a need to search through all the customers, you would reference the summary table to locate the customer record. You could retrieve the order detail for that customer by executing a distributed query against the containing that customer's data. For more information about data-dependent routing, refer to the article, "Microsoft TechNet SQL TechCenter: Scaling Out SQL Server with Data Dependent Routing" at *http://www.microsoft.com/technet/prodtechnol/sql/2005/scddrtng* You can also refer to the article, "Scaling Out SQL Server with Data-Dependent Routing" *http://www.dell.com/downloads/global/power/ps3q05-20050100-Auger.pdf.*

Using Service-Oriented Database Architecture

Based on the widely adopted concept of Service-Oriented Architecture (SOA), Service-Oriented Database Architecture (SODA) combines SOA with the new features available in SQL Server 2005. SODA allows your database application to use independent and reusable services available through the database itself. This means the database is operating as a service provider.

SOA involves a collection of services that communicate with each other. The services themselves are autonomous and do not rely on the state from other services to function. However, they must have the ability to communicate with each other using XML messages, and SOA allows them to do that. SODA offers a way for SQL Server 2005 to implement the service-oriented architecture.

The benefit to using SODA is that you have a flexible solution in which services can easily be moved to another server if necessary. It also handles a high volume of transactions and database updates. Most important, applications can take advantage of features built into SQL Server 2005, such as the following:

- **Service Broker**   Provides queuing along with reliable and secure messaging to applications using SQL Server 2005. It can be used to coordinate services asynchronously and provide a scalable and robust solution.
- **Query Notifications**   Allows an application to request that a notification is sent when the results of a query change. This is useful when refreshing cached data. Instead of refreshing the data on a scheduled basis, the application can refresh the cache only when the data has actually changed.
- **Native XML Web Services**   Through HTTP endpoints, you can expose SQL Server data directly through XML Web services. Instead of residing on an Microsoft Internet Information Services (IIS) server, the Web services reside on SQL Server itself and are built using stored procedures or user-defined functions.
- **Notification Services**   Allows you to send notifications to subscribers concerning events within the application. The notifications can be sent to a variety of devices according to the subscribers' preferences.
- **SQLCLR**   The SQL Common Language Runtime (CLR) allows you to create and compile .NET Framework code that executes on the SQL Server. This is where the logic for your service provider resides. You can use SQLCLR to create high-level functions that replace Transact-SQL stored procedures and user-defined functions.

The drawback to implementing a solution using SODA is that it requires many application changes, and a good deal of the code will reside in the database in the form of SQLCLR code. Because so much of the business logic resides with the database, you are essentially tied to that

particular database. However, if you work with SQL Server 2005 exclusively and know
will always be the case, it might not be an issue for you.

To demonstrate how SODA works, assume you want to build a service-oriented data sol
using the *AdventureWorks* database. You want to separate the data and services that are us
handle initial sales orders from the work orders. In this case, if the database handling
orders goes down or is overloaded, sales orders will not be affected.

To accomplish this task, you will first need to partition the data used to handle sales o
and work orders. The tables associated with these processes will be moved to separate
bases. Reference tables that are used by both processes will be replicated to each dat
using peer-to-peer replication. You can also use replication to copy product and custome
to each database server.

When a sales order is entered into the system, one or more records are created in the
order tables. A sales order message is then placed into a queue using Service Broke
message is forwarded to the database that handles work orders. If the database is not
able, then the message will be queued until the server is available. If the database is
able, then the message will be processed and a response will be sent to the user th
Notification Services.

Transparently Distributing Data and Workload

In some cases, you might not have access or the ability to change an existing application
application might be suffering from performance problems, but making major changes
code is not an option. This section features techniques that can be used to scale your ap
tion transparently, which means few or no application changes are required.

Using a Scalable Shared Database

This is a new feature with SQL Server 2005 that allows you to indicate whether a datab
read-only. Typically, this is used for reporting or data-warehousing databases in whic
know that no updates are required. *Data-warehousing databases* are used to store large am
of data and are typically stored in a multidimensional format. You can create a scalable s
database that is used by up to eight different SQL Server instances to execute long-ru
queries or generate reports.

IMPORTANT   System requirements

Only Microsoft Windows Server 2003, Service Pack 1 or later can support the creation of a sc
shared database. You will also need to use SQL Server 2005 Enterprise Edition.

To enable a scalable shared database, it must be mounted on a read-only volume and accessed over a storage area network (SAN). The availability of the *SAN protocol* is new with the Enterprise Edition of SQL Server 2005. It allows you to cluster servers together and deliver high availability to your database applications.

Once the volume is mounted and the database built, you can attach the database to an instance of SQL Server. This is when it becomes available as a scalable shared database. It can then be accessed by clients using reporting servers.

BEST PRACTICES   **Reporting servers need to be identical**

All reporting servers should be running under the same operating system and service pack. If upgrades or updates are needed, make sure they are applied to all servers.

Even though the database is read-only, you will need to periodically refresh the data within the database. To update the database, you will need to detach all instances and attach only one instance in read/write mode. The best way to do this is to alternate the update cycles between two different volumes. While the first volume is being updated, the second one can be reattached to the production server to prevent application downtime.

Using Peer-to-Peer Replication

One of the best ways to target multiple servers is by using replication. In many cases, no application changes are necessary, and by using multiple servers, applications are allowed to scale to whatever level is necessary. There are many types of replication, but one that you might want to consider is peer-to-peer replication. Peer-to-peer replication is a new feature added with SQL Server 2005. This low-overhead solution allows you to maintain copies of a database on multiple servers, while still allowing for updates.

In peer-to-peer replication, each server will access its own copy of the database, but only one of the servers at a time will be allowed to update the data. Once the server updating the database has made the changes, a new copy of the database will be sent to the peers. If any of the other peers has made a similar change before the change is propagated to the others, a conflict could occur. For this reason, you want to implement this solution on servers where there is a low update frequency. In cases where there is a high update frequency, you might want to consider another scale-out option or consider using another replication type, such as merge replication. Merge replication does provide conflict resolution, but it consumes more server resources.

In peer-to-peer replication, each peer acts as both a publisher and a subscriber. There is no master publisher that copies updates to read-only subscribers. Each peer is able to make updates and then copy the changes to all other peers. Because conflict resolution is not built-in, the only way to avoid conflicts is by using a concept known as *data stewardship* involves assigning ownership of the data and then creating rules that define how that will be updated.

A good example of where peer-to-peer replication is effective is in the case of a large com with offices scattered across the country. Each office has its own application and dat servers, but they all need to share customer account information. Peer-to-peer replic would allow each office to maintain a separate copy of the database. The office that opene customer account would be the only one allowed to update the data for that custom other offices would be able to read the customer data and place orders for that custome only the original office would own the customer account. In addition, the office that plac order would be the only one allowed to update that order. The application would be re sible for determining which office is allowed to update a customer or order record.

For this scenario to work, all the databases must maintain the same data schema. The in ual peer databases should not contain any additional tables or objects that are not part central schema. Before any subscriptions are created, a publication that allows peer-to replication should be created. When the subscriptions are created, they need to be initi using a backup as opposed to a snapshot. Using a backup is a fast and easy way to pop the subscription database.

In this lesson, we will not go into detail surrounding replication and specifically config peer-to-peer replication. For more information regarding this topic, refer to the article, to: Configure Peer-to-Peer Transactional Replication" at *http://msdn2.microsoft.com/ /library/ms152536.aspx.*

Moving Code to a Different Tier

You have probably heard or read about using a multi-tiered architecture to develop enter wide applications that accommodate a large number of concurrent users. Typically, the be a user presentation tier to represent the user interface and a middle tier to encapsula business logic. The middle tier will communicate with the final layer, the data tier, to and update data for the end user. By moving functionality to different tiers, you can in code reusability and interoperability.

In some cases, you might be able to gain a performance advantage by moving complex ness logic from the middle tier to the SQL Server platform. SQL Server 2005 introduc ability to execute code for the .NET Framework CLR on SQL Server itself. This mear can write code using Microsoft Visual Basic .NET, C#, or J# and execute it on the SQL S To determine in which tier code will operate most efficiently, you might have to execut tions of the code in both environments and compare the results. For more inform about the considerations to make regarding this decision, refer to the article, "The Database Administrator's Guide to the SQL Server Database Engine .NET Common Language Runtime Environment" at *http://www.microsoft.com/technet/prodtechnol/sql/2005/clr4dbas.mspx.*

You will need to enable CLR integration before using it. You can do so with the SQL Server Surface Area Configuration tool. You will need to select the Surface Area Configuration For Features link and then expand the node for the instance of SQL Server 2005 you wish to enable. If you select CLR Integration, you should see a dialog box such as the one in Figure 8-3.

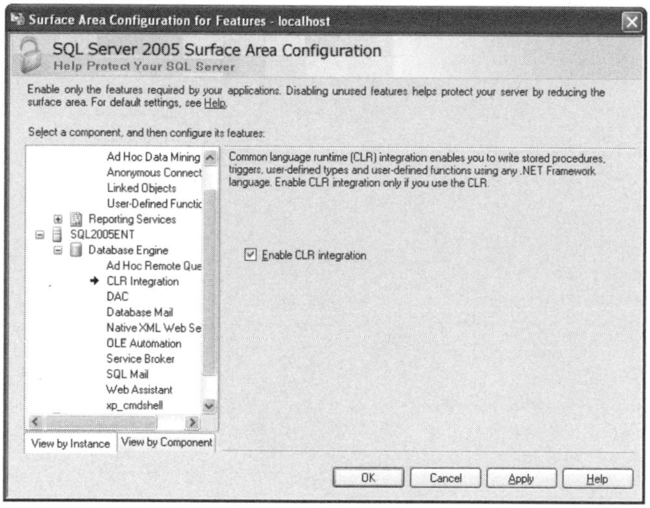

Figure 8-3   Enable CLR Integration using the SQL Server Surface Area Configuration tool

By default, this feature is disabled, so you will need to select the Enable CLR Integration check box and click Apply to save the changes. Alternatively, you can execute the following Transact-SQL statement from a new query window inside of SQL Server Management Studio:

```
sp_configure N'clr enabled', 1
GO
RECONFIGURE
GO

SELECT * FROM sys.configurations
WHERE [Name] = N'clr enabled'
```

Once CLR has been enabled, you can create a CLR stored procedure by using an ordinary text editor such as Windows Notepad. For example, you could type the following code into Notepad and then save the file as CLRStoredProcedure.cs or CLRStoredProcedure.vb:

```csharp
//C#
using System;
using System.Data;
using Microsoft.SqlServer.Server;
using System.Data.SqlTypes;

public class CLRStoredProc
{
    [Microsoft.SqlServer.Server.SqlProcedure]
    public static void GetTomorrowsDate()
    {
        System.DateTime tomorrow = System.DateTime.Now;
        System.TimeSpan ts = new System.TimeSpan(1, 0, 0, 0);
        SqlContext.Pipe.Send(Convert.ToString(tomorrow.Add(ts)));
    }
}
```

```vbnet
'VB
Imports System
Imports System.Data
Imports Microsoft.SqlServer.Server
Imports System.Data.SqlTypes


Public Class CLRStoredProc
    <Microsoft.SqlServer.Server.SqlProcedure> _
    Public Shared Sub GetTomorrowsDate()
        Dim tomorrow As System.DateTime
        tomorrow = System.DateTime.Now()
        Dim ts As New System.TimeSpan(1, 0, 0, 0)
        SqlContext.Pipe.Send(Convert.ToString(tomorrow.Add(ts)))
    End Sub
End Class
```

Notice that the *CLRStoredProc* method uses the *SqlContext* object to send a command thr
the SQL pipe. The *SQLContext* object is used to provide access to the context of the caller
the managed code executes in the SQL Server. The *SqlPipe* is one of three objects ava
through the *SqlContext*. This represents the pipe in which results flow back to the clien
can execute any one of the following methods:

- **Send**   Used to send data straight to the client. The data can either be a result set
  a *SqlDataReader* object or a string message.
- **ExecuteAndSend**   Used to execute a command using a command object and then
  the results back to the client.
- **SendResultsStart**   Used to send data that did not originate from a *SqlDataReader* c
  back to a client. Accepts a *SqlDataRecord* object as input and marks the beginning
  result set.

- **SendResultsRow**   Used in conjunction with *SendResultsStart* to send a row of data back to the client.
- **SendResultsEnd**   Used in conjunction with *SendResultsStart* and *SendResultsRow* to send data back to the client. This method is used to set *SqlPipe* back to its original state.

SQL Server provides command-line compilers that can be used to generate an assembly from a code file. If you are using Visual Basic, you will use vbc.exe, and if you are using C#, you will use csc.exe. To use the compiler, go to a Visual Studio 2005 Command Prompt and enter a command such as the following example. Replace <dir> with the location that you've created for testing this example. You also have the option of creating a directory named c:\TK442\Chapter8\Code\Lab1, which will be used in a lab exercise later in the chapter.

```
//C#
csc /target:library .<dir>\SQLStoredProc.cs
```

```
'VB
vbc /target:library <dir>\SQLStoredProc.vb
```

By executing the compiler, you will generate a dynamic-link library (DLL) file that is placed in the target library by default, <dir>\. You will then need to create an assembly in SQL Server that lets you access the stored procedure. You do so by executing a Transact-SQL statement, such as the following, from a new query window:

```
Use AdventureWorks;
CREATE ASSEMBLY SQLStoredProc from <dir>\SQLStoredProc.dll' WITH PERMISSION_SET = SAFE
```

The final step is to create a stored procedure that references the *SQLStoredProc* assembly. For example, the following Transact-SQL statement can be used to reference the assembly using its external name:

```
Use AdventureWorks;
CREATE PROCEDURE GetTomorrowsDate
AS
EXTERNAL NAME SQLStoredProc.CLRStoredProc.GetTomorrowsDate
```

Now that the procedure has been created, we can execute it just like any Transact-SQL stored procedure. For example, the following Transact-SQL statement will return tomorrow's date in the messages window:

```
EXEC GetTomorrowsDate
```

Rewriting Algorithms

It has long been established that Transact-SQL is a set-based language and not an object-ori(
one. For this reason alone, you should restrict the amount of complex business logic
resides in Transact-SQL stored procedures, user-defined functions, and triggers. Even th
there are scenarios where Transact-SQL performs more quickly than code in the .NET F
work, it is generally best to restrict use of Transact-SQL for queries. (For more inform
about this, refer to Lesson 2, "Designing a Cursor Strategy" and Lesson 3, "Designing Effi
Cursors," in Chapter 3, "Designing a Cursor and Caching Strategy.")

SQL Server 2005 introduced the ability to execute .NET Framework code on SQL S(
which we covered in the previous section. Now that you have this option, you might ne
consider whether moving some of the business logic to the database server is a good
SQLCLR is not a magic bullet, and just because it is offered does not mean you should re
all your code to utilize it. If you just need to retrieve data, then it is quicker and more effi
to use Transact-SQL. However, if you need to retrieve data and perform complex opera
against that data, then SQLCLR might be a better option.

Lab: Scaling Database Applications

In this lab, you will experiment with techniques used to scale out a database applicatio
the first exercise, you will create a partition function that is used to indicate how a partit
divided. In Exercise 2, you will create a SQLCLR user-defined function.

The completed code examples, in both Visual Basic and C#, are available in the \Labs\(
ter 08 folder on the companion CD.

IMPORTANT   Lab requirements

You will need to have SQL Server 2005 installed before you can complete this lab. Refer to th
Introduction for setup instructions.

▶ **Exercise 1: Create a Partition Function**

In this exercise, you will create a partition function that is used to horizontally partitio
data in the Production.Product table. The data will be partitioned by ProductNumber, v
is a character-based column. The data will be placed into separate filegroups that reside o
same instance of SQL Server.

1. Open Microsoft SQL Server Management Studio.
2. Connect to the instance of SQL Server 2005 that contains the *AdventureWorks* data
3. Right-click the *AdventureWorks* database, and select Properties. Select the Fileg(
    page. (Refer to Figure 8-4.)

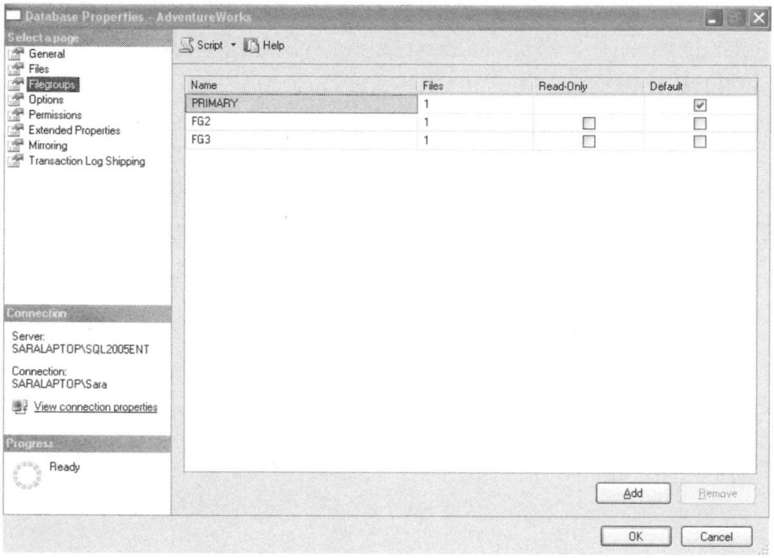

Figure 8-4 The Filegroups page as displayed in the Properties dialog box for the *Adventure-Works* database

4. Click Add, and enter FG2 as the name of the new filegroup. Add another filegroup named FG3.

5. Select the Files page, and click Add to add a new file. The new file will be named AdventureWorks_Data_FG2, the File Type will be data, and the Filegroup will be FG2. Add another file named AdventureWorks_Data_FG3 with a File Type of data and the Filegroup FG3. When finished, click OK to save your changes to the database.

6. Select New Query.

7. Select AdventureWorks from the Available Databases drop-down list box. Add the following code to the query window:

```
CREATE PARTITION FUNCTION
    pfnProduct (nvarchar(25))
AS RANGE LEFT FOR VALUES ('FL', 'LN')
```

8. Click the Execute button, and ensure that the function is created successfully.

9. Replace the code added in step 7 with the following:

```
CREATE PARTITION SCHEME
    pscProduct
AS PARTITION pfnProduct
    TO ('Primary', 'FG2', 'FG3')
```

10. Click the Execute button, and ensure that the scheme is created successfully.

11. From Object Explorer, expand the Production.Product table, and then the indexes
     within the *AdventureWorks* database. Right-click the AK_Product_ProductNumber i
     and select Properties.

12. From the Properties dialog box, select the Storage page. Select the Partition sc
     option, and ensure that the partition scheme named pscProduct is selected. (Refer
     ure 8-5.) Enter ProductNumber as the Table Column, and click OK to save the cha

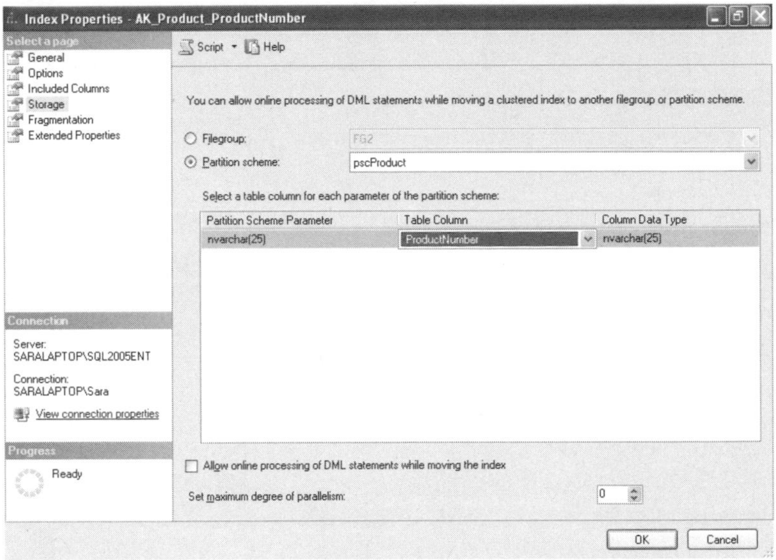

Figure 8-5   The Storage page for the AK_Product_ProductNumber index properties

13. Return to the new query window, and execute the following query:

```
select * from sys.partitions where object_name(object_id) = 'Product'
```

14. You should see results similar to those in the following table:

Partition ID	Object ID	Index ID	Partition Number	Hobt ID	R
72057594056867840	1429580131	1	1	72057594056867840	5
72057594056998912	1429580131	3	1	72057594056998912	5
72057594057064448	1429580131	4	1	72057594057064448	5
72057594057129984	1429580131	17	1	72057594057129984	5
72057594057195520	1429580131	2	1	72057594057195520	1
72057594057261056	1429580131	2	2	72057594057261056	2
72057594057326592	1429580131	2	3	72057594057326592	1

15. Notice that in this table, the last three rows are associated with our newly created partition. The table was partitioned into three groups of the following sizes: 137, 204, and 163.

▶ **Exercise 2: Create a CLR User-Defined Function**

In this exercise, you will create a user-defined function using .NET Framework code. The code will be created using a Windows text-based editor and compiled using the Visual Basic or C# command line compiler. You will then create an assembly in SQL Server and execute the newly created user-defined function just as you would a user-defined function created with Transact-SQL.

BEST PRACTICES   For demonstration purposes only

For demonstration purposes, the user-defined function in this exercise performs a data access query. Generally, you will not use SQLCLR for basic data access. In this case, Transact-SQL is a better alternative.

---

1. Open SQL Server Management Studio.

2. Connect to the instance of SQL Server 2005 that contains the *AdventureWorks* database.

3. Select New Query.

4. Select *AdventureWorks* from the Available Databases drop-down list box. Add the following code to the query window:

```
sp_configure N'clr enabled', 1
GO
RECONFIGURE
GO

SELECT * FROM sys.configurations
WHERE [Name] = N'clr enabled'
```

5. Click the Execute button, and ensure that the query executed successfully.

6. Open Windows Notepad, and copy in either the C# or VB code shown below:

```
//C#
using System;
using System.Data;
using Microsoft.SqlServer.Server;
using System.Data.SqlClient;
using System.Data.SqlTypes;

public class TK442Chapter8
{
    [Microsoft.SqlServer.Server.SqlFunction(DataAccess=DataAccessKind.Read,
IsDeterministic=true)]
    public static Int32 GetProductID(String prodNumber)
```

```csharp
    {

    SqlCommand cmd;
    Int32 ret = 0;

        //Connect to the context connection
    SqlConnection conn = new SqlConnection("Context Connection=true");
    conn.Open();


    cmd = new SqlCommand("SELECT ProductID FROM Production.Product " +
        " WHERE ProductNumber = @prodNumber", conn);
        cmd.Parameters.AddWithValue("@prodNumber", prodNumber);

    try
    {
        //Execute the command and return the results
        SqlDataReader dr = cmd.ExecuteReader();
        while(dr.Read())
        {
            ret = Convert.ToInt32(dr[0]);
        }

    }
    catch(SqlException ex)
    {
        //Process the exception
        SqlContext.Pipe.Send("The Following error was encountered: " +
            ex.Message);
    }

    return ret;

    }
}

'VB
Imports System
Imports System.Data
Imports System.Data.SqlClient
Imports Microsoft.SqlServer.Server
Imports System.Data.SqlTypes


Public Class TK442Chapter8
    <Microsoft.SqlServer.Server.SqlFunction(DataAccess:=DataAccessKind.Read,
IsDeterministic:=true)> _
    Public Shared Function GetProductID(ByVal prodNumber as String) As Int32
```

```
Dim cmd As SqlCommand
Dim ret As Int32 = 0

    'Connect to the context connection
Dim conn as New SqlConnection("Context connection=true")
conn.Open()

cmd = New SqlCommand("SELECT ProductID FROM Production.Product " & _
    " WHERE ProductNumber = @prodNumber", conn)
    cmd.Parameters.AddWithValue("@prodNumber", prodNumber)


Try

        'Execute the command and return the results
        Dim dr As SqlDataReader = cmd.ExecuteReader()
        Do While dr.Read()
            ret = Convert.ToInt32(dr(0))
        Loop
Catch ex as Exception
        'Process the exception
        SqlContext.Pipe.Send("The Following error was encountered: " & _
            ex.Message)
End Try

    Return ret
    End Function
End Class
```

7. Save the files with the name TK442Chapter8Lab1.cs or TK442Chapter8Lab1.vb to the directory C:\TK442\Chapter8\Code\Lab1\.

IMPORTANT Local directory required

If you have not already created a directory on your local drive, do so now and use the path from this step. This path will be referenced in later steps. If you choose to use a different path, make sure you reference the new path in the next steps.

---

8. Open a Visual Studio 2005 Command Prompt. From the command window, execute the following command:

//C#
```
csc /target:library c:\TK442\Chapter8\Code\Lab1\TK442Chapter8Lab1.cs
```

'VB
```
vbc /target:library c:\TK442\Chapter8\Code\Lab1\TK442Chapter8Lab1.vb
```

9. Ensure that the command completes successfully and returns no errors. When plete, there should be a file named TK442Chapter8Lab1.dll in the C:\T \Chapter8\Code\Lab1 directory.

10. Return to Microsoft SQL Server Management Studio, and execute the following mand from the new query window for the *AdventureWorks* database:

```
CREATE ASSEMBLY TK442Chapter8Lab1
FROM 'c:\TK442\Chapter8\Code\Lab1\TK442Chapter8Lab1.dll'
WITH PERMISSION_SET = SAFE
```

11. Ensure that the query executed successfully. Replace the code in step 10 with the f ing code:

```
CREATE FUNCTION GetProductID(@prodNumber nvarchar(25))
RETURNS int
EXTERNAL NAME TK442Chapter8Lab1.TK442Chapter8.GetProductID
```

12. Ensure that the query executed successfully. Replace the code in step 10 with the f ing code:

```
Select dbo.GetProductID('AR-5381')
```

13. Ensure that the previous query returns a value of 1.

Quick Check

1. Name and explain the two basic kinds of partitioning.
2. What is the purpose of a partition scheme?
3. What two methods can be used to specify the name of a linked server in a que
4. What is the purpose of a Distributed Partition View (DPV)?
5. Which scale-out technique uses middleware to route requests to the appropri database server?
6. Which SQL Server 2005 features can applications built with the Service-Orien Database Architecture (SODA) take advantage of?
7. Which scale-out technique is best for transparently distributing data across mu ple servers?
8. What does SQLCLR provide?

Quick Check Answers

1. Vertical partitioning involves removing columns from a table and creating separate tables to store the data. Horizontal partitioning involves removing rows from a table based on a key partitioning column.

2. A partition scheme is used to specify to which filegroups a partition will be assigned. The partition function associated with this scheme will also be provided because this specifies a range of values that will fall within each partition.

3. For a query involving a linked server, you can either use a four-part name or the *OPENDATASOURCE* function, which is used to execute an ad hoc query against a remote server.

4. A Distributed Partition View (DPV) is used to bring together data that was horizontally partitioned into a single view for the client. The query for the view is built using UNION statements that join together one or more linked servers that contain the partitioned data.

5. Data Dependent Routing (DDR) uses the application or middleware to route requests to the appropriate server where the data has been partitioned. Lookup tables are used to associate the data with the table based on a partition key value.

6. Applications built using the SODA scale-out technique can take advantage of SQLCLR, Notification Services, Query Notifications, Service Broker, and Native XML Web Services.

7. A Scalable Shared Database is a read-only database that was built on a SAN and can service up to eight different instances of SQL Server. No application changes are needed to implement this scale-out technique.

8. SQLCLR allows developers to write managed code using the .NET Framework and execute the assembly on SQL Server. Stored procedures, user-defined functions, and triggers can be written using Visual Basic, C#, or J#. In cases where complex operations must be performed on the data, SQLCLR can enhance application performance.

Lesson 2: Resolving Performance Problems

Estimated lesson time: 60 minutes

Even if your application was carefully designed and meticulously developed and deploy is still prone to performance problems. Performance problems can arise from a change operational environment, the addition of data, or improper use of indexes. You need to what tools can be used to analyze application performance and be able to make recomm tions on how to improve the application.

Analyzing Application Performance

There are several tools that can be used to troubleshoot poorly performing applicatio addition to the commonly used tools such as SQL Server Profiler and Windows System itor, SQL Server 2005 provides dynamic management views (DMVs) that expose stati data through relational row sets. This section will review these tools and reveal how the be used to diagnose commonly encountered problems.

Using SQL Server Profiler

SQL Server Profiler is a tool that allows you to capture detailed information about an occurring in a SQL Server database. An event represents an action such as logging in server and executing a query or a stored procedure. Each event is associated with a class as *Audit Login* and *Audit Logout*. These event classes are used to audit server activity, anc are two of the default events selected when you start a new trace.

A trace is like a recording in which you first define what events and columns should be itored. From the point a trace is started, data will be collected and stored in either a tabl file. The data collected from a trace can be analyzed to reveal information about how the Server database is performing. Typically, a trace will be associated with a goal, such as lo for long-running queries.

You can execute SQL Server Profiler in one of two ways. From SQL Server Management Studio, select SQL Server Profiler from the Tools menu. Alternatively, you can go to Start, All Programs, SQL Server 2005, Performance Tools, and SQL Server Profiler. Either way, you will encounter a blank window with a menu bar.

Templates provide a way to pre-load a trace with the events and columns associated with a particular goal. A default template is provided, along with several others. (See Table 8-3.) You can use the templates provided with SQL Server or create your own, saving them to a file with a .tdf file extension.

Table 8-3   Templates Included with SQL Server Profiler

Template Name	Goal	Event Category/Event Class
Standard (default)	Monitor general database activity	Security Audit/Audit Login Security Audit/Audit Logout Sessions/Existing Connection Stored Procedures/RPC:Completed TSQL/SQL:BatchStarting TSQL/SQL:BatchCompleted
SP_Counts	Capture stored procedure information over a period of time	Stored Procedures/SP:Starting
TSQL	Debug client-based applications	Security Audit/Audit Login Security Audit/Audit Logout Sessions/Existing Connection Stored Procedures/RPC:Completed TSQL/SQL:BatchStarting
TSQL_Duration	Identify long-running queries	Stored Procedures/RPC:Completed TSQL/SQL:BatchCompleted
TSQL_Grouped	Investigate queries from a particular user	Security Audit/Audit Login Security Audit/Audit Logout Sessions/Existing Connection Stored Procedures/RPC:Starting TSQL/SQL:BatchStarting

Table 8-3   Templates Included with SQL Server Profiler

Template Name	Goal	Event Category/Event Class
TSQL_Replay	Perform benchmark testing	Cursors/CursorClose Cursors/CursorExecute Cursors/CursorOpen Cursors/CursorPrepare Cursors/CursorUnprepare Security Audit/Audit Login Security Audit/Audit Logout Sessions/Existing Connection Stored Procedures/RPC Output Parameter Stored Procedures/RPC:Complete Stored Procedures/RPC:Starting TSQL/Exec Prepared SQL TSQL/Prepare SQL TSQL/SQL:BatchCompleted TSQL/SQL:BatchStarting
TSQL_SPs	Confirm that procedures are being recompiled	Security Audit/Audit Login Security Audit/Audit Logout Sessions/ExistingConnection Stored Procedures/RPC:Starting Stored Procedures/SP:Completed Stored Procedures/SP:Starting Stored Procedures/StmtStarting TSQL/SQL:BatchStarting
Tuning	Create a workload that is used by the Database Tuning Engine Advisor tool.	Stored Procedures/RPC:Complet Stored Procedures/SP:StmtCom-pleted TSQL/SQL:BatchCompleted

To start a new trace, select New Trace from the File menu. You will first be prompted to connect to the SQL Server. You can connect to either the Database Engine or Analysis Ser Once connected, you will need to select properties for your trace, such as the trace name plate, and optional start and stop times. You will also specify whether the trace is saved to or a table. (See Figure 8-6.)

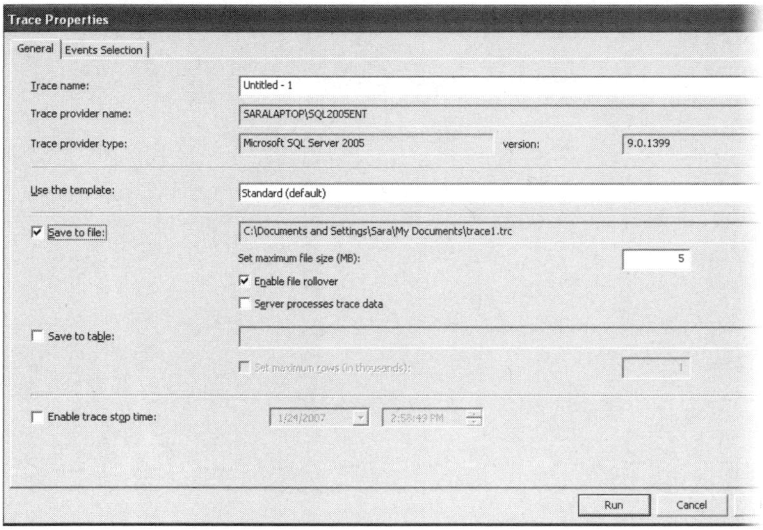

Figure 8-6 General trace properties for a new trace created with SQL Server Profiler

When you select a template on the General tab, certain events are automatically selected on the Events Selection tab. See Table 8-3 for a list of the templates included with SQL Server. If you prefer to select your own events and columns, you can choose Blank as the template. At this point, from the Events Selection tab, you will have to select which events and columns will be included in your trace. (See Figure 8-7.)

To specify a new event using an existing template, you must first select the Show all events check box. This will display all events grouped by event category. Click the plus icon next to a category in the Events column to expand that node and see the events within the category. If a category contains selected events, the node will already be expanded.

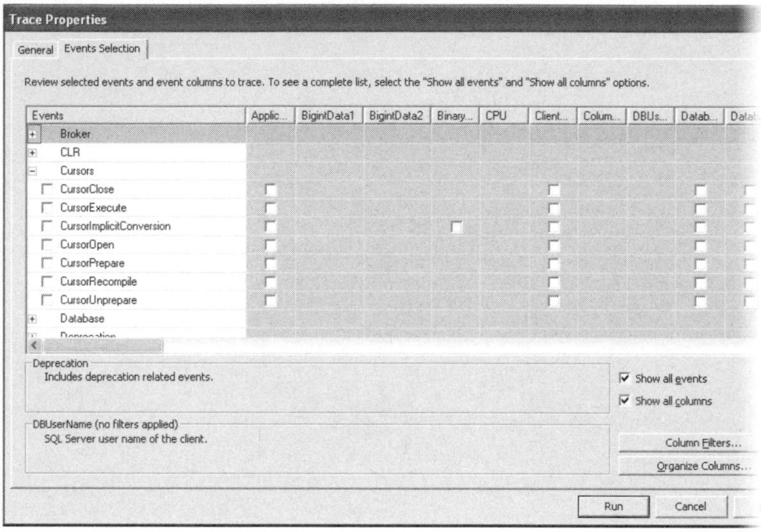

Figure 8-7   Events Selection tab for a new trace that is based on the blank template

When selecting a new event, you must also select the columns to be captured for that The columns are displayed as check boxes; you can select the Show All Columns check see them all displayed. Not all columns will be available for every event. For example, the umn named Reads is used to track the number of logical reads performed by the serv behalf of the event. This column is available for events such as *Audit Logout*, but it is not able to the activation event for Service Broker.

The Events Selection tab allows you to specify column filters. This can be useful if you ne run a trace that monitors a single application. The server you are monitoring might be us several applications. To ensure that the trace records events for one particular applicatio could add a filter for the ApplicationName column where the name is like the name of yo get application.

Once you have specified the trace properties, you will click Run to begin the recording. A point, the trace will begin and you will see a split-screen window. (See Figure 8-8.) Unles specified a start and stop time, the trace will run until you click the Stop Selected Trace b (the red stop icon on the toolbar) to stop the selected trace. While the trace is running events specified in the trace will appear in the top window, so you can watch the trace a running.

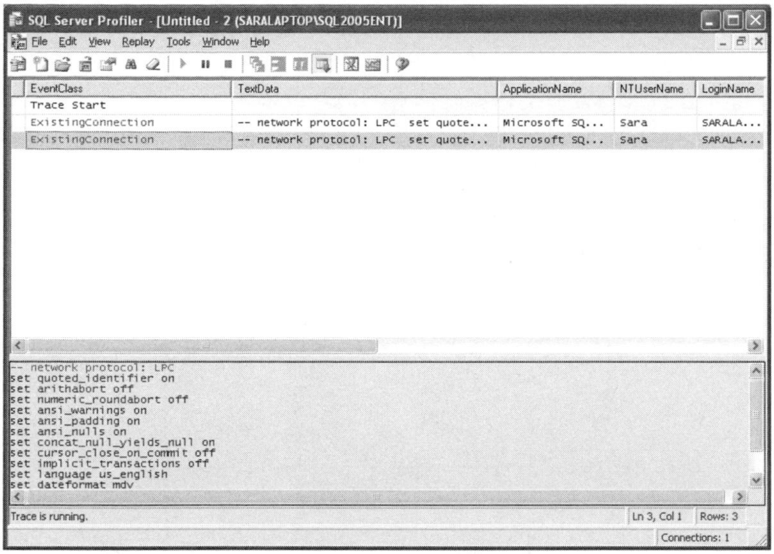

Figure 8-8 Events Selection tab for a new trace that is based on the blank template

Typically, you will run a trace at a time when you know the application is experiencing problems. Because SQL Server Profiler will consume server resources while running a trace, you do not want to allow the trace to run any longer than necessary. Once the trace is stopped, you can manually review the trace file or use it as input for the Database Engine Tuning Advisor tool.

BEST PRACTICES Use filters and run trace remotely

Typically, you will be performing a trace against a production server. An active SQL Server will fill up a trace file very quickly. Use filters, if possible, to restrict the number of entries collected. Also, try to limit the number of events and columns selected.

SQL Server Profiler will consume additional server resources while running a trace. If possible, use a separate server to monitor your production server remotely.

Using System Monitor

Windows System Monitor, also known as PerfMon or Performance Monitor, is a graphical tool provided with Windows that can be used to monitor all aspects of a server's health. Like SQL Server Profiler, System Monitor provides results in real time, so you can monitor a server as it is experiencing problems. To start System Monitor, go to Start, All Programs, Administrative Tools, and Performance. Alternatively, you can type **perfmon.msc** from a command prompt. By default, System Monitor will display activity for the current machine. (See Figure 8-9.)

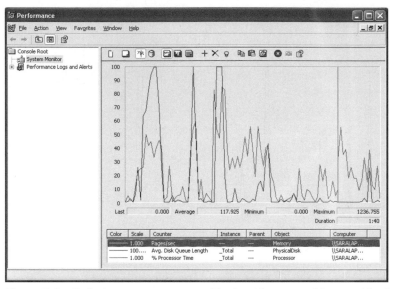

Figure 8-9   Default counters measured by local instance of System Monitor

System Monitor uses performance counters to represent the measurement of a sp
object or system component. For example, the *processor* object has a counter that ca
the percentage of processor time for a particular instance. Upon execution, System M
will begin monitoring three default counters (as shown in Table 8-4) for the cu
machine.

Table 8-4   Default Performance Counters for System Monitor

Counter	Description	Object	Ins
Pages/sec	Represents the rate at which pages are read and written to the hard disk and can indicate system delays.	Memory	—
Avg. Disk Queue Length	This is the average number of read and write requests that are queued. If this number consistently exceeds a value of 2, you could have an IO bottleneck.	Physical Disk	_To
% Processor Time	Indicates the amount of processor activity by displaying the percentage of busy time. This counter should not exceed 80% per CPU.	Processor	_To

To add additional counters, click the Add button (the plus sign on the toolbar) abo
graph to open the Add Counters dialog box and select a performance object. Each

represents a subsystem to be monitored and has one or more counters associated with it. Each counter might be associated with a particular instance, such as the ASP.NET worker process. In some cases, the counters are associated with all instances, which is represented as _Total. In cases where the object is not associated with an instance, the instance list box will be unavailable.

IMPORTANT **Permissions required**

Your Windows user account will need to be a member of the local Administrators group or Performance Log Users group for the server being monitored, or a member of the Domain Admins group for the network.

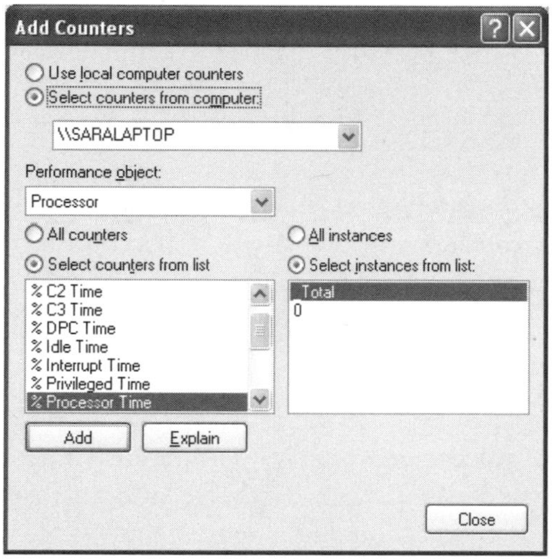

Figure 8-10 Add Counters dialog box used to add performance counters to a System Monitor graph

The next section, "Investigate Performance Problems," lists some additional performance counters that can be helpful for investigating specific problems with your server.

Exam Tip To understand how System Monitor works, you can download a free tool from MSDN called the Performance Monitor Wizard. This tool will help you select configuration settings and determine which counters are best. The utility is available at *http://www.microsoft.com/downloads /details.aspx?FamilyID=31fccd98-c3a1-4644-9622-faa046d69214&displaylang=en&Hash=7YTJ6NC.*

Using a Dynamic Management View

A dynamic management view (DMV) can be included in a SELECT query to return in[...]
tion about the health of your server and databases. New to SQL Server 2005, DMVs e[...]
statistical information as a result set. The information included in each view can be crit[...]
diagnosing problems with your SQL Server.

IMPORTANT   Permissions required

You will need the SELECT permission for each object, along with the VIEW SERVER STATE or
DATABASE STATE permission to use a DMV in a SELECT query. Which permission is required
depends on whether the DMV is server-scoped or database-scoped.

SQL Server 2005 provides dozens of views to represent all areas of SQL Server. Each[...]
bears a prefix of dm_, and to reference the view in a SELECT query, you must use the tw[...]
name. For example, the following query can be used to access the dm_exec_connection[...]

```
SELECT * FROM sys.dm_exec_connections
```

The previous query will return information about all open connections. This will inc[...]
time stamp for the connection time, last read and write operations, and a count of the n[...]
of reads and writes. This DMV is just one of several built-in views that can be used to dia[...]
the health of your SQL Server.

Investigating Performance Issues

The previous section identified tools that you can use to analyze the performance of you[...]
Server. Collecting the necessary information is the easy part. The hard part is iden[...]
where a performance issue might lie. Ideally, you should be able to identify issues befo[...]
users suffer the consequences. This will allow you to proactively monitor and tune you[...]
Server and ensure that all your database applications perform at their best.

Creating a Performance Baseline

A *performance baseline* is a chart or log that represents a period of time when the SQL[...]
was performing acceptably. The baseline can be created with Windows System Moni[...]
SQL Server Profiler. You can then refer to the result if the SQL Server begins to experien[...]
formance problems. By comparing the results from two collection periods, you can id[...]
outliers that might indicate a problem.

Before creating a baseline, you will need to determine which performance counters or profiler events will be captured. Microsoft recommends that the performance counters listed in Table 8-5 are included in your performance baseline. You should also include the counters listed in Table 8-6. These counters will represent your System Monitor baseline; subsequent logs should contain the same counters.

Table 8-5   Performance Counters Recommended by Microsoft for Performance Baseline

Object\Counter	Description
Memory\Pages/sec	Rate at which pages are read from or written to disk to resolve hard page faults
Network Interface\Bytes total/sec	Rate at which bytes are sent and received for the local connection
PhysicalDisk\Disk Transfers/sec	Rate at which read and write operations are performed for the physical disk selected in the instance list box
PhysicalDisk\Avg. Disk Queue Length	Average number of read and write requests that were queued for the sample interval
SQL Instance:Memory Manager\Total Server Memory	Total amount of memory the server is consuming
SQL Instance:Access Methods\Full Scans/sec	Number of unrestricted full table or index scans
SQL Instance:Buffer Manager\Buffer Cache Hit Ratio	Percentage of pages that were found in the buffer pool without having to incur a read from the disk
SQL Instance:Databases\Log Growths	Total number of log growths for the database specified in the Instances list box
SQL Instance:Databases\Percent Log Used	Percentage of space used by the log for the database specified in the Instances list box
SQL Instance:Databases\Transactions/sec	Number of transactions started for the database specified in the Instances list box
SQL Instance:General Statistics\User Connections	Number of users connected to SQL Server
SQL Instance:Latches\Average Latch Wait Time	Average wait time for waiting latch requests
SQL Instance:Locks\Average Wait Time	Average wait time for waiting lock requests

Table 8-5 Performance Counters Recommended by Microsoft for Performance Baseline

Object\Counter	Description
SQL Instance:Locks\Lock Waits/sec	Number of lock requests that were forced wait for the lock to be granted
SQL Instance:Locks\Number of Deadlocks/sec	Number of lock requests that resulted in deadlock
SQL Instance:Memory Manager\Memory Grants Pending	Number of processes waiting for a works memory to be granted

For baselines created with Windows System Monitor, you will need to specify a sampling val. By default, a performance counter is sampled every second. You can change this in of time to the number of seconds you prefer.

Table 8-6 Key Counters for Diagnosing Problems

Object\Counter(s)	Used to Diagnose
SQL Instance:SQL Statistics\SQL Re-compilations *SQL Instance*:SQL Statistics\Batch Requests/sec	Indicates whether there are compiles and compiles occurring. The ratio between the two numbers should be low.
SQL Instance:Cursor Manager by Type\Cursor Requests/sec	Indicates the ratio between hits and looku and can reveal how many cursors are bein lized. If this number is high, you might be cursors poorly and causing an unnecessar den on system resources.
Memory\Available bytes	Indicates if there is enough physical mem available to the server. This value should high as possible, relative to the baseline.
Memory\Commit Limit Paging File\%Usage Paging File\%UsagePeak	Indicates whether there is enough virtual ory available to the server. The two paging counters should not be high relative the b line, and the commit limit should be high because this represents the maximum am of memory that can be committed withou extending the page file space.
Physical Disk\Avg. Disk Sec/Read Physical Disk\Avg. Disk Sec/Write Physical Disk\%Disk Time	Indicates whether there is a possible I/O neck on the server. The average disk coun should not exceed 50 ms, and the disk tir counter should not exceed 50 percent.

Table 8-6 Key Counters for Diagnosing Problems

Object\Counter(s)	Used to Diagnose
SQL Instance:General Statistics\User Connections	Indicates the number of users connected to the instance. This can be useful in determining if you have connections that are not being closed. The amount should not be high relative to a baseline.

In addition to the performance counters listed in Tables 8-5 and 8-6, you might need to use DMVs to investigate outliers. Table 8-7 lists key DMVs that can be used to diagnose problems with your SQL Server.

Table 8-7 Key Dynamic Management Views for Diagnosing Problems

Dynamic Management View(s)	Used to Diagnose
sys.dm_db_file_space_usage sys.dm_db_session_space_usage	Returns space information about a database and can be used to monitor the space in the tempdb. Session Space Usage can then be used to get information about a particular session.
sys.dm_db_index_operational_stats sys.dm_db_index_usage_stats	Operational Stats returns index usage statistics and can be used to identify excessive blocking. Usage Stats returns statistics about all indexes in use and can be useful for monitoring index usage.
sys.dm_exec_cursors sys.dm_exec_connections	Returns detailed information about all open cursors for a specific session. This can be used to identify poor cursor usage. When combined with the Connections view, you can track down a specific problem connection.
sys.dm_exec_query_optimizer sys.dm_exec_query_stats	The Optimizer Info view returns information about the query optimizer and can help determine if too much time is spent doing compiles. Query Stats returns aggregate data about cached query plans and can be used to identify inefficient query plans. This view can also help identify which request is generating the most I/O and potentially causing an I/O bottleneck.
sys.dm_os_memory_clerks	Returns information about all active SQL Server memory clerks. Memory clerks are used by components to allocate memory, so this can be used to identify a memory issue.

Table 8-7   Key Dynamic Management Views for Diagnosing Problems

Dynamic Management View(s)	Used to Diagnose
sys.dm_os_schedulers	Returns information about tasks for each schedule can be used to identify runaway tasks, which migh cate a CPU bottleneck.
sys.dm_os_waiting_tasks	Returns information about tasks waiting for resou and can be used to identify slow-running queries.

Several scenarios cause the performance of SQL Server to diminish. In some cases, there
be multiple issues that contribute to a problem. Following are issues commonly encou
with SQL Server:

Inefficient queries or slow-running queries   These can be caused by missing in
because the absence of an index forces the query optimizer to perform a table scan.
scans are expensive in terms of resources, and you want to avoid them if at all possible

Another possibility is that the table(s) is using an inefficient query plan. This might
when there are changes to the statistical information, but it can also occur when query
are utilized. Query hints override the query plan selected by the query optimizer, and
ally, this is not a good idea. Query hints should only be used by experienced database
opers in situations where there is a compelling reason to use one.

You might also check to see whether the table(s) contains too much data. The database
need to be partitioned. Typically, it might take millions or billions of records before sign
delays are experienced.

A final possibility is that the database was designed poorly. If tables are not normalized a
relationships exist between related tables, you could experience delays in returning da

Excessive blocking   This can occur when the wrong isolation level is used for a transa
Transactions are utilized when there is a need to update data and prevent others from
fying the data at the same time. There are several types of isolation levels allowed b
Server. Read uncommitted is the least restrictive; serializable is the most restrictive.

If a transaction is held open for longer than necessary, it can cause delays for an appli
with high activity. Transactions should be opened and closed as quickly as possible to
unnecessary delays.

I/O and CPU bottlenecks   Resource bottlenecks can occur for various reasons, and
they occur suddenly, it is generally not caused by insufficient hardware. Both I/O an
bottlenecks can occur if you are using a poor execution plan or there are missing ind
problem can also occur if SQL Server was not configured with enough memory. You

also consider how the physical files are allocated. Log files and data files should rarely exist on the same physical disks, and multiple data files can reside on separate physical disks as well.

Limited space for tempdb   Continuously monitoring the tempdb helps to prevent your SQL Server from running out of space and experiencing errors. There are several things that can cause SQL Server to run low on space for the tempdb. For example, applications might hold transactions open too long, stored procedures and user-defined functions might create and drop a large number of temp tables, and query plans might create too many temporary objects.

Memory issues   Memory can refer to physical or virtual memory, whether internal or external. Although it might be necessary to add more memory to the SQL Server, issues might also be resolved by adjusting the demands for major memory consumers, adjusting the server configuration, and increasing the swap file size.

Orphaned connections   A common mistake for new and even some experienced database developers is to leave connections open too long or not to close them at all. If a database connection is not specifically closed, it can remain open for some time before it times out and is released. Connections that are not specifically released are known as orphaned connections; they can cause an unnecessary consumption of resources.

For more information about analyzing and resolving SQL Server performance problems, refer to the TechNet article "Troubleshooting Performance Problems in SQL Server 2005" at *http://www.microsoft.com/technet/prodtechnol/sql/2005/tsprfprb.mspx*.

Analyzing Performance

In this lab, you will analyze the performance of a single Web page. You will create an ASP.NET project that retrieves data from the database using a *DataSet*. Using the Web Application Stress Tool (available from *http://www.microsoft.com/downloads*), you will simulate execution of the Web page while running a trace with SQL Server Profiler.

The completed code examples, in Visual Basic, C#, and Transact-SQL, are available in the \Labs\Chapter 08 folder on the companion CD.

IMPORTANT   Lab requirements

You will need to have SQL Server 2005 and Visual Studio 2005 installed before you can complete this lab. Refer to the Introduction for setup instructions.

▶ **Exercise 1: Use Profiler to Analyze Performance**

In this exercise, you will create a new ASP.NET project that will be used to connect t
AdventureWorks database, retrieve product data for all products, populate a *DataSet*, anc
use that data to populate a *dataGridView* control. The Microsoft Web Application Stres:
will be used to simulate activity for the project. You will then run a trace using SQL Profile
view the results.

1. Open Visual Studio 2005.
2. On the File menu, select New, Project.
3. In the New Project dialog box, expand the *Other Project Types* node and select Visua
    dio Solutions. Type **TK442Chapter8** for the name of your blank solution, and plac
    a directory of your choosing. Click OK.
4. On the File menu, select Add, New Web Site. Select ASP.NET Web site as the templat
    type **http://localhost/TK442Chapter8CSharp** or **http://localhost/TK442Chapte**
    as the project name. Set the language by selecting Visual Basic, Visual C#, or Vis
    from the language drop-down list box. By default, Visual Studio will select the lan
    specified when it was first configured.
5. From the Source pane, add the following code below the form tag:

    ```
    <asp:Button ID="btnGetProducts" runat="server" Text="Get Products" />
    <asp:GridView ID="GridView1" runat="server">
    </asp:GridView>
    <asp:Label ID="lblError" runat="server"></asp:Label>
    ```

6. Right-click the Default.aspx file from Solution Explorer, and select View Code. Ac
    following code at the top of the code pane:

    ```
    //C#
    using System.Data;
    using System.Data.SqlClient;


    'VB
    Imports System.Data
    Imports System.Data.SqlClient
    ```

7. Add the following code beneath Inherits System.Web.UI.Page, modifying conn
    strings to match your environment:

    ```
    //C#
    protected void btnGetProducts_Click(object sender, EventArgs e)
        {
            DataSet dsProducts = new DataSet("Products");
            SqlDataAdapter adapter = new SqlDataAdapter();

            //Initiate the connection to SQL Server
            String connString = @"server=.\SQL2005ENT;" +
    ```

```
                        "uid=sa;pwd=gator;" +
                        "Database=AdventureWorks";
    SqlConnection conn = new SqlConnection(connString);

    //Define the query that will be executed
    SqlCommand cmd = new SqlCommand("SELECT * FROM Production.Product" +
        " WHERE SafetyStockLevel > 500", conn);

    try
    {
        //Populate the adapter with results of the query
        adapter.SelectCommand = cmd;
        adapter.Fill(dsProducts);

        //Set the datasource for the GridView control on the form
        GridView1.DataSource = dsProducts.Tables[0];
        GridView1.DataBind();

    }
    catch (Exception ex)
    {
        //write error to the label
        lblError.Text = ex.Message;
    }
    finally
    {
        if (adapter != null)
        {
            adapter.Dispose();
            adapter = null;
        }

        if (cmd != null)
        {
            cmd.Dispose();
            cmd = null;
        }

        if (conn != null)
        {
            if (conn.State == ConnectionState.Open)
            {
                conn.Close();
            }
            conn = null;
        }
    }
}
```

```vb
'VB
Protected Sub btnGetProducts_Click(ByVal sender As Object, ByVal e As System.Event
Handles btnGetProducts.Click
        Dim dsProducts As New DataSet("Products")
        Dim adapter As New SqlDataAdapter()

        'Initiate the connection to SQL Server
        Dim connString As String = "server=.\SQL2005ENT;" & _
                                    "uid=sa;pwd=gator;" & _
                                    "Database=AdventureWorks"
        Dim conn As New SqlConnection(connString)

        'Define the query that will be executed
        Dim cmd As New SqlCommand("SELECT * FROM Production.Product" & _
            " WHERE SafetyStockLevel > 500", conn)

    Try
        'Populate the adapter with results of the query
        adapter.SelectCommand = cmd
        adapter.Fill(dsProducts)

        'Set the datasource for the dataViewGrid control on the form
        GridView1.DataSource = dsProducts.Tables(0)
        GridView1.DataBind()

    Catch ex As Exception
        lblError.Text = ex.Message
    Finally
        If Not (adapter Is Nothing) Then
            adapter.Dispose()
            adapter = Nothing
        End If

        If Not (cmd Is Nothing) Then
            cmd.Dispose()
            cmd = Nothing
        End If

        If Not (conn Is Nothing) Then
            If (conn.State = ConnectionState.Open) Then
                conn.Close()
            End If
            conn = Nothing
        End If

    End Try

End Sub
```

8. Save the project by selecting File, Save All.

9. Press Ctrl+F5 to build the project without debugging. Ensure that the project builds successfully. The default Web page should appear after the project compiles and executes. You should see a button labeled "Get Products." Click this button. You should see the data results displayed in the *GridView* control.

10. Open SQL Server Profiler by selecting Start, All Programs, Microsoft SQL Server 2005, Performance Tools, SQL Server Profiler.

11. Select File, then New Trace.

12. Enter the connection information for the server that contains the *AdventureWorks* database.

13. From the Trace Properties dialog box, enter a name for the Trace and select the Save to table check box. You will then be prompted to log in to the SQL Server 2005 database again.

14. From the Destination Table dialog box, select *AdventureWorks* as the database and enter the name TraceResults as the table. Click OK to continue. Do *not* close SQL Server Profiler or the Trace Properties dialog box.

15. Open the Microsoft Web Application Stress Tool by selecting Start, All Programs, then Microsoft Web Application Stress Tool. If you have not already installed this utility, refer to the setup instructions in the Introduction.

16. Click Record in the Create New Script dialog box.

17. Click Next and then Finish to begin the recording. A blank Microsoft Internet Explorer page should appear. Type the following in the URL address bar:

    ```
    //C#
    http://localhost/TK442Chapter8CSharp/Default.aspx
    ```

    ```
    'VB
    http://localhost/TK442Chapter8VB/Default.aspx
    ```

18. Click the Get Products button, and ensure that the products are displayed.

19. Return to the Web Application Stress Tool, and click Stop Recording. This will create a new recorded script that you can use to simulate user activity. Do *not* close the Web Application Stress Tool.

20. Return to the Trace Properties dialog box, and click Run to start the trace. Do *not* close or stop the SQL Server Profiler trace.

21. Return to the Web Application Stress Tool, and click Run from the Scripts me
    default, the script will take one minute to complete. Wait until it finishes before cc
    ing to the next step.

22. Return to SQL Server Profiler, and click Stop from the Replay menu to end th
    recording. SQL Server Profiler will now contain a result window that lists several r
    and columns recorded during the trace. Scroll through the results, and take note
    columns EventClass, TextDate, CPU, Reads, Writes, and Duration.

23. Open SQL Server Management Studio, and connect to the database that contai
    AdventureWorks database.

24. Select the *AdventureWorks* database from the database drop-down list box.

25. Select New Query, and enter the following query:

    ```
    SELECT *
    FROM dbo.TraceResults
    ```

26. The results stored in the TraceResults table are the same that were displayed i
    Server Profiler. Storing the results in SQL Server allows you to query the data and
    tially combine results with dynamic management functions.

Quick Check

1. How can SQL Server Profiler help you to troubleshoot database applications?
2. What other system tool can be used to troubleshoot database applications?
3. What new feature in SQL Server 2005 allows you to return information about
   health of your SQL Server?

Quick Check Answers

1. SQL Server Profiler can help you by allowing you to record a trace in which spe
   SQL Server events are monitored and recorded. This information can be invalu
   when determining the cause of a specific problem, such as a server slowdown

2. Windows System Monitor is the tool that allows you to graphically monitor pe
   mance counters that are associated with server objects in real time.

3. Dynamic management view (DMV) can be included in a SELECT statemen
   expose statistical information as a result set. There are dozens of them availa
   they all start with the "dm_" prefix.

e Scenario: Diagnosing a Performance Problem

Six months ago, you were part of a development team that deployed a large and complex ASP.NET application into production. The Web application is used by customers of a large insurance company to get rate quotes for insurance. Built with multiple tiers, the Web application accesses a SQL Server 2005 database that has been partitioned across multiple servers using Data-Dependent Routing.

For the past six months, the application has been performing well and no slowdowns have been reported. All of the sudden, the application started experiencing sporadic but dramatic slowdowns. When the application was moved into production, key performance counters were identified and performance baselines established for all database servers. You have been asked to quickly determine what is causing the problem and make a recommendation for resolving the issue. What steps do you take to analyze the cause of the problem?

gested Practices

Objective 5.3: Scale database applications

■ **Practice 1**   See if you can get access to multiple servers or workstations in your organization and perform the following steps:

❏ Install SQL Server 2005 on these machines if it is not already available.

❏ Reference the *AdventureWorks* database already available on one of the SQL Servers. Determine how you can partition the data in the Person.Contact table.

❏ Select a partitioning column that was not already used in this chapter and move a portion of the data to at least one other server.

❏ Create linked servers that point to the other SQL Servers.

❏ Create a distributed partition view that joins the data from all servers into a single view using the UNION clause.

Objective 5.4: Resolve performance problems

■ **Practice 1**   Refer to the lab in the second lesson. Use the Web application and script created with that exercise to perform another load test. This time, execute System Monitor and add performance counters listed in Table 8-4 to create a baseline. After the test completes, review the results and record them to a log file.

References

- Scaling Out SQL Server 2005
  http://msdn2.microsoft.com/en-us/library/aa479364.aspx
- Data Partitioning in SQL Server 2005 – Part III
  http://www.databasejournal.com/features/mssql/article.php/3643726
- Use hardware to partition tables horizontally in SQL
  http://articles.techrepublic.com.com/5100-9592_11-5796600.html
- Scaling Out SQL Server with Data-Dependent Routing
  http://www.dell.com/downloads/global/power/ps3q05-20050100-Auger.pdf
- How SQL Server Enables Service-Oriented Database Architectures
  http://www.microsoft.com/technet/prodtechnol/sql/2005/sqlsoda.mspx
- Scaleable Shared Databases Are Supported by SQL Server 2005
  http://support.microsoft.com/default.aspx?scid=kb;en-us;910378
- The Database Administrator's Guide to the SQL Server Database Engine .NET Co
  Language Runtime Environment
  http://www.microsoft.com/technet/prodtechnol/sql/2005/clr4dbas.mspx
- Managing Data Access Inside SQL Server with ADO.NET and SQLCLR
  http://msdn2.microsoft.com/en-us/library/ms345135.aspx
- Troubleshooting Performance Problems in SQL Server 2005
  http://www.microsoft.com/technet/prodtechnol/sql/2005/tsprfprb.mspx
- 10 Baselining Tips for SQL Server: Lessons From the Field
  http://www.sql-server-performance.com/gv_baselining_tips.asp
- Monitoring and Tuning for Performance
  http://msdn2.microsoft.com/en-us/library/ms189081.aspx
- Establishing a Performance Baseline
  http://technet2.microsoft.com/WindowsServer/en/library/9277f422-eb8c-4c14 9fe09f80fd191033.mspx?mfr=true

ipter Summary

- Horizontal data partitioning is a method of moving data from one table or database to other data repositories. Data can be partitioned across multiple filegroups on the same server or moved to databases on remote servers.

- Targeting multiple database servers is an effective way to scale out an application and allow it to accommodate more users. You can use several techniques to scale out your application. You might have to use one or more of the following to achieve the desired result: scalable shared database, peer-to-peer replication, linked servers, distributed partition views, data-dependent routing, and service-oriented data architecture.

- You can use SQLCLR to execute managed code for the .NET Framework on your SQL Server. In some cases, this can provide a performance advantage. You can write code using Visual Basic .NET, C#, or J#.

- To analyze and resolve database application performance problems, you should use tools such as Windows System Monitor, SQL Server Profiler, and the newly included distributed management views.

se Scenario Answers

pter 1: Selecting a Data Access Strategy

Because the new application will only need to access data from a SQL Server database and you are targeting the .NET Framework, you can use the ADO.NET data provider. It is unlikely you will need to take advantage of the newer features available with SQL Server, given the application is being converted from an older application and given your time constraints. For that reason, it is not necessary to consider SNAC as a data provider. You can also use TCP/IP as the network protocol to provide the fastest access to the data across the Internet.

You can also suggest that they use Visual Basic .NET as the language because the development team is already accustomed to using prior versions of Visual Basic. This should help to speed the conversion time.

pter 2: Creating a Plan Guide

In cases where you are not able to modify Transact-SQL directly, you can still improve query performance using a plan guide. The plan guide is used to override the execution plan automatically generated by the query optimizer. As long as the execution plan you come up with returns the same results and performs better than the original query, this is a good way to affect performance without altering the code.

pter 3: Evaluating Cursor Performance

It might not be necessary to replace all the cursors in this poorly performing application. The best place to start is by identifying those areas of the application that are experiencing the largest delays. You could use SQL Server Profiler to record a trace while the application executes some of the slower functions. The trace recording can be used as input for the Database Engine Tuning Advisor, as an alternative to replacing the cursor. You might be able to resolve the application problems by simply applying a few indexes.

If the application performance continues to suffer, then you should consider replacing some of the cursors with set-based alternatives. You would start by identifying those cursors that take the longest to execute. For these long-running stored procedures, try to find a way to replace the cursor with one of the alternatives mentioned in Lesson 2, "Designing a Cursor Strategy." Compare the execution times for the alternative with the original cursor to determine

if the change was successful. You might just have to do this procedure with a few of the c
to achieve the desired performance results. There is a tradeoff to consider between de
ment time and application performance.

Chapter 4: Automating a Data-Mining Solution

The data-mining features available with SQL Servers Analysis Services (SSAS) enable
locate trends in large sets of data for the purpose of making predictions. You could utiliz
to create a data-mining solution that processed the sales history data and predicted wha
ucts the customer would likely purchase.

In order to keep the recommendations up-to-date, and based on the latest sales data, th
mining solution would need to be automated so that it was re-processed on a nightly o
hourly basis. Analysis Management Objects (AMO) could be used to accomplish this tas
only could you develop code that automated the processing of the mining model, b
code could be added to your ASP.NET application to query the mining model for predi
These predictions would then be presented to the customer as customized product r
mendations.

Chapter 5: Validating Data Integrity

Implement foreign key constraints between child and parent objects (such as from em
to department) to stop parent objects from being deleted if they contain child objects.
ment a check constraint on the product price to validate that prices cannot be less tha
After implementing these updates on a test environment, test the application against t
environment, and look for run-time errors caused by these added constraints.

Chapter 6: Optimizing Locking

- **The blocked lists**   The problem with the lists in the application being blocked
  peak hours is that they are being blocked by write transactions. Solving this proble
  either be accomplished by using the read uncommitted transaction isolation leve
  is, allowing dirty reads), or by implementing either the read committed snaps
  snapshot isolation level. Because there is no mention of dirty reads being allowe
  should assume that they are not allowed. The snapshot isolation level will cause r
  sions to be kept for more time than the read committed snapshot isolation level b
  only versions from the beginning of the transaction can be used. This will caus
  space to be used in the *tempdb* system database; it will also cause more informa

written to *tempdb*. This means that the read committed snapshot isolation level is the best solution to this problem. (If it can't be decided that dirty reads in the lists are acceptable, read uncommitted will provide the best performance.)

- **The inconsistent reports**   The reports that contain inconsistent data are either experiencing non-repeatable or phantom reads. To solve this problem, the queries used in a report need to be combined in a transaction and use the repeatable read, serializable, or snapshot isolation level. Because the repeatable read isolation level doesn't protect against phantom reads, it will solve the problem only if the problem is non-repeatable reads. Both repeatable read and serializable drastically increase locked resouces. The reports are run against the same database as the order entry application; they should be avoided because they are highly likely to introduce blocking and deadlock problems. The snapshot isolation level will protect against both non-repeatable and phantom reads without introducing blocking or deadlock issues. Because the reports don't update data, update conflicts will not be a problem.

pter 7: Optimizing Query Performance

To find out which stored procedures are performing poorly, you should examine the output of a SQL Trace (through Profiler or the trace stored procedures). Queries with value in the Duration column that is too high need to be optimized. When optimizing these queries, execute them in SQL Server Management Studio, examine their graphical execution, and consider rewriting the queries as well as redesigning the indexes on the queried tables. To reduce the query execution times from up to 30 minutes down to a couple of seconds, you will most likely have to do something other than design appropriate indexes. First, examine if these long response times are due to the finance queries being blocked by other users. If this is the issue, one solution may be to replicate the data to another SQL Server instance and execute the finance queries against this instance instead of the production server. If blocking is not the problem, either consider de-normalizing the tables to allow for shorter response times or using Analysis Services Cubes as a source for the finance department's queries.

pter 8: Diagnosing a Performance Problem

Because the problem has occurred suddenly and appears sporadically, it is not likely to be a memory issue. However, nothing should be overruled at this point. The first thing you should do is to execute Windows System Monitor using the key counters included in the baseline. Save the log results to the database or a log file. You will need to continue monitoring until the performance problem has been observed. Note the time when the issue occurred and when

the monitoring stopped. At the same time, run a trace using the events from the baseline
SQL Server Profiler and log it to the database or a log file.

Then, compare the resulting counter and trace logs to the log files created for the perform
baseline. Note outliers and investigate to determine if they are indicative of the probl
might be necessary to execute queries using various dynamic management views to inves
an outlier. It might also be necessary to repeat the monitoring until you determine i
cause. Once you identify a suspected cause, make the appropriate changes and repe
monitoring to determine if the outliers are still present. Continue this process until yo
confident that the problem has been identified and resolved. You should then create
performance baseline for all database servers. This will be used for any issues that migh
in the future.

pendix A

erences

ign Appropriate Data Access Technologies

- Learning ADO.NET
  http://msdn2.microsoft.com/en-us/data/aa937699.aspx
- Learning Microsoft Data Access Components (MDAC)
  http://msdn2.microsoft.com/en-us/data/aa937703.aspx
- Learning SQL Native Client
  http://msdn2.microsoft.com/en-us/data/aa937705.aspx
- Usage Scenarios for SQL Server 2005 Native Web Services
  http://msdn2.microsoft.com/en-us/library/ms345140.aspx
- How to Use the ODBC.NET Managed Provider in Visual Basic.NET and Connection Strings
  http://support.microsoft.com/kb/310985/
- How to Use the ODBC.NET Managed Provider in C# .NET and Connection Strings
  http://support.microsoft.com/kb/310988
- SQL Server OLE DB Programmer's Reference
  http://msdn2.microsoft.com/en-us/library/aa198360(SQL.80).aspx

ign an Appropriate Data Access Object Model

- ADO.NET: More than a Matter of ABCs
  http://www.samspublishing.com/articles/article.asp?p=102202&seqNum=2&rl=1
- Comparison of ADO.NET and ADO
  http://msdn.microsoft.com/library/default.asp?url=/library/en-us/vbcon/html/vbconA-DOPreviousVersionsOfADO.asp

e Queries

- Administering a Full-text Search
  http://msdn2.microsoft.com/en-us/library/ms142557.aspx

- An Overview of SQL Server 2005 for the Database Administrator
  http://www.microsoft.com/technet/prodtechnol/sql/2005/sqlydba.mspx
- Using the USE PLAN Query Hint
  http://msdn2.microsoft.com/en-us/library/ms186954.aspx
- Forcing Query Plans
  http://www.microsoft.com/technet/prodtechnol/sql/2005/frcqupln.mspx
- Invoke UDFs that Accept Tables with SQL Server 2005's APPLY Operator
  http://builder.com.com/5100-6388_14-6108869.html
- New T-SQL Features in SQL Server 2005, Part 1
  http://www.sqlservercentral.com/columnists/sramakrishnan/2734.asp
- Returning Ranked Results with Microsoft SQL Server 2005
  http://www.4guysfromrolla.com/webtech/010406-1.shtml
- Optimizing Distributed Queries
  http://msdn2.microsoft.com/en-us/library/ms180972.aspx
- XQuery 1.0: An XML Query Language
  http://www.w3.org/TR/xquery/
- Understanding SQL Server Full-Text Indexing
  http://www.developer.com/db/article.php/3446891
- Lesson 5 XML Integration with SQL Server 2005
  http://www.programmersheaven.com/2/SQL-server-2005-school-lesson-5

Design Caching Strategies

- ASP.NET Caching
  http://www.ondotnet.com/pub/a/dotnet/2002/12/30/cachingaspnet.html
- .NET Data Caching
  http://aspnet.4guysfromrolla.com/articles/100902-1.aspx
- ASP.NET Caching: Techniques and Best Practices
  http://msdn2.microsoft.com/en-us/library/aa478965.aspx
- Working with Query Notifications
  http://msdn2.microsoft.com/en-us/library/ms130764.aspx

ign a Cursor Strategy

- Performance Tuning SQL Server Cursors
  http://www.sql-server-performance.com/cursors.asp
- Application Development Trends—The SQL Server 2005 Paradigm Shift
  http://www.adtmag.com/article.aspx?id=11148&page=
- SQL Server Query Design: 10 Mistakes to Avoid
  *http://searchsqlserver.techtarget.com/loginMembersOnly/1,289498,sid87
  _gci1229788,00.html?NextURL=http%3A//searchsqlserver.techtarget.com
  /tip/0%2C289483%2Csid87_gci1229788%2C00.html*
- The Curse and Blessings of Dynamic SQL
  http://www.sommarskog.se/dynamic_sql.html
- How to Perform SQL Server Row-by-Row Operations Without Cursors
  http://www.sql-server-performance.com/dp_no_cursors.asp
- Using SQL Server Cursors
  http://www.mssqlcity.com/Articles/General/UseCursor.htm
- SQL Server Clinic: T-SQL Performance Problems and Solutions
  *http://searchsqlserver.techtarget.com/tip/1,289483,sid87_gci1170220
  _ tax301334,00.html?adg=301324&bucket=ETA?track=sy41*

ign Applications that Administer a SQL Server Service

- Data Mining with SQL Server 2005 by ZhaoHui Tang and Jamie MacLennan (Wiley, 2005)
- SQL Server Analysis Services
  http://msdn2.microsoft.com/en-us/library/ms175609.aspx
- FIX: Error message when you try to use the SqlClient class in an ADO.NET 2.0-based application to connect to an instance of SQL Server 2005: "New request is not allowed to start because it should come with valid transaction descriptor"
  http://support.microsoft.com/kb/916002
- Installing Sample Integration Services Packages
  http://msdn2.microsoft.com/en-us/library/ms160898.aspx

- How To: Create a Publication (RMO Programming)
  http://msdn2.microsoft.com/en-us/library/ms146941.aspx
- How To: Creating, Modifying, and Deleting Subscriptions (RMO Programming)
  http://msdn2.microsoft.com/en-us/library/ms147918.aspx
- How To: Synchronize a Pull Subscription (RMO Programming)
  http://msdn2.microsoft.com/en-us/library/ms147890.aspx
- How To: Define an Article (RMO Programming)
  http://msdn2.microsoft.com/en-us/library/ms146883.aspx
- How to: Create a Push Subscription (RMO Programming)
  http://msdn2.microsoft.com/en-US/library/ms146863.aspx
- How to: Synchronize a Push Subscription (RMO Programming)
  http://msdn2.microsoft.com/en-us/library/ms146910.aspx
- Multiple Active Result Sets (MARS) in SQL Server 2005
  http://msdn2.microsoft.com/en-us/library/ms345109.aspx
- Asynchronous Command Execution in ADO.NET 2.0
  http://www.aspspider.net/resources/Resource244.aspx
- Asynchronous Command Execution in ADO.NET 2.0
  http://msdn2.microsoft.com/en-us/library/ms379553(VS.80).aspx

Scale Database Applications

- Scaling Out SQL Server 2005
  http://msdn2.microsoft.com/en-us/library/aa479364.aspx
- Data Partitioning in SQL Server 2005 – Part III
  http://www.databasejournal.com/features/mssql/article.php/3643726
- Use Hardware to Partition Tables Horizontally in SQL
  http://articles.techrepublic.com.com/5100-9592_11-5796600.html
- Scaling Out SQL Server with Data-Dependent Routing
  http://www.dell.com/downloads/global/power/ps3q05-20050100-Auger.pdf
- Microsoft TechNet SQL TechCenter: Scaling Out SQL Server with Data Depe Routing
  http://www.microsoft.com/technet/prodtechnol/sql/2005/scddrtng.mspx

- How SQL Server Enables Service-Oriented Database Architectures
  http://www.microsoft.com/technet/prodtechnol/sql/2005/sqlsoda.mspx
- Scaleable shared databases are supported by SQL Server 2005
  http://support.microsoft.com/default.aspx?scid=kb;en-us;910378
- The Database Administrator's Guide to the SQL Server Database Engine .NET Common Language Runtime Environment
  http://www.microsoft.com/technet/prodtechnol/sql/2005/clr4dbas.mspx
- Managed Data Access Inside SQL Server with ADO.NET and SQLCLR
  http://msdn2.microsoft.com/en-us/library/ms345135.aspx#mandataac_topic7

olve Performance Problems

- Troubleshooting Performance Problems in SQL Server 2005
  http://www.microsoft.com/technet/prodtechnol/sql/2005/tsprfprb.mspx
- 10 Baselining Tips for SQL Server: Lessons From the Field
  http://www.sql-server-performance.com/gv_baselining_tips.asp
- Monitoring and Tuning for Performance
  http://msdn2.microsoft.com/en-us/library/ms189081.aspx
- Establishing a Performance Baseline
  http://technet2.microsoft.com/WindowsServer/en/library/9277f422-eb8c-4c14-89b5-9fe09f80fd191033.mspx?mfr=true

nage Concurrency by Selecting the Appropriate Transaction ation Levels

- Using Snapshot Isolation
  http://msdn2.microsoft.com/en-us/library/tcbchxcb.aspx

ign Code that Uses Transactions

- The Rational Guide to SQL Server 2005 Service Broker by Roger Wolter (Rational Press, 2006).

Optimize and Tune Queries for Performance

■ Creating Indexes on Computed Columns
 http://msdn2.microsoft.com/en-us/library/ms189292.aspx

■ Creating Indexed Views
 http://msdn2.microsoft.com/en-us/library/ms191432.aspx

Design Code that Validates Input Data and Permissions

■ Microsoft SQL Server 2005 Books Online: "Security Functions (Transact-SQL)."
 http://msdn2.microsoft.com/en-us/library/ms186236.aspx

L Server 2005 Architecture and Internals

To become a true IT professional-level database developer, candidates need to know more than just the basics about the product with which they are working. SQL Server is no exception to this rule, and given how it's grown into a full-fledged application server, there are a number of internals topics that are relevant to a successful database developer and that aren't covered in today's training materials or instructor-led classes due to the amount of time and depth required to cover them properly. See Figure B-1 for a look at the internals topics covered in this index.

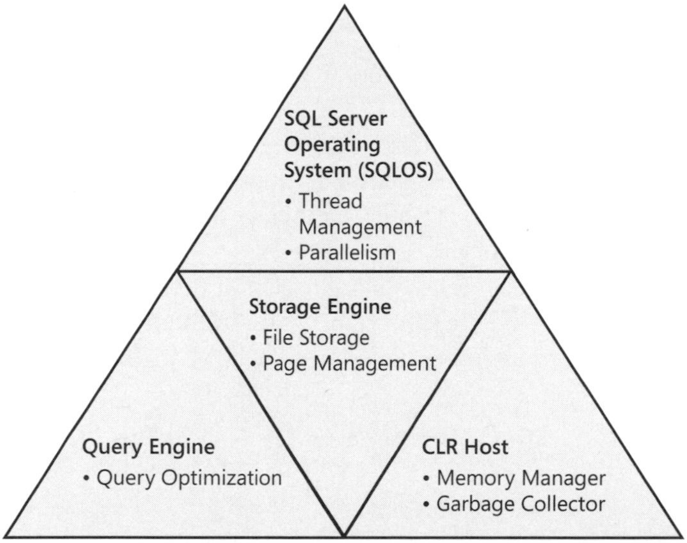

Figure B-1   SQL Server internal components covered by this appendix

This appendix will cover many of the internals topics that could not be covered in-depth in the chapters of the book. It is important to note that much of the detail contained within this appendix is in-depth. While the exams themselves do not necessarily test to the level of detail contained here, the information is highly relevant; knowledge in these areas can make the difference between a passing grade on the exam and mastery of SQL Server development.

Topics covered in this appendix are as follows. Mastery of each of these topics can help solidify a database developer's understanding of SQL Server 2005, and therefore increase his or her chances of doing well on the certification exam.

- **Hardware Trends and Their Effect on SQL Server 2005**   Hardware manufacturers are stantly looking for new ways to improve system performance. SQL Server 2005 advantage of many of these new trends; developers must be aware of what is happe behind the scenes.

- **SQL Operating System (SQLOS)**   SQLOS is the layer between the operating system SQL Server itself. SQLOS is new in SQL Server 2005. Developers who understand SQLOS operates are much more successful in writing solid, high-performing code.

- **Common Language Runtime (CLR) Host**   The CLR host is what enables develope write .NET code such as C# .NET and Visual Basic .NET, and integrate that code s lessly with SQL Server. Understanding the strengths and weaknesses of the CLR is very important when designing code objects that utilize .NET code within Server.

- **SQL Server 2005 Storage Engine**   The storage engine is the heart of the database se The storage engine is responsible for physically storing and retrieving information i most efficient manner. Every developer should understand his or her database's p cal structure.

- **SQL Server 2005 Query Engine**   The query engine is responsible for moving between the storage engine and the user. The query engine is composed of several and database developers must have an understanding of each of these parts if the going to write efficient, scalable code.

- **SQL Server 2005 Index Internals**   Indexes are used to assist both the query and sto engines to construct efficient queries and return data in the most efficient mai Developing good indexing strategies is an important part of any database develo workload.

  New index types in SQL Server 2005 include enhanced full-text indexes and index XML data types. It is essential for developers to understand exactly how these new i types function.

- **Database Encryption**   SQL Server 2005 provides a host of new features related to rity and encryption. A good understanding of these technologies and their usa vital.

Hardware Trends and Their Effect on SQL Server 2005

When SQL Server 7.0 was developed, Microsoft realized that they had to build an abstra layer between the Microsoft Windows operating system kernel and the user-mode applic that would become SQL Server. They faced many challenges but solved them through the ation of the User Mode Scheduler (UMS). The UMS worked by essentially "fooling" Wind in effect, it enabled SQL Server to control Windows resources such as thread allocations. This worked very well on the hardware of the day, and the UMS concept was carried forward into SQL Server 2000. Unfortunately, as hardware became more sophisticated, the limitations of the UMS became apparent.

dware Building Blocks

The heart of any computer system, the central processing unit (CPU or "processor"), is the hardware component that is responsible for executing tasks. To execute tasks, the processor utilizes a unit of work known as a thread. If a program is written to be multithreaded, it can split itself into two or more simultaneously running tasks. Multiple threads can be executed in parallel on many computer systems. This multithreading generally occurs by time slicing, wherein a single processor switches between different threads, which means the processing only appears to be simultaneous. On a machine with multiple processors (or processor "cores"), threading can be achieved via multiprocessing, which means that different threads can literally execute simultaneously on different cores. Windows supports the use of threads as well as a technique known as fiber mode scheduling, which is also known as "lightweight pooling." Fibers are scheduled by the application itself and run in the context of a thread, enabling multiprocessing.

dware Trends

Computer hardware today is increasingly diverse, and it is very difficult to develop applications that exploit the hardware for performance and scalability. It wasn't that long ago that computers with multiple CPUs were rare and used only in sophisticated business environments. Today, multiple CPU cores are commonplace, and features such as Symmetric Multi Processing (SMP) are often present in household systems.

Manufacturers continue to find ways around the limitations of their hardware platforms and build these solutions into new systems at astonishing rates. For example, it has been generally accepted that 4 GB of RAM is the upper limit of supportable memory for 32-bit CPUs, but that hasn't stopped innovators from pushing for more.

Using Non-Uniform Memory Architecture (NUMA) is becoming a standard method to enable support of more than 4 GB of RAM. Some processor manufacturers have built CPU architectures that support cache-coherent or CC-NUMA architectures that enable utilizing large amounts of memory and cache for the CPU, making NUMA available on even low-end systems. Larger enterprise computer systems with as many as 64 CPUs and 512 GB or more memory are becoming more common today. As the number of CPUs within a machine increases, hardware manufacturers are beginning to standardize on CC-NUMA architectures.

NUMA Architecture

Modern computer systems generally have more than one system bus, each serving a set o
cessors (or processor cores). Each set of processors has its own memory, known as local 1
ory, and might have its own input/output (I/O) channels as well. This is known as a N
group. Each group can access memory associated with the other groups as well. Me1
associated with other groups is known as foreign memory (or remote memory). The ra
the cost of accessing foreign memory to the cost of accessing local memory is calle(
NUMA ratio. The higher the NUMA ratio, the slower the access to the memory.

The main benefit of NUMA is scalability. The NUMA architecture was designed to surpas
scalability limits of SMP architectures. With SMP, all memory access is located on the
memory bus. This works fine for a relatively low number of processors, but not wher
have several (more than 16) cores competing for access to the shared memory bus. N
alleviates these bottlenecks by limiting the number of CPUs on any one memory bus and
necting the various nodes with a high-speed bus.

SQL Server 2005 has been designed to fully support NUMA and CC-NUMA architec
without special configuration. Generally speaking, this is true for systems with 16 cor
fewer. When dealing with systems that have more than 16 cores, special care must be tak
configure SQL Server 2005 to most efficiently utilize the NUMA architecture.

Implications of Hardware on Software Design

Because hardware vendors are continuously pushing the limits of what they can achieve
their architecture, more and more limitations are being uncovered that must be overcon
either new hardware-management techniques or software workarounds. Current hard
trends such as the move towards NUMA architectures have significantly affected soft
designs. To get adequate performance and scalability, software developers have to exp1
take advantage of hardware features, which is not an easy task within the Windows oper
system because only kernel-mode applications have direct access to the hardware. To
advantage of the hardware while at the same time keeping SQL Server a user-mode ap]
tion, Microsoft decided to replace the UMS with a new component called the SQL Oper
System (SQLOS).

SQLOS

Put simply, SQLOS is a user-mode application that is actually a miniature operating
tem. SQLOS is designed to abstract the complexities of the underlying hardware wh
the same time providing a rich programming environment that enables the develope
SQL Server to take full advantage of hardware features and functionality. SQLOS pro

operating system-like services such as a non-preemptive scheduling, memory management, deadlock detection, and exception handling.

OS Architecture

SQLOS is made up of three major components: nodes, schedulers, and tasks. Nodes represent the resource that is being addressed, such as a CPU or memory resources. Schedulers represent the work item queue for that resource, such as a thread. Tasks represent the actual work item for that resource, such as performing an operation or reading a memory register. There is a strict hierarchical relationship among these, as shown in Figure B-2.

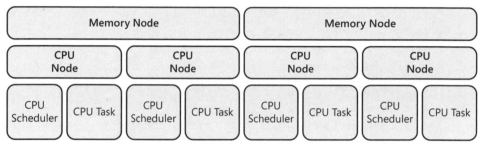

Figure B-2   The hierarchical relationship between SQLOS nodes, schedulers, and tasks

It is important to understand how the underlying architecture of SQLOS is represented on various types of hardware. In SMP systems, for example, all CPU nodes share only one memory node. In NUMA systems, multiple memory nodes each sponsor multiple CPU nodes. (For example, a 16-core system most likely contains four memory nodes, each "sponsoring" four CPU nodes.) When SQL Server first starts, it examines the underlying hardware configuration and dynamically constructs the SQLOS structure. This information is reported in the SQL Server Log, which can be viewed from the *Management* node in SQL Server Management Studio as follows:

```
SQL Server is starting at normal priority base (=7). This is an informational message only. No
user action is required.
Detected 4 CPUs. This is an informational message; no user action is required.
Using locked pages for buffer pool.
Using dynamic lock allocation.  Initial allocation of 2500 Lock blocks and 5000 Lock Owner
blocks per node.  This is an informational message only.  No user action is required.
Multinode configuration: node 0: CPU mask: 0x000000000000000c Active CPU mask:
0x000000000000000c. This message provides a description of the NUMA configuration for this
computer. This is an informational message only. No user action is required.
Multinode configuration: node 1: CPU mask: 0x0000000000000003 Active CPU mask:
0x0000000000000003. This message provides a description of the NUMA configuration for this
computer. This is an informational message only. No user action is required.
```

This log demonstrates the default SQLOS configuration for a four-processor machine w
GB of RAM, showing two memory nodes, each hosting two CPU nodes. What this m
from a practical standpoint, is that even though 8 GB of RAM is present in the system, 4 (
RAM is associated with one set of processors, and 4 GB of RAM is associated with anothe

In SQL Server 2005, all user access to data occurs through memory buffers known a
buffer cache. This is especially important to note on systems that support NUMA, becaus
total memory in the system is equally divided among NUMA memory nodes, and the ma
of that memory is allocated to buffer cache. Due to the fact that Windows does not ha
Application Programming Interface (API) that enables SQLOS to directly allocate phy
memory to NUMA nodes, SQLOS must use a dynamic approach to allocating memory.
means that the behavior of SQL Server 2005 will sometimes differ on systems that have
started versus systems that have been running for a while. From a practical standpoint
means that developers must be aware of how memory is divided among NUMA node:
how to properly partition application access to the system so that any one node is not c
taxed by their application.

Due to the nature of the SQLOS hierarchy, the memory node is probably the most impo
node for developers to be aware of, as it is the node that controls the system resources. Th
lowing query, which uses the sys.dm_os_memory_clerks Dynamic Management
(DMV), shows how many memory nodes SQLOS has configured as well as the amou
memory assigned and allocated to each.

```
SELECT
    memory_node_id AS [Memory Node],
    SUM(single_pages_kb) AS [Single Pages KB],
    SUM(multi_pages_kb) AS [Multi Pages KB],
    SUM(virtual_Memory_reserved_kb) AS [Reserved Virtual Memory KB],
    SUM(virtual_memory_committed_kb) AS [Virtual Memory Committed KB],
    SUM(awe_allocated_kb) AS [AWE Memory Allocated KB]
FROM sys.dm_os_memory_clerks
GROUP BY memory_node_id;
```

Executing this SQL script will result in a result set that details the amount and type of i
ory that is allocated to each memory node. See Figure B-3 for the result of this query on a
processor machine with 8 GB of total RAM.

	Memory Node	Single Pages KB	Multi Pages KB	Reserved Virtual Memory KB	Virtual Memory Committed KB	AWE Memory Allocated KB
1	0	11480	11168	0	0	544528
2	1	142136	17256	8426672	21680	258616

Figure B-3 Displaying the SQLOS memory node configuration and allocations

If the query returns a single row, it indicates that your system is not configured to use NUMA. In some cases, hardware vendors have implemented NUMA architectures that are not detectable by SQLOS. This can lead to performance problems very quickly. To alleviate this problem, SQL Server 2005 has the capability to manually configure NUMA-like support. This is known as "soft-NUMA."

Configuring SQL Server Soft-NUMA Support

The primary instance in which you should consider utilizing soft-NUMA is when you suspect that there is an I/O-related performance problem when running applications but you also believe that your I/O subsystem is properly configured. This is a common problem among high-volume systems that are configured to utilize Storage Area Networks (SANs). Each NUMA node has its own I/O thread that is responsible for reading and writing data on the disk and another thread, known as a lazy writer, that is responsible for managing the state of the SQL Server buffer cache. For systems in which NUMA is not automatically detected by SQLOS, configuring soft-NUMA can significantly affect I/O performance. Another reason to consider soft-NUMA is for multiple-instance support. Each instance of SQL Server on a single machine shares NUMA nodes by default, so when dealing with multiple instances and more than 8 GB on a machine, using soft-NUMA can lead to performance gains.

Configuring soft-NUMA support in SQL Server 2005 is a two-step process. The first step is setting the processor affinity mask. A processor affinity mask is a structure that is used to bind a specific processor to a specific memory node. The second step is adding a registry value to map NUMA nodes onto specific processors.

Configuring soft-NUMA support also requires an understanding of binary and hexadecimal math. For example, if you have a system with eight processors and two instances of SQL Server 2005 running, and you want to assign four processors to each instance, you would set the processor affinity of the first instance to 15 decimal (00001111 binary), and the processor affinity of the second instance to 240 decimal (11110000 binary). Processor affinity on the first instance can be set with the sp_configure stored procedure as follows:

```
EXEC sp_configure 'show advanced options',1
RECONFIGURE
GO
EXEC sp_configure 'affinity mask',15;
Processor affinity on the second instance can be set as follows:
EXEC sp_configure 'show advanced options',1
RECONFIGURE
GO
EXEC sp_configure 'affinity mask',240;
```

IMPORTANT Configuring NUMA support on more than 32 processors

The above sp_configure options are specific to systems with 32 or fewer processors. If you are working with a system that has more than 32 processors and you want to configure the affinity mask, you must use both the affinity mask option shown above and the affinity64 mask. For more information, see the SQL Server 2005 Books Online article "affinity64 mask Option" at *http://msdn2.microsoft.com/en-us/library/ms188291.aspx*.

In addition to using hexadecimal math, you can also use the Microsoft SQL Server 2005 agement Studio to configure processor affinity, as shown in Figure B-4.

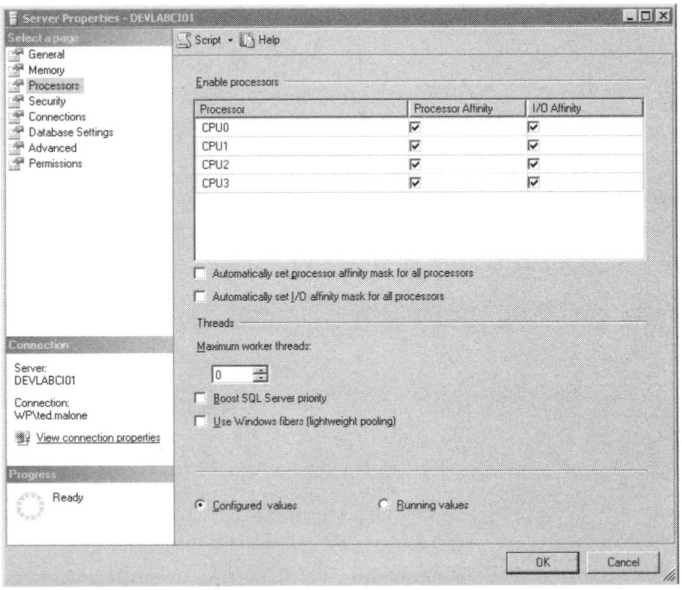

Figure B-4 Configuring the processor affinity using the Microsoft SQL Server 2005 Management Studio Server Properties dialog box

Once the processor affinity is set, soft-NUMA can be configured as desired using a registry setting. In HKEY_LOCAL_MACHINE\SOFTWARE\Microsoft\Microsoft SQL Server\90\N Configuration\Nodex, where the first node is Node0, the second node is Node1, and so single DWORD named CPUMask has a value set to the hexadecimal representation of the binary affinity mask. For example, if you want to assign two NUMA memory nodes, each two processors, to the first instance from the above scenario, you would create registry en for Node0 and Node1 and set the CPUMask values to 0x03 hexadecimal (00000011 bir and 0x0c hexadecimal (00001100 binary), respectively. To assign a single NUMA memo node (with all four processors) to the second instance, create a registry entry for Node2 set the CPUMask value to 0xF0 (11110000 binary). Soft-NUMA support can also be used in systems that support hardware NUMA to control the processor-to-memory affinity.

IMPORTANT Configure processor affinity

SQL Server 2005 provides the ability to dynamically configure processor affinity, but soft-NUMA support requires a restart of SQL Server to take effect.

SQLOS provides a granular level of control over NUMA configurations, giving experienced database developers good control over how their applications perform on high-end hardware. Unfortunately, processor affinity and soft-NUMA are not the only places where SQLOS needs to step in on high-end systems. In the SQLOS hierarchy, schedulers play a very important role in deciding what tasks are executed and when.

SQL Server Task Scheduling

When an application connects to SQL Server, it is assigned a server process identifier (SPID). All information that must be maintained for the life of the connection is managed in internal data structures associated with the SPID. As an instance of SQL Server receives batches from clients, it breaks the batch into one or more tasks, and then associates each task with an available worker thread from a pool of worker threads. A worker thread is bound to the task for the lifetime of the task. A worker thread runs the request on the associated SQL scheduler. If there are no free worker threads and the configuration value "max worker threads" has not been reached, the instance of SQL Server allocates a new worker thread for the new batch. If there are no free threads or fibers available and the max worker threads value has already been reached, the instance of SQL Server blocks the new task until a worker thread is freed.

After a worker is associated with a task, it remains associated with the task until the task is completed; for example, until the last of the result sets generated by the batch has been returned to the client. At that time, the worker thread is freed and can be paired with the tasks associated with the next batch.

The database engine must actively perform work for a connection only from the time a batch is received until the results have been returned to the client. During this period, there might be times when the batch does not require active processing. For example, there might be times during which the database engine must wait for a read operation to retrieve the data required for the current query, or must wait for another batch to release a lock. The task-to-worker association is maintained even when the task is blocked on some resource.

Whenever the database engine starts to process a task associated with a batch, it schedules the worker thread associated with the task to perform the work. After the worker thread has completed the work for the task, an instance of SQL Server dispatches the worker thread to the next task that is ready to work. A SPID remains constant for a connection for the life of connection. Long-running connections might have their individual batch tasks execute many different worker threads. For example, the tasks from the first batch might be exec by worker1, but the tasks from the second batch could be executed by worker2. Some ments can be processed in parallel. In this case, a batch might have multiple tasks that are cuted by multiple worker threads at the same time.

SQLOS Schedulers

Due to the nature of SQLOS, only one task can execute on a given CPU at any given tin it is the job of the scheduler to determine which task can run. Most tasks that SQL S must execute begin with a user request. (There are several system tasks that run.) requests generally begin with a client system making a request of the server. The problem this approach is that all user requests are generally funneled into a single TCP/IP conne (the IP Sockets protocol uses port 1433 by default) which, by default, assigns requests to NUMA node scheduler in a "round-robin" fashion. The theory behind this approach i the workload will be evenly spread out among all schedulers. However, for systems tha port multiple applications, database developers might want tighter control over which N nodes their applications use.

IMPORTANT   TCP/IP port affinity

When considering whether to configure TCP/IP port affinity, database developers must have thorough understanding of how their application consumes system resources. Normally, the de configuration is more than sufficient for most applications.

Configuring TCP/IP Port Affinity   One of the new features in SQL Server 2005 is the a to create TCP/IP endpoints. Usually, these endpoints are used to host native Web ser however, they can also be used to configure additional Tabular Data Stream (TDS) endp for use with "normal" client communication. For very high-activity systems that suppor tiple applications, it might be desirable to create a single TCP/IP connection to the serv each NUMA memory node, and bind applications to each connection in a logical fas such as grouping applications that have similar data-access patterns. Creating a TCP/II nection for SQL Server involves the following steps:

1. Create an endpoint for a specific TCP/IP port.
2. Grant permissions to the new endpoint.
3. Configure SQL Server to listen on the new port.

To create the endpoint, execute the CREATE ENDPOINT command as follows. (In this ple, the endpoint is named "CustomConnection" and is configured to listen to TCP port on any IP address in the system.)

```
CREATE ENDPOINT [CustomConnection]
STATE = STARTED
AS TCP
   (LISTENER_PORT = 1500, LISTENER_IP =ALL)
FOR TSQL();
```

IMPORTANT   Re-enable access to the default port

Whenever a new endpoint is created for T-SQL, SQL Server assumes that the default endpoint (TCP port 1433) is no longer being used. If you still want to be able to utilize the default port, you must re-enable access by using the command GRANT CONNECT ON ENDPOINT::[TSQL Default TCP] to [public] to grant access to the public role.

Once the endpoint is created, proper permissions must be assigned to the users who will connect by using the GRANT command as follows:

```
GRANT CONNECT ON ENDPOINT::[CustomConnection] to [corp\SQLSupport] ;
```

The final step in configuring additional TCP/IP ports is to add the newly configured endpoint to the listener by performing the following steps:

1. Start SQL Server Configuration Manager.
2. Expand the SQL Server 2005 *Network Configuration* node.
3. Expand the *Protocols* node.
4. In the right pane, select the TCP/IP protocol, right-click, and select Properties.
5. On the IP Addresses tab, under IPAll, enter the new port number, as shown in Figure B-5.

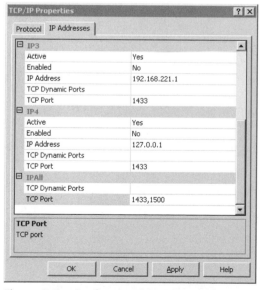

Figure B-5   Configuring SQL Server 2005 to listen on an additional TCP port

Once the new port (or ports) are created, they can be bound to specific NUMA memory by appending the node mask to the port number in the TCP/IP configuration. For exa on a system with three NUMA nodes and two TCP/IP ports, where it is desired to bin first two nodes to the default port and the third node to the port just created, the defaul would utilize a node mask of 0x3 (00000011), and the second port would utilize a node of 0x4 (00000100), as shown in Figure B-6.

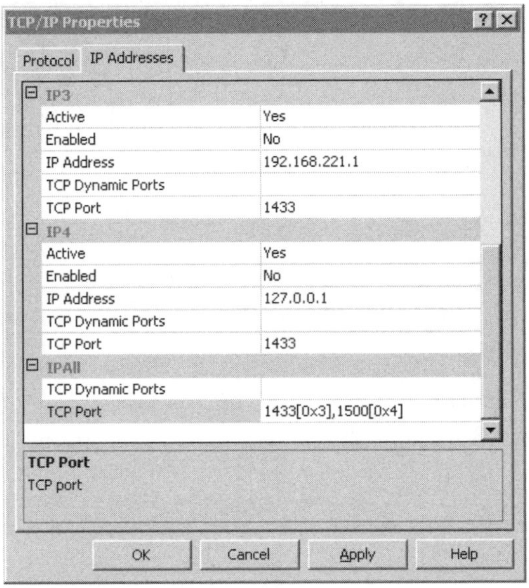

Figure B-6   Configuring SQL Server 2005 to utilize IP Port affinity

Getting each SQLOS node and scheduler to the optimal configuration is a challenge fo the most experienced database developer and is very different for each system, dependi usage characteristics. Fortunately, SQL Server 2005 and SQLOS provide a rich manag structure that enables developers and administrators to understand exactly how the sys behaving at any given point in time.

Using SQLOS to Determine Application Performance Characterist

One challenge that database developers face when developing applications is unders ing how the application performs while in production. To accurately understand th formance characteristics of an application, the developer needs to know the specific of any wait states that occur during the execution of the application. At the most level, waits can be broken down into two categories: signal waits or resource waits. In SQL Server, signal waits occur when the scheduler is waiting on a processor resource to schedule the task, and resource waits occur when the task has been assigned to a processor resource but are waiting for disk or memory resources. When examining overall waits for an application, if there is a high ratio of signal to resource waits (that is, if there are many more signal waits than resource waits), it might signify an inefficient use of processor resources. If there is a high ratio of resource to signal waits, that can indicate an inefficient use of disk resources. To begin the process of evaluating application performance, developers need to understand which of these wait types is most prevalent. Fortunately, SQLOS provides a window into the system that is granular enough that developers are able to use it to answer the question.

IMPORTANT SQLOS vs. SQL Server 2000 UMS

With SQL Server 7 and SQL Server 2000 and the UMS, developers could never tell whether application performance problems were a result of signal waits or resource waits. Many times a developer would use a tool such as Windows System Monitor, notice that the processor was very busy, and assume that she needed to upgrade her machine to a faster processor. In reality, because of how UMS accomplishes thread manipulation, the problem was really caused by a slow disk subsystem, and upgrading to a faster processor simply exacerbated the problem. With SQLOS, this problem no longer exists, but developers must know how to utilize the new functionality in SQLOS to understand signal waits versus resource waits.

The following query utilizes the sys.dm_os_wait_states DMV to query SQLOS and report on resource versus signal waits:

```
SELECT signal_wait_time_ms=sum(signal_wait_time_ms)
    ,'%signal waits' = cast(100.0 * sum(signal_wait_time_ms) / sum (wait_time_ms) AS NUMERIC
(20,2))
    ,resource_wait_time_ms=sum(wait_time_ms - signal_wait_time_ms)
    ,'%resource waits'= cast(100.0 * sum(wait_time_ms - signal_wait_time_ms) / sum
(wait_time_ms) AS NUMERIC(20,2))
FROM sys.dm_os_wait_stats;
```

Executing this query on a SQL Server 2005 machine will return a result set that provides details on the percentage of overall waits and whether they are signal or resource waits, as shown in Figure B-7. Generally, systems that exhibit a low signal-to-resource wait exhibit the best overall performance.

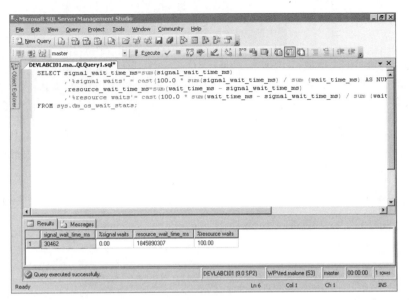

Figure B-7   Using SQL Server 2005 Dynamic Management Views to query SQLOS wait types

When performing "normal" performance-monitoring tasks (for a discussion of normal p
mance monitoring, see Chapter 8, "Improving Database Application Performance," Les
"Resolving Performance Problems"), database developers can isolate a specific SPID
causing performance issues, such as excessive blocking or excessive memory consum
Using SQLOS, developers can dig deeper into the process to determine the exact stat
that is executing, as well as the resource utilization by the process. The following que
lizes the sys.dm_exec_requests DMV to query all non-system processes and report on s
resource utilization (to isolate a specific process, replace the ">50" in the WHERE claus
the specific process ID you wish to view):

```
SELECT r.session_id
       ,status
       ,substring(qt.text,r.statement_start_offset/2,
            (CASE WHEN r.statement_end_offset = -1
            then len(convert(nvarchar(max), qt.text)) * 2
            ELSE r.statement_end_offset END - r.statement_start_offset)/2)
       AS query_text
        ,qt.dbid
        ,qt.objectid
        ,r.cpu_time
        ,r.total_elapsed_time
        ,r.reads
        ,r.writes
```

```
        ,r.logical_reads
        ,r.scheduler_id
FROM sys.dm_exec_requests r
cross apply sys.dm_exec_sql_text(sql_handle) AS qt
WHERE r.session_id > 50
ORDER BY r.scheduler_id, r.status, r.session_id;
```

Executing this query on SQL Server 2005 will provide detail on all system activity and resource consumption, as shown in Figure B-8.

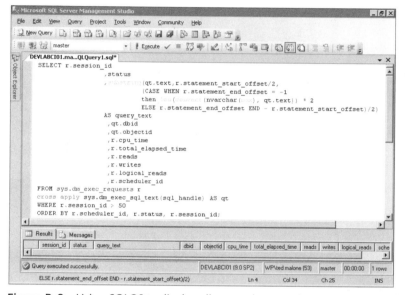

Figure B-8   Using SQLOS to display all currently executing statements and their resource utilization

Using the above query, database developers can isolate specific statements that are causing performance issues, as well as gain insight into how the various statements are distributed among SQLOS memory nodes and schedulers.

Once a database developer learns about how SQL Server is processing his queries and utilizing resources, he might want to consider creating a system configuration strategy that can be used to deploy his application. Part of the system configuration strategy is to understand how evenly the load on the system is distributed. SQLOS can report on the distribution state of the current system workload and what type of load factor each scheduler is experiencing. This is done via the sys.dm_os_schedulers DMV. The following code can be used to query SQLOS to determine the distribution of current tasks and their associated workload:

```
SELECT
  scheduler_id,
  cpu_id,
  current_tasks_count,
  runnable_tasks_count,
  pending_disk_io_count,
  current_workers_count,
  active_workers_count,
  work_queue_count,
  load_factor
FROM sys.dm_os_schedulers
WHERE scheduler_id < 255;
```

The output of this query is shown in Figure B-9.

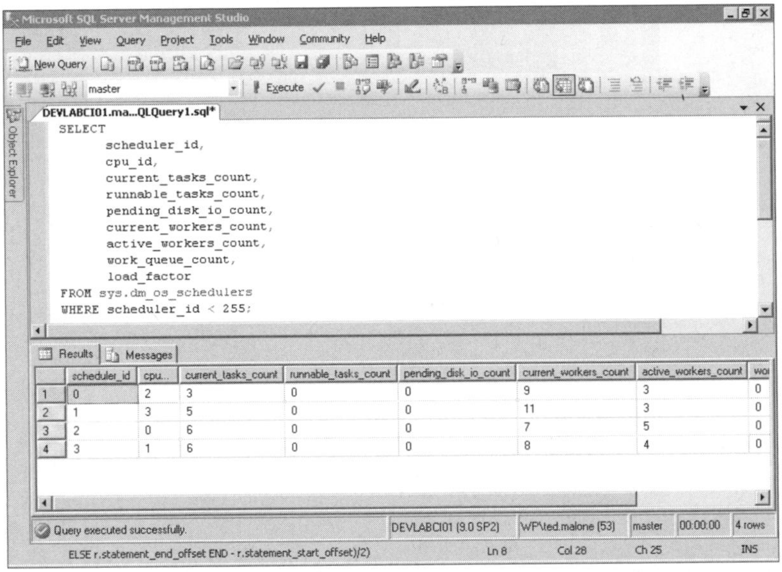

Figure B-9   Querying SQLOS to determine the current system workload distribution

One very interesting column in the result set is "load factor." Load factor indicates th
ceived load on a scheduler. This value is used to determine whether a new task should
on this scheduler or another scheduler. This value is useful for debugging purposes w
appears that schedulers are not evenly loaded. In SQL Server 2000, a task is routed to
ticular scheduler. However, in SQL Server 2005, the routing decision is made based
load on the scheduler. SQL Server 2005 also uses a load factor of nodes and schedu

help determine the best location to acquire resources. When a task is enqueued, the load factor is increased. When a task is completed, the load factor is decreased. Using the load factors helps SQLOS to evenly distribute system workload.

On multiprocessor systems, performance problems can arise due to the way the SQL Optimizer chooses to parallelize a particular query plan. When a query is first examined by the optimizer, a decision is made regarding whether the query should be run serially or there are instead portions of the query that can run in parallel. The number of query portions that the optimizer chooses to run in parallel is known as the degree of parallelism. SQL Server 2005 automatically detects the best degree of parallelism for each query. It does this based on the following criteria, which are evaluated in the following order:

1. Whether SQL Server is running on a computer that has more than one processor.
2. Whether sufficient threads are available. Each query or index operation requires a certain number of threads to execute. Executing a parallel plan requires more threads than a serial plan, and the number of required threads increases with the degree of parallelism.
3. The type of query or index operation executed. Index operations that create or rebuild an index, or drop a clustered index, and queries that use processor cycles heavily are the best candidates for a parallel plan. For example, joins of large tables, large aggregations, and sorting large result sets are good candidates. For simple queries, which are frequently found in transaction-processing applications, the additional coordination required to execute a query in parallel outweighs the potential performance boost. To distinguish between queries that benefit from parallelism and those that do not benefit, SQLOS compares the estimated cost of executing the query or index operation with the cost threshold for parallelism value.
4. Whether there are a sufficient number of rows to process. If the query optimizer determines that the number of rows is too low, it does not introduce parallel operations.
5. Whether current distribution statistics are available. In earlier versions of SQL Server, the database engine abandoned parallel plans if the available statistics prevented the database engine from providing the highest degree of parallelism. In SQL Server 2005, if the highest degree of parallelism is not possible, lower degrees are considered before the parallel plan is abandoned. For example, when you create a clustered index on a view, distribution statistics cannot be evaluated, because the clustered index does not yet exist. In this case, the database engine cannot provide the highest degree of parallelism for the index operation. However, some operators, such as sorting and scanning, can still benefit from parallel execution.

IMPORTANT SQL Server 2005 Enterprise Edition supports parallel index operations

Only SQL Server 2005 Enterprise Edition supports parallel index operations.

At execution time, SQLOS determines whether the current system workload and con
tion information previously described enable parallel execution. If parallel execution i
ranted, the database engine determines the optimal number of threads and sprea
execution of the parallel plan across those threads. When a query or index operation
executing on multiple threads for parallel execution, the same number of threads is use
the operation is completed. The database engine re-examines the optimal number of
decisions every time an execution plan is retrieved from the procedure cache. For exa
one execution of a query can result in the use of a serial plan, a later execution of the
query can result in a parallel plan using three threads, and a third execution can resu
parallel plan using four threads.

The query below, which uses the sys.dm_ DMV, provides details for the tasks th
assigned to specific schedulers and can be used to determine the current state of queri
have been parallelized. (When a query is parallelized, there will be multiple entries
result set with the same session_id and request_id values.)

```
SELECT
    request_id,
    session_id,
    task_address,
    task_state,
    context_switches_count,
    pending_io_count,
    pending_io_byte_count,
    pending_io_byte_average,
    scheduler_id,
    exec_context_id,
    worker_address,
    host_address
FROM sys.dm_os_tasks
    WHERE session_id > 50
ORDER BY session_id, request_id;
```

The output of this query is shown in Figure B-10.

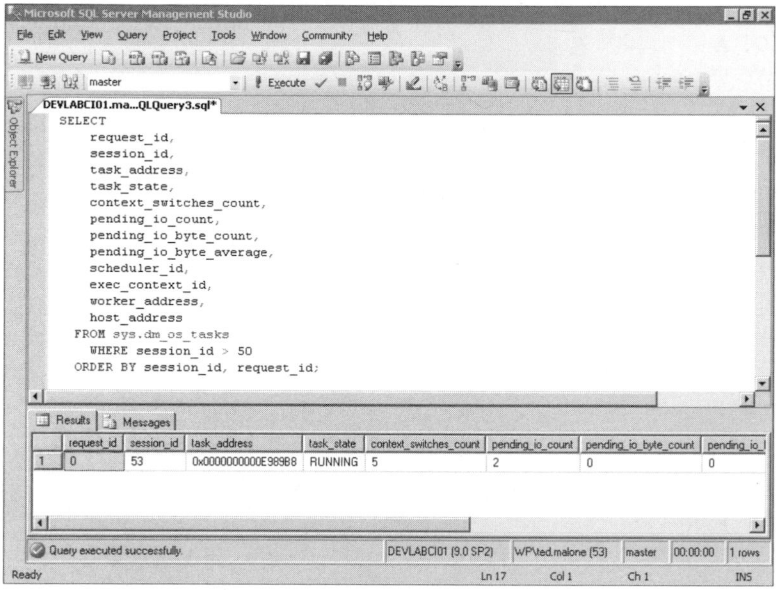

Figure B-10 Querying SQLOS to determine the degree of parallelism of currently executing queries

In some cases, queries that have been parallelized can perform more poorly than the same query running in a serial fashion. The easiest way to determine whether parallelism is causing system performance issues is to follow the normal performance tuning procedures described in Chapter 8, and look for CXPacket waits. If a specific SPID is experiencing CXPacket waits, run the query above and note the statement that is executing on that SPID. If it is determined that a specific statement or batch is causing a problem with CXPacket waits, use the MAXDOP 1 query option for that batch and execute it again to see if it performs better.

As discussed earlier in this appendix, all user access to data in SQL Server occurs through the buffer cache. When a query is executed, the query engine first checks to see whether the data needed is already present in the buffer cache. If it isn't present, a request is made for the storage engine to read the data into buffer cache. Because the buffer cache is a finite resource, SQLOS must manage the buffer cache very carefully. Developers can assist SQLOS by controlling how their applications access data (for example, group access to similar objects as much as possible), which can help minimize data movement within the buffer cache. SQLOS provides a mechanism in the form of the sys.dm_os_buffer_descriptors DMV that enables developers to peer into buffer cache and determine which objects currently have pages in buffer cache. The following query will provide a list of all objects and the number of pages from that object currently in buffer cache:

```
SELECT count(*)AS cached_pages_count
    ,name ,index_id
FROM sys.dm_os_buffer_descriptors AS bd
    INNER JOIN
    (
        SELECT object_name(object_id) AS name
            ,index_id ,allocation_unit_id
        FROM sys.allocation_units AS au
            INNER JOIN sys.partitions AS p
                ON au.container_id = p.hobt_id
                    AND (au.type = 1 OR au.type = 3)
        UNION ALL
        SELECT object_name(object_id) AS name
            ,index_id, allocation_unit_id
        FROM sys.allocation_units AS au
            INNER JOIN sys.partitions AS p
                ON au.container_id = p.hobt_id
                    AND au.type = 2
    ) AS obj
        ON bd.allocation_unit_id = obj.allocation_unit_id
WHERE database_id = db_id()
GROUP BY name, index_id
ORDER BY cached_pages_count DESC;
```

The output of this query is shown in Figure B-11.

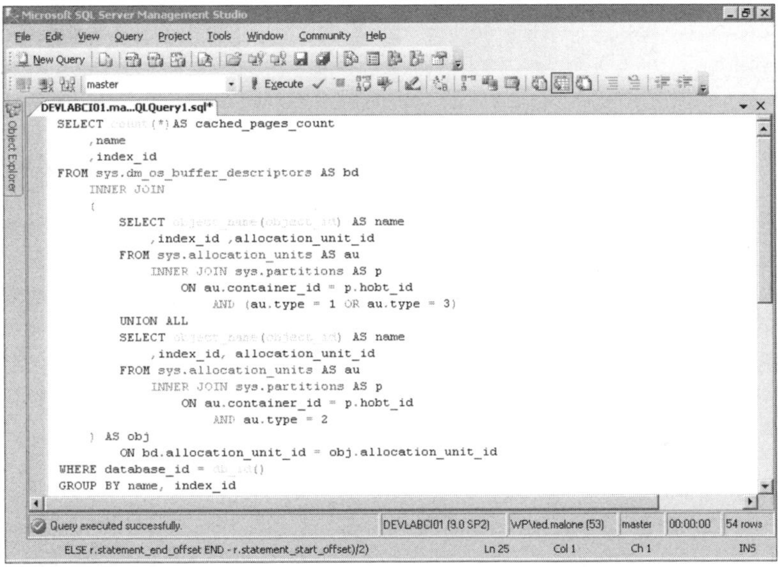

Figure B-11 Determining the objects that have data currently stored in buffer cache

Having a solid understanding of how database objects are used relative to buffer cache can have a major impact on how developers build applications to interact with data. This is especially important on systems that have limited memory.

mmon Language Runtime (CLR) Host

Before Microsoft introduced the .NET Framework, they took pains to ensure that the framework itself would be non-proprietary and suitable for international standardization. To accomplish this, Microsoft introduced a standard known as the Common Language Infrastructure (CLI), which specified how applications written in different high-level languages could operate in multiple system environments without changing any of the high-level code. For more information on the Common Language Infrastructure standard, see "The CLI Specification" on MSDN at *http://msdn2.microsoft.com/en-us/netframework/aa497266.aspx*.

Microsoft's implementation of the CLI is known as the common language runtime (CLR). The CLR is responsible for compiling code into Intermediate Language (IL), and then managing the execution of the code. The CLR is a component of the Microsoft .NET Framework. The .NET Framework consists of several key components such as Assemblies, just-in-time compiler, and the Common Type System. Although not an actual component of the .NET Framework, the Framework does rely on the use of namespaces, which is also described here.

- **Namespaces** Namespaces in the .NET Framework are a logical grouping of code classes that enable developers to pick and choose which components they wish to use. For example, the *Microsoft.SqlServer* namespace contains .NET Framework classes that support SQL Server programming.
- **Assemblies** Assemblies are the smallest unit of deployment within a .NET application. Assemblies are used to group logical functions into a single execution environment.
- **Just-in-Time (JIT) Compiler** The JIT compiler is responsible for compiling the IL code generated by the CLR and preparing it for execution.
- **Common Type System (CTS)** The CTS is responsible for ensuring that object classes known as types can be understood across languages. For example, a "String" type in C#.NET is compatible with a "String" in Visual Basic .NET because of the CTS.

With SQL Server 2005, Microsoft decided to make the features of the .NET Framework available to developers using SQL Server. This presented a challenge due to the way SQL Server and SQLOS interact with the operating system. To overcome this challenge, Microsoft developed a CLR host, which enables SQL Server to host the CLR. This enables developers to build applications that are executed by the CLR, but don't require a context switch to the underlying operating system to execute. In SQL Server 2000 and earlier, if developers wanted to utilize other programming languages to develop objects within SQL Server, they needed to create extended stored procedures (XPs). The problem with extended stored procedure that they executed "out of band" of the SQL Server process, and if something went wrc was possible for the XPs to cause the entire system to crash. By creating the CLR hos enabling developers to write native .NET Framework code within the SQL Server exec environment, this problem was alleviated. (Note that the SQLCLR host only access operation system through SQLOS and never directly.)

This section describes how best to take advantage of this technology from the perspect a database application developer, comparing CLR integration techniques with existim gramming language support in SQL Server: Transact-SQL (T-SQL) and XPs.

Design Goals for the CLR Host

When Microsoft designed the CLR host for SQL Server 2005, they had several design including reliability, scalability, security, and performance.

Reliability

Code executing in the CLR should not be permitted to perform operations that compr the integrity of the database engine, such as displaying a message box requesting a response or exiting the process. CLR code should not be able to directly access SQLOS ory buffers or internal data structures. This is the only way to ensure subsystem integri reliability.

When managed code in the .NET Framework APIs encounters critical exceptions, such a of-memory or stack overflow, it is not always possible to recover and ensure consister correct actions for their implementation. These APIs raise a thread abort except response to these failures.

When hosted in the CLR host, thread aborts are handled as follows: the CLR detec shared state in the application domain in which the thread abort occurs. The CLR does t checking for the presence of synchronization objects. If there is shared state in the appli domain, then the application domain itself is unloaded. The unloading of the appli domain stops database transactions that are currently running in that application doma rolls them back. Because the presence of shared state can widen the impact of such c exceptions to user sessions other than the one triggering the exception, Microsoft has steps in SQL Server and the CLR have taken steps to reduce the likelihood of shared st

Scalability

To support the scalability goals defined for SQL Server, SQLOS and the CLR have differen els for scheduling and memory management. SQLOS supports a cooperative, non-preer threading model in which the threads voluntarily yield execution periodically, or when they are waiting on locks or I/O. The CLR uses a preemptive threading model. If CLR code running inside the CLR host could directly call the operating system threading APIs, then it would not integrate well into the SQLOS task scheduler and could degrade the scalability of the system. The CLR does not distinguish between virtual and physical memory, but enables SQLOS to directly manage memory.

The different models for threading, scheduling, and memory management present an integration challenge for SQL Server. The architecture needs to ensure that the scalability of the system is not compromised by CLR code calling application APIs for threading, memory, and synchronization operations directly.

CLR interacts directly with SQLOS to create threads, both for running user code and for its own internal use. To synchronize between multiple threads, the CLR calls SQLOS synchronization objects. This enables the SQLOS scheduler to schedule other tasks when a thread is waiting on a synchronization object. For example, when the CLR initiates garbage collection, all of its threads wait for garbage collection to finish. Because the CLR threads and the synchronization objects they are waiting on are known to the SQLOS scheduler, SQL Server can schedule threads that are running other database tasks not involving the CLR. This also enables SQL Server to detect deadlocks that involve locks taken by CLR synchronization objects and employ traditional techniques for deadlock removal. CLR code runs preemptively in SQL Server. The SQLOS scheduler has the ability to detect and stop threads that have not yielded for a significant amount of time. The ability to hook CLR threads to SQLOS threads implies that the SQLOS scheduler can identify "runaway" threads in the CLR and manage their priority. Such runaway threads are suspended and put back in the queue. Threads that are repeatedly identified as runaway threads are not permitted to run for a given period of time so that other executing workers can run.

The CLR utilizes SQLOS for allocating and de-allocating its memory. Because the memory used by the CLR is accounted for in the total memory usage of the system, SQL Server can stay within its configured memory limits and ensure the CLR and SQLOS are not competing with each other for memory. SQL Server can also reject CLR memory requests when system memory is constrained and ask CLR to reduce its memory use when other tasks need memory.

Security

CLR code running in the database must follow SQL Server authentication and authorization rules when accessing database objects such as tables and columns. In addition, database administrators should be able to control access to operating system resources, such as file and network access, to database code. This becomes important because managed programming languages used by the CLR provide functions to access such resources. The system must provide a secure way for CLR code to access machine resources outside the database engine proc

Code Access Security (CAS) is implemented in the CLR host through the use of asse level attributes. These attributes are deployed to the database within the assembly attributes and their function are shown in Table B-1.

Table B-1   CLR Host Assembly Permissions

Permission Set	SAFE	EXTERNAL_ACCESS	UNSAFE
Code Access Security	Execute Only	Execute + External Access	Unrestrict
Programming model restrictions	Yes	Yes	No
Verifiability	Yes	Yes	No
Ability to call native code	No	No	Yes

SAFE is the most reliable and secure mode with associated restrictions in terms of the p ted programming model. SAFE assemblies are given enough permission to run, perform putations, and are granted access to the local database. SAFE assemblies need to be veri type safe and are not permitted to call unmanaged code.

UNSAFE is for highly trusted code that can only be created by database administr This trusted code has no code access security restrictions, and it can call unmar (native) code. For additional information on SAFE and UNSAFE assemblies, visit h *msdn2.microsoft.com/en-us/library/ms189524.aspx.*

EXTERNAL_ACCESS provides an intermediate security option; it permits code to a resources external to the database, but it still has the reliability guarantees of SAFE.

SQL Server uses the host-level CAS policy layer to set up a host policy that grants one three sets of permissions based on the permission set stored in SQL Server catalogs. Ma code running inside the database always gets one of these code access permission sets.

The CLR host loads assemblies belonging to the same owner in the same application do By virtue of a set of assemblies running in the same application domain, assemblies are a discover each other at execution time using the Microsoft .NET Framework reflection ap tion programming interfaces or other means, and they can call into them in late-bound ion. Because such calls are occurring against assemblies belonging to the same owner, are no SQL Server permissions checked for these calls. The placement scheme of assen in application domains is designed primarily to achieve scalability, security, and iso goals; however, Microsoft has not guaranteed that this functionality will be present in versions of SQL Server.

Services

The CLR provides a number of services to help achieve the design goals of CLR integration with SQL Server, such as type safety verification, Application Domains, Code Access Security and Host Protection Attributes.

Type Safety Verification

Type-safe code is code that accesses memory structures only in well-defined ways. For example, given a valid object reference, type-safe code can only access objects exactly as they are defined, reducing memory access errors (or general protection faults). When assemblies are loaded in the CLR, prior to the MSIL being compiled using JIT compilation, the runtime performs a verification phase that examines code to determine its type safety.

Application Domains

The CLR supports the idea of application domains as zones of execution within the SQLOS process where managed code assemblies can be loaded and executed. The application domain boundary provides isolation between assemblies. The assemblies are completely isolated in terms of their ability to interact with one another. Application domains are also the mechanism for loading and unloading code. Code can be unloaded from memory only by unloading an entire application domain.

Code Access Security (CAS)

The CLR security system provides a way to control the kinds of operations managed code can perform by assigning permissions to code. Code access permissions are assigned based on the signature, or strong name of the code.

The CLR offers a system-wide policy that can be set by the system administrator. This policy defines the permissions for any managed code running on the system. In addition, the CLR host provides additional security to specify additional restrictions on managed code. If a managed API in the .NET Framework exposes operations on resources that are protected by a code access permission, the API will demand that permission before accessing the resource. This demand causes the CLR security system to trigger a comprehensive check of every assembly in the chain. Only if the entire call chain has permission will access to the resource be granted.

Host Protection Attributes (HPAs)

The CLR provides a mechanism for interacting with managed APIs that are part of the .NET Framework and have certain attributes that might be of interest to a host of the CLR. For

example, the *SharedState* attribute indicates whether the API exposes the ability to cre
manage static class fields. *Synchronization* indicates whether the API exposes the ability t
form thread management. *ExternalProcessMgmt* indicates whether the API exposes a v
control the host process. Given these attributes, the developer can specify a list of HPAs
as the *SharedState* attribute, that should be disallowed in the hosted environment. In this
the CLR denies attempts by user code to call APIs that are annotated by the HPAs in th
hibited list.

CLR Database Object Types

In SQL Server 2005, several database object types can be implemented in CLR code. `
object types are as follows:

- **CLR Stored Procedures**   These are stored procedures that utilize CLR code inste
  TSQL code. They have the same execution characteristics as a T-SQL stored proce
  for example, the process to execute a CLR stored procedure from client code is ide
  to executing a TSQL stored procedure.
- **CLR Triggers**   These are database triggers that utilize CLR code instead of TSQL
  Using CLR triggers, database developers can implement complex logic that is not `
  ble in T-SQL. CLR triggers function identically to T-SQL stored procedures.
- **User-Defined Types (UDTs)**   User-Defined Types are a way for database develop
  apply object orientation into database code. For example, database developer
  implement a custom class in .NET code that has all of the attributes required to rep
  a specific object. This class can then be created as a UDT and used to create a co
  and store data in a SQL Server 2005 table.
- **CLR Table-Valued Functions (TVFs)**   CLR table-valued functions have one very impo
  advantage over TSQL TVFs: They do not need a temporary work table to store r
  and can begin streaming the data back immediately. This is especially important fo
  perceptions of performance for large data sets.
- **User-Defined Aggregates (UDAs)**   User-Defined Aggregates are useful when devel
  applications that perform complex mathematical operations. T-SQL can perform
  ematical functions, but it is not designed for that purpose. Using UDAs, database
  opers can exert tight control over how aggregate calculations are performed.

CLR vs. Transact-SQL

Transact-SQL (T-SQL) is the native programming language supported by SQL Serve
compliant with both the American National Standards Institute (ANSI) and Interna
Organization for Standardization (ISO) standards for SQL and contains data-manipu

features and data-definition features. The data-manipulation features can be broadly categorized into two parts: a declarative query language (composed of SELECT/INSERT /UPDATE/DELETE statements) and a procedural language (WHILE, assignment, triggers, cursors, etc.). Generally, CLR support in SQL Server provides an alternative to the procedural portion of T-SQL.

Even without CLR support, it is important to recognize that database applications should use the declarative query language as much as possible. This portion of the language is able to leverage the power of the query processor, which is best able to optimize and perform bulk operations. Developers should only resort to CLR programming to express logic that cannot be expressed within the query language. All of this remains true with CLR support in SQL Server: the CLR should not be used to write procedural code that can be expressed using the declarative features of the T-SQL language. Developers should be aware that there are a number of significant enhancements to the T-SQL query language in SQL Server 2005 that augment the power of the T-SQL query language; they should ensure that they are taking full advantage of them before writing procedural code, whether in the CLR or otherwise. New features in T-SQL that should be considered before writing CLR code are the ability to write recursive queries to traverse recursive hierarchies in a table; new analytical functions such as *RANK* and *ROW_NUMBER* that enable ranking rows in a result set; and new relational operators such as *EXCEPT*, *INTERSECT*, *APPLY*, *PIVOT*, and *UNPIVOT*. Developers should view the CLR as an efficient alternative for logic that cannot be expressed declaratively in the query language.

In T-SQL, query language statements such as SELECT, INSERT, UPDATE, and DELETE are simply embedded within procedural code. CLR code uses the ADO.NET data access provider for SQL Server (SqlClient). Using this approach, all query language statements are represented by dynamic strings that are passed as arguments to methods and properties in the ADO.NET API. Because of this, data access written using the CLR can be more verbose than T-SQL. More importantly, because the SQL statements are encoded in dynamic strings, they are not compiled or validated until they are executed, which affects both the debugging of the code and its performance. It is important to note that both T-SQL-based and CLR-based programming models use the same SQL query language; only the procedural portions differ.

One issue that developers have with programming CLR code inside of SQL Server is the fact that data access is not as easy as it is with T-SQL. In T-SQL, returning data is as simple as using a SELECT statement. With the CLR and the Native Data Access Provider, developers must use a *SqlPipe* object to return data to the client, as shown below:

```csharp
//C#
using System;
using System.Data;
using System.Data.SqlClient;
```

```
using System.Data.SqlTypes;
using Microsoft.SqlServer.Server;


public partial class StoredProcedures
{
    [Microsoft.SqlServer.Server.SqlProcedure]
    public static void SqlPipeTest()
    {
        // Connect through the context connection.
        using (SqlConnection connection = new SqlConnection("context connection=true"))
        {
            connection.Open();

            SqlCommand command = new SqlCommand(
                "SELECT VendorID, AccountNumber, Name FROM Purchasing.Vendor " +
                "WHERE CreditRating <= @rating", connection);
            command.Parameters.AddWithValue("@rating", rating);

            // Execute the command and send the results directly to the client.
            SqlContext.Pipe.ExecuteAndSend(command);

        }
    }
}
```

```
'VB
    <Microsoft.SqlServer.Server.SqlProcedure()> _
Public Shared Sub StoredProcExecuteCommand(ByVal rating As Integer)
    Dim command As SqlCommand
    ' Connect through the context connection
    Using connection As New SqlConnection("context connection=true")
        connection.Open()
        command = New SqlCommand( _
            "SELECT VendorID, AccountNumber, Name FROM Purchasing.Vendor " & _
            "WHERE CreditRating <= @rating", connection)
        command.Parameters.AddWithValue("@rating", rating)
        ' Execute the command and send the results directly to the client
        SqlContext.Pipe.ExecuteAndSend(command)
    End Using
End Sub
```

The code uses a *SqlConnection* and a *SqlCommand* to execute a stored procedure and return the data to the client using a *SqlPipe* object. This is a very simple example of the structure required to return data to client applications from within CLR objects.

The *SqlPipe* object coupled with the context connection enables all data access to be tained within the SQLOS process. This has a very succinct advantage over using X accomplish similar tasks. In previous releases of SQL Server, XPs were the only alternat

T-SQL with which to write server-side code with logic that was difficult to write in T-SQL. CLR integration provides a more robust alternative to XPs. In addition, with CLR integration, many stored procedures can be better expressed as table-valued functions, enabling them to be invoked and manipulated using the query language.

Following are some of the benefits of using CLR procedures rather than XPs:

- Security control. SQL Server administrators have little control over what XPs can or cannot do. Using the Code Access Security (CAS) model, a SQL Server administrator can assign one of three permission buckets—SAFE, EXTERNAL_ACCESS, or UNSAFE—to exert varying degrees of control over the operations that managed code is permitted to perform.

- Reliability. Managed code, especially in the SAFE and EXTERNAL_ACCESS permission sets, provides a more reliable programming model than XPs do. Verifiable managed code ensures that all access to objects is performed through strongly typed interfaces, reducing the likelihood that the program accesses or corrupts memory buffers belonging to SQL Server.

- Data access. With XPs, an explicit connection back to the database—a loop-back connection—must be made to access the local SQL Server database. In addition, this loop-back connection must be explicitly bound to the transaction context of the original session to ensure that the XP participates in the transaction in which it is invoked. Managed CLR code can access local data using a more natural and efficient programming model that takes advantage of the current connection and transaction context.

- Additional data types. The managed APIs support new data types (such as *XML, (n)varchar(max)*, and *varbinary(max)*) introduced in SQL Server 2005, while the ODS APIs have not been extended to support these new types.

- Scalability. The managed APIs that expose resources such as memory, threads, and synchronization are implemented on top of the SQL Server resource manager, enabling SQL Server to manage these resources for CLR code. Conversely, SQL Server has no view or control over the resource usage of an XP. If an XP consumes too much CPU time or memory, there is no way to detect or control this from within SQL Server. With CLR code, SQL Server can detect that a given thread has not yielded for a long period of time and force the task to yield so that other work can be scheduled. Consequently, using managed code provides for better scalability and robustness.

As mentioned above, CLR routines can outperform XPs when the intent is to simply obtain some data and return it to the client. For code that does not involve data access or sending results, comparing the performance of XPs and managed code is a matter of comparing managed code with native code. In general, managed code cannot beat the performance of native code in these scenarios. Furthermore, there is an additional cost during transitions

from managed to native code when running inside SQL Server because SQL Server r
to do additional maintenance on thread-specific settings when switching context bet
native code and back. Consequently, XPs can significantly outperform managed code
ning inside SQL Server for cases where there are frequent transitions between mar
and native code.

CLR Code That Solves Common Problems

One of the challenges that database developers face when considering whether to use
code or T-SQL is deciding what problems will be solved within the code. For example, a
mon problem faced by database developers is how to parse a string of input and use the
vidual elements. In .NET code, this is easy using the *Split()* function; however, in T-SQ
problem requires looping string manipulation. The following code demonstrates a CLR
that accepts input in the form of semicolon-delimited strings and returns a single row for
delimited string in the input:

```csharp
//C#
using System;
using System.Data;
using System.Data.SqlClient;
using System.Data.SqlTypes;
using Microsoft.SqlServer.Server;

public partial class UserDefinedFunctions
{

[Microsoft.SqlServer.Server.SqlFunction(FillRowMethodName="FillRow",TableDefinition="va
nvarchar(60)")]
    public static IEnumerable SplitString(SqlString str)
    {
        return str.Value.Split(';');
    }

    public static void FillRow(object row, out string str)
    {
        str = (string)row;
    }
}
```

```vb
'VB
Imports System
Imports System.Data
Imports System.Data.SqlClient
Imports System.Data.SqlTypes
Imports Microsoft.SqlServer.Server

Partial Public Class UserDefinedFunctions
```

```
<Microsoft.SqlServer.Server.SqlFunction(FillRowMethodName:="FillRow", _
    TableDefinition:="value nvarchar(60)")> _
Public Shared Function SplitString(ByVal str As SqlString) As IEnumerable

    Return str.Value.Split(";"c)
End Function

Public Shared Sub FillRow(ByVal row As Object, _
    ByRef str As String)

    str = CType(row, String)
End Sub
```

End Class

Using the TVF in a T-SQL stored procedure is a very simple process. For example, if the UI of an application captured line items for an order in a semicolon-delimited string, a T-SQL stored procedure could be created to accept the full string (with delimiters) and then call the TVF to break apart the string for insert into the LineItems table, as shown in the following T-SQL code:

```
CREATE PROCEDURE Insert_Order @cust_id int, @lineitems nvarchar(8000)
AS
BEGIN
    INSERT LineItems
    SELECT * FROM dbo.SplitString(@lineitems)
END
```

Another common problem developers face is when to use T-SQL aggregate functions versus using middle tier code to perform aggregations. T-SQL aggregates can be very efficient when the bounds of the aggregation are known at design time; however, it is sometimes appropriate to aggregate data based on a variable. For example, the following code demonstrates a CLR aggregate that can aggregate data based on the value of a column:

```
//C#
using System;
using System.Data;
using System.Data.SqlClient;
using System.Data.SqlTypes;
using Microsoft.SqlServer.Server;


[Serializable]
[Microsoft.SqlServer.Server.SqlUserDefinedAggregate(Format.Native)]
public struct DomesticSales
{
    private double m_domesticSales;
```

```csharp
    public void Init()
    {
        m_domesticSales = 0;
    }

    public void Accumulate(SqlString Country)
    {
        if (Country == "USA")
        {
            ++m_domesticSales;
        }

    }

    public void Merge(DomesticSales Group)
    {
        m_domesticSales += Group.m_domesticSales;
    }

    public double Terminate()
    {
        return m_domesticSales;
    }


}
```

```vbnet
'VB
Imports System
Imports System.Data
Imports System.Data.SqlClient
Imports System.Data.SqlTypes
Imports Microsoft.SqlServer.Server


<Serializable()> _
<Microsoft.SqlServer.Server.SqlUserDefinedAggregate(Format.Native)> _
Public Structure DomesticSales
    Private m_DomesticSales As Double

    Public Sub Init()
        m_DomesticSales = 0
    End Sub

    Public Sub Accumulate(ByVal Country As SqlString)
        If Country = "USA" Then m_DomesticSales = m_DomesticSales + 1
    End Sub

    Public Sub Merge(ByVal value As DomesticSales)
        value.m_DomesticSales = m_DomesticSales
```

```
        End Sub

        Public Function Terminate() As Double
            Return m_DomesticSales
        End Function
End Structure
```

:iding When to Use CLR Code

The decision regarding whether to use a stored procedure in conjunction with the *SqlPipe* object or a TVF depends on several factors: usability requirements, the source of the data, the need for side effects, and the typing requirements for the results.

Usability

It might be desirable to reuse or further manipulate results produced inside a TVF or a stored procedure. Table-valued functions are more versatile from a usability perspective, as the return type of a TVF is a relational rowset that can be used in any place where such a construct is permitted. In particular, it can be used in the FROM clause of SELECT statements, and as such, the results produced can benefit from the usability of SELECT in subqueries, INSERT...SELECT statements, derived tables, table expressions, etc. However, using the T-SQL language, stored procedures can be composed only as part of the INSERT...EXEC combination that enables produced results to be stored in a permanent or temporary table. The INSERT operation represents an actual copy of the data, which will likely have a performance impact. If usability and reuse of results from within the server is a requirement, TVFs are a better alternative. If the results produced need to only be streamed back to the client or middle tier, either approach is reasonable.

Source of the Data

The source of the data being returned is another important factor in deciding between T-SQL-based implementations and CLR-based implementations. Results can be produced either by reading from some source in the local instance using the ActiveX Data Object (ADO).NET provider, or from a source external to SQL Server. For external sources, a CLR-based implementation is a better choice than T-SQL because of the ease with which the logic accessing the external data can be implemented. In the case of generating results based on a query executed on the local instance using the ADO.NET provider, a stored procedure would generally execute a query, iterate through the result, and perform some operation on the rows before sending them back through a *SqlPipe*.

Operations with Side Effects

In general, operations that produce side effects, such as DML statements or transaction
ations, are disallowed from user-defined functions, including table-valued functions. 1
operations might be desired, however. For example, one might wish to set a SAVEP(
transaction, perform some operation, and roll back to the SAVEPOINT in case an error oc

Typing of Results and Number of Results

The description of results produced by a CLR-stored procedure through *SqlPipe* differs
that of a CLR TVF and is consistent with results in T-SQL. A TVF is strongly typed, and a:
of the registration (CREATE FUNCTION) statement, it must statically define the type
return value.

Transaction Management in CLR Code

Another factor when deciding whether to use CLR objects is determining how transac
will be handled. The Microsoft .NET Framework 2.0 (which SQL Server 2005 requires) i
duced a new namespace called *System.Transactions*. *System.Transactions* greatly extend
transaction-management capability of the .NET Framework. One major enhancement
System.Transactions provides is the concept of a current transaction, which is available thr
System.Transaction.Current. To maintain consistency with the .NET Transaction Framev
CLR code operates in the same fashion. If a transaction was active at the point where SQI
code is entered, then the transaction will be surfaced to the SQLCLR API through the
tem.Transactions.Transaction class. Specifically, *Transaction.Current* will be non-null. In
cases, you don't need to access the transaction explicitly. For database connections, ADO
will check *Transaction.Current* automatically when the connection is opened and will enli:
connection in that transaction transparently unless developers specify otherwise. How
there are a few scenarios in which you might want to use the transaction object directly,
as when you want to abort the external transaction from within your stored procedu
function. In this case, you can simply call *Transaction.Current.Rollback()*. If you want to e
a resource that doesn't do automatic enlistment, or for some reason wasn't enlisted durin
tialization, you might also use the transaction object directly.

The following code demonstrates CLR code using explicit transactions through the
tem.Transactions namespace:

```csharp
//C#
namespace TK442AppendixCodeCSharp
{
    using System.Data;
    using System.Data.SqlClient;
    using System.Transactions;
```

```csharp
using Microsoft.SqlServer.Server;

public partial class StoredProcedures
{
    [Microsoft.SqlServer.Server.SqlProcedure()]
    public static void SampleSP()
    {

        // start a transaction block
        using (TransactionScope tx = new TransactionScope())
        {

            // connect to the context connection
            using (SqlConnection conn = new SqlConnection("context connection=true"))
            {
                conn.Open();

                // do some changes to the local database
            }

            // connect to the remote database
            using (SqlConnection conn = new SqlConnection(
                                "server=MyServer; database=AdventureWorks;" +
                                "user id=MyUser; password=MyPassword"))
            {
                conn.Open();

                // do some changes to the remote database
            }

            // mark the transaction as complete
            tx.Complete();
        }
    }
}
}
```

```vbnet
'VB
Imports System.Data
Imports System.Data.SqlClient
Imports System.Transactions
Imports Microsoft.SqlServer.Server

Partial Public Class StoredProcedures
    <Microsoft.SqlServer.Server.SqlProcedure()> _
    Public Shared Sub SampleSP()

        ' start a transaction block
        Using tx As New TransactionScope()
```

```
      ' connect to the context connection
      Using conn As New SqlConnection("context connection=true")
          conn.Open()

          ' do some changes to the local database
      End Using

      ' connect to a remote server (don't hardcode the conn string in real code)
      Using conn As New SqlConnection("server=MyServer; database=AdventureWorks;"
                                      "user id=MyUser; password=MyPassword")
          conn.Open()

          ' do some changes to the remote database
      End Using

      ' mark the transaction as completed
      tx.Complete()
    End Using
  End Sub
End Class
```

The previous code shows the simplest way of using *System.Transactions*. Simply surroun
code that needs to be part of a transaction with a transaction scope. Notice that toward
end of the block, there is a call to the *Complete* method on the scope indicating that this
of code executed its part successfully and it's okay to commit the transaction. If you wa
abort the transaction, simply don't call *Complete*. The *TransactionScope* object will do the
thing" by default. That is, if there was already a transaction active, then the scope will ha
within that transaction; otherwise, it will start a new transaction.

The pattern is fairly simple: The transaction scope will either pick up an already active
action or will start a new one. It is very important to ensure the code calls the *disp*
method when code execution is complete, so make sure that the transaction code is wit
using block, or make sure to explicitly dispose of the object. There is no requirement t
the newer transaction models with SQLCLR code; the existing .NET Framework 1.x
explicit SQL Server transactions still exist.

These transactions can be nested, in the sense that your stored procedure or function r
be called within a transaction, and it would still be valid for you to call *BeginTransa*
(Note that this does not mean you get "true" nested transactions; you'll get the same b
ior that you'd get when nesting BEGIN TRAN statements in T-SQL.) There is a differ
between transactions started in T-SQL stored procedures and the ones started in SQL
code: SQLCLR code cannot unbalance the transaction state on entry/exit of a SQLCLR
cation. This brings up a couple of limitations:

- You cannot start a transaction inside a SQLCLR frame and cannot commit it or roll it back; SQL Server will generate an error during frame exit. Similarly, you cannot commit or roll back an outer transaction inside SQLCLR code.
- Any attempt to commit a transaction that you didn't start in the same procedure will cause a run-time error.

Any attempt to roll back a transaction that you didn't start in the same procedure will doom the transaction (preventing any other side-effect operation from occurring), but the transaction won't disappear until the SQLCLR code is unloaded.

Transactions can be a very powerful tool in the arsenal of database developers, but you must take care to understand exactly how they work when integrating with CLR code.

Determining CLR Code Statistics

Another factor to weigh when deciding whether to use CLR objects is determining the memory utilization of CLR code. Sometimes a developer will choose to implement a CLR object only to realize that performance suffers due to excessive memory consumption. Unfortunately, there aren't any easy ways to determine how much memory a CLR object will consume before it is deployed, but every developer should make an effort to measure memory consumption of all CLR objects during the development cycle before they are placed into production. The easiest way to measure CLR memory consumption is by querying the sys.dm_os_memory_clerks DMV, as shown in the following code:

```
SELECT
    single_pages_kb +
    multi_pages_kb +
    virtual_memory_committed_kb AS [TotalMemory]
FROM sys.dm_os_memory_clerks
WHERE type = 'MEMORYCLERK_SQLCLR';
```

The column "single_pages_kb" details memory allocated in the SQL Buffer Pool, "multi_pages_kb" details memory allocated by the SQL CLR host that is outside the SQL Buffer pool, and "virtual_memory_committed_kb" details memory allocated by the CLR directly through the bulk allocation interface. The memory is mostly used for the managed .NET garbage collector heap and the JIT compiler heap, and it is also stored outside of the SQL Buffer Pool.

Once you know how much memory SQL CLR is using on the server, it would be nice to know how much memory SQL CLR is permitted to use. When there is memory pressure on the server, SQL CLR will try to release memory by explicitly running garbage collection and possibly unloading objects from memory that are not currently used.

There are two types of memory pressure to monitor:

- Physical memory pressure based on the amount of available system memory
- Virtual address space memory pressure based on the number of available v addresses

Physical memory pressure is pretty straightforward; if your server is under load and rur low on available memory, Windows will issue a LowMemoryResourceNotification, v SQL Server will recognize and handle. Virtual address space memory pressure is more cult and generally more limiting to SQL CLR because it might cause memory pressure when there is enough physical memory available. This might happen because, as was above, most SQL CLR memory allocations occur outside of the SQL Buffer Pool in w called the MemToLeave area. The size of this area of memory is set by the -g flag on SQL S startup, but by default, it is at least 256 MB.

Another item that database developers want to closely manage is how much time CLR o spend executing. You can determine this by executing the following query:

```
SELECT
    (SELECT text FROM sys.dm_exec_sql_text(eqs.sql_handle)) AS query_text,
    eqs.*
FROM sys.dm_exec_query_stats AS eqs
WHERE eqs.total_clr_time > 0
ORDER BY eqs.total_clr_time DESC
```

The output of this query will provide the exact statement and how much time is spent e> ing in CLR, as well as offer statistics on various resource consumption by the statement.

Another item that database developers will want to keep track of is the number of CLR a; blies that have been deployed to a database. It is a good idea to minimize the numk assemblies deployed to any given database by ensuring that only those assemblies th; currently used are deployed to the database. The following query provides the assemblie have been deployed to a database:

```
SELECT
    a.[name],
    ad.[appdomain_name],
    clr.[load_time]
FROM sys.dm_clr_loaded_assemblies AS clr
JOIN sys.assemblies AS a
    ON clr.assembly_id = a.assembly_id
INNER JOIN sys.dm_clr_appdomains AS ad
    ON clr.appdomain_address = ad.appdomain_address
```

The CLR offers database developers a very powerful tool to solve many of the perple problems of the day. Understanding how the CLR functions and when to use CLR v T-SQL code is an important part in the overall application design cycle.

This section has discussed how the CLR functions, when to consider using CLR code, how transactions function, and how to obtain various management statistics related to the SQL CLR.

Server 2005 Storage Engine

The storage engine is another important aspect of SQL Server 2005 for developers to master. SQL Server 2005 ultimately reads and writes data to disk. The storage engine is the component that is responsible for the management of the task of reading and writing data across all databases in the SQL Server instance. The storage engine has been designed to be "invisible" to the user in that they are not aware of its existence, except, of course, when something goes wrong. The storage engine is responsible for the following tasks:

- Managing physical data and log files on the disk subsystem
- Reading data from database storage files and loading it into buffer cache
- Reading data from buffer cache and storing it to disk
- Tracking atomicity of all transactions
- Writing transaction log data to the log file
- Ensuring the data is in a consistent state when the instance starts
- Performing database backup operations when instructed
- Performing database restore operations when instructed
- Miscellaneous file-management tasks

As you can see, the database storage engine is a very busy component within the SQL Server 2005 architecture. The database storage engine incorporates an industry-standard set of algorithms known as "Algorithms for Recovery and Isolation Exploiting Semantics" or ARIES. ARIES was first developed in the late 1980s by scientists at IBM and, later, Microsoft incorporated them into SQL Server. Because the database storage engine is based on such mature standards, it is very efficient in its operation.

age Engine Architecture and Terminology

To understand the vast amount of documentation and information that exists for the database storage engine, database developers should be familiar with the following terms:

- **ACID properties**   The ACID (Atomicity, Consistency, Isolation, and Durability) properties are a core requirement for SQL Server; anyone developing applications within SQL Server should understand them. ACID properties are:
  - ❑ **Atomicity**   A transaction must be an atomic unit of work; either all of its data modifications are performed or none of them are performed.

❑ **Consistency**   When completed, a transaction must leave all data in a cons
state. In SQL Server 2005, all rules must be applied to the transaction's mo
tions to maintain data integrity. All internal data structures, such as B-tree in
or doubly linked lists, must be correct at the end of the transaction.

❑ **Isolation**   Modifications made by concurrent transactions must be isolated
modifications made by all other concurrent transactions. A transaction eithe
the data in the state it was in before another concurrent transaction modifiec
it sees the data after the second transaction has completed, but it does not s
intermediate state. This is referred to as serializability because it provides th
tem with the capability to reload the starting data and replay a series of tra
tions to end up with the data in the same state it was in after the or
transactions were performed.

❑ **Durability**   After a transaction has completed, its effects are permanently in
in the system. The modifications persist even in the event of a system failure

■ **Point in Time**   Point in Time is generally used to refer to the ability to restore a dat
to a specified point in time due to a hardware or software failure.

■ **Stable Media**   Stable media is often confused with physical storage. SQL Server d
stable media as storage that can survive system restart or common failure. Many
end disk subsystems provide high-speed cache facilities to reduce the latency of rea
write operations. This cache is often supported by a battery-powered backup facilit
battery backup provides the necessary power to maintain the data in the cache fc
eral days, but implementations vary by manufacturer. Manufacturers can switch ov
teries to increase the life of the cache when necessary.

The key is that after the system problem has been corrected, the pending writes
cache are treated as if the failure or restart never occurred. Most manufactu
implementations immediately flush pending writes to physical disk during the r
operations.

■ **Write Ordering**   Write ordering (or write dependency) is the capability of the I/C
system to preserve the order of I/O operations. As described previously, stable i
can include caching. If a point in time is studied, the stable media should revea
served I/O order characteristics.

The order of the I/O operations associated with SQL Server must be maintainec
system must maintain write ordering, or it breaks the WAL protocol described i
appendix. (The log records must be written out in correct order and the log re
must always be written to stable media before the data pages that the log records
sent are written.) After a transaction log record is successfully flushed, the asso
data page can then be flushed as well. If the subsystem permits the data page to
stable media before the log record does, data integrity is breached.

For example, if a computer running SQL Server had to restart after the data page had reached stable media but before the log record, the database recovery might fail. Because the log record for a page modification does not exist, the recovery process cannot determine the proper transactional state of the page. Worse, the log record did not get flushed to stable media, so the recovery process is not aware that the page requires rollback and it cannot attempt to correct the problem, thereby leaving the database in an unknown state.

- **Multichannel and Load-Balancing Systems** Many high-end storage environments, such as Storage Area Networks, implement load-balanced systems that can have multiple channels to support I/O requests. These systems must maintain support for I/O ordering. Many of these systems support I/O ordering with a stable media cache and subsequently combine and/or split I/O requests across available subsystem resources to complete the storing to physical media.

- **Torn I/O or Pages** Torn I/O is often referred to as a torn page in SQL Server documentation. A torn I/O occurs when a partial write takes place, leaving the data in an invalid state. SQL Server data pages are 8 KB in size. A torn data page for SQL Server occurs when only a portion of the 8 KB is correctly written to or retrieved from stable media.

    SQL Server always checks I/O completion status for any operating system error conditions and proper data transfer size and then handles errors appropriately. Torn pages generally arise after system outages where the subsystem does not complete the entire 8-KB I/O request.

    Disk drive manufacturers generally limit data transfer guarantees to sector boundaries of 512 bytes, so if the stable media is a physical disk and the controller does not contain a cache with battery backup capabilities, the I/O request is limited to the final spin/ transfer rate of the physical drive. Therefore, if an I/O is issued to write 8 KB (for a total of sixteen 512-byte sectors), but only the first three sectors make it to stable media, then the page becomes torn, which results in data corruption. A subsequent read of the 8-KB page would bring in 3 sectors of the new version of the page and 13 sectors of an older version.

    SQL Server can enable torn page detection on a per-database basis. A portion of the first 512-byte sector of the page contains the page header. When torn page detection is enabled, the header member contains information about each of the other 512-byte sectors or segments of the 8-KB page. When the page is read in, the torn page information is used to detect a torn page situation.

    Torn page detection incurs minimal overhead and is a recommended practice for SQL Server installations.

- **Log Parity** Hardware manufacturers guarantee sector-size writes, so SQL Server action log files are always written with sector-size alignment. Each sector of the tra tion log contains a parity flag. This flag can be used to determine the last sector tha correctly written.

  During a recovery operation, the log file(s) are scanned for the final sector that wa ten; the log records can then be used to return the database to the appropriate tra tional state.

- **Mirroring and Remote Mirroring** Mirroring is a common data redundancy and gency recovery practice. Mirroring can be implemented at a software or hardware Mirroring installations have historically been physical implementations of l(attached hardware cabinets. Recent advances in remote mirroring technologies made it possible to maintain mirrors across long distances.

  Several types of mirroring implementations are on the market. Some implementa are cache-based; others ensure that the I/O takes place at all mirrored locations I the I/O request is considered complete. Whatever the implementation, write orc must be maintained.

  SQL Server considers a mirror to be a stable-media, point-in-time copy of the pr data. Point in time is an important aspect of this. Strict maintenance of the WAL re ments must occur on the mirrored subsystem to maintain the ACID properties data. The mirrored subsystem must mimic the exact points in time as experienced primary data.

  For example, many high-end installations contain multiple I/O storage devices. I base log files are placed on one mirror set and data files on another mirror set, ordering cannot be directly maintained across the separate hardware components. out extended capabilities, the log and data page write order on the mirror devices c be maintained with point-in-time capabilities. Extended mirror capabilities are n to ensure that write ordering can be maintained across multiple physical mir devices. These are often referred to as Mirror Groups or Consistency Groups.

- **Forced Unit Access (FUA)** Forced Unit Access (FUA) occurs when a file is opene using *CreateFile*) with the *FILE_FLAG_WRITETHROUGH* flag. SQL Server ope database and log files with this flag.

  The flag indicates that on any write request, the FUA bit should be sent with the re to the subsystem. This bit indicates to the subsystem that data must reach stable before the I/O is to be considered complete and the operating system signaled th I/O is complete. No intermediate cache should be used that is not considered media. In other words, the write should go directly to the stable media; this proc called writethrough.

This prevents problems that occur when a cache (such as a disk cache that is not battery backed up) accepts the I/O and informs SQL Server that the I/O is complete, when in fact it has not yet been stored to stable media. Without this capability, SQL Server could not rely on the system to support WAL protocol needs.

IMPORTANT How FUA requests are handled

Integrated Drive Electronics (IDE) disk specifications and implementations do not have clear standards for how the FUA request is handled. Small Computer System Interface (SCSI) disk specifications and implementations use the FUA request to disable physical disk caches and other caching mechanisms. In many IDE implementations, the FUA request is simply discarded by the IDE hardware, thereby making this type of subsystem unsafe to use with SQL Server or with any other product that relies on the FUA behavior. Because of the need to honor the FUA setting, some IDE drive manufacturers have utilities that permit IDE drive caches to be disabled, making them safe for use with SQL Server.

■ **Data Pages**   The SQL Server database page size is 8 KB. Each page contains a header with fields such as Page Number, Object Id, LSN, Index Id, Torn bits, and Types. The actual row data is located on the remaining portion of the page. The internal database structures track the allocation state of the data pages in the database.

■ **Page Number**   A page number is a value from 0 through ((Max File Size/8 KB)-1). The page number multiplied by 8 KB provides the offset in the file to the first byte in the page.

When a page is read from disk, the page number is immediately checked to ensure that the proper offset was returned (the page number in the header is compared to the expected page number). If the value isn't as expected, SQL Server will generate Error 823.

■ **Object ID**   This is the ID of the object to which the page is assigned within the schema of the database. A page can be assigned to only a single object. When the page is read from disk, the object ID is checked on the page. If the object ID does not match the expected object ID, SQL Server will generate Error 605.

■ **Extents**   SQL Server generally allocates space an extent at a time. An extent is eight 8-KB pages, or 64 KB. SQL Server often performs reads in extent-sized (64 KB or 128 KB) boundaries as well.

■ **Buffer Pool**   The buffer pool is also referred to as the BPool. The BPool consumes the majority of the user mode address space, leaving relatively little virtual address range free for thread stacks, dynamic-link libraries (DLLs), and other activities. The buffer pool is reserved in large chunks, but the working page size of 8 KB is maintained to match the database page size.

■ **Hardware Read Cache**   The hardware read cache is commonly a read-ahead cache by the controllers. Depending on the size of the available cache, the read-ahead ca used to retrieve more data than the actual read request might have requested.

The hardware read cache and read-ahead cache will be helpful to an application v data is commonly of a contiguous nature and is retrieved in a reasonably contig manner, such as OnLine Analytical Processing (OLAP) scans or a reporting applic

Because the hardware read cache removes some of the cache memory that could be to support write requests, it can have a negative effect on OnLine Transaction Proce (OLTP) installations that require that data be written at high rates.

IMPORTANT   Read-ahead and size constraints

Some controllers will not do read-ahead if the size of the read request is larger than 1 If the primary application is SQL Server, the hardware read-ahead activity does not pro any benefit because I/O read requests can occur for sizes larger than 16 KB. Check with hardware vendor for complete details and recommendations when running SQL Serve

---

■ **Hardware Write Cache**   The hardware write cache not only caches write request also fulfills read requests if the data is still available in the hardware write cache. 1 a commonly used I/O caching mechanism.

Hardware write cache capabilities can be critical in maintaining OLTP perform goals. With the proper battery backup and algorithms, the hardware write cach secure the data safely (on stable media) as well as increase the speed of SQL Ser hiding much of the true physical I/O time.

■ **Write-Ahead Logging (WAL) Protocol**   A key to ACID property maintenance is the protocol. The WAL protocol requires that all transaction log records associated v particular data page be flushed to stable media before the data page can be flushed ble media.

SQL Server 2005 uses 8-KB data pages and sector-aligned transaction log buffers.

■ **Log Sequence Number**   The log sequence number (LSN) value is a three-part, un incrementing value. It is used for maintaining the sequence of the transactic records in the database. This enables SQL Server to maintain the ACID properties a perform appropriate recovery actions.

When a modification occurs, a log record is generated with a new LSN value. The LSN value is stored in the data page header so the last log record and matching data can be associated with each other.

- **Latching** SQL Server uses latches to provide data synchronization. A latch is a user-mode reader-writer lock implemented by SQL Server. Each data page in memory has a buffer (BUF) tracking structure. The BUF structure contains status information (Dirty, On LRU, In I/O) as well as a latch structure.

    Locking maintains the appropriate lock activity; latching controls physical access. For example, it is possible for a lock to be held on a page that is not in memory. The latch is only appropriate when the data page is in memory (associated with a BUF).

    SQL Server 2005 utilizes the Win32 APIs *WriteFileGather* and *ReadFileScatter* for access to the disk subsystem. The *WriteFileGather* function gathers data from multiple discontinuous buffers and writes the data to a file. The *ReadFileScatter* function reads data from a file and distributes the data into multiple discontinuous buffers.

    These APIs enable SQL Server to avoid multiple physical I/O requests. For example, during the checkpoint process, up to sixteen 8-KB pages can be flushed with a single WriteFileGather invocation. Previous versions of SQL Server had to issue an I/O request for each data page, or would have to sort and buffer a larger request itself, leading to possible performance problems on busy systems.

IMPORTANT Scatter-Gather I/O

Scatter-gather capabilities are hardware specific. When the hardware does not support scatter-gather capabilities, the operating system must intervene and issue separate I/O requests. To maximize SQL Server I/O performance, ensure that your subsystem natively supports scatter-gather I/O operations.

- **Lazy Writer** The lazy writer in SQL Server 2005 attempts to locate up to 16 unique pages for each sweep to return to the free list. If the page reference count has dropped to zero, the page is eligible for return to the free list. If the page is marked dirty, the log records and page date will be flushed to disk.

    Thus, it is possible for the lazy writer to flush 16 * 16 pages to disk in a single sweep. This is efficient because many of the pages will remain in the SQL Server buffer pool but are now in a clean state. I/O is done in the background from the primary SPID. When the lazy writer needs additional buffers for the free list, the buffers might not need to be flushed to disk, but are returned to the free list.

- **Checkpoint** The SQL Server 2005 checkpoint process periodically sweeps the buffer pool for buffers that contain pages from a specified database and flushes all dirty buffers to stable media. This makes recovery quicker because roll-forward operations have less physical work to complete.

As described earlier, the checkpoint process uses the same I/O approach to post up pages in a single I/O. Because the I/O is posted (OVERLAPPED), checkpoint do wait for each I/O request to complete immediately. Checkpoint continues to posted and completed I/Os, but attempts to maintain a high level of outstanding (for example, 100 write requests continuously outstanding). This maximize throughput and reduces checkpoint runtime.

Before the introduction of *WriteFileGather*, SQL Server sorted the buffers for a spe database in page order and issued I/O requests in page order. This required many ical I/O requests because the page order of the flush is not in contiguous memor tion order. However, it often kept the physical subsystem mechanisms in ph locations that are in close proximity to make the I/O requests complete faster.

With the older design, an elevator seek can be a problem. Issuing many I/Os ir order generally results in a similar "on disk" order, resulting in table "hot spots spots are not as much of a problem in SQL Server 2005.

With *WriteFileGather*, SQL Server can sweep the buffer pool without requirin physical ordering relationship to the pages on disk. By gathering 128 KB (sixteer pages) in a group, SQL Server is able to transfer blocks of data with far fewer ph I/O requests. This allows the checkpoint process to maintain its speed, while th dom nature of the I/O requests deters any elevator seeking that could affect oth operations.

All databases, except for *tempdb*, are checkpointed. *Tempdb* does not require recov is re-created every time SQL Server starts), so flushing data pages to disk is not o for *tempdb*, and SQL Server avoids doing so.

Checkpoint protects the system from I/O flooding by serializing checkpoint proc Only one checkpoint at a time can run to completion. The checkpoint and lazy processes also communicate with each other to control I/O queue depths.

- **Eager Write**   SQL Server 2005 uses eager writes to post data pages associated wit imally logged or bulk operations. This enables the async capabilities of the I/O pa to keep the dirty pages flowing to disk without dirtying large and unwanted porti the buffer pool. The same mechanism as that used by the lazy writer and checkpoir cesses to post I/O operations is used.

IMPORTANT Efficient I/O

Lazy writer, checkpoint, and eager write do not wait for the I/O to immediately complete. They always post the I/O with *WriteFileGather* with the OVERLAPPED option and continue with other work, checking for I/O completion success at a later point in time. This enables SQL Server to maximize both CPU and I/O resources for the appropriate tasks.

Server Database Engine Physical Operations

Understanding how the SQL Server database engine physically reads and writes data to the disk is important for any database developer who wants to understand how his or her application will perform. It is very easy, however, to get lost in the vast sea of information about ARIES technologies and the intricacies of SQL Server implementation. The most important facet for developers to take away is how data and log pages are flushed to disk.

Flushing Data Pages to Disk

The three primary mechanisms shown below trigger the flush of a data page to disk. However, each mechanism uses the same internal routine in the buffer pool to achieve the transfer.

- Lazy write (least recently used (LRU) and memory-pressure based)
- Checkpoint (recovery-interval based)
- Eager write (nonlogged I/O based)

To efficiently flush writes to disk, *WriteFileGather* is used. This enables SQL Server to bundle consecutive dirty pages into a single write request. SQL Server performs the following steps to flush a single page:

1. It latches the page to prevent further modifications.
2. It ensures that log records up to and including the LSN on the page are flushed to stable media.
3. It establishes proper entries for the *WriteFileGather* invocation.

SQL Server performs the following steps to set up another page for flushing and repeats for up to 16 total pages (inclusive of the first page):

1. SQL Server does a hash lookup for the next contiguous page. For example, if the page to be flushed were page 100, SQL Server searches for page 101 in the buffer hash array.
2. If it does not locate the page, then the end of contiguous I/O block is established and the I/O is posted.

3. If it locates the page, it acquires the latch to prevent further modifications if the might be dirty.

4. It checks to ensure that the page is dirty and needs to be written. If it isn't, SQL S releases the latch and considers the end of contiguous I/O block as established and mits the asynchronous I/O request.

If the page is dirty, SQL Server follows the steps described earlier that detail how it flus single page. After the set of pages to be flushed is determined, the *WriteFileGather* funct invoked to post (Async / OVERLAPPED) the I/O request with the associated callback tion to complete the I/O operation.

When SQL Server determines that *HasOverlappedIoCompleted* returns TRUE, *GetOverlc Results* is used to gather completion information from the system and the callback funct invoked. The callback makes an appropriate determination regarding the success of th operation and releases the latch on each page.

Flushing Log Pages To Disk

The process for flushing log records to disk is very similar to the way that data pag written. The log manager is responsible for all writes for all transaction log records databases.

When a request to flush all log records up to a certain LSN is requested by any worker system, the request is queued to the log manager. The worker then waits for a response the log manager specifying that the I/O has completed successfully. The log manager ret from the queue and formats the request; it then posts the I/O on sector-aligned bounda

The I/O is posted with *WriteFile* using the OVERLAPPED (async) mechanisms. The log ager can then return to service other queued requests. When the I/O is completed, the pletion routine is run to check the success of the write. If the write is successful, the w workers can be signaled to continue their operations.

Write ordering is critical at this stage. Because multiple log write requests can be post the same transaction log, the LSN order must be maintained.

For example, pages 5, 10, and 20 are modified by separate transactions. Page 5 was mo first, then 10, and then 20. LSN flush requests occurred for page 5, 10, and 20 and we in motion in the same order. If the log record(s) for page 5 and 20 are flushed to stable r only the flush to LSN for page 5 is considered done and SQL Server might only flush p The LSN 10 must be flushed to stable media before 10 and then 20 can be considered flushed to the LSN.

Read-Ahead

SQL Server uses sophisticated algorithms to retrieve data pages that are going to be used in the immediate future. For example, if you run a query that can use an index to determine applicable rows, a read-ahead might occur on the actual data pages that are needed to complete the select list. As index entries are identified, SQL Server can post OVERLAPPED I/O operations for the data pages that will be used in upcoming steps of the query plan. For example, this is how a query using a bookmark lookup operator uses read-ahead. (More information about the bookmark lookup is included later in this appendix.)

This example is just one of many read-ahead situations that SQL Server can use. Enabling the index searching to continue while the data page I/O is in progress maximizes the CPU and I/O of the system. The I/O is often completed by the time it is needed, so other steps in the plan have direct memory access to the needed data and do not have to stall while waiting on I/O. When a read-ahead is posted, it can be from 1 to 1,024 pages. SQL Server limits a single read-ahead request depth to 1,024 pages.

SQL Server uses the following steps to set up read-ahead:

1. It obtains the requested amount of buffers from the free list.
2. For each page:
   a. It determines the in-memory status of the page by doing a hash search.
   b. If it's found to be already in memory, SQL Server sets up the read-ahead request to immediately return the buffer to the free list upon I/O completion.
   c. It establishes the proper I/O request information for *ReadFileScatter* invocation.
   d. It acquires I/O latch to protect buffer from further access.
   e. If the page is not found in hash search, then SQL Server inserts it into the hash table.
3. It issues the ReadFileScatter operation to read the data.

When the I/O operation is complete, each page is sanity checked for a valid page number and torn page errors. In addition, various other data integrity and safety checks are performed. The I/O latch is then released so the page is available for use if it is located on the hash chain. If the page was determined to be already in memory, the page is immediately discarded to the free list.

This process shows the key factors of SQL Server I/O patterns. Read-ahead goes after pages that can already be in memory or not allocated. Because SQL Server maintains the in-memory buffers and hash chains, SQL Server tracks the page's state. Importantly, read-ahead processing opens the door for overlapping read and write requests at the hardware level.

If a page is already in memory when the read-ahead request is posted, the contiguous r—
still needed and is faster than breaking up read requests into multiple physical requests
Server considers the read to be unusable for the page in question, but many of the
around it might be usable. However, if a write operation is in progress when the read is po
the subsystem has to determine which image of the read to return. Some implementa
return the current version of the page before the write is complete; others make the read
until the write completes; and yet others return a combination, showing partially new
and partially old data. The key is that SQL Server will discard the read as unusable b
subsystem needs to maintain the proper image for subsequent read operations. T
progress write, when completed, must be the next read image returned to the server ru
SQL Server.

IMPORTANT Read-ahead vs. parallel query plans

Do not confuse read-ahead with parallel query plans. Read-ahead occurs independently of th
allel query plan selection. The parallel plan might drive I/O harder because multiple workers
driving the load, but read-ahead occurs for serial and parallel plans. To ensure that parallel wc
do not work on the same data sets, SQL Server implements the parallel page supplier to hel
ment the data requests.

Having a good understanding of the internal workings and architecture of the SQL
2005 database storage engine helps database developers to develop applications tha
overcome the weaknesses of the storage engine as well as take advantage of its strength

SQL Server 2005 Query Engine

Simply put, the SQL Server 2005 query engine, sometimes known as the relational eng
responsible for efficiently answering requests from users and providing output. The
engine is made up of the following components, as shown in Figure B-12:

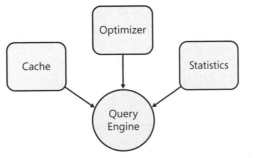

Figure B-12 The SQL Server 2005 query engine components

- **Query Optimizer**   The Query Optimizer is responsible for constructing an efficient "plan of attack" to answer queries.
- **Procedure Cache Manager**   The Procedure Cache Manager is responsible for managing the storage and retrieval of query execution plans that the optimizer has constructed.
- **Statistics Manager**   The Statistics Manager is responsible for maintaining statistical information on indexes to ensure that the most up-to-date information is used when constructing a query plan.

Each of these components works together to construct the most efficient plan, or set of instructions, to provide to the storage engine for data retrieval and storage.

One of the most prevalent design goals for the SQL Server 2005 query engine was to make it invisible to the user. The hope was that developers would never need to know about the internal workings of the query engine, and it would just do its job without interaction. In previous versions of SQL Server, developers of large-scale applications spent a fair amount of time trying to fool the query engine into generating more efficient query plans. This practice led to a number of query hints and options being embedded in T-SQL code that helped instruct the query engine. Unfortunately, due to the improvements in the SQL Server 2005 query engine, this practice can lead to less-efficient queries, and as the applications are upgraded to SQL Server 2005, many developers are finding that their applications are running more slowly. Developers need to understand exactly how the query engine processes data in SQL Server 2005 to make the best choices for creating efficient queries within their applications.

ry Engine Processing

The most basic query type is the SELECT query. SELECT simply instructs the database engine to retrieve certain data based on the criteria specified in the FROM and WHERE clauses. A SELECT statement is nonprocedural, in that it does not state the exact steps that the query engine should use to retrieve the requested data. This means that the query engine must analyze the statement to determine the most efficient way to extract the requested data. This is referred to as query optimization. The component that does this is called the query optimizer. The input to the optimizer consists of the query, the database schema (table and index definitions), and the database statistics. The output of the optimizer is a query plan.

A SELECT statement only defines the following:

- The format of the result set. This is specified mostly in the select list. However, other clauses, such as ORDER BY and GROUP BY, also affect the final form of the result set.
- The tables that contain the data. This is specified in the FROM clause.

- How the tables are logically related. This is defined in the JOIN specifications, might appear in the WHERE clause or in an ON clause following FROM.
- The conditions that the rows in the source tables must satisfy to qualify for the ment. These are specified in the WHERE and HAVING clauses.

A query execution plan is a definition of the following:

- The sequence in which the source tables are accessed.
- Typically, there are many sequences in which the query engine can access the base to build the result set. For example, if the SELECT statement references three tabl database server could first access Table1, use the data from Table1 to extract ma rows from Table2, and then use the data from Table2 to extract data from Table also possible that the query engine could choose Table3 first. This is important be database developers must construct queries that do not rely on data being retrie any specific order.
- The methods used to extract data from each table.

Generally, there are different methods for accessing the data in each table. If only a few with specific key values are required, the database server can use an index. If all the r the table are required, the database server can ignore the indexes and perform a table s all the rows in a table are required, but there is an index whose key columns are in an O BY, performing an index scan instead of a table scan might save a separate sort of the set. If a table is very small, table scans might be the most efficient method for almost all to the table.

The process of selecting one execution plan from potentially many possible plans is re to as optimization. The query optimizer is one of the most important components c Server 2005. While some overhead is used by the query optimizer to analyze the que select a plan, this overhead is typically balanced out when the query optimizer picks a cient execution plan.

The SQL Server query optimizer is a cost-based optimizer. Each possible execution pl an associated cost in terms of the amount of resources used to answer the query. The optimizer must analyze the possible plans and choose the one with the lowest estimate SELECT statements can have thousands of possible execution plans. In these cases, the optimizer does not analyze all possible combinations. Instead, it uses complex algorit find an execution plan that has a cost reasonably close to the minimum possible cost.

The SQL Server query optimizer does not choose only the execution plan with the resource cost; it chooses the plan that returns results to the user with a reasonable resources and that returns the results the most quickly. For example, processing a qu parallel typically uses more resources than processing it serially, but it completes the more quickly. The SQL Server optimizer will use a parallel execution plan to return results if the load on the server will not be adversely affected.

The query optimizer relies on distribution statistics when it estimates the resource costs of different methods for extracting information from a table or index. Distribution statistics are retained for columns and indexes. They indicate the selectivity of the values in a particular index or column. For example, in a table representing people, many people can live in the same city and even have the same last name, but each person has a unique Social Security Number (SSN). An index on the SSN is more selective than an index on the city or last name. If the index statistics are not current, the query optimizer might not make the best choice for the current state of the table.

The query optimizer is important because it enables the database server to adjust dynamically to changing conditions in the database without requiring input from the developer or administrator of the application. This enables developers to focus on developing the query and trusting that the query optimizer will build an efficient execution plan for the state of the database every time the statement is run.

To put it all together, the query engine performs the following steps:

1. The parser scans the SELECT statement and breaks it into logical units such as keywords, expressions, operators, and identifiers.

2. A query tree, sometimes referred to as a sequence tree, is built describing the logical steps needed to transform the source data into the format required by the result set.

3. The query optimizer analyzes different ways the source tables can be accessed. It then selects the series of steps that returns the results the most quickly while using fewer resources. The query tree is updated to record this exact series of steps. The final, optimized version of the query tree is called the execution plan.

4. The relational engine starts executing the execution plan. As the steps that require data from the base tables are processed, the relational engine requests that the storage engine pass up data from the rowsets requested from the relational engine.

5. The relational engine processes the data returned from the storage engine into the format defined for the result set and returns the result set to the client.

The basic steps described for processing a SELECT statement apply to other SQL statements such as INSERT, UPDATE, and DELETE. UPDATE and DELETE statements both have to target the set of rows to be modified or deleted. The process of identifying these rows is the same process used to identify the source rows that contribute to the result set of a SELECT statement. The UPDATE and INSERT statements might both contain embedded SELECT statements that provide the data values to be updated or inserted.

SQL Server 2005 has a pool of memory that is used to store both execution plans and buffers. The percentage of the pool allocated to either execution plans or data buffers f ates dynamically, depending on the state of the system. The part of the memory pool t used to store execution plans is referred to as the procedure cache.

One important aspect of the query execution steps is the fact that once the "best" query is generated, it is stored in procedure cache so that subsequent executions of the query d have to generate the plan.

Query Plan Cache and Retrieval

SQL Server 2005 execution plans have two main components: the *query plan* and the *tion context*, as shown in Figure B-13.

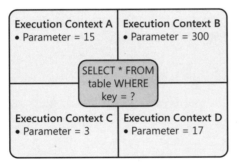

Figure B-13   The SQL Server 2005 Query Execution Plan Architecture

The purpose of these components is as follows:

- Query Plan. The bulk of the execution plan is a re-entrant, read-only data structure by any number of users. This is referred to as the query plan. No user context is s in the query plan. There are never more than one or two copies of the query p memory: one copy for all serial executions, and another for all parallel execution parallel copy covers all parallel executions, regardless of their degree of parallelism

- Execution Context. Each user that is currently executing the query has a data stru that holds the data specific to their execution, such as parameter values. This data ture is referred to as the execution context. The execution context data structur reused. If a user executes a query and one of the structures is not being used, it is tialized with the context for the new user.

When any SQL statement is executed in SQL Server 2005, the query engine first through the procedure cache to verify that an existing execution plan for the same SQL ment exists. SQL Server 2005 reuses any existing plan it finds, saving the overhead of r piling the SQL statement. If no existing execution plan exists, SQL Server 2005 generates a new execution plan for the query.

SQL Server 2005 has an efficient algorithm to find any existing execution plans for any specific SQL statement. In most systems, the minimal resources that are used by this scan are less than the resources that are saved by being able to reuse existing plans instead of compiling every SQL statement.

One of the problems with the cache architecture that the SQL Server query engine uses for execution plan storage is that memory is a finite resource. To ensure that the procedure cache memory is utilized in the most effective manner, the query engine must manage the lifetime of query plans stored in procedure cache.

Procedure Cache Storage Management

After an execution plan is generated, it stays in the procedure cache. SQL Server 2005 ages old, unused plans out of the cache only when additional memory is required. Each query plan and execution context has an associated cost factor that indicates how expensive the structure is to compile. These plans also have an age field. Every time the object is referenced by a connection, the age field is incremented by the compilation cost factor. For example, if a query plan has a cost factor of 10 and is referenced two times, its age becomes 20. The lazy writer process periodically scans the list of objects in the procedure cache. The lazy writer then decrements the age field of each object by one on each scan. It will take 20 passes of the lazy writer process to age out a plan with an age of 20. The lazy writer process deallocates an object if the following conditions are met:

- The memory manager requires memory and all available memory is currently being used.
- The age field for the object is 0.
- The object is not currently referenced by a connection.

Because the age field is incremented every time an object is referenced, frequently referenced objects do not have their age fields decremented to 0 and are not aged from the cache. Objects infrequently referenced are soon eligible for deallocation, but are not actually deallocated unless memory is required for other objects.

Certain changes in a database can cause an execution plan to be either inefficient or invalid, based on the new state of the database. The query engine detects the changes that invalidate an execution plan and marks the plan as not valid. A new plan must then be recompiled for the next connection that executes the query. The conditions that cause a new plan to be created are:

- Schema changes made to a table or view referenced by the query
- Changes to any indexes used by the execution plan
- Updates on statistics used by the execution plan, generated either explicitly from a ment, such as UPDATE STATISTICS, or generated automatically
- Dropping an index used by the execution plan
- An explicit call to sp_recompile
- Large numbers of changes to index keys
- For tables with triggers, if the number of rows in the inserted or deleted tables significantly
- Executing a stored procedure using the WITH RECOMPILE option (which mear stored procedure won't take advantage of the procedure cache)

Most recompilations are required either for statement correctness or to obtain poter faster query execution plans.

In previous versions of SQL Server, whenever a statement within a batch causes recor tion, the whole batch, whether submitted through a stored procedure, trigger, ad-hoc bat prepared statement, is recompiled. In SQL Server 2005, only the statement inside the that causes recompilation is recompiled. Because of this difference, recompilation cou SQL Server 2000 and SQL Server 2005 are not comparable. Also, there are more ty recompilations in SQL Server 2005 because of its expanded feature set.

Statement-level recompilation benefits performance because, in most cases, a small num statements causes recompilations and their associated penalties, in terms of CPU tim locks. These penalties are therefore avoided for the other statements in the batch that c have to be recompiled.

The SQL Server Profiler *SP:Recompile* trace event reports statement-level recompilatic SQL Server 2005. This trace event reports only batch recompilations in previous versior can lead to confusion if not examined closely. Also, in SQL Server 2005, the TextData cc of this event is populated so that more information is returned by the trace.

SQL Server 2005 also adds a new trace event called *SQL:StmtRecompile* that reports ment-level recompilations. This trace event can be used to track and debug recompila Whereas *SP:Recompile* generates only for stored procedures and triggers, *SQL:StmtRecc* generates for stored procedures, triggers, ad-hoc batches, batches that are executed by sp_executesql, prepared queries, and dynamic SQL.

The following profiler trace events are relevant for observing and debugging plan caching, compilation, and recompilation behaviors:

- Cursors: CursorRecompile. Useful for observing recompilations caused by cursor-related batches.

- Objects: Auto Stats. Useful for observing the statistics updates caused by SQL Server's "auto-stats" feature.

- Performance: Show Plan All For Query Compile. Useful for tracing batch compilations. It does not distinguish between a compilation and a recompilation. It produces show-plan data in textual format

- Performance: Show Plan XML For Query Compile. Useful for tracing batch compilations. It does not distinguish between a compilation and a recompilation. It produces showplan data in XML format

- Stored Procedures: SP:Recompile. Useful for detecting when a recompilation occurs.

See Chapter 8, "Improving Database Application Performance," for a more complete discussion of the SQL Server Profiler. For more information on how SQL Server 2005 caches query execution plans, see the TechNet article, "Batch Compilation, Recompilation, and Plan Caching Issues in SQL Server 2005" at *http://www.microsoft.com/technet/prodtechnol /sql/2005/recomp.mspx*.

You can use the following query to list all query plans that are currently cached by the query engine and how often they are used:

```
SELECT
    cacheobjtype,
    objtype,
    pagesused,
    usecounts,
    sd.[name],
    sql
FROM sys.syscacheobjects so
JOIN sys.sysdatabases sd
ON so.dbid = sd.dbid;
```

The output of this query returns a result set with one row for each object, as well as some statistical information on how the object is used. The query also returns the SQL Statement that was used to generate the plan. This can be very helpful when examining which queries are most frequently run on a busy system.

SQL Server 2005 caches query plans for a variety of statement types submitted to it for e
tion. Query plan caching causes query plan reuse, avoids compilation penalty, and u
plan cache better. Some coding practices hinder query plan caching and reuse, and the
should be avoided. (This is unlike previous versions of SQL Server, where hints were the
way to ensure the optimizer was doing its job.) SQL Server detects opportunities for
plan reuse. In particular, query plans can become non-reusable for two reasons: Schema
object appearing in a query plan can change, thereby making the plan invalid; and d
tables, referred to by a query plan, can change enough to make a plan sub-optimal. SQL S
detects these two classes of conditions at query execution time and recompiles a bat
pieces of it as necessary. Bad T-SQL coding practices can increase recompilation freq
and adversely affect SQL Server's performance.

SQL Server 2005 Index Internals

It doesn't generally help database developers to have an in-depth understanding of the
engine or the storage engine without also having an in-depth understanding of how d
tables is indexed and how those index structures affect query performance.

There are two types of indexes in SQL Server. In NonClustered indexes, the data in the
is a pointer to the actual data, as shown in Figure B-14. In Clustered indexes, the data s
in the table column is physically stored in the index page, as shown in Figure B-15.

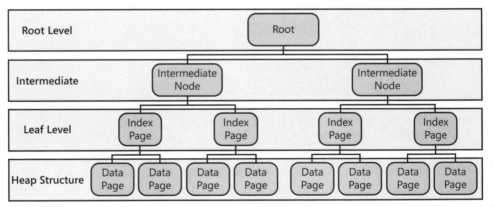

Figure B-14   The SQL Server 2005 NonClustered Index Structure

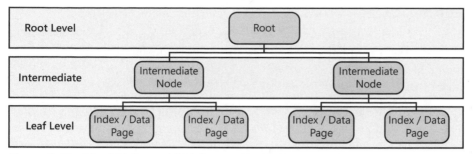

Figure B-15   The SQL Server 2005 Clustered Index Structure

As discussed earlier, the most basic unit of storage in SQL Server is a data page. Data pages are organized into extents, and extents are referenced by tables. In SQL Server 2005, tables are organized into one or more partitions, and each partition is stored in either a heap, which is simply a non-grouped data page, or clustered index structure. (See Chapter 7, "Optimizing SQL Server 2005 Performance," Lesson 2, "Optimizing Index Strategies," for more information on indexes.) The pages within the heap or clustered index structure are organized into allocation units, depending on the type of data contained within the row of data. (For example, TEXT and IMAGE data are stored in different allocation units than VARCHAR data.)

Server 2005 Index Organization

SQL Server 2005 supports a single Clustered Index per table and up to 249 NonClustered indexes per table. Indexes in SQL Server 2005 utilize a structure known as a Balanced Tree (B-Tree). A B-Tree structure is a structure where navigating from the root of the structure to any point should take exactly the same number of intermediate steps no matter what end point is chosen. Each page in an index B-tree is called an index node. The top node of the B-tree is called the root node. The bottom level of nodes in the index is called the leaf nodes. Any index levels between the root and the leaf nodes are collectively known as intermediate levels. In a clustered index, the leaf nodes contain the data pages of the underlying table. The root and intermediate level nodes contain index pages holding index rows. Each index row contains a key value and a pointer to either an intermediate-level page in the B-tree, or a data row in the leaf level of the index. The pages in each level of the index are linked in a doubly linked list. Data is either organized into a Clustered Index or a Heap.

Heap Structures

A heap is a table without a clustered index. Heaps have one row in sys.partitions, index_id = 0 for each partition used by the heap. By default, a heap has a single part When a heap has multiple partitions, each partition has a heap structure that contair data for that specific partition.

Depending on the data types in the heap, each heap structure will have one or more alloc units to store and manage the data for a specific partition. At a minimum, each heap will one IN_ROW_DATA allocation unit per partition. The heap will also have one LOB_I allocation unit per partition, if it contains large object (LOB) columns. It will also hav ROW_OVERFLOW_DATA allocation unit per partition, if it contains variable-length col that exceed the 8,060-byte row size limit.

The column first_iam_page in the sys.system_internals_allocation_units system view p to the first Index Allocation Map (IAM) page in the chain of IAM pages that manage the allocated to the heap in a specific partition. SQL Server 2005 uses the IAM pages to through the heap. The data pages and the rows within them are not in any specific orde are not linked. The only logical connection between data pages is the information recorc the IAM pages.

Table scans or serial reads of a heap can be performed by scanning the IAM pages to fir extents that are holding pages for the heap. Because the IAM represents extents in the order that they exist in the data files, this means that serial heap scans progress sequer through each file. Using the IAM pages to set the scan sequence also means that rows fro heap are not typically returned in the order in which they were inserted.

Clustered Index Structures

Clustered indexes have one row in sys.partitions, with index_id = 1 for each partition us the index. By default, a clustered index has a single partition. When a clustered index ha: tiple partitions, each partition has a B-tree structure that contains the data for that specifi tition. For example, if a clustered index has four partitions, there are four B-tree struc one in each partition.

Depending on the data types in the clustered index, each clustered index structure wil one or more allocation units in which to store and manage the data for a specific partiti a minimum, each clustered index will have one IN_ROW_DATA allocation unit per par The clustered index will also have one LOB_DATA allocation unit per partition if it cor large object (LOB) columns. It will also have one ROW_OVERFLOW_DATA allocatior per partition if it contains variable-length columns that exceed the 8,060-byte row size

The pages in the data chain and the rows in them are ordered on the value of the clustered index key. All inserts are made at the point where the key value in the inserted row fits in the ordering sequence among existing rows.

For a clustered index, the root_page column in sys.system_internals_allocation_units points to the top of the clustered index for a specific partition. SQL Server moves down the index to find the row corresponding to a clustered index key. To find a range of keys, SQL Server moves through the index to find the starting key value in the range and then scans through the data pages using the previous or next pointers. To find the first page in the chain of data pages, SQL Server follows the leftmost pointers from the root node of the index.

Non-Clustered Index Structures

Non-clustered indexes are very similar in structure to clustered indexes with the following key differences:

- The data rows of the underlying table are not sorted and stored in order based on their non-clustered keys.
- The leaf layer of a non-clustered index is made up of index pages instead of data pages.

non-clustered indexes can be defined on a table or view with a clustered index or a heap. Each index row in the non-clustered index contains the non-clustered key value and a row locator. This locator points to the data row in the clustered index or heap having the key value.

The row locators in non-clustered index rows are either a pointer to a row or are a clustered index key for a row, as explained below:

- If the table is a heap, which means it does not have a clustered index, the row locator is a pointer to the row. The pointer is built from the file identifier (ID), page number, and number of the row on the page. The whole pointer is known as a Row ID (RID).
- If the table has a clustered index, or the index is on an indexed view, the row locator is the clustered index key for the row. If the clustered index is not a unique index, SQL Server 2005 makes any duplicate keys unique by adding an internally generated value called a uniqueifier. This four-byte value is not visible to users. It is only added when required to make the clustered key unique for use in non-clustered indexes. SQL Server retrieves the data row by searching the clustered index using the clustered index key stored in the leaf row of the non-clustered index.

Non-clustered indexes have one row in sys.partitions with index_id >1 for each partition by the index. By default, a non-clustered index has a single partition. When a non-clus index has multiple partitions, each partition has a B-tree structure that contains the rows for that specific partition. For example, if a non-clustered index has four partitions, are four B-tree structures, with one in each partition.

Depending on the data types in the non-clustered index, each non-clustered index stru will have one or more allocation units in which to store and manage the data for a specifi tition. At a minimum, each non-clustered index will have one IN_ROW_DATA allocatio per partition that stores the index B-tree pages. The NonClustered index will also hav LOB_DATA allocation unit per partition if it contains large object (LOB) columns. Additic it will have one ROW_OVERFLOW_DATA allocation unit per partition if it contains var length columns that exceed the 8,060-byte row size limit. For more information about a tion units, see Table and Index Organization at *http://msdn2.microsoft.com/en-us/l /ms189051.aspx*. The page collections for the B-tree are anchored by root_page pointers sys.system_internals_allocation_units system view.

Included Columns Index

In SQL Server 2005, you can extend the functionality of non-clustered indexes by adding key columns to the leaf level of the non-clustered index. By including non-key column can create non-clustered indexes that cover more queries. This is because the non-ke umns have the following benefits:

- They can be data types not permitted as index key columns.
- They are not considered by the database engine when calculating the number of key columns or index key size.

An index with included non-key columns can significantly improve query performance all columns in the query are included in the index either as key or non-key columns. F mance gains are achieved because the query optimizer can locate all the column values v the index; table or clustered index data is not accessed, resulting in fewer disk I/O opera

Understanding the physical structure of indexes in SQL Server 2005 helps database de ers to optimize both the creation and use of proper indexes specific to their application

Optimizing Index Structures

One of the biggest challenges database developers face is how to optimize their indexes to obtain the most efficient query response. When developing indexes for database applications, the following guidelines should be considered:

- Always look at the query plan first. It will show you the optimal current execution plan from the query engine's point of view. Find the most expensive part of the execution plan and start optimizing from there. However, even before that, make sure that the statistics on all tables in your query are up-to-date by running the update statistics command on all tables in your query.

- If you see table scan, optimize. Table scan is the slowest possible way of execution. Table scan means not only that no index is used, but that there is no clustered index for this table at all. Even if you can only replace table scan with clustered index scan, it is still worth it.

- If you see clustered index scan, find out whether it can be replaced with index seek. For that, find the conditions applied to this table. Usually, conditions exist for two or three fields of the table. Find out the most selective condition (that is, the condition that would produce the smallest number of records if applied alone), and see whether an index on this field exists. Any index that lists this field first will qualify. If there is no such index, create it and see whether the query engine picks it up.

- If the query engine is not picking up the existing index (that is, if it is still doing a clustered index scan), check the output list. It is possible that seek on your index is faster than clustered index scan, but involves bookmark lookup that makes the combined cost greater than use of a clustered index. Clustered index operations (scan or seek) never need bookmark lookup, because a clustered index already contains all the data. If the output list is not big, add those fields to the index and see whether the query engine picks it up. Please remember that the combined size is more important than the number of fields. Adding three integer fields to the index is less expensive than adding one *varchar* field with an average data length of 20.

- If you see bookmark lookup, it means that your index is not covering. Try to make it covering if it makes sense. (See the preceding bullet.) The execution plan selected by the query engine might not be the best one. The query engine makes certain assumptions about disk subsystem and CPU cost versus IO cost. These assumptions can sometimes be incorrect. If you don't believe that the query engine's selection is the best one, run a query in the loop for 10 to 15 minutes with automatic selection, change the query to use your index (you will have to use index hint to force it), and then run it for 10 to 15 minutes again. Compare the results to see which one works better.

- Avoid any calculations or operations on the columns where possible. Some opera
will prevent the use of the index on this field even if it exists—for example, usin
LTRIM or *RTRIM* functions on string data will seriously affect performance. For exa
instead of using the condition cast (DateField as varchar(20)) = @dateString, try tc
vert @dateString to an expression of datetime type first, and then compare it to
Field. When it is not possible to avoid functions or calculations on the column, u
index built on that expression. This can be done in two ways:
  - Create a calculated field based on your expression.
  - Create a view and build an index on it.

Indexed views are a good way to further increase the speed of the query if you are not sat
with the results. Indexed view is a clustered index built over the view's select list. You car
define additional indexes for the indexed view, just as you can for any regular table. Inc
views take disk space and have some maintenance overhead (every time underlying t
change, the indexed view also has to change), but they usually provide a good boost in p
mance, even after all other optimization techniques are exhausted.

Full-Text Indexes

A full-text index is another type of index used in SQL Server 2005. Full-text indexes
from "normal" SQL Server indexes because they are stored outside the confines of the
base storage engine. Full-text search facilitates fast and flexible indexing for keyword-t
query of text data stored in a SQL Server database. Unlike the T-SQL LIKE predicate, v
only works on character patterns, full-text queries perform a linguistic search agains
data, operating on words and phrases based on rules of a particular language.

The performance benefit of using full-text search can be best realized when querying ag
a large amount of unstructured text data. A T-SQL LIKE query against millions of rows o
data can take minutes to return; whereas, a full-text query can take only seconds o
against the same data, depending on the number of rows that are returned.

Full-text indexes might be built not just on columns that contain text data, but also ag
formatted binary data, such as Microsoft Word documents, stored in a BLOB-type colun
these cases, it is not possible to use the LIKE predicate for keyword queries.

With the growing popularity of storing and managing textual data in a database, ful
indexes have become more common. Common uses of full-text search include Web-t
applications, document-management systems, and other applications that need to pr
text-search capabilities over data stored in a SQL Server database.

The full-text engine for SQL Server is what enables SQL Server 2005 to utilize full-text indexes. This engine is in turn built on Microsoft Search technology and is tightly integrated into the SQL Server 2005 Database Engine. For more information on the full-text search engine or full-text indexes, see the MSDN article "SQL Server 2005 Full Text Search: Internals and Enhancements" at *http://msdn2.microsoft.com/en-us/library/ms345119.aspx.*

L Indexes

XML index is another new index type that developers need to be aware of in SQL Server 2005. SQL Server 2005 introduced the *XML* data type that can be used to store structured and unstructured XML data within a column in a SQL Server database. XML documents can be very large. (SQL Server can store up to 2GB in an XML column.) XML data can be queried using new XQuery functionality in SQL Server 2005. To return results efficiently, SQL Server 2005 now supports a special type of index known as an XML index.

XML indexes are broken down into two types:

- Primary XML Index. A primary XML index is a representation of the nodes in the XML data stored in the column. Primary XML indexes are physically stored as additional rows in the XML column. A primary XML index is very similar in function and structure to a Clustered index.
- Secondary XML Index. A secondary XML index is an additional index that is either created on the *PATH, PROPERTY,* or *VALUE* nodes within the primary XML index. Secondary XML indexes are very similar in function and structure to a NonClustered index.

Primary XML Indexes

The primary XML index is a shredded and persisted representation of the XML BLOBs in the *xml* data type column. For each XML binary large object (BLOB) in the column, the index creates several rows of data. The number of rows in the index is approximately equal to the number of nodes in the XML binary large object. Each row stores the following node information:

- Tag name, such as an element or attribute name.
- Node value.
- Node type, such as an element node, attribute node, or text node.
- Document order information, represented by an internal node identifier.
- Path from each node to the root of the XML tree. This column is searched for path expressions in the query.
- Primary key of the base table. The primary key of the base table is duplicated in the primary XML index to enable efficient join operations with the base table.

This node information is used to evaluate and construct XML results for a specified quer the purposes of optimization, the tag name and the node type information are stored a ger values.

The query processor uses the primary XML index for queries that involve *xml* data type ods and returns either scalar values or the XML subtrees from the primary index itself.

Secondary XML Indexes

If your queries generally specify path expressions on *xml* type columns, a PATH seco index might be able to speed up the search. As described earlier, the primary index is h when you have queries that specify the *exist()* method in the WHERE clause. If you PATH secondary index, you might also improve the search performance.

Although a primary XML index avoids having to shred the XML binary large objects a time, it might not provide the best performance for queries based on path expres Because all rows in the primary XML index corresponding to an XML BLOB are sea sequentially for large XML instances, the sequential search might be slow. In this case, h a secondary index built on the path values and node values in the primary index can s cantly speed up the index search. In the PATH secondary index, the path and node valu key columns that enable more efficient seeks when searching for paths.

If queries are value based, for example, /Root/ProductDescription/@*[. = "WidgetA"] or ductDescription[@Name = "Widget A"], and the path is not fully specified or it includes a card, you might obtain faster results by building a secondary XML index that is built on values in the primary XML index.

The key columns of the VALUE secondary index are (node value and path) of the pr XML index. If your workload involves querying for values from XML instances without ing the element or attribute names that contain the values, a VALUE secondary index be useful.

Queries that retrieve one or more values from individual XML instances might benefit f PROPERTY secondary index. This occurs when you retrieve object properties by usir *value()* method of the *xml* type and when the primary key value of the object is known PROPERTY secondary index is built on columns (PK, path, and node value) of the pr XML index, where PK is the primary key of the base table. For more information on indexes and their usage, see the MSDN Article "XML Indexes in SQL Server 2005"at h *msdn2.microsoft.com/en-us/library/ms345121.aspx.*

tabase Encryption

One of the major new features in SQL Server 2005 is the new security model for database encryption. Developers need to understand exactly how the new encryption model functions. One of the most common feature requests in earlier versions of SQL Server was for the ability to natively encrypt and decrypt data stored in the database. As SQL Server became more popular for online shopping and other data storage that required robust encryption techniques, Microsoft decided that it should be a functional part of SQL Server 2005.

The data encryption functionality in SQL Server 2005 is very closely compliant with the international X.509 v3 certificate standard, which means that any application built using X.509 certificate encryption can utilize SQL Server 2005's built-in encryption methods. The database encryption is built on a hierarchy of certificates, keys, and data, as shown in Figure B-16.

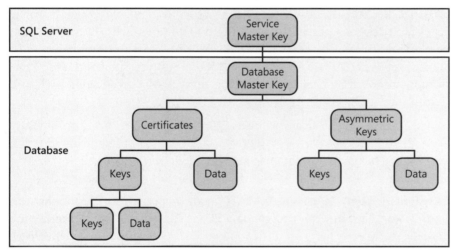

Figure B-16   The SQL Server 2005 database encryption hierarchy

tificates

A public key certificate is a digitally signed object that binds the value of a public key to the identity of the person, device, or service that holds the corresponding private key. Certificates are issued and signed by a certification authority (CA). The entity that receives a certificate from a CA is the subject of that certificate. Certificates contain the following information:

- The public key of the subject.
- The identifier information of the subject, such as the name and e-mail address.

- The validity period. This is the length of time that the certificate is considered va
  certificate is valid only for the period of time specified within it; every certificate cor
  Valid From and Valid To dates. These dates set the boundaries of the validity p(
  When the validity period for a certificate has passed, a new certificate must be requ
  by the subject of the now-expired certificate.
- Issuer identifier information.
- The digital signature of the issuer. This signature attests to the validity of the bi
  between the public key and the identifier information of the subject.

A primary benefit of certificates is that they relieve hosts of the need to maintain a set of
words for individual subjects. Instead, the host merely establishes trust in a certificate is

When a host, such as a secure Web server, designates an issuer as a trusted root authorit
host implicitly trusts the policies that the issuer has used to establish the bindings of c
cates it issues. In effect, the host trusts that the issuer has verified the identity of the certi
subject. A host designates an issuer as a trusted root authority by putting the self-signe
tificate of the issuer, which contains the public key of the issuer, into the trusted root c
cation authority certificate store of the host computer. Intermediate or subord
certification authorities are trusted only if they have a valid certification path from a tr
root certification authority.

The issuer can revoke a certificate before it expires. Revocation cancels the binding of a p
key to an identity that is asserted in the certificate. Each issuer maintains a certificate-re
tion list that can be used by programs when they are checking the validity of any given
icate. SQL Server 2005 encryption uses the following key types for encryption:

- **Asymmetric keys**   An asymmetric key is made up of a private key and the correspor
  public key. Each key can decrypt data encrypted by the other. Asymmetric encry
  and decryption are fairly expensive operations, but they provide a higher level of se(
  than symmetric encryption. An asymmetric key can be used to encrypt a symmetr
  for storage in a database.
- **Symmetric keys**   A symmetric key is one key that is used for both encryptior
  decryption. Encryption and decryption by using a symmetric key is fast and is su
  for routine use with sensitive data in the database.

figuring SQL Server for SSL

One of the most common uses of certificate-based security in SQL Server 2005 is configuring and utilizing Secure Sockets Layer (SSL) communication between clients and the server. SQL Server 2005 can use SSL to encrypt data that is transmitted across a network between an instance of SQL Server and a client application. The SSL encryption is performed within the protocol layer and is available to all SQL Server clients.

SSL can be used for server validation when a client connection requests encryption. If the instance of SQL Server is running on a computer that has been assigned a certificate from a public certification authority, identity of the computer and the instance of SQL Server is vouched for by the chain of certificates that lead to the trusted root authority. Such server validation requires that the computer on which the client application is running be configured to trust the root authority of the certificate that is used by the server. Encryption with a self-signed certificate is possible, but a self-signed certificate offers only limited protection.

Enabling SSL encryption increases the security of data transmitted across networks between instances of SQL Server and applications. However, enabling encryption does slow performance. When all traffic between SQL Server and a client application is encrypted using SSL, the following additional processing is required:

- An extra network round-trip is required at connect time.
- Packets sent from the application to the instance of SQL Server must be encrypted by the client Net-Library and decrypted by the server Net-Library.
- Packets sent from the instance of SQL Server to the application must be encrypted by the server Net-Library and decrypted by the client Net-Library.

For SQL Server to utilize certificates for SSL encryption, they must be valid and must meet the following conditions:

- The certificate must be in either the local computer certificate store or the current user certificate store.
- The current system time must be after the Valid From property of the certificate and before the Valid To property of the certificate.
- The certificate must be meant for server authentication. This requires the Enhanced Key Usage property of the certificate to specify Server Authentication (1.3.6.1.5.5.7.3.1).

- The certificate must be created by using the KeySpec option of AT_KEYEXCHA
  Usually, the certificate's key usage property (KEY_USAGE) will also include key
  pherment (CERT_KEY_ENCIPHERMENT_KEY_USAGE).
- The Subject property of the certificate must indicate that the common name (CN)
  same as the host name or fully qualified domain name (FQDN) of the server com
  If SQL Server is running on a failover cluster, the common name must match the
  name or FQDN of the virtual server and the certificates must be provisioned on all
  in the failover cluster.

To configure SQL Server to use SSL, you must perform the following steps in order:

- Install a valid certificate into the certificate store of the SQL Server machine.
- Start the SQL Server Configuration Manager, as shown in Figure B-17.

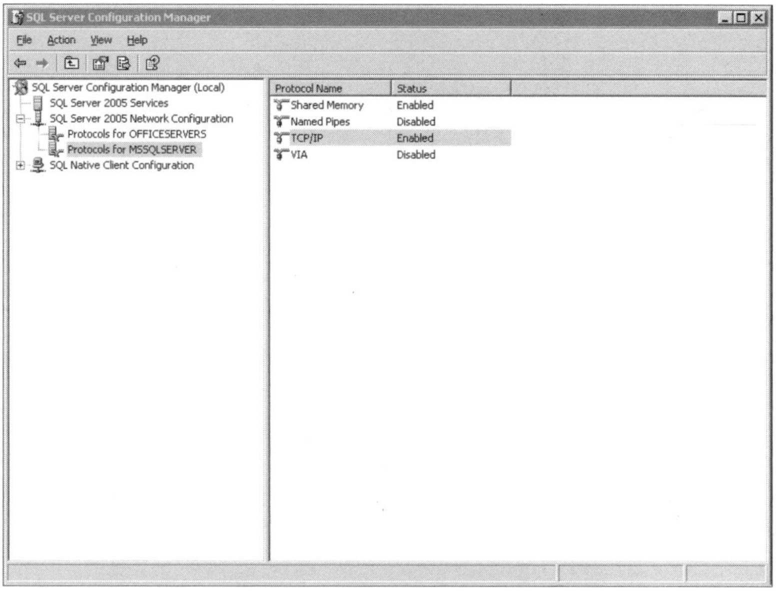

Figure B-17   Using the SQL Server Configuration Manager

- Expand the SQL Server 2005 Network Configuration node, right-click on the *Pro*
  node.

■ Select the certificate you want to use from the Certificate drop-down list box and click OK, as shown in Figure B-18.

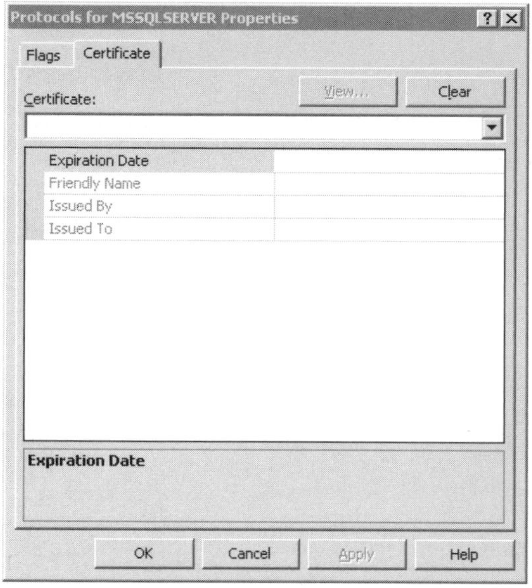

Figure B-18 Using the SQL Server Configuration Manager to install a certificate

Once SQL Server is configured for SSL communications, clients can be configured to support encrypted communication between them and the SQL Server, ensuring that the data transmitted is secure.

ossary

application programming interface (API)
Represents a set of functions and methods that other developers can use to access the functionality within another application.

asynchronous processing Considered an efficient way of processing, asynchronous processing allows operations to perform in parallel.

authentication Process of verifying the identity for both the sender and receiver of a message. Once the user has been validated, they are considered authenticated.

caching Process of storing data into a cache object until it is needed again. The cache object is an in-memory representation of the data that can serve as the data source for Web page and Microsoft Windows form objects.

catalog view Contains metadata about objects found in a SQL Server instance.

catch If an error occurs while within a *try* block, the execution control is transferred to the *catch* block adjacent to the *try* block.

check constraint A database object that can be applied to columns to enforce domain integrity.

class identifier (CLSID) Represents a unique, read-only identifier that is used to identify an object. In the windows registry, the CLSID is used to identify a specific program.

clustered index An index whose leaf level is the actual data page of the table.

constraint A database object that can be applied to tables to enforce different types of data integrity.

cubes Used with online analytical processing (OLAP), data cubes are multidimensional structures built from one or more tables in a relational database(s).

data definition language (DDL) A component of structured query language (SQL) used to create and delete databases and database objects such as tables and indexes.

data partitioning Process of moving data from a single server to one or more different data repositories. This can be vertical, in which data from a single table is split into multiple tables, or horizontal, in which the number of rows in a table are restricted and partitioned by one or more columns.

data source name (DSN) Refers to the logical name of an open database connectivity (ODBC) data source. The data source name identifies connection information and the correct driver to utilize.

data stewardship Necessary for resolving conflicts in peer-to-peer replication, data stewardship involves assigning an owner to data that resides on multiple servers and creating rules for how the data should be updated.

data warehousing database Structure that is used to store large amounts of data in a format that is easily accessible. Typically, data is stored in a multidimensional format in which users can drill down into the data.

deadlock Occurs when multiple connections that hold locks are waiting for locks to be released that are held by the other transactions, that is, the transactions are waiting for each other to release locks.

dimensions A collection of attributes used to describe the data within an OLAP cube. Dimensions are helpful to users trying to browse data within a cube.

dirty row When discussing transaction isolation levels, a dirty read has occurred if data that has not yet been committed by one transaction is read by another transaction.

distributed queries This type of query is used to retrieve data from multiple heterogeneous data sources using the OLE DB data provider.

estimated query cost Estimated query cost is a metric used to measure query performance.

extended markup language (XML) Simple and flexible text format used to represent data. XML was designed by the World Wide Web Consortium (W3C).

federation Represents a group of servers that cooperate in order to share data that is dispersed among those servers. The purpose of a federation is to share the load of an application across multiple servers.

foreign key constraint A database object that enforces data reference integrity between (or within) tables.

mining model Built from a mining structure, the mining model applies an algorithm to the data and processes it so that predictions can be made.

mining structure Used to describe that data from which a mining model will be built. This data can come from one or more relational or multidimensional data sources.

named instances Represent additional instances of SQL Server; used to uniquely identify the instance.

network library Set of dynamic link library (DLL) files that support a particular network protocol and allow you to pass data across the network through packets.

network protocol Represents a set of ru used to facilitate communication betw applications across a network. The rule specify how the applications perform authentication, detect errors, and send sages to each other.

non-clustered index An index whose le level stores only the columns included index (key columns and included colu and holds pointers to the rows in the table.

non-trusted constraints Constraints th not guaranteed to have verified the da integrity for all rows in a table.

normalization Logical design process in which data is separated into multiple, related tables. The process allows data to perform optimally.

object linking and embedding (OLE DB) Interface designed by Microsoft to effic access diverse data sources. OLE DB c sists of several COM interfaces, which e data providers to access each data sou

online analytical processing (OLAP) Pro whereby raw data is stored in a multid sional format so that it can be analyze ily by decision-makers.

open database connectivity (ODBC) Int face used to provide access to data sou that provide an ODBC driver. The driv software file that provides instructions how to access the data source.

performance baseline Represents a cha log that is used to mark an application it was performing satisfactorily. This b line can be compared to logs captured the application is performing poorly to tify the problem area.

phantom read A phantom read (or pha row) describes the occurrence of data returned by a statement in a transactic which was not returned by an earlier s ment (with the same WHERE clause) within the same transaction.

primary key constraint   A database object that enforces value uniqueness for one or more columns in a table. Used to enforce entity integrity.

proxy code   Code used to call a Web service. The proxy represents a local object with the same interface as the Web service itself.

pseudo code   Used to represent actual code as real English. This simplifies the code and makes it easier to read.

read locks   In SQL Server, this is equal to shared locks.

replication   Process of copying data and database objects from one data source to another across a network. This is done to synchronize two databases or to maintain a remote copy of a database

rule   A database object that can be applied to columns or alias data types to enforce domain integrity. Is deprecated and should not be used.

scalability   Used to indicate that an application can handle an increased workload to accommodate a growing number of users. Scalability is accomplished by either scaling up (by increasing the hardware capacity of the current server) or scaling out, (by increasing the number of servers).

scalar function   User-defined function in which a single data value is returned, such as a string or an integer.

schema stability lock   A table-level lock taken to assert that a table's schema cannot be changed while the lock is held.

searchable arguments   Refers to the WHERE portion of a SELECT query in which a column is compared to a variable or a constant value. The query optimizer uses the searchable argument to determine the optimal execution path.

secure sockets layer (SSL)   To secure communications across the network, SSL certificates can be registered for a socket, which is an IP address and port.

Simple Object Access Protocol (SOAP)   Designed by the World Wide Web Consortium (W3C), this transport protocol provides a standard way to send messages between applications using XML.

storage area network (SAN) protocol   This new protocol available with SQL Server 2005 allows you to cluster together multiple servers to provide high availability to your database applications.

table-valued function   User-defined function in which a table is returned as a result, as opposed to a single data value.

try   If an error occurs while within a *try* block, the execution control is transferred to the *catch* block adjacent to the *try* block.

unique constraint   A database object that enforces value uniqueness for one or more columns in a table. Used to enforce entity integrity.

dex

Additional SQL Server Resources for Administrators

Published and Forthcoming Titles from Microsoft Press

Microsoft® SQL Server™ 2005 Reporting Services *Step by Step*
Hitachi Consulting Services • ISBN 0-7356-2250-7

SQL Server Reporting Services (SRS) is Microsoft's customizable reporting solution for business data analysis. It is one of the key value features of SQL Server 2005: functionality more advanced and much less expensive than its competition. SRS is powerful, so an understanding of how to architect a report, as well as how to install and program SRS, is key to harnessing the full functionality of SQL Server. This procedural tutorial shows how to use the Report Project Wizard, how to think about and access data, and how to build queries. It also walks the reader through the creation of charts and visual layouts to enable maximum visual understanding of the data analysis. Interactivity (enhanced in SQL Server 2005) and security are also covered in detail.

Microsoft SQL Server 2005 Administrator's Pocket Consultant
William R. Stanek • ISBN 0-7356-2107-1

Here's the utterly practical, pocket-sized reference for IT professionals who need to administer, optimize, and maintain SQL Server 2005 in their organizations. This unique guide provides essential details for using SQL Server 2005 to help protect and manage your company's data—whether automating tasks; creating indexes and views; performing backups and recovery; replicating transactions; tuning performance; managing server activity; importing and exporting data; or performing other key tasks. Featuring quick-reference tables, lists, and step-by-step instructions, this handy, one-stop guide provides fast, accurate answers on the spot, whether you're at your desk or in the field!

Microsoft SQL Server 2005 Administrat◀ Companion
Marci Frohock Garcia, Edward Whalen, and Mitchell Schroeter • ISBN 0-7356-2198-5

Microsoft SQL Server 2005 Administrator's Companic comprehensive, in-depth guide that saves time by p the technical information you need to deploy, admin mize, and support SQL Server 2005. Using a hands-on rich approach, this authoritative, one-volume referer provides expert advice, product information, detaile procedures, and real-world troubleshooting tips from enced SQL Server 2005 professionals. This expert guic you how to design high-availability database system for installation, install and configure SQL Server 2005, services and features, and maintain and troubleshoc database system. It covers how to configure your sys your I/O system and model and optimize system cap The expert authors provide details on how to create defaults, constraints, rules, indexes, views, functions, procedures, and triggers. This guide shows you how administer reporting services, analysis services, notif services, and integration services. It also provides a ◀ of information on replication and the specifics of sn◀ transactional, and merge replication. Finally, there is coverage of how to manage and tune your SQL Serv including automating tasks, backup and restoration bases, and management of users and security.

Microsoft SQL Server 2005 Analysis Ser *Step by Step*
Hitachi Consulting Services • ISBN 0-7356-21◀

One of the key features of SQL Server 2005 is SQL S◀ Analysis Services—Microsoft's customizable analysis business data modeling and interpretation. Just com Server Analysis Services to its competition to unders the great value of its enhanced features. One of the harnessing the full functionality of SQL Server will b◀ Analysis Services for the powerful tool that it is—inc creating a cube, and deploying, customizing, and ex basic calculations. This step-by-step tutorial discusse get started, how to build scalable analytical applica◀ how to use and administer advanced features. Intera (which is enhanced in SQL Server 2005), data transla security are also covered in detail.

Microsoft SQL Server 2005 Express Edition
Step by Step
Jackie Goldstein • ISBN 0-7356-2184-5

Inside Microsoft SQL Server 2005:
The Storage Engine
Kalen Delaney • ISBN 0-7356-2105-5

Inside Microsoft SQL Server 2005:
T-SQL Programming
Itzik Ben-Gan • ISBN 0-7356-2197-7

Inside Microsoft SQL Server 2005:
Query Processing and Optimization
Kalen Delaney • ISBN 0-7356-2196-9

For more information about Microsoft Press® books and other learning products,
visit: **www.microsoft.com/mspress** *and* **www.microsoft.com/learning**

ditional SQL Server Resources for Developers
shed and Forthcoming Titles from Microsoft Press

crosoft® SQL Server™ 2005 Express Edition
p by Step
kie Goldstein ● ISBN 0-7356-2184-5

h yourself how to get data-
projects up and running
kly with SQL Server Express
on—a free, easy-to-use
base product that is based
QL Server 2005 technology.
lesigned for building simple,
amic applications, with all
rich functionality of the SQL
er database engine and
g the same data access APIs,
as Microsoft ADO.NET, SQL
ve Client, and T-SQL.
ther you're new to database
ramming or new to SQL Server, you'll learn how, when, and
to use specific features of this simple but powerful data-
development environment. Each chapter puts you to work,
ding your knowledge of core capabilities and guiding you
ou create actual components and working applications.

crosoft SQL Server 2005 Programming
p by Step
nando Guerrero ● ISBN 0-7356-2207-8

Server 2005 is Microsoft's
-generation data manage-
t and analysis solution that
ers enhanced scalability,
ability, and security features
terprise data and analytical
ications while making them
r to create, deploy, and
age. Now you can teach
self how to design, build, test,
by, and maintain SQL Server
bases—one step at a time.
ad of merely focusing on
ribing new features, this book shows new database
rammers and administrators how to use specific features
n typical business scenarios. Each chapter provides a highly
ical learning experience that demonstrates how to build
base solutions to solve common business problems.

Microsoft SQL Server 2005 Analysis Services
Step by Step
Hitachi Consulting Services ● ISBN 0-7356-2199-3

One of the key features of SQL Server 2005 is SQL Server Analysis Services—Microsoft's customizable analysis solution for business data modeling and interpretation. Just compare SQL Server Analysis Services to its competition to understand the great value of its enhanced features. One of the keys to harnessing the full functionality of SQL Server will be leveraging Analysis Services for the powerful tool that it is—including creating a cube, and deploying, customizing, and extending the basic calcula- tions. This step-by-step tutorial discusses how to get started, how to build scalable analytical applications, and how to use and ad- minister advanced features. Interactivity (enhanced in SQL Server 2005), data translation, and security are also covered in detail.

Microsoft SQL Server 2005 Reporting Services
Step by Step
Hitachi Consulting Services ● ISBN 0-7356-2250-7

SQL Server Reporting Services (SRS) is Microsoft's customizable reporting solution for business data analysis. It is one of the key value features of SQL Server 2005: functionality more advanced and much less expensive than its competition. SRS is powerful, so an understanding of how to architect a report, as well as how to install and program SRS, is key to harnessing the full functional- ity of SQL Server. This procedural tutorial shows how to use the Report Project Wizard, how to think about and access data, and how to build queries. It also walks through the creation of charts and visual layouts for maximum visual understanding of data analysis. Interactivity (enhanced in SQL Server 2005) and security are also covered in detail.

Programming Microsoft SQL Server 2005
Andrew J. Brust, Stephen Forte, and William H. Zack
ISBN 0-7356-1923-9

This thorough, hands-on reference for developers and database administrators teaches the basics of programming custom appli- cations with SQL Server 2005. You will learn the fundamentals of creating database applications—including coverage of T-SQL, Microsoft .NET Framework, and Microsoft ADO.NET. In addition to practical guidance on database architecture and design, application development, and reporting and data analysis, this essential reference guide covers performance, tuning, and availability of SQL Server 2005.

---

le Microsoft SQL Server 2005:
Storage Engine
n Delaney ● ISBN 0-7356-2105-5

le Microsoft SQL Server 2005:
QL Programming
Ben-Gan ● ISBN 0-7356-2197-7

Inside Microsoft SQL Server 2005:
Query Processing and Optimization
Kalen Delaney ● ISBN 0-7356-2196-9

Programming Microsoft ADO.NET 2.0 Core Reference
David Sceppa ● ISBN 0-7356-2206-X

---

re information about Microsoft Press® books and other learning products,
www.microsoft.com/mspress *and* **www.microsoft.com/learning**

Press products are available worldwide wherever quality computer books are sold. For more information, contact your book or
retailer, software reseller, or local Microsoft Sales Office, or visit our Web site at **www.microsoft.com/mspress**. To locate your
urce for Microsoft Press products, or to order directly, call 1-800-MSPRESS in the United States. (In Canada, call **1-800-268-2222**.)

Additional Resources for Developers: Advanced Top and Best Practices

Published and Forthcoming Titles from Microsoft Press

Code Complete, Second Edition
Steve McConnell • ISBN 0-7356-1967-0

For more than a decade, Steve McConnell, one of the premier authors and voices in the software community, has helped change the way developers write code—and produce better software. Now his classic book, *Code Complete*, has been fully updated and revised with best practices in the art and science of constructing software. Topics include design, applying good techniques to construction, eliminating errors, planning, managing construction activities, and relating personal character to superior software. This new edition features fully updated information on programming techniques, including the emergence of Web-style programming, and integrated coverage of object-oriented design. You'll also find new code examples—both good and bad—in C++, Microsoft® Visual Basic®, C#, and Java, although the focus is squarely on techniques and practices.

More About Software Requirements: Thorny Issues and Practical Advice
Karl E. Wiegers • ISBN 0-7356-2267-1

Have you ever delivered software that satisfied all of the project specifications, but failed to meet any of the customers expectations? Without formal, verifiable requirements—and a system for managing them—the result is often a gap between what developers think they're supposed to build and what customers think they're going to get. Too often, lessons about software requirements engi-neering processes are formal or academic, and not of value to real-world, professional development teams. In this follow-up guide to *Software Requirements*, Second Edition, you will discover even more practical techniques for gathering and managing software requirements that help you deliver software that meets project and customer specifications. Succinct and immediately useful, this book is a must-have for developers and architects.

Software Estimation: Demystifying the I
Steve McConnell • ISBN 0-7356-0535-1

Often referred to as the "black art" because of its co and uncertainty, software estimation is not as hard or as people think. However, the art of how to create e and schedule estimates has not been very well publi *Software Estimation* provides a proven set of proced heuristics that software developers, technical leads, managers can apply to their projects. Instead of arca and rigid modeling techniques, award-winning auth McConnell gives practical guidance to help organiza achieve basic estimation proficiency and lay the gro continue improving project cost estimates. This bool avoid the more complex mathematical estimation a but the non-mathematical reader will find plenty of guidelines without getting bogged down in complex

Debugging, Tuning, and Testing Microsoft .NET 2.0 Applications
John Robbins • ISBN 0-7356-2202-7

Making an application the best it can be has long be consuming task best accomplished with specialized tools. With Microsoft Visual Studio® 2005, developer available a new range of built-in functionality that e them to debug their code quickly and efficiently, tur timum performance, and test applications to ensure ibility and trouble-free operation. In this accessible on book, debugging expert John Robbins shows de how to use the tools and functions in Visual Studio t advantage to ensure high-quality applications.

The Security Development Lifecycle
Michael Howard and Steve Lipner • ISBN 0-73

Adapted from Microsoft's standard development pr Security Development Lifecycle (SDL) is a methodolo helps reduce the number of security defects in code stage of the development process, from design to re book details each stage of the SDL methodology an its implementation across a range of Microsoft softwa Microsoft Windows Server™ 2003, Microsoft SQL Se Service Pack 3, and Microsoft Exchange Server 2003 Pack 1, to help measurably improve security feature direct access to insights from Microsoft's security tea lessons that are applicable to software development worldwide, whether on a small-scale or a large-scale includes a CD featuring videos of developer training

---

Software Requirements, Second Edition
Karl E. Wiegers • ISBN 0-7356-1879-8

Writing Secure Code, Second Edition
Michael Howard and David LeBlanc • ISBN 0-7356-1722-8

CLR via C#, Second Edition
Jeffrey Richter • ISBN 0-7356-2163-2

For more information about Microsoft Press® books and other learning products, visit: **www.microsoft.com/mspress** *and* **www.microsoft.com/learning**

System Requirements

We recommend that you use a test workstation, test server, or staging server to comple exercises in each lab. The following are the minimum system requirements your com needs to meet to complete the practice exercises in this book. For more information, s "Introduction."

Hardware Requirements

The following hardware is required to complete the lab exercises:

- Personal computer with a 600 MHz Pentium III compatible or faster processor
- 512 MB of RAM or more (1 GB or more recommended)
- 350 MB free hard disk space for the SQL Server installation
- 450 MB additional free hard disk space if you plan to install SQL Server Books (and sample databases
- CD-ROM drive or DVD-ROM drive
- Super VGA (1,024 x 768) or higher resolution video adapter and monitor
- Keyboard and Microsoft mouse or compatible pointing device

Software Requirements

The following software is required to complete the lab exercises:

- One of the following operating systems:
  - Microsoft Windows 2000 Server Service Pack 4 (SP4)
  - Windows 2000 Advanced Server SP4
  - Microsoft Windows Server 2003, Standard Edition SP1
  - Windows Server 2003, Enterprise Edition SP1
  - Windows Server 2003, Datacenter Edition SP1
- SQL Server 2005. A 180-day evaluation of SQL Server Enterprise Edition is incluc the companion DVD with this book and is available as a free download from the M Web site at *http://www.microsoft.com/sql/downloads/trial-software.mspx*.
- The *AdventureWorks* database; available as a separate download with the SQL Server samples from the Microsoft Downloads site at *http://www.microsoft.com/downloads*

- Visual Studio 2005 or Visual Studio 2005 SP1. A free 90-day evaluation of Visual Studio 2005 Professional Edition is available for download from the MSDN Web site at *http://msdn2.microsoft.com/en-us/vstudio/bb188238.aspx*. Visual Studio 2005 SP1 works with Visual Studio 2005 Standard Edition, Professional Edition, and Team Edition and is available from the Microsoft Downloads site.

- Microsoft Data Access Components (MDAC) 2.8; available for free download from *http://www.microsoft.com/downloads/details.aspx?FamilyID=6c050fe3-c795-4b7d-b037-185d0506396c&DisplayLang=en*.

- Microsoft Web Application Stress Tool; available for free download from *http://www.microsoft.com/downloads/details.aspx?familyid=E2C0585A-062A-439E-A67D-75A89AA36495&displaylang=en*.

- Microsoft Internet Explorer 6.0 SP1 or later.

- Internet Information Services (IIS) 5.0 or later.

What do you think of this book?

We want to hear from you!

Do you have a few minutes to participate in a brief online survey?

Microsoft is interested in hearing your feedback so we can continually improve our b and learning resources for you.

To participate in our survey, please visit:

www.microsoft.com/learning/booksurv

...and enter this book's ISBN-10 number (appears above barcode on back cover*).
As a thank-you to survey participants in the United States and Canada, each month we randomly select five respondents to win one of five $100 gift certificates from a leadi online merchant. At the conclusion of the survey, you can enter the drawing by provi your e-mail address, which will be used for prize notification only.

Thanks in advance for your input. Your opinion counts!

* Where to find the ISBN-10 on back cover

Example only. Each book has unique ISBN.

www.microsoft.com/learning/booksurve